The Transf
of Meanin

ENCOUNTERS

Series Editors: **Ana Deumert**, *University of Cape Town, South Africa,* **Zane Goebel**, *University of Queensland, Australia* and **Anna De Fina**, *Georgetown University, USA.*

The Encounters series sets out to explore diversity in language from a theoretical and an applied perspective. So the focus is both on the linguistic encounters, inequalities and struggles that characterise post-modern societies and on the development, within sociocultural linguistics, of theoretical instruments to explain them. The series welcomes work dealing with such topics as heterogeneity, mixing, creolization, bricolage, cross-over phenomena, polylingual and polycultural practices. Another high-priority area of study is the investigation of processes through which linguistic resources are negotiated, appropriated and controlled, and the mechanisms leading to the creation and maintenance of sociocultural differences. The series welcomes ethnographically oriented work in which contexts of communication are investigated rather than assumed, as well as research that shows a clear commitment to close analysis of local meaning making processes and the semiotic organisation of texts.

All books in this series are externally peer-reviewed.

Full details of all the books in this series and of all our other publications can be found on http://www.multilingual-matters.com, or by writing to Multilingual Matters, St Nicholas House, 31-34 High Street, Bristol BS1 2AW, UK.

ENCOUNTERS: 19

The Transformative Materiality of Meaning-Making

David Parkin

MULTILINGUAL MATTERS
Bristol • Blue Ridge Summit

DOI https://doi.org/10.21832/PARKIN1470
Library of Congress Cataloging in Publication Data
A catalog record for this book is available from the Library of Congress.
Names: Parkin, David J. – author.
Title: The Transformative Materiality of Meaning-Making/David Parkin.
Description: Bristol, UK; Blue Ridge Summit, PA: Multilingual Matters, 2021. | Series: Encounters: 19 | Includes bibliographical references and index. | Summary: 'This book explores verbal and non-verbal communication from a social anthropological viewpoint, drawing on ethnographic data from fieldwork in eastern Africa. It gives an overview of developments since the 1960s in the anthropology of language use and how these have influenced the author's thinking' – Provided by publisher.
Identifiers: LCCN 2021015234 (print) | LCCN 2021015235 (ebook) | ISBN 9781800411463 (paperback) | ISBN 9781800411470 (hardback) | ISBN 9781800411487 (pdf) | ISBN 9781800411494 (epub)
Subjects: LCSH: Language and culture – Africa, East. | Sociolinguistics.
Classification: LCC P35.5.A353 P48 2021 (print) | LCC P35.5.A353 (ebook) | DDC 306.4409676 – dc23
LC record available at https://lccn.loc.gov/2021015234
LC ebook record available at https://lccn.loc.gov/2021015235

British Library Cataloguing in Publication Data
A catalogue entry for this book is available from the British Library.

ISBN-13: 978-1-80041-147-0 (hbk)
ISBN-13: 978-1-80041-146-3 (pbk)

Multilingual Matters
UK: St Nicholas House, 31-34 High Street, Bristol BS1 2AW, UK.
USA: NBN, Blue Ridge Summit, PA, USA.

Website: www.multilingual-matters.com
Twitter: Multi_Ling_Mat
Facebook: https://www.facebook.com/multilingualmatters
Blog: www.channelviewpublications.wordpress.com

The policy of Multilingual Matters/Channel View Publications is to use papers that are natural, renewable and recyclable products, made from wood grown in sustainable forests. In the manufacturing process of our books, and to further support our policy, preference is given to printers that have FSC and PEFC Chain of Custody certification. The FSC and/or PEFC logos will appear on those books where full certification has been granted to the printer concerned.

Typeset by Riverside Publishing Solutions Ltd.
Printed and bound in the UK by the CPI Books Group Ltd.
Printed and bound in the US by NBN.

For Jan Blommaert who inspired and encouraged so many and left a rich intellectual legacy for future generations to work on.

Contents

Acknowledgements

Below are the dates and details of publications included as chapters in the volume. Acknowledgement is here made of permission to reproduce these publications granted by the publishers as indicated. I especially thank Ben Rampton, Jan Blommaert, Max Spotti, Karel Arnaut, Steve Vertovec, Sirpa Leppänen, Roxy Harris and Charles Briggs and other members of the International Consortium on Language Superdiversity (InCoLaS) for their stimulation and the encouragement that enabled me to bring together this collection. I am grateful to many people who have contributed to the 'mission' of increasing the scope and awareness of linguistic anthropology in the United Kingdom and European mainland: David Shankland, Director of the Royal Anthropological Institute, welcomed the possibility of putting on a series of seminars on anthropology and language at the RAI in 2013–2014; thereafter, Alex Pillen collaborated tirelessly in setting up the RAI Anthropology and Language Committee; and Elisabeth Hsu, David Zeitlyn and Ramon Sarro helped initiate similar seminars at the School of Anthropology and Museum Ethnography (SAME), then headed by David Gellner at the University of Oxford. Finally, I thank colleagues at SAME and All Souls College for fruitful discussion and generous help in preparing this work, and Anna Roderick for steering it through the publication process.

List and Dates of Publications Included in the Volume

Part 1: Chapters 1–6

2016 Multilingual classification to translingual ontology: a turning point. In K. Arnaut, J. Blommaert, B. Rampton and M. Spotti (eds) *Language and Superdiversity* (pp. 71–88). New York and Abingdon, UK: Routledge.

1977 Stabilized and emergent multilingualism. In H. Giles (ed.) *Language, Ethnicity and Inter-group Relations* (pp. 186–210). London and New York: Academic Press.

1971 Language choice in two Kampala housing estates. Chapter 20. In W.H. Whiteley (ed.) *Language Use and Social Change* (pp. 347–363). London: University of Oxford Press for International African Institute.

1974b Language switching in Nairobi. Chapter 8. In W.H. Whiteley (ed.) *Language in Kenya* (pp. 167–188). Nairobi: Oxford University Press.

1980 The creativity of abuse (Curl lecture l979). Man 15: 45–64.

1976 Exchanging words. In B. Kapferer (ed.) *Exchange and Meaning* (pp. 163–190). Philadelphia: Institute for the Study of Human Affairs.

Part 2: Chapters 7–11

1984 Political language. *Annual Review of Anthropology* 13, 345–65.

1994 Language, government and the play on purity and impurity: Arabic, Swahili and the vernaculars in Kenya. In R. Fardon and G. Furniss (eds) *African Languages, Development and the State* (pp. 227–245). London: Routledge.

1985a Being and selfhood among intermediary Swahili. In J. Maw and D. Parkin (eds) *Swahili Language and Society* (pp. 247–260). Beiträge zur Afrikanistik. Band 23. Vienna. Institut für Afrikanistik der Universität.

1985b Controlling the U-turn of knowledge. In R. Fardon (ed.) *Power and Knowledge* (pp. 49–60). Edinburgh: Scottish Academic Press.

1989 The politics of naming among the Giriama. In R.D. Grillo (ed.) *Social Anthropology and the Politics of Language* (pp. 61–89). Sociological Review Monograph No. 36. London and New York: Routledge.

Part 3: Chapters 12–17

1992 Unpacking anthropology (review article of E. Ardener “The voice of prophecy”) in *Journal of the Anthropological Society of Oxford* 23 (1), 57–65.

2015 Revisiting: Key words, transforming phrases and cultural concepts. In *Working Papers in Urban Languages and Literacies*. Paper 164. Kings College, London.

2017 Loud ethics and quiet morality among Muslim healers in Eastern Africa. *Africa* 87 (3), 537–553.

1985c Reason, emotion and the embodiment of power. In J. Overing (ed.) *Reason and Morality* (pp. 135–151). Tavistock, London: ASA Monograph No. 24. Tavistock.

2000 The power of incompleteness: innuendo in Swahili women’s dress. In B. Masquelier and J-L Siran (eds) *Pour une Anthropologie de l’Interlocution: Rhétoriques du Quotidien*. Paris: L’Harmattan.

1991 Simultaneity and sequencing in the oracular speech of Kenyan diviners. In P. Peek (ed.) *African Divination Systems* (pp. 174–189). Bloomington: Indiana University Press.

Introduction

The book explores verbal and non-verbal communication from a social anthropological viewpoint and not just from that of linguistic anthropology. This is unusual because social anthropologists in Europe do not normally focus on the detailed analysis of language use, which is undertaken much more by sociolinguists (see Meyerhoff (2018) for a recent detailed and comprehensive overview) and by scholars in the new, mainly British, field of linguistic ethnography (Rampton, 2007a, 2007b). American linguistic anthropology is an important sub-field in North America but is not much pursued in Europe, even though elements of it influence and overlap with European linguistic ethnography and sociolinguistics. Even by 2016, Arnaut *et al.* note that 'linguistic anthropology has very little institutional presence outside the US, and it is hard to find any graduate programmes in linguistic anthropology in Europe' (2016a: 7). Intensive ethnography is, however, common ground in these interrelated perspectives, recently shared even more by an interest in 'superdiversity', a concept referring to the consequences since the late 1990s of unprecedented global population movement and sociolinguistic mixture transcending previous patterns (see Arnaut *et al.*, 2017; Goebel, 2015; Vertovec, 2007).

The ethnographic data in this book are mostly from an earlier period and are drawn from fieldwork in eastern Africa, where I have spent overall a number of years since the 1960s and have learned to varying levels of competence some of its languages, most fluently Swahili and to a lesser extent Giriama and Luo. I am able therefore to give an overview of developments since then in the social anthropology of language use and how these have influenced the chapters in this book (cf. Whiteley, 1971, 1974). Theoretically, the argument is that language and other forms of communication involve semiotic transactions between interlocuters; that such communicative exchanges do more than convey information; and that they give identity to the recipients of such transactions who reciprocate by defining speakers. The density and situational totality of such semiotic exchange can moreover be regarded as a kind of materiality through its performative impact on social interaction, through interlocuters' bodily sensorial transmission of energy (akin to the notion of 'bio-speech community'; Black, 2019), and through the more conventional graphic materiality of text or image.

The book's title: *The Transformative Materiality of Meaning-Making* is intended to convey this multimodal semiotic density of interaction and communicative exchange. This distinctive approach has been arrived at as follows.

A paper published in 1976, and reproduced in the present volume as Chapter 6, is called 'Exchanging words'. A prompt was Levi-Strauss's characterisation of myth as the exchange of words and as one of three universal forms of exchange. The paper aroused queries at that time as to whether words could 'really' be likened to so-called material objects and transacted. The words in question were in fact East African ethnographically presented 'role-terms': i.e. consistent lexical labels for regularly recurring activities of which the most recognisable are defined occupations carried out by persons of the 'tinker, tailor, soldier' type. Underlying the questioning scepticism was an admittedly fading faith in the dichotomy of idealism and materiality: the sceptics claimed that words are ideal constructs and can only refer to but not become objects. Speech act theory and its concepts of illocutionary and perlocutionary force, semantic anthropology and philosophical developments have since those days served to dissolve that dichotomy in favour of regarding idealism and materiality as mutually constituted and as together having material impact. We are indeed well used to the idea of sacred words and magical spells purportedly having (sometimes harmful) physical and mental effect (Favret-Saada, 1980 (1977); Tambiah, 1968). Moreover, semiosis, as comprising cross-over non-verbal as well as verbal communication, has more than just physical or material effect but is itself materially constituted through interlocuters and their signs, in the same way that a high density of human interaction (e.g. a placard-carrying crowd, social gathering or interlocuters in conversation) can be thought of as a kind of materiality (Parkin, 2007a). This materiality of both agency and consequence is moreover made through reciprocal movement as the semiotic signs of voice, image, gesture, facework and bodily posture are exchanged between people in communication, a range of multisensory modes extensively analysed by Finnegan (2002).

Although benefitting from diverse developments in the broad field of linguistic anthropology, the chapters in this volume most directly relate historically to the 'ethnography of speaking/communication' pioneered by Dell Hymes and John Gumperz (Blommaert, 2018; Gumperz & Hymes, 1972, 1964; Hymes, 1964, 1983 [1974]), for it was these scholars who helped shift an early anthropological interest in language classification to one of language as ontological, i.e. as identifying and so creating persons and things. The themes covered in the chapters subscribe to this approach to communication. They have arisen over time from detailed ethnographic interest in events unsought but encountered in the field which are revealed to be instantiated and made 'real' through speech and other forms of verbal and non-verbal communication. It is an interest shared by all anthropologists by definition. However, there is considerable variation in the extent to which a focus on language and communication is prioritised, as in this volume, as a way of showing how the voices, bodies and inter-subjectivities that make up social interaction are irreducibly consubstantial and material.

Arnaut *et al.* (2016a: 7–8) recognise the overlap between their notion of the mainly European and recently established linguistic ethnography and that of the longer-established American linguistic anthropology (see also Rampton, 2007a, 2007b, 2008, 2009). They see the latter as historically based on fieldwork 'away from home' while practitioners of European linguistic ethnography 'focus on environments where researchers work and/or have grown up or spent much of their lives … motivated by an interest in linguistic configurations, inequalities and divisions noticed locally, more or less "on the doorstep" … in engagement with, for example, local refugee centres and immigration and asylum procedures, work-place production and interviewing processes, complementary schools, primary and secondary education, literacy programmes and popular cultural production'.

While acknowledging the influence of the ethnography of speaking/communication on the new linguistic ethnography, Rampton spells out a distinctive feature which is relevant to themes covered by the present volume. He says 'Linguistic ethnography is…investigating communication within the *temporal unfolding* of social processes …' (Rampton, 2007b: 3, my emphasis). It is '… a view of *situated communication* that pays particular attention to the efforts individuals make to get other people to recognise their feelings, perceptions, interests etc. Every moment in the *unfolding* of communicative action is unique and never-to-be-repeated, but this also involves linguistic forms, rhetorical strategies, semiotic materials and institutional genres that have achieved a degree of stability, status and resonance in the world …' (Rampton, 2007b: 4, my emphasis). For me, the key criterion here is the paradoxical notion of 'temporal unfolding' of a never-to-be repeated 'situated communication' in the context of stability, a juxtaposition of the immediate and continuous making up the complete utterance or speech event. Taken thus, it seems at first to resonate with the Saussurian contrast respectively with unique parole and enduring langue, but it goes much further in seeing the two as mediated by the play of interpersonal feelings, perceptions, strategies and (common and conflicting) interpersonal interests. The sense of an 'unfolding' may be extended to include things which emerge from a previous state (as a butterfly emerging from a cocoon), a kind of poiesis (cf. Arnaut *et al.*, 2017: 3–24). An act of communication, or more specifically a speech event, may be viewed in this way as some examples from the chapters of the present volume show. What may be called a *critical* speech or communication event refers to the actual moment of transformation, triggered by any number of communication factors such as change of accent/pronunciation, topic, mood, misunderstanding, misinterpretation, accidental usage, bodily/facial movement or gesture, textual or pictorial declaration or speaker's deliberate provocation (see especially Part 1). The volume's aim is thus to show that communication is not just affirmative but is a socio-ontological process of 'coming-into-being' through 'instantiation', on which more below. I see these aspects as packed into the ethnographic notion of 'situated communication'.

The publication dates of the seventeen chapters in the current volume range from 1971 to 2017. Before and during this period, especially since World War II, there were major developments and changes both in anthropology and the study of language in society. As regards language study, Boerllstorff's informative compendium (2011) of 66 selected articles from 1888 to 2010 drawn from the American Anthropologist can be used as a rough guide of some such developments, some of which have a bearing on the collected chapters. From Boerllstorff, we see that from about the late 1940s and early 1950s, there is a reduction in articles and books dealing with the classification of languages, whether typological or genetic. Guthrie published his monumental *The Classification of the Bantu Languages* in 1948 which was followed in 1955 by Greenberg's equally major *Studies in African Linguistic Classification* (preceded in previous years by journal articles on the subject). Interest in language classification has continued but as an increasingly specialised field separate from more ethnographically focused work on the sociocultural dimensions of language. Thus, in 1949, a work entitled 'Ethnolinguistics and the study of culture' (Silva-Fuenzalida, 1949) was followed by a majority emphasis in publications on such topics as 'verbal expression', 'dialect differences', 'dialect stratification' and 'speech variations' with the path-breaking work of Gumperz (1958, 1961) and Hymes (1964) being produced from the early 1960s and, as noted above, named 'the ethnography of speaking/communication', together with cognate study at the same time, including an early, partially feminist, perspective by Susan Ervin-Tripp on 'language, topic and listener' (1964).

Language classification by itself had thus diverged from the increasing interest in the then increasing turn towards language as live discourse premised on communicative exchange, cultural precepts and context of situation. The 1960s also saw the birth of 'ethnoscience' as methodology for explaining culturally distinctive language-use rules (see Frake, 1964). At the same time, Labov's famous research (1964, 1977) questioned claims that certain diatypes did not consistently follow grammatical rules and demonstrated the communicative logic of non-standard English in Harlem, New York. The 1970s and 1980s moved towards poetics and verbal art as performance with seminal contributions by Bauman and Briggs (1990), Bauman (1975), Briggs (1985) and Scherzer (1987) and thence in the 1990s to a consideration of 'language ideologies', an interest which has continued to present time (e.g. Chernela, 2003; Friedman, 2003; Friedrich, 1989; Haviland, 2003; Keane, 2018; Laitin & Gomez, 1992; Makihara, 2004; Schieffelin *et al.*, 1998; Stromberg, 1990). A related concern with literacy also emerged (Besnier, 1991; Street, 1985). From the 1970s until the present, in anthropology, abstract concepts originating from or echoing philosophy have increasingly been applied theoretically across different communicative exchanges and performances. They include 'intentionality' (Duranti, 1993, 2015), 'indexicality' (Silverstein, 1976), 'pragmatics' (Levinson, 1983), 'entextualisation' (Bauman & Briggs, 1990; Silverstein, 2014; Wolfgram, 2012); 'contextualisation' (Silverstein, 1992), and many others. Such concepts may vary by author, sometimes extending out from a focus on the linguistic or textual. For instance, Wolfgram applying and widening his view of entextualisation to the analysis of scholarly medical traditions, declares that '… the concept of entextualization that I draw upon and develop here is not limited to the writing and deployment of text but rather the appropriation, circulation, and transformation of *discourse* more generally (that is, it includes but is not limited to text)' (Wolfgram, 2012: 215, my emphasis). The introduction of the key theoretical concept of 'discourse' (see Silverstein & Urban, 1996) extends issues of communication to that of multimodality and semiosis, including use of the five senses. This is an interest implicit in some chapters in the present volume and of special concern in the increasing contemporary research into sign languages.

Although influenced by early work in linguistic anthropology, the current collected papers reflect changes drawn more directly from social anthropology. For instance, 'transactionalism' was a social anthropological approach developed in the 1960s and 1970s, which analysed social interaction as a form of exchange in which individuals or groups sought to extract profit or benefits from those they interacted with at minimal cost to themselves (Bailey, 1969; Barth, 1966). The chapters in Part 1 analyse conversations in these terms, emphasising the fragile balance between competitive and cooperative communication and the danger in this of miscommunication.

Occurring at the same time as the emergence of transactionalism, political anthropology turned towards an interest in what was called 'local level politics' (Swartz, 1968) with an emphasis on interpersonal and small group encounters, conflicts and goals rather than the analysis of large-scale states or other socially extensive political formations. The interpersonal and small group perspectives were sometimes identified as examples of 'methodological individualism' and are combined in a number of the chapters, which view language and communicative exchanges or transactions as a form of interpersonal micro-politics.

This concern in the 1960s with micro-politics shaded into the analysis of political language which is the subject of the chapters constituting Part 2 of the book. Along with oratory and rhetoric, political language was much studied in the 1970s and 1980s (from Bloch (1975) to Paine (1981); Brenneis & Myers, 1984; Brenneis, 1986a, 1986b; Briggs, 1985; Grillo, 1989; Parkin, 1975, 1984) and comprehensively revisited a generation later (Stasch, 2011). The early interest raised questions about selfhood and personhood through the realisation that controllers of political language and rhetoric and their audiences were mutually identified and constituted by how they were spoken to and how they listened and, if at all, responded. A key issue is the distinction (in practice sometimes elided) between so-called formal and informal modes of communication, including types of greeting and honorifics, as discussed in Part 1. A derived issue is the extent to which speakers or interlocuters follow or neglect social rules governing communicative interaction, and the expectations and responses of educational and political authorities to either rule conformity or divergence, including the part played by government and other language ideologies (Parkin, 1975; cf. Blommaert, 2009).

Part 3 includes chapters exploring the implications of the fact that, underlying any political engagement is the play of power, which is sometimes implicit rather than evident in communication and plays a role in how meanings are encoded and decoded. Here, meaning draws on more than words and lexicon and rests on key cultural concepts which are as much unsaid as said yet which, like stigma, sometimes powerfully influence thought and action and may lurk in unexpected contexts. A number of the chapters here describe cases where such apparent semantic invisibility, so to speak, has effect through indirect cultural allusion both outside and within language. The influence of Ardener is here often evident in the chapters. For about 15 years from the beginning of the 1970s until the mid-1980s, Ardener published a number of theoretically developing articles different in focus from most other anthropological approaches to language appearing beforehand (see Chapter 12; Parkin, 1982; and Ardener's posthumous collection (1989a) edited by Chapman).

Taken as a whole, the volume covers a view of communicative exchange as working within but also transcending rule-governed behaviour and so, through its material effect, creating new 'ways of being'. In keeping with the ethnographic focus as analytical starting-point, all the chapters draw on fieldwork data from the peoples I have worked among: Luo, Giriama and Swahili in eastern Africa in both rural and urban areas from 1962 to present time. The remarkable increase in speed and scale of digital communication in the 21st century through social media, the internet and mobile phones (see McIntosh (2010) on Giriama) post-date the fieldwork and so are not documented in the chapters. The resultant explosion of internationally shared sporting events and of mutually identifiable forms of global popular culture and communication make human interaction across the world more accessible and potentially liberating. An instance is the cross-cultural 'buffalaxed' or parodied videos, recordings, lyrics and dancing of 'the other' and the international sharing of hip-hop and rap (Leppänen & Elo, 2016; Varis & Wang, 2016). But this development rides on the new digital technology which can be harnessed by states and other corporate institutions to exert greater communicative control over people. Research is likely on the consequences of this ambiguity. Is it a radical or fundamental change in global means of communication? Or is it simply an accelerated concentration of pre-existing and continuing templates of sociality? The former seems the more likely development. The chapters in this volume may then be read as describing past and generally more localised communicative exchange as being historically the precursor of unprecedented densities and scale of communication within which small group interlocution may or may not flourish.

The three broadly thematic parts each consist of five or six chapters focused on small groups and are preceded by a short introduction. Apart from a few typological corrections and clarifications, the chapters are reproduced in their original form, the better to indicate the influence of their micro-historical contexts. However, they are not in the chronological order of their publication since the intention is rather to show the connection between ideas which might be interspersed and not always follow directly from one to the other.

It is here relevant to mention an interview carried out by Karel Arnaut and Roxy Harris (2013), although not included in the present volume, which gives an informal overview of some of the intellectual paths taken, from an early interest in transactionalism to, later, the broader canvas of semiosis and its multimodal role in enabling interlocuters to copy, modify or reject each other's modes of communication and lifestyles.

Part 1

Communication as Transaction and Becoming

Chapter 1 was first published as Parkin (2016). Though recent, it is included early in the current volume because it is a kind of summation of developments beginning from the time in the 1960s when transactionalism informed my approach to the analysis of language and communication. The chapter is distinctive in making explicit that communication exchanges do more than convey meanings, directions and expectations, they also play a role in defining and re-defining the personhood of interlocuters. It documents the shift from an early concern with the classification of languages to more ontological issues of human 'becoming' through communicative interaction. It appeared in a volume arising from the work, inspired by Vertovec (2007), of the International Consortium on Language and Superdiversity (InCoLaS) (Arnaut *et al.*, 2016b), which has been especially important in the immediate post-millennial years and has, in many respects, taken up ethnographically the mantel of language and communication that social anthropology touched on but did not carry far.

Performativity and materiality are part of the 'becoming' in the interactions discussed in Chapter 1. Thus, when London teenagers imitate and embody the communicative styles, gestures and identities of a 'cool' and therefore exalted reference group in their circle, this is a kind of understated performance, not like a full-blown ritual, but performative nevertheless. It is language and body together physically prompting members of the circle to change positions and postures as well as speech modes, idioms and accents, and is to that extent language and communication as materiality, similar in a way to illocutionary force as being material effect and not just proposition.

Chapter 2. While such examples of situated communication capture moments, Chapter 2 (Parkin, 1977) presents a case from the 1960s in

Nairobi, Kenya, of youth groups over time dividing along putative class lines presaged beforehand in their perceived choice of dominant lingua franca. As youngsters they play football, speak a form of the 'non-tribal' language of Swahili and are uninterested in the 'tribal' divisiveness of their adult elders. But as they grow into adolescence they split into 'gangs' now differentiated on the basis of whether they speak, or claim to speak, Swahili or English. Gangs claiming to use mainly Swahili have failed to attend school through lack of fees and call themselves uneducated and unable to get good jobs and therefore socially rebellious, while the English gangs claim to be educated and to be able to aspire to better job opportunities and 'respectable' citizenship. There is a kind of template of such incipient class differentiation which is contoured by the value-laden distinctiveness of Swahili and English as low and high diatype, respectively. It is instantiation of class through a public perception of lingua franca hierarchy.

It has to be noted that the relative statuses of English and Swahili have changed since this fieldwork was carried out in the 1960s: it might be difficult nowadays to refer to Nairobi or so-called 'up-country' Swahili as a low diatype. The distinction between speech pattern or varieties as either 'high' or 'low' must be seen nowadays as presupposing too much homogeneity between varieties and of ignoring the dynamic and changing overlap between such varieties. These are better analysed as differences of communicative style. As a prestigious language of Muslim coastal East Africa with a classical literary pedigree and a range of regional varieties, Swahili has always had elevated status along the coast. Tanzania's post-independence further elevation of the language has helped spread its rising reputation inland as well, including Kenya, Uganda and the Democratic Republic of Congo via Rwanda and Burundi. That said, socioeconomic differences continue under conditions of politico-inequality to be reflected in hierarchical judgements about people's apparent language competence, including the colonial and postcolonial legacy of privileging supposedly 'high' competence in English in contexts defined by differential access to authority, power and wealth. Various chapters depict this earlier prestige hierarchy between English and Swahili. A relatively new form of mixed English-Swahili with vernacular inclusions, called Sheng, now occupies the place of so-called low diatype of Swahili in East African cities such as Nairobi, according to current East African language scholars, some of whom see it as a 'working class' youth language (Bosire (2009), Githiora (2018) and Mazrui (1995) for detailed analyses). Although the chapters in this section were written before Sheng was popularly named and widely recognised as a distinctive speech variety, Chapter 2 on youth groups (already mentioned) includes mixed English-Swahili usage in the 1960s that can be regarded as part of a prototype emerging from the 1950s of Sheng, as being indeed early Sheng.

Chapter 3 documents some social implications of this early English-Swahili prestige hierarchy. Language-based differentiation and instantiation can of course lead not to harmonious imitation or integration but to conflict. The case described in this chapter (Parkin, 1971) is from 1962 of a well-educated tenant new to a low-income housing estate speaking at its association meeting in English to the annoyance of the other tenants, most of whom did not know English and so angrily accused him of not observing the convention that only Swahili should be used. A further example is of six male drinking companions nearly coming to blows in a bar in what I call a 'conversational arena of prestige competition'. They are educated, in well-paid jobs and speak English fluently, which they use among themselves, preferring to do so despite being able to use their respective northern Uganda Nilotic dialects. Their preference to use English goes beyond an expression of high status. Much of their interaction consists of friendly banter and teasing, including a game to out-perform each other's command of English through witty statements and clever use of vocabulary. The game gets out of hand when one of the men is losing badly in the competition and unexpectedly turns on one of the teasers, insulting him severely and provoking him to great anger. The high emotionalism, quarrel and near violence are only stifled when they calm the offended companions through use of their respective vernaculars. The switch from English to vernacular is thus from dangerous to less risky language use.

Chapter 4. The framework of competitive jocularity and gamesmanship is in fact a recurrent feature of cross-ethnic talk and communication as well as that between English-speaking prestige contestants. Chapters four and five provide instances of such language competition. Chapter 4 (Parkin, 1974b) takes an example from the 1960s of market vendors and customers of different ethnic groups acting like rivals and making language concessions and appeasements in order to secure bargains or clients' custom. Their banter is hedged around with humorous references as to whether or not the rival speaker is really competent in the language of the other. Banter among relative strangers is a common means of camouflaging underlying interpersonal tensions, especially those deriving from perceived differences of ethnicity or socioeconomic class. Traditionally, in much of Africa, institutionalised joking relationships played this role and the instances in this chapter occur in the wider context of pronounced polyethnic consciousness often displayed in humorous exchanges.

Chapter 5. Politeness, like joking, may moderate interpersonal tensions, but sometimes institutionalised impoliteness can, paradoxically, also perform this role. Politeness and impoliteness can in fact be seen, not always as diametrically opposed, but as ends of a continuum of communicative exchange, between which there are other institutionalised examples of reciprocal address. In this chapter (Parkin, 1980) the topic of insult or abuse is treated theoretically. It shows how greetings, honorific address and formal and informal joking relationships constitute a cluster of ambivalent verbal encounters which sit dangerously on the edge of acceptability and severe insult but which nevertheless, through their very risky experimentality, innovate through creative suggestions about social status and relationships. Much of the ethnography is taken from my work on Giriama in Kenya but also considered are the extensive studies in linguistic anthropology on greetings, the reciprocal power semantic (e.g. *tu* versus *vous*) and other formulaic exchanges, including as already mentioned Labov's analysis (1977) of the logic of non-standard English in Harlem, New York, through youths' reciprocally competitive exchanges called 'sounding' and other names.

Chapter 6 concludes this section with a critique but also sympathetic application of Barth's transactional analysis, using Giriama role terms (Parkin, 1976). It continues to address the question of how we can refer to communication, including verbal language, as essentially a kind of materiality and, through its performativity, 'making' persons through the role relationships they are deemed lexically to hold. That is to say, the institutionalisation of social activity, through the terms used to designate publicly acknowledged occupational and other roles, structures the presentation of people. Thus rendered as objects rather than subjects or agents in communication, role-defined persons are transacted: the many roles they play 'become' what they are and are liable to be constantly shuffled.

In short, Part 1 suggests that communication consists of reciprocal transactions which are ontological material, sometimes withholding interlocuters' agency and so always liable to achieve their effect through emotional charge.

1 From Multilingual Classification to Translingual Ontology: A Turning Point

Superdiversity and Language

In addressing the issue of 'superdiversity' as defined by Vertovec in 2007, subsequent work indirectly addressed an historical turning point (see contributions to Arnaut *et al.*, 2016, Arnaut *et al.*, 2017, Toivanen and Saarikivi 2016). The late 1980s and early 1990s saw major geo-political changes coinciding with those of rapid communications technology and the maturing of the digital age. There was the fall of the Berlin war in 1989, which Ernest Gellner called the most momentous occasion since the French revolution; the ensuing collapse of communism; its conversion to a new kind of capitalism in China following that country's reforms of the 1980s; the remarkably swift effect of India's own economic reforms; and the ending of apartheid in South Africa. That these politico-economic events occurred within a few years of each other is a good illustration of the knock-on effects of crises in relation to each other. Not necessarily related, at least in the first instance, was the way in which an already slowly growing globalisation following World War II was further helped through increasing use of mobile phones and the internet, a change that accelerated at a pace and to a geographic extent that left us bewildered in the very moment of experiencing it. The so-called 'Arab Spring' of 2011, allegedly partly organised through digital communication, was a precursor of more of the like, as were the burgeoning new patterns of international population movement, with new, smaller and more ethno-culturally diverse groups of migrants caulked upon earlier, long-standing migratory patterns. National boundaries, for all the attempts of powerful nations to patrol them, are becoming more porous. They are part of a global demographic shift in the making, punctuated by savage curbs but redefining ineluctably and irreversibly the very idea of a self-recognising population.

It is true that prior to the late 1980s, there was already a speed of communication and contact that made it feasible to speak of a new kind of globalisation different in these respects from any predecessors. But in this earlier globalisation, politico-economic and sociocultural diversity was seen as made up of supposedly discrete elements brought together in conjunction and not yet so merged as to lose their respective remembered lines of differentiation. The diversity then was really that of parallelisms and pluralities. Ethnic pluralism, cultural pluralism, medical pluralism and linguistic pluralism referred in liberal quarters to the side-by-side relations of distinctive entities or knowledges that were encouraged to celebrate their distinctiveness and, despite real differences between them of power, privilege and resources, to take their place as equals before each other. Ideologies cannot last for long without material or substantive reinforcement and, cross-cut by increasing inequalities, the ideal-based pluralisms gave way at their edges to fuzzy boundaries or no boundaries at all. Echoing Rampton (2016: 91) we can say that the current situation is one in which old predictabilities have dissolved and certain forms, acts and social categories no longer co-occur in the patterns that were once expected.

A key notion here is what Arnaut (2016: 60–62) calls a new kind of post-panoptic governmentality that has developed since the late 1980s and which tries to control this diversity. This is different from an earlier view of governmentality as, ultimately, a centre controlling subject populations and institutions. The new post-panoptic hegemonic discourse is of rules, regulations, exactions and punitive stigma set up by various, and often unrelated, interests seeking to curb and direct what they see as the random spread of new migratory, linguistic and semiotic agents and activities. Arnaut importantly reminds us not to forget, however, that alongside this new ramifying hegemonic configuration, superdiversity has also opened up spaces for creativity of a kind not easily available beforehand when society was internally made up of relatively constant and therefore constraining boundaries, (e.g. of class, ethnic,educational and professional differentiation and commensurate lifestyles). Some of this 'new' creativity is seen as in fact the 'recycling' of the many disparate and overlapping elements that make up what we call social and linguistic communication and interpretation in so-called postmodernity. To extend the metaphor, but also to invite contestation, it is as if the bricoleur is seen as having taken up much of the space in public culture and opinion previously occupied by the scientist.

The concept of superdiversity tries to capture the implications of the alleged development from the co-existing, side-to-side (and sometimes back-to-back) relations of relatively bounded entities to the reverberative, criss-crossing, and subdivision of different parts of these entities. In the field of linguistic ethnography, the latter is a process that Rampton (1995; 2010) has called crossover speech or crossing, in which a range of diverse linguistic particles are borrowed, transformed, returned and employed as communicative 'resources', to use the notion much evident in, for instance, Arnaut *et al.* (2016) and which I examine below. The resources make up what Blommaert and Backus (2011) call a speech 'repertoire', and which are deployed in what Jørgensen and others (2016: 137–154) call 'polylanguaging' and Creese and Blackledge (2010) refer to as 'translanguaging'. The key position adopted in Arnaut (2016 and 2017) is that such processes are more than just code-switching. To coin a phrase, everyday speech is becoming more and more a matter of constant polythetic classification with social impact, as speakers juggle the limits of face-to-face intelligibility at any one time with new styles of expression made up of ever-changing linguistic resources. Varis and Xuan (2016: 218–221) similarly talk of a struggle between semiotic creativity and normativity. As Rampton showed for urban Britain, ethnicity from the 1980s and 1990s began to lose its predominance as a driver of youth speech in favour of social class and the crossing of different speech 'styles', a class-based heteroglossic vernacular that seems to have lasted into some speakers' middle age and is not just a cyclical generational characteristic (Rampton 2006; 2011).

So what is the difference between this relatively recent theoretical position and, say, early 1960/1970s descriptions by Joshua Fishman (1966; 1971) of 'language shift, maintenance and stabililty' and the code-switching studied by those such as John Gumperz (1961; 1982) and Dell Hymes (1962) as part of an 'ethnography of speaking'?

From Multilingual Classification to Ontological Processes

One difference between crossover speech and code-switching (seen as speech alternating within single sentences between use of morphemes recognisable as deriving from different languages) is of focus. We can say that, while the earlier studies of detailed cases of code-switching could be called micro-sociolinguistics, the approach of Rampton and his colleagues is that of nano-sociolinguistics. It is concerned with conversation analysis (CA), whose constituent features are smaller than those making up codes and require longer within any stretch to decipher. It underlines a tendency and perhaps a need, given the greater complexity of superdiversity, to analyse minute fractions of the borrowings and exchanges characteristic of much speech in late modern urban settings.

This perspective is a methodological response to the new and more varied population and linguistic flows whose intermingling of boundaries and identities invites a closer look at how elements of a communicative act cohere. Language ideology, its forms, and the way these are expressed in social interaction constitute a three-part interrelationship (some would say dialectic). Thinking of this interrelationship as a triangle (see e.g. Hanks 1996: 230), we can say that it has been stretched into more triangular shapes than was the case before the polycentric normative effects of modern superdiversity. Wide differences among interlocutors as to the relative value, modes of articulation, and interpersonal relevance of particular speech features need not nowadays seem to be a 'foreign' incursion into a 'mainstream' speech variety but can be thought of as belonging within a broad notion of 'normality'.

For example, Rampton (2013) examines the speech of a man who only started speaking English in the UK as an adult. He shows that the man's 'learned' English unconventionally combines features which are however spread among other speakers who would not be regarded as learners. The point is that it is nowadays harder to separate as a category those who have learned English as a second language from other speakers, because these other speakers may also use such combinations in English as a first language. They are together making use of the variety of language resources available through superdiversity.

Consider not only Rampton's examples but also those of Jørgensen *et al.* (2016: 138–141) in their analysis of the deployment of fractional features. In one of their cases, overlapping features of standard Danish, youth Danish, English, Spanish, Turkish and Arabic are used by three Copenhagen girls in the space of just a few exchanges of conversation. As in youth language generally, such features are adopted rapidly (and in some cases discarded swiftly), many of them stylised for effect, a development to which I return below. It is difficult consistently to attribute the variable use of these features to changing topics or conversational domains.

Gumperz and some of his colleagues acknowledged this in the 1970s. On the one hand, drawing on his earlier work, Gumperz recognised that there were occasions when a particular speech variety and a particular social event or setting would go together and that a change in the language or variety might change the social setting, and vice versa (Blom and Gumperz 1970; Gumperz and Hernandez-Chavez 1972). On the other hand, he also provided contrary instances of conversational code-switching between words of English and Spanish where such close correlations did not apply nor could be predicted. He showed, moreover, that switching between codes or varieties did more than communicate the meaning of the particular words used, but also metaphorically drew on the social associations each variety might have – to articulate a particular speech variety was to take on some of the stereotypical social characteristics of its speakers. Gumperz here took a step in a movement away from classification, and nowadays this is even greater. As evident in Arnaut (2016 and 2017) and also Vigouroux and Mufwene (2008), the features making up codes can no longer be regarded as unambiguously belonging to particular languages, for they are imperceptibly merged with other features of different provenances and do not necessarily alter by topic.

Fishman's interest was more macroscopic than the later Gumpez and was tied to the idea of a language as belonging to a group whose speakers would each share a loyalty to their distinctive language (Parkin 1974; Spotti 2011a). He described language shift and stability. This illustrates the most obvious case of languages seen as relatively bounded entities subject to change from contact with others or able to withstand such change or, as in some of Fishman's examples, incorporating some changes while preserving an 'original' essence. Fishman's recorded material, especially on the relation in urban United States between Spanish and English, is exemplary and did indeed at that time suggest both an ideological and practiced distinctiveness of two languages seen analytically as well as indigenously separable, a distinctiveness that then, as now, has ideological-cum-political significance in defining acceptable citizenship. It is a view of integrated speech, in Jørgensen's terms (2016: 140), in which a noticeable degree of language distinctiveness is maintained, and which educators and policy makers assume is 'natural'.

So, just as the world has allegedly undergone the transition within a generation from (urban) diversity to superdiversity as a result of historical developments, is there a commensurately different linguistic horizon today in much of the world from that which existed in, say, the 1960s and 1970s, to say nothing of even earlier periods?

It would be indulgent to dwell long on one's own researches at that time in the cities of Nairobi in Kenya and Kampala, Uganda. But it should be mentioned that migration to each city, as in many African cities consequent on the expulsion in the early 1960s of French, British and Belgian colonialism (Portugese fifteen years later), consisted heavily of new migrants from rural areas many of who were, if not monoglot, at least defined in terms of a self-perceived single 'mother tongue' vernacular hedged around with other languages used at trading centres and markets. Nairobi under the British, after all, discouraged Africans from becoming permanent residents in the city and so urban ethno-linguistic admixture was small compared with today. A non-colonial 'traditional' city like

Kampala was, by contrast, already ethnically and linguistically mixed, though even there LuGanda, the language of the dominant BuGanda kingdom, was seen by everyone as the ideological standard to which one should aspire if one wanted the benefits of Ganda 'citizenship'. But it was the British and other imperialists of Africa who insisted on falsely demarcating peoples as unambiguously belonging to 'tribes'. It was false because pre-colonial movement, trade, inter-marriage and alliances had precluded set boundaries and borders (Southall 1970). But in imposing them, the imperialists in fact created a sense of bounded ethno-linguistic distinctiveness that became partially reinforced in practice and has become the bane of modern national politics.

The colonial project of ethno-linguistic essentialism did not in practice curb language mixing, and indeed studies were made of it in Nairobi and Kampala (Parkin 1971 and 1974). But colonial essentialising did foster an ideological view on the part of African speakers of the coexistence of not just ethnic groups, but also languages as discrete entities, which could be found in allegedly 'pure' form somewhere, perhaps in a notional rural heartland. There was, in other words, the coexistence of, on one hand, an ideology of linguistic pluralism and individual purity, and on the other hand, increasing heteroglossia, especially with greater urban migration. Such language mixing may indeed be said now to have grown more complex in conjunction with denser urban settlement, and yet still juxtaposed to colonially derived ideas of language separateness and purity. The two, language ideologies of purity, and crossover talk, continue today, reflecting a similar duality in Europe.

Pre-colonial extensive African networks of trade, political absorption, movement to new farming, pastoral and hunting land, and intermarriage did spread the use of a number of vernaculars. To that extent, there was some indigenous linguistic diversity. But it was hardly on the scale of modern superdiversity. For, by the latter, we understand the situation in late modern urban settings, and, with in 2020 just over half of the world's population living in urban areas and with two thirds predicted by 2050, there clearly has been a qualitative shift. More research on older archives and records is needed to say more about this shift and to compare earlier with present periods.

Underlying such history of apparent polylingual change is a theoretical distinction. In the English language we can interrogate the verb, 'identify', with reference to the ways in which allegedly different speech varieties are classified and have effect on social relations. For a speaker to identify a speech variety as different from others is to classify it as one might an object. The act sets up a classificatory grid that is ideological insofar as it is based on a perception and claim that may depart from the fact that the variety is not really that neatly distinctive of others and in some respects overlaps with them. By contrast, for a speaker to identify *with* a speech variety is to embody it or, perhaps, to be embodied by it, with echoes of empathy and Levy-Bruhl's notion of '*participation*' by which the speaker and the variety share in each other's being: I do not just speak it, for it is part of my being even when I do not speak it. To identify *with* is then ontological and not just classificatory.

I raise this distinction because I have the impression that earlier sociolinguistics tended towards the 'objective' classification of speech varieties and their social and conceptual correlates. A primary task was to show how speakers make, or are induced to make, choices as between varieties or registers according to the sociocultural domain in which they are operating or the topic on which they are speaking. As mentioned above, the later Gumperz was different in that his approach to metaphorical code-switching understood varieties as coming from different settings and informing speakers with identities built on such variation. It was to that extent moving towards a view of conversations as ontological processes and not just one of speakers collectively classifying and being classified by the languages around them. The publications cited above (Arnaut 2016, 2017 et alia) on sociolinguistic diversity are in part heirs to Gumperz but go further and strongly depict the use of not just spoken language but also other semiotic resources (text, visual, dress, music). Their usage is seen as intrinsic to and part of the migratory and social superdiversity that for at least a generation characterises cities and can be seen as a kind of further diversification of pre-existing diversity. Such constant involution of semiotic resources lends itself to what Blommaert and Maly (2016: 197–217) call 'ethnogaphic lingustic landscape analysis' (ELLA). ELLA investigates not just the 'permanent' features of language and signs in a Ghent neighbourhood but also those that come and go quickly and would be ignored as unimportant in conventional studies of language diversity, but which are in fact intrinsic to the sociodemographic layers and dynamics of the neighbourhood.

I deal with the notion of semiotic resources in more detail below. But I should here briefly note that it is different from the notion of urban language resources as used in the late 1960s in Nairobi by Parkin (1974), who explicitly adopted a transactionalist market model in which sellers and buyers of different, unambiguously defined ethnic groups at a market made challenges and concessions to each other by including parts of each other's language in a game to gain custom or a lower price. The resources were seen as directly deriving from ethnic languages whose boundaries were maintained despite the reciprocal borrowing in the market transactions. It was a view of resources in the economic sense and of ethnic groups regarded by townsfolk as distinctive of each other. The classificatory predominated over the ontological, with only strains of the latter identified (e.g. Parkin 1971).

The Semiotic Creation of Identity

People's use of semiotic resources as described in the work of Arnaut *et al.* does not unambiguously classify social strata and ethnic groups but creates and draws from communicative outlines that cut across them and blur their contours. Although to some extent evident earlier in Parkin (1977), the concept of semiotic resources is increasingly seen as relevant to the characterisation of late urban modernity. Put simply. it is a shift of analytical focus from mainly verbal 'language' to verbal and non-verbal 'semiosis.' Two findings emerge. One is that contemporary polylanguaging is an ontological act on the part of speakers to empower themselves or to project a desired or appropriate personal image, perhaps in accordance with some kind of network membership but not tied to a particular speech domain or topic in the broader sense given above. The other is that this creation of identity is through semiotic stylisation, which by non-standard means projects new identities or reinforces existing ones, sometimes allowing (rapid) change from one to the other.

The distinction between the earlier tendency to classify on the basis of language varieties and the current or recent concern to show individuals' ontological and stylistic deployment of semiotic resources is not watertight. But it does seem to constitute a broad if overlapping shift. Referring again to John Gumperz, Levinson says Gumperz in his early days was:

> "interested in how social groups express and maintain their otherness in complex societies. Gumperz started as a dialectologist interested in tracking down the forces of standardization and particularly those of differentiation, and it was the search for where these forces are located that has led him inexorably from the macrosociological to the micro-conversational perspective; it was a long journey from the study of regional standards, to ethnic groups, to social networks, to the activation of social boundaries in verbal interaction, to discourse strategies" (Levinson 1997: 1; 2003: 31; and see Gumperz 1982; 1984).

Levinson points out that Gumperz's later work on code-switching tried to reconcile the macro- (the group classification effect) with the micro- (the discursively strategic) through analysis of the individual speaker. He also wanted to explain how a speaker's utterance could be interpreted in different and sometimes conflicting ways among interlocutors depending on their own respective backgrounds. In this attempt, he turned to 'the careful analysis of prosody, the neglected acoustic cues that might help to explain how we can possibly mean so much by uttering so little' (Levinson 2003: 33). I recall Gumperz in London in the 1980s describing how the distinctive prosody of immigrant South Asian bus conductors in speaking to passengers sometimes came across as impolite and even hostile, marking and so making them different from the indigenous 'mainstream'. They were regarded by passengers as not just different speakers of English but as different persons of different behavioural disposition (personal communication).

A recent example of how the ontological may be at the root of misunderstood polylanguaging is provided by Blommaert (2009). He shows how, in the United Kingdom, an asylum seeker claiming Rwandan nationality did not speak Rwandan (KiNyaRwanda or OruNyaRwanda) as his first language. For a person not to know well the language of their official nationality is quite common in that region of east-central Africa where wars and drastic population displacement have thrust people into numerous speech enclaves away from their or their parents' natal origin, often to the detriment of any so-called 'mother tongue', to use that Eurocentric misnomer. The British Home Office rejected the application on the grounds that a person must have an original nationality and should therefore be able to speak the language of that nationality. In this case a man's alleged mother tongue should not only define his very being, its apparent absence disqualifies him from acceptable being, a classic case of the analytical falsity of 'methodological nationalism' (where the modern nation, state, society or ethnic group is regarded as the natural analytical or investigative starting-point) .

Let me give some examples of the ontological turn in linguistic ethnography. Similar to Blommaert's description above of the Rwandan refugee in the United Kingdom, Spotti (2016: 266–273) analyzes the case of an Arabic-speaking Sudanese asylum seeker. He shows how Dutch and other European immigration authorities use language tests that focus on immigrant applicants' accents and/or the use of certain words in their speech as clues to where they come from. The authorities are therefore not just discovering who the asylum seekers are but are in effect (re-)constructing their identities. This assumed perfect fit of language to territory simply does not reflect the actual linguistic diversity, as would be evident even in a European capital.

In anticipation of such tests, there has grown a whole industry of private Dutch language courses for applicants, who are in effect being constructed in this way as acceptable Dutch citizens (Spotti 2011(b)). It is not enough to know the host society's cultural norms. Proficiency in an idealised version of its language is also required. Moreover, for immigration authorities, applicants who can demonstrate such linguistic competence through being tested are in effect being assessed as to whether they may become a productive member of the society.

In this way, the language makes the person, or perhaps remakes him/her. Roberts's analysis of British job interviews (2016) shows how they are a form of institutional gatekeeping. It describes how judgements about immigrants' fitness as potential employees (and, by implication, citizens) becomes based on a standardised mode of linguistic competence and often disregards their work experience in another country prior to coming to the UK. The interviewees are in effect penalised for not using the language of assumed competence despite their previous skills. They are judged as not being the 'right' person for the job according to interviewers subliminally affected by applicants' lack of so-called mainstream accent, prosody and lexicon, and despite late modern legal and institutional prohibition of such discriminatory barriers as ethnicity and class.

The irony, as with all the various European entry tests, is that ordinary everyday speech of most or many citizens bears sometimes limited resemblance to the formal language which the applicants have to learn. The heteroglossic urban vernaculars characteristic of all European cities nowadays are in fact what the new immigrants will have to learn for everyday purposes, including that of getting a job and being the productive member of society that is desired by government. But urban mixed vernaculars have ambivalence. They may not help the applicant in a formal job interview where language proficiency based on measurable, standard features is demanded. They may however help the immigrant get a job in the so-called informal employment sector where forms of non-standard English are in common use among small-scale employers of both indigenous and immigrant origin. Moreover, it can be suggested that use of the urban mixed vernaculars may among some people offer a kind of resistance to official government language and educational policy (cf. Urla 1995 on Basque), rather like breakaway religions in some societies resisting formally established faiths. In absorbing these urban vernaculars, people set themselves apart as a separable category. An extension of the irony, therefore, is that it is not the monoglot English, Dutch or other mainstream European language that is likely to define the person, whether new immigrant or long-settled, but their capacity for polylanguaging through knowledge of urban mixed vernaculars, as is the case to some degree for much of the population. So-called BBC standard English is, after all, consistently spoken by only a minority of the country's population.

The case of African marabouts' self-advertisements in France shows how even writing styles can effect an ontological 'realignment' of the person. According to Vigouroux (2011), the marabouts deliberately cultivate the impression of poor French literacy in their written advertisements for their clairvoyant and divinatory skills, for this is how best to persuade potential French clients that they are truly authentic African practitioners, conforming therefore to French stereotypes of them. Thus self-classified, they take on the behavioural characteristics of the stereotype in their relations with customers. As Vigouroux pithily puts it (2011: 53): '... *ways of writing* become iconic of ... *ways of being*. She further says, 'Distinctive ways of writing ... are an essential part of marabouts' *doing being African*' (2011: 58).

Shading into speaking and writing as elements of semiosis are the visual signs and productions that punctuate most forms of everyday discourse. Blommaert and Rampton (2016: 22–23) provide an example of a calligraphic text found on a building in Antwerp which advertises rental accommodation and is written in two forms of Chinese language script. The traditional script probably indicates the writer as a long-standing Chinese immigrant from outside the People's Republic of China (PRC) while the more modern script seems aimed at newer arrivals from within the PRC. It also gives the rent in Yuan rather than Euro and overall suggests a transition in the population of the Chinese diaspora as well as telling us something of the writer and the intended addressees. The visual is implicated in the linguistic in such a way, then, that two quite different social subcategories are defined within the wider category of Chinese incomer: new ones from the PRC and older ones from outside it. They are defined separately according to different language scripts whose effect is visual as much as it is textual.

That meaning is thus multi-modal has been a rich source for understanding different kinds and intensities of communication, whether of propositions or moods (e.g. phatic communion). But, like semiosis and indeed as part of it, ontological person-making is also multi-modal. It may start with a person being fitted into a stereotypical class or category of persons on the basis of visual and acoustic signs distinguishing them. But, ingrained in habitus over time, each person so classified reproduces, exaggerates, and believes in the semiotic features allegedly making up that stereotype.

In addition to the example of the Antwerp advert linguo-visually setting up two categories of Chinese, there is that of the YouTube genre of 'buffalaxed videos' described by Leppänen and Häkkinen (2016: 110–136). These are made up of fragments of films and music videos taken from different cultural backgrounds. The production as a whole is subtitled in the language of the maker which is however homophonic with words drawn from other languages in which the video clips are presented. These original languages are commonly unknown to the video producer and viewer. The juxtaposition and co-occurrence of homophonic subtitles and original language snippets lend themselves to interpretation as new meanings, and so provide what the authors call 'affordances' in which identities and relationships can be represented or, as I would suggest, can be made. Every viewer can find something in the mixture which speaks to their own identity. Indeed it is a form of identity-making which transcends, through its superdiversity, that of conventional contours of ethnicity. It also achieves much of its effect through humour which belittles the many forms of Otherness, justified as harmless fun by some but rejected by others as politically incorrect.

It is an ambivalent genre for which stand-up comedians are noted. Comedians are successful to the extent that they can draw a line between the acceptable and unacceptable while straddling but not crossing it. But their reputations can plunge should they fail in this by saying something regarded by enough people as unambiguously 'racist', 'classist', 'sexist' or 'ageist'. These labels are the modern demarcators not just of moral behaviour but of the proper person, who avoids being so labelled and vice versa. The videos are then more than representational. As is evident through the use of the ecological concept of affordances, they allow viewers to see how they might fit into ontological spaces provided by the mix of identity and relationship possibilities: as in one example, is one gay or straight in one's relationship to an available girl?

The ontological is about being and presence and, as such, is commonly expressed through the body or body parts. Goffman throughout his work shows how the 'presentation of self' is not just the giving out of cognitive cues but is also to do with posture, gesture, physical and bodily orientation, distance in relation to others, and facework or ways of looking at and speaking with. In China the metaphor of 'face' has been much documented as a fundamental feature of status qualification: appearance is everything – at whatever level of social class; and it is seen and assessed from the 'front', whether of a house or a person, for the 'back' has no face and value and can even be neglected. While most societies have a similar form of interpersonal evaluation, the notion of face in China does seem to have special significance in occupying an inordinate area of peoples' concerns in daily interaction (Cf. Hu 1944; Qi 2011).

What is interesting, therefore, in Dong's account (2016: 174–94)) is the importance of 'voice' in contemporary China. Of Bakhtinian origin, this is her term and not that of her informants, though they are perfectly aware of the effects of different modes of language articulation. She uses voice in a conjoined metaphorical and direct manner to refer mainly to types of language use. But we may see how it can be extended in other situations to include differences between high and low status speech varieties, as in Dong's case, and of dialect, pronunciation, pitch, talk-speed, politeness, prosody, and other features of speech, including its absence, i.e. silence, as also being semiotic. 'Face' appears to be about maintaining integral and honourable selfhoods between equals, as for instance between a shop buyer and seller. The main concern is not to lose face more than gaining face. 'Voice' tends towards the assertive insofar as it seeks to advance or defend selfhood and is less concerned to maintain it or create equality between speaker and listener. We may speculate on whether superdiversity and greater interpersonal competition for goods, life-styles and influence in rapidly urbanising, capitalist China has made 'voice' a more prevalent feature of semiotic interaction than 'face' which belongs more to an earlier premise of equality[1].

Dong's account is set among Chinese elite migrants who define themselves in terms of class and status hierarchy. Her self-selected group of wealthy Saab automobile owners reject use and even knowledge of such regional speech varieties as Shanghainese, which they regard as limited in its communicative and status value. The Saab car defines them as an exceptional elite whose expensive consumer interests converge and who come together in order to save the Saab company from bankruptcy and themselves from loss of their status symbol. As cosmopolitans rejecting the regional language as demeaning, they celebrate instead their knowledge both of Putonghua, the national Chinese language, and English. Dong's theoretical point is that having the 'right voice' enables people to be heard more widely than through regional vernaculars such as Shanghainese. It gives them what she calls repertoires of mobility, one throughout China by means of Putonghua and the other internationally through English.

This is an important argument about the dynamics of voice and social stratification and is analysed with the broad sweeps of the brush that current socio-linguistic stratification in China invite. One can apply the same argument more microscopically however to situations on which we have data. For example, differences of accent in the United Kingdom, where much class prejudice, antagonism and rejection rest on the polarisation of so-called lower class and middle class pronunciations (e.g. 'estuary' and 'posh'), pitch and tone, with regional accents variably rated, sometimes treated as lower class and sometimes as standing outside it. Similarly, though in terms of regional rather than class differentiation,

Swahili in Kenya is broadly distinguished as either up-country (*ya bara*) or coastal (*ya pwani*), the latter regarded as 'correct' and 'pure' and the former as at best of pragmatic usefulness only. Such distinctions belie the complicated realities. Coastal Swahili is itself further distinguished both regionally through its many, sometime mutually unintelligible forms, and as to whether it contains more Arabic than Bantu expressions. It is likewise difficult to talk unambiguously of up-country Swahili, given such rapid transformations of the Sheng type, which challenge the very idea of a single Swahili diatype. Estuary English similarly varies across much of central and southern England and in fact may overlap with regional types and residues, with middle class posh English rated above estuary but below 'royal' or 'aristocratic' speech of the 'hise', 'trizers' (for 'house' and 'trousers') variety.

Here we see 'voice' as the individual speaker's ability or inability to communicate successfully in a specific situation, doing so through adoption of a particular conventionalised 'style', the appropriateness of which determines the success or failure of the communication. As Rampton notes, 'style/voice tension is experienced in many social sites, as people struggle to match their expressive resources to the requirements of the situation' (personal communication March 2012).

'Voice' in this sense may then hover over the possibility either of deriving from or building on the stylisations of social categories which, like the speech varieties and registers, are in fact much more diverse than their stereotypes. 'Higher' speech forms embedded unambiguously in social hierarchies seem moreover to move up and away when threatened from below. Thus once the voice immediately below begins to approach in imitation the one above it, the latter develops new aspects of voice, principally pronunciation but also other speech elements and lexicon. Rampton's findings in London suggest that this process will become ever more complicated through superdiversity, as older ethnic and class differences are cut across by new kinds of hierarchised speech forms under the pressure of, and in partial 'resistance', to standard language regimes.

An interesting question is whether voice, as an expression of assertiveness, will develop a kind of autonomy of movement that precedes the creation of recognised social groupings. That is to say, will new experimental forms of voice, as defined above, be used at a pace which exceeds that of observable social differentiation? To put it simply, is class in the older sense already lagging behind voice in some late modern cities such as London, at least among the young and those older speakers exposed earlier to the process? Imagine a lower class speaker of either immigrant or indigenous origin working in the City of London, retaining their version of Estuary but, with like-speaking colleagues, setting themselves up as a desirably successful reference group in money-making skills and conspicuous consumption. Certainly media exploitation of class and regional styles, as in television adverts and some soaps, often celebrates what were once low status attributes.

Back with Dong's case, we note that the elite status of the Saab owners is threatened by the possibility that a reduction in the price of the automobile will bring in 'other' people who can now afford it but who are not regarded as of their status. The elite then distances itself further through even more consumerism by buying expensive wines, cigars and playing golf in addition to continuing to buy Saab cars. Through semiosis a status category of relatively unconnected individuals develops a common interest and agency. Semiosis thus mediates the transition from classification to ingrained ontology. It is the equivalent of the British upper classes traditionally altering pronunciation, prosody and vocabulary in order to distance themselves from evident imitation by lower strata, a subtle process which occurs slowly and perhaps largely unconsciously.

Continuing with China we have a case where 'vernacular' does not connote the regional limitations that the Saab owners ascribe to Shanghainese. Varis and Wang (2016: 218–236) show how a particular form of hip-hop rapping in Beijing makes use of various global vernacular varieties. They make up a mix and create what the authors call supervernaculars. These are 'global ways of fashioning identities, forms of communication, genres, etc., recognizable for members of emergent super-groups'. They share indexical orders, and 'super-communities' are constructed through them. This coordination and bringing together of the different bits and pieces of global vernaculars is made possible through the internet, or at least the internet makes it possible for the mix to reach very many more people than would otherwise be the case.

The difference between the more face-to-face 'club' of Saab owners and the internet hip-hop rappers and audience, both within China, illustrates two uses of English. Saab club English complements Putonghua but both are viewed as relatively distinct and bounded, for that is how they can be stratified. Shanghainese is rejected and cannot therefore 'muddy' either of the two main languages, whose discrete boundedness is therefore reinforced through non-interference by the vernacular. By contrast, English for the Beijing rapper 'is the supervernacular template', into which are inserted the chosen elements of Chinese and Korean (related to current Chinese enthusiasm for Korean pop culture). Moreover, this template provides 'affordances' (Leppänen and Häkkinen 2016; Varis and Wang 2016), because it is made up of such a variety of language use, clothing and other signs taken from different sources that speakers can creatively make up new combinations in the rapping lyrics and images. The thrust of Varis and Wang (2016) is indeed to show how such creativity jostles with normative constraints in a kind of search for authenticity: 'true' rap or hip-hop is Afro-American and yet is presented with a Chinese accent and so is also 'really' Chinese, possessing rebelliousness and yet working within limits of Chinese public acceptability. One image presented in Varis and Wang (2016) is of 'a young Afro male, suggesting an alignment with "hip-hop authority" embodied in blackness – being and doing "black".' It reminds us again of the marabouts doing and being 'African' in order to conform to Parisians' stereotypes of them. This is clearly an ontological consequence, i.e. creating an identity, which draws on semiotic resources. It is to the theme of these resources, central to all the presentations in Arnaut *et al.* (2016), that I now turn.

Semiotic Resources, Repertoire and Style

The concern with resources presupposes speakers as agents. They are agents not in the unsubtle or logocentric sense of calculating beforehand the effects of speech, but as having an effect on listeners without necessarily intending that effect. Insofar as we can distinguish it, this is communicative intention which is implicit to speaking in context. In other words, we may intend something but may also elaborate on meaning as we go along, as part of performing the utterance. Putting this crudely, we often know the full sense of what we have said only after we have said it and observed its effect on the listener, sometimes to our dismay but usually without cause or wish to reflect on that sense. Resources are, by definition, there to be used or exploited, and so we must be talking about processes of speaking which draw on them as part of the speech act but without singular, aim-directed consciousness.

This view of the relationship between resources and action departs from a much earlier view prevalent in the 1960s of transactional analysis. This argued that actors are impelled to maximise gains at minimal cost, using resources consisting not just of material goods but also of emotions, reputations, and interactional skills (Barth 1966). In Nairobi in the late 1960s, Parkin (1974) looked at the use of language resources in an urban market place. There sellers and buyers of different, unambiguously defined ethnic groups made challenges and concessions to each other by including parts of each other's language in a serious game to gain custom or a lower price. The resources were seen as directly deriving from ethnic languages whose boundaries were maintained despite the reciprocal borrowing in the market transactions. It was a view of resources in the economic sense and of ethnic groups regarded by townsfolk as distinctive of each other. The classificatory predominated over the ontological, with only strains of the latter identified (e.g. Parkin 1971). Whereas that view focused on actors' strategies, with language resources waiting as objects to be gathered for use, the chapters in Arnaut *et al.* (2016) place greater emphasis on the wider range of semiotic resources as comprising the non-verbal as well as verbal, how they are created and used for new forms of communication, and on how they are inextricably part of the (changing) selfhoods of their speakers.

Their approach is concerned with the evolution of environments of linguistic opportunity resulting from the superdiversity of semiotic modes and sensibilities operating together. This approach does of course set up (the outlines of) social categories of users, as discussed above. I perceive however something near to a generative explanation: superdiversity produces 'affordances' and opportunities for semiotic crossovers which produce further diversity at an often bewildering pace, as seemingly befits the current global age. A couple of authors even talk of superdiversity as a generative logic which is not unreasonable at a certain level of analysis but raises the question of what are the triggers of choice and change among speakers.

Perhaps this is to ask how semiotic resources become what Blommaert and others have referred to as a semiotic repertoire (Blommaert and Varis 2011; 2012). That is to say, resources exist out there ready to be garnered; a repertoire is a particular ordering of them. How do we get from the first to the second? And how do speakers/communicators avoid the hazards of being unfamiliar with harvestable signs and voices and of not understanding them. In other words, resources may be out there but we cannot always know them well enough to arrange and use them to good effect. More confidently, Varis and Wang (2016) in their study of the internet in China emphasise that in tandem with the creativity afforded by linguistic superdiversity, the meanings produced through semiotic signs are nevertheless systematic, stratified and context-specific and conform to conventional normative patterns. Similarly, Dong (2016: 180) asserts that 'Linguistic resources are never distributed in a random way. … (they) are distributed according to the logic of the social system, and sociolinguistic analysis has from its inception addressed these non-random aspects of distribution'.

How does the creativity involved in building up and presenting new multi-modal semiotic repertoires engage with normativity? Creativity presupposes non-normative innovation, i.e. by transcending the non-random norms. So how can we be creative, i.e. non-normative, if meaning is drawn from the normative? The answer seems to be that it is by taking norms out of their conventionalised patterns, mixing them and presenting them for effect. The effect would seem to be to highlight a message or to package it in a special way. Its packaging is therefore likely to be a matter of style as well as of communication. That is to say, the way we communicate and create 'truths' about ourselves and our interlocutors is conveyed by a changing variety of styles and is not governed by a uniform logic.

This emphasis on style comes out directly or indirectly in many ways, most evidently as an aspect of the various forms of youth speech and pop-culture, including visual, acoustic and dress, and especially as a feature of late modern urban society. It is true that 'style' has a standard linguistic connotation of identifying a linguistic variety. Jørgensen *et al.* (2016: 145–151) suggest that, in this sense, it is one of a number of unacceptably delimited ways of analysing language, because it does not reflect the reality of speech for which the idea of semiotic resources is necessary instead. Style is of course also used in a number of different ways, for example as mode or register, covering form, interaction and ideology and not just delimited speech varieties. There is also the distinctive, everyday social connotation of trying to impress an audience, of being a discursive strategy, or style or stylisation as ontologically enacted. Arnaut *et al.* (2016) give many examples: the use of English and Afro images in Chinese hip-hop/rap; of highly rated Creole among South London schoolchildren; the choice of 'cool' music and lyrics from different cultures as in the buffalaxed videos; the display of magic in 'doing African' of the Paris marabouts; the status-conscious brandishing of cigars, wine, cars and golf club membership among the Chinese Saab owners; and, reaching out for the classification that may provide the conditions for national acceptance, the almost ceremonial parading of lavish language test certificates for migrants and asylum seekers in European cities. Being culturally defined, the absence of style contributes to communicative disadvantage or is regarded as linguistic incompetence, as among the immigrant job-seekers unfamiliar with British styles described by Roberts (2016: 237–260)

Style for impression-management is clearly both semiotic resource and part of a repertoire. It is likely also to be consubstantial with bodily use and images, as the examples just given suggest. The linguistic is part of this semiotics but seems almost to be drowned in its multi-modality. However, we can see such multi-modality as creating a stylised semiotic package, in which speech, texts, non-verbal sounds and the visual intertwine. The packages serve two main demands made of interlocutors: to act ontologically in the sense of interacting with others on the same semiotic wavelength; and to impress listeners and bystanders. That they also classify, instruct, persuade, admonish and promise seems to me to follow in the wake of style in actual social contexts in conditions of late modern urban superdiversity.

Our interest may indeed be in a general semiology, of which language is but one strand, possibly absent altogether in, say, silent rituals lacking verbal and textual comment. But, as a matter of heuristic choice rather than of theoretical stance, it can be argued that language normally provides an empirically convenient starting-point for tracing out the other different visual and acoustic sign systems that accompany, substitute for, blend with and shadow speech. The caveat is not to return to bounded, essentialised speech varieties and languages as the initial building blocks of what we observe and study.

Acknowledgements

I thank Ben Rampton for very extensive and insightful comments on this chapter, most of which I have been able to address, Jan Blommaert and Max Spotti for some useful references, and Karel Arnaut for comment and advice.

Note

(1) Based on an observation made by Rampton.

References

Arnaut, K. (2016) Superdiversity: elements of an emerging perspective. In K. Arnaut, J. Blommaert, B. Rampton and M. Spotti (eds) *Language and superdiversity*. New York and Abingdon: Routledge.

Arnaut, K, M.S. Karrebaek, M. Spotti and J. Blommaert (eds) (2017) *Engaging superdiversity: recombining spaces, times and language practices*. Bristol. Blue Ridge Summit: Multilingual Matters.

Blom, J.P. and Gumperz, J.J. (1970) “Social Meaning in Linguistic Structures.” In John J. Gumperz and Dell Hymes (eds) *Directions in Sociolinguistics*. New York: Holt, Rinehart and Winston.

Blommaert, J. (2009) Language, asylum and the natural order. *Current Anthropology* 50 (4), 415–441.

Blommaert, J. and Maly, I. (2016) Ethnographic linguistic landscape analysis and social change: a case study. In K. Arnaut, J. Blommaert, B. Rampton and M. Spotti (eds) *Language and superdiversity*. New York and Abingdon: Routledge.

Blommaert, J. and Rampton, B. (2016) Language and superdiversity. In K. Arnaut, J. Blommaert, B. Rampton and M. Spotti (eds) *Language and superdiversity*. New York and Abingdon: Routledge.

Blommaert, J. and Varis, P. (2011) *Enough is enough: The heuristics of authenticity in superdiversity*. Tilburg Papers in Cultural Studies, 2. Tilburg University.

Blommaert, J. and Varis, P. (2012) Culture as accent. *Tilburg Papers in Cultural Studies. Paper*, 18. Tilburg University.

Creese, A. and Blackledge, A. (2010) Translanguaging in the bilingual classroom: A pedagogy for learning and teaching? *The Modern language journal* 94 (1), 103–115.

Dong, J. (2016) Mobility, voice, and symbolic restratification: an ethnography of 'elite migrants' in urban China. In K. Arnaut, J. Blommaert, B. Rampton and M. Spotti (eds) *Language and superdiversity*. New York and Abingdon: Routledge.

Fishman, J.A. (1966) *Language loyalty in the United States; the maintenance and perpetuation of non-English mother tongues by American ethnic and religious groups*. The Hague: Mouton.

Fishman, J.A. (1971) *Bilingualism in the barrio*. Bloomington: Indiana University Press.

Gumperz, J. (1961) Speech variation and the study of Indian civilization. *American Anthropologist* 63, 976–988.

Gumperz, J. (1982) *Discourse strategies*. Cambridge: Cambridge University Press.

Gumperz, J. (1984) Communication and Social Identity. In A. Jacobson-Widding (ed.) *Identity: Personal and Socio-Cultural*. Uppsala Studies in Cultural Anthropology 5.

Gumperz, J. and E. Hernández-Chavez (1972) "Bilingualism, bidialectalism, and classroom interaction", in C. Cazden, V. John and D. Hymes (eds) *Functions of Language in the Classroom*. New York: Teachers College Press 84–108.

Hanks, W. (1996) *Language and Communicative Practices*. Colorado: Westview Press.

Hu, Hsien Chin (1944) The Chinese Concept of "Face". *American Anthropologist* 46 (1), 45–64.

Hymes, D. (1962) The ethnography of speaking. In Thomas Gladwin and William C. Sturtevant (eds) *Anthropology and human behaviour*. Washington D.C.: Anthropological Society of Washington, pp. 13–53.

Jorgensen, J.N, M.S. Karreboek, L.M. Madsen and Moeller, J.S. (2016) In In K. Arnaut, J. Blommaert, B. Rampton and M. Spotti (eds) *Language and superdiversity*. New York and Abingdon: Routledge.

Leppänen, S. and Elo, A. (2016) Buffalaxing the other: superdiversity in action on You Tube. In K. Arnaut, J. Blommaert, B. Rampton and M. Spotti (eds) *Language and superdiversity*. New York and Abingdon: Routledge.

Levinson, S.C. (1997) A review of John J. Gumperz's contribution to the academic community. In Susan Eerdmans (ed). *Discussing communication analysis 1*. Lausanne: Beta Press.

Levinson, Stephen C. (2003) Contextualising 'contextualization cues'. *Language and interaction: Discussions with John J. Gumperz*. S.L. Eerdmans, C.L. Prevignano, and P.J. Thibault (eds) pp. 31–39. Amsterdam: John Benjamins.

Parkin, D.J. (1971) Language choice in two Kampala housing estates. In W.H. Whiteley (ed.) *Language use and social change*. London: University of Oxford Press for International African Institute, pp. 347–363.

Parkin, D.J. (1974) Chapters 5–8 in W.H. Whiteley (ed.) Language in Kenya. Nairobi and London: University of Oxford Press.

Parkin, D.J. (1977) Stabilized and emergent multilingualism. In H. Giles (ed.) Language, Ethnicity and Inter-Group Relations. London and New York. Academic Press.

Qi, Xiaoying (2011) Face: a Chinese Concept in a Global Sociology. *Journal of Sociology* 47, 279–296

Rampton, B. (1995) *Crossing: language and ethnicity among adolescents*. London: Longman.

Rampton, B. (2006) *Language in late modernity: interaction in an urban school*. Cambridge: Cambridge University Press.

Rampton, B. (2010) An everyday poetics of class and ethnicity in stylization and crossing. In *Working Papers in Urban Language & Literacies*, 59. London: King's College, University of London.

Rampton, B. (2011) From 'Multi-ethnic adolescent heteroglossia' to 'Contemporary urban vernaculars'. *Working papers in urban languages and literacies*, 61. London: King's College, University of London.

Rampton, B. (2013) Styling in a language learned later in life. *The Modern Language Journal* 97 (2), 360–382.

Rampton, B. (2016) Drilling down to the grain in superdiversity. In K. Arnaut, J. Blommaert, B. Rampton and M. Spotti (eds) *Language and superdiversity*. New York and Abingdon: Routledge.

Roberts, C. (2016) Translating global experience into institutional models of competency: linguistic inequalities in the job interview. In K. Arnaut, J. Blommaert, B. Rampton and M. Spotti (eds) *Language and superdiversity*. New York and Abingdon: Routledge.

Southall, A.W. (1970) The illusion of tribe. *Journal of Asian and African studies* 5, 28–50.

Spotti, M. (2011a) Modernist language ideologies, indexicalities and identities: Looking at the multilingual classroom through a post-Fishmanian lens. *Applied Linguistics Review* 22, 29–50.

Spotti, M. (2011b) Ideologies of success for superdiverse citizens: The Dutch testing regime for integration and the online private sector. *Diversities* 13 (2), 39–52.

Spotti, M. (2016) Sociolinguistic shibboleths at the institutional gate: language, origin, and the construction of asylum seekers' identities. In K. Arnaut, J. Blommaert, B. Rampton and M. Spotti (eds) *Language and superdiversity*. New York and Abingdon: Routledge.

Urla, J. (1995) Outlaw language: creating alternative public spheres in Basque free radio. *Pragmatics* 5 (2), 245–61.

Varis, P. and Wang, X. (2016) Superdiversity on the internet: a case from China. In K. Arnaut, J. Blommaert, B. Rampton and M. Spotti (eds) *Language and superdiversity*. New York and Abingdon: Routledge.

Vertovec, S. (2007) Super-diversity and its implications. *Ethnic and Racial Studies* 29 (6), 1024–54.

Vigouroux, C.B. (2011) Magic marketing: performing grassroots literacy. In J. Blommaert, B. Rampton, M. Spotti (eds) Language and Superdiversities. *Diversities*. Vol 13. No 2. UNESCO Online journal.

Vigouroux, C.B. and Mufwene, S.S. (2008) *Globalization and language vitality: perspectives from Africa*. London and New York: Continuum.

2 Emergent and Stabilised Multilingualism: Polyethnic Peer Groups in Urban Kenya

Ethnicity implies the mutual recognition of cultural and linguistic differences between social groups in interaction with each other. Where such differences persist for generations, they take on an oppositional quality: the vernacular and culture of one group are seen as in various ways opposed to those of another group. As if obeying a law of phonemic construction, the very distinctiveness of a culture and vernacular or code may only be conceptualised through such opposition. When opposed in this way, languages, codes and cultures frequently become associated as the distinctive property of ethnic groups in politico-economic competition, conflict, or outright confrontation.

In ethnic confrontation the vernacular or speech variety of whichever emerges as the dominant group is likely to become the primary language of authority and state. The relationship of English to Welsh in Britain, of Canadian English to Canadian French, or of varieties of American English to Mexican Spanish, are a few of the many familiar and well documented examples (e.g. Giles 1977). In these kinds of admittedly changing and yet relatively "established" situations of ethnic confrontation, each vernacular or speech variety is unambiguously associated with one or other ethnic group. But in many parts of the Third World, particularly those which have recently been under colonial rule, there exists a second kind of ethnic and linguistic situation. It can be called emergent.

Emergent multilingualism includes use of a colonial lingua franca together with an indigenous, usually pre-colonial, lingua franca. They are used alongside different vernaculars or mother tongues in ethnically mixed speech communities of recent creation. But, unlike these ethnic vernaculars, the colonial and indigenous lingua francas are not unambiguously regarded by members of the speech community as the property of any one ethnic group nor even of a distinct "class" or status group. Some main examples from Africa are: English and Swahili in Eastern Africa (Whiteley, 1974, Abdulaziz-Mkilifi, 1972), French and Swahili in Central Africa (Polome, 1971), English and Fangalo (not pre-colonial) also in Central Africa (Cole, 1964), French and Wolof in Western Africa (Wioland and Calvet, 1967; Calvet, 1971), and English and "Pidgin" English/Creole also in Western Africa (Scotton, 1976). These are examples of extensive lingua francas which are no longer, and sometimes never were, regarded as exclusively the mother tongue of particular ethnic or other sociocultural groups.

This multilingual situation is emergent in the sense that these ethnically and socioculturally unattached lingua francas have at least the potential for becoming recognised as the distinctive property of a particular ethnic or sociocultural group (e.g. English of an elite or of an ethnic group transformed into a dominant collectivity, and Swahili of an urban proletariat in, say, up-country Kenya). Though still emergent in this sense, use of these lingua francas does already carry their social connotations as either High, Low or Middle diatypes. These overarching connotations of the lingua francas influence the acquisition and use of their vernaculars by members of ethnic groups in the polyethnic settings which are so common in African and other Third World towns.

In this chapter, I want to substantiate this ideal-type distinction between emergent and established or, as I would prefer to call it, stabilised multilingualism. By the use of the term stabilised, I do not mean to imply that the linguistic situation is unchanging. Far from it, for that is never possible. But, accepting that language stability (see Fishman, 1964, 1967) is a relative concept only of significance in comparative analysis, I find its use legitimate. I also prefer the term emergent rather than evolving, to avoid any assumptions of linear development contained in the latter. Finally, as a matter of convenience, the terms "multilingualism" (including "bilingualism") and "language" are also taken to refer to mutually intelligible but otherwise distinct varieties of a single language, known as diglossia when there are two, triglossia when three, and so on (Ferguson, 1959).

My argument is two-fold. First, that in emergent polyethnic and multilingual situations, the pattern of language-use relationships enjoys, so to speak, great autonomy as long as some of its constituent languages remain detached, as yet, from unambiguous associations with specific groups. The pattern of language-use relationships can here be visualised as a relatively free-floating system of values and connotations. Yet, internally, the pattern of language-use relationships is such that a change in the connotations of, say, English, must affect or be affected by change in the connotations of, say, Swahili or a vernacular to which it is conceptually opposed.

Second that the pattern of values and connotations emerging from opposed language-use relationships may provide a kind of template along the lines of which social groups may later become distinguished. To put this point simply, emergent multilingualism as I have defined it may precede and so prepare the ground for marked social differentiation. This is a radical modification of an hypothesis advanced by Fox (1968). Fox saw the adoption of loanwords as preparing the ground for later cultural assimilation. I argue that it is people's conceptualisation of how languages in their speech environment are related to each other, rather than whether or not they actually borrow words, syntax or phonology, which provide the outlines on which new sociocultural groups may be based. I am here ascribing a degree of collective consciousness to language-use relationships, an emerging sense of "them" and "us", which is prior to that of other observable cultural features by which groups are normally assumed to express their distinctiveness, e.g. customs, life-styles and even myths.

In the Kenyan case I describe here, some adolescents vehemently claim to be "Swahili-speakers" and others to be "English-speakers". But this distinction does not accurately reflect their actual use of either language. It reflects their perception of an educational and socioeconomic cleavage emerging between disadvantaged adolescents, expressed as Swahili-speaking, and "privileged" adolescents, expressed as Englishspeaking. This putative difference of Swahili and English usage cuts across the bonds of everyday vernacular usage which, for each ethnic group, continues to have great practical as well as moral significance.

Thus, the conceptually opposed High and Low diatypes, English and Swahili, anticipate the expression of status groups which cut across the distinctive ethnic groups variously in alliance or rivalry.

I am not departing from the conventional view that economic and material property interests are the basis of persisting differences between self-perpetuating groups. But I suggest that an early, perhaps the earliest, expression of such differences is likely to become located in a pre-existing pattern of opposed language-use relationships.

Stabilised Multilingualism and Ethnic Polarisation

The degree and nature of change in a multilingual situation may usefully be understood by tracing speech differences between the generations making up a community. For this reason, I focus in this chapter on the distinctive use of language by children and adolescents. The two cases chosen to develop the argument are from Harlem, USA, which has two mutually intelligible diatypes, and Nairobi, Kenya, which has a plurality of mutually unintelligible ones. In spite of such a fundamental difference, of diglossia on the one hand and multilingualism on the other, we find similar factors operating to define the role of language use within the two speech communities. This underlying similarity derives from the oppositional quality which speakers themselves attribute to the diatypes regardless of their number and degree of mutual lexical intelligibility. I begin by abstracting two general propositions from Labov's famous critique of the theory that Harlem schoolchildren are verbally deprived, and then apply them to the Nairobi case.

First, Labov stresses the necessity for analysing adolescent culture in order to understand that their speech is alternative but not inferior to dominant and therefore "standard" middle class suburban speech. Seen in its own terms and not according to grammatical criteria derived from middle class speech of predominantly White origin, Labov shows that (*sic*) "Non-standard Negro English" (NNE) cannot be said to lack the capacity for logical expression, as has been suggested. It is necessary to understand the ethnic ghetto's adolescent culture because the peer group exerts more influence over the individual's speech than does the school. Thus, while the adolescent rejected by the peer group for his personal deficiencies may respond well to the middle class norms of school and so come to speak what is regarded as standard English, "the healthy, vigorous popular child with normal intelligence" (Labov 1972) is by definition a central member of the peer group and, in solidarity with the rest, is likely to reject school and standard English and to continue to emphasise use of his peer group vernacular. In this process of speech formation, the family is reported as also, like the school, exerting less influence than the peer group, especially from the age of nine or ten. In other words, three variable influences operate: school, family and peer group. The peer group is dominant and the school, a mainly White middle-class institution, is potentially divisible. This is the first proposition. Second, Labov's study isolates the normative framework of standard English as middle class and predominantly White, and NNE as lower class and predominantly Black. We can abstract from this the general and unsurprising proposition that the polarisation of ethnic and class interests and solidarity is likely to be accompanied by a polarisation of speech styles.

Polarisation may occur along two dimensions. First, it may be an expected concomitant of the life- cycle. Thus, in the ongoing political and cultural confrontation between Black/lower class and White middle class in and around Harlem, children progressively emphasise contrasting speech styles as they pass from early and late childhood, through adolescence, and into adulthood. Labov (1972) reports, for instance, that four to seven year old Black children are more likely to use the full form of the copula "is" (e.g. "it is mine" (standard English) rather than "it mine" (NNE)) than older children and adolescents, indicating that the maturation process is accompanied by a rejection of "White middle class" speech influences and the formulation of an alternative, low-level rule which limits redundancy.

Another, partial, example of this process of life-cycle polarisation, though of North American bilingualism rather than diglossia, is apparent in a study by Gumperz and Hernandez. They note that Mexican American teenagers prefer to use English among themselves, but revert to Spanish when they marry (in Whiteley 1971). This reversion to the mother tongue as a main language among peers seems to indicate acceptance by adults of their distinctive "Mexican" ethnic identity in the wider, to some extent stratified, polyethnic situation. It is what we might expect of stabilised bilingualism, in which use of the High diatype, English, is unambiguously associated with a dominant group speaking it as its mother tongue. In this respect, the use of NNE in Harlem corresponds with the use of Spanish. Both are emphasised at mature points in the lifecycle, adolescent in the case of Harlem, and adult among the Mexican Americans, possibly as a result of growing awareness by the individual of the relatively unchanging ethnic power and opportunity structure, and of the likely unalterability of his own ethnic identity. The Harlem rejection of Standard English and commitment to NNE at adolescence rather than adulthood suggests an early awareness of ethnic unalterability, as might be expected of a Black American community.

These are both examples of the predictable dimension of ethnic speech polarisation which occurs in a relatively unchanging situation of political and cultural confrontation.

Emergent Multilingualism and Ethnic Polarisation

In situations of emergent multilingualism, there is a second more comprehensive dimension of ethnic speech polarisation. It arises from significant changes in the relationship to each other of ethnic groups: those formerly in confrontation may come into alliance, and vice versa. It can only occur when more than two ethnic collectivities are identified in the total social system. This identification is not usually unambiguously clear to outsiders but, as a "folk" classificatory system, may exert great symbolic power over insiders and be used to explain misfortune. Thus, members of ethnic groups X and Y together blame their misfortunes on the alleged dominance of Z group, while the latter attribute their misfortunes to the believed subversion of either or both X and Y; later on, the direction of accusations may be altered following a shift in the dominance pattern, in which X, say, is regarded as supreme, and so on. In much of independent Africa, such polyethnicity is a common characteristic of large towns, and alternating relationships of alliance and confrontation are found in some of them. Polarisation may occur between groups AB and CD during one historical period, and between AC and BD during a subsequent period, possibly settling to a more enduring pattern. Nairobi, the cultural capital of Kenya, is one city in East Africa in which this has happened.

Nairobi: A Political Profile

The population (1969 census) of Nairobi is 509,286, of whom 82% are African, 14% Asian and 4% European. Four ethnic groups make up most of the African population: Kikuyu 45%, Luo 15%, Luyia 15% and Kamba 14%, with "other" groups making up the rest. Intermarriage between these four groups is infrequent and their cultural distinctiveness has been emphasised even more in the increasing competition for jobs and housing in the current era of great scarcity. Without going into details, it can reasonably be claimed that immediately before and after Kenya's independence in 1963, the Kikuyu and Luo were allies dominating one political party, the Kenya African National Union (KANU), which also included the Kamba, while the Luyia and other smaller groups (not heavily represented in Nairobi) were allies making up the opposing political party, the Kenya African Democratic Party (KADU). KADU voluntarily disbanded itself in 1964. Thereafter, however, KANU became increasingly dominated by Kikuyu and, gradually, Luo associated themselves with a new political party, the Kenya Peoples Union (KPU), which was set up in 1966 by some foremost Luo leaders.

Thus, the Luo and Kikuyu, once allies, were now politically opposed. The Luyia, who share a common home boundary with the Luo in western Kenya, became politically "closer" to the Luo, not to the extent of joining the KPU in large numbers but by the positions taken by their political representatives. The Kamba, who are linguistically and culturally close to the Kikuyu nevertheless became a distinct power block, sometimes standing in political opposition to the Kikuyu but likely also, at an interpersonal level, to translate their cultural affinity with Kikuyu into more practical expressions of solidarity in the competitive environment of Nairobi (e.g. job-finding, business relationships, co-residence) (see Table 1).

In other words, there has been a complete reversal of the formal alliances, with Kikuyu and the Luo now opposed to the Luo and Luyia in alliance, and with Kamba ambivalently placed but, in many informal

Table 1[1]

1963→	1964→	1966→	1969→	→1969→
Kenya's independence KANU (Luo, Kikuyu and Kamba)		KANU (Kikuyu, Kamba and Luyia)		KANU Effective one-party political system
KADU (Luyia and others)	KADU Voluntarily disbanded	KPU Luo New political party	KPU banned	

contexts, drawn to the Kikuyu. To be precise, while broadly accurate, these are the folk classifications of people themselves in Nairobi and are really abstractions from the more complex political reality. They represent peoples' perceptions of the changes of ethnic political polarisation. As I shall show below, one reflection of these perceived political changes is the way in which quadri-ethnic children's play groups eventually become divided into adolescent groups of Luo and Luyia on the one hand, and of Kikuyu and Kamba on the other. Within each of these adolescent "alliances", family and school create further divisions.

A Nairobi Speech Community

I can begin to show these developments by looking at a public housing area in Nairobi of men, women and children, in which all four ethnic groups are well represented: Kikuyu 14%, Kamba 16%, Luyia 26% and Luo 39%. It can be seen that this housing estate (called Kaloleni) is unusual in accommodating a majority of western Kenyans, the Luo and the Luyia, in a town otherwise dominated by Kikuyu. However, the recreational and school relationships of older children and adolescents spread beyond this housing estate. The estate is therefore one in which city-wide Kikuyu numerical preponderance is counterbalanced by the estate's own preponderance of Luo and Luyia, with Kamba roughly equalling their proportion in the city. Another unusual characteristic of the housing estate is that each of the ethnic groups (though less so among the Kamba) contains a significant proportion of families which have been raised more in the city than in the rural areas from which the parents of nearly all of them originally migrated. Most of the children attend or have attended school in Nairobi (though with much variation in years of attendance), and so the estate provides a good laboratory situation, in a general context of ethnic polarisation, for analysing the interaction of peer group, family and school as variable influences on their speech formation.

Before presenting the case material on which this analysis is based, I provide a brief speech profile of the inhabitants. The vernaculars of the Kikuyu, Kamba and Luyia are of the Bantu family, while that of the Luo is Nilotic. Kikuyu and Kamba speech are very close, (lexically, syntactically and phonologically), and after a few years in Nairobi, speakers can understand each other reasonably well. The shared rural border of the Luo and Luyia peoples has resulted, according to self-reports (Parkin, 1974), in over a quarter of Luyia male household heads in Kaloleni being able to converse in Luo in addition to their own vernacular, with a much smaller proportion (7%) of Luo speaking Luyia. Swahili is spoken at varying levels by nearly everyone on the estate, among many men to a surprisingly high level of fluency, and may be regarded as the main lingua franca. English is spoken to a "reasonable" conversational level (i.e. "fluently") by over 40% of the men but by less than 10% of women.[2] Most children of school age attend school. All learn English, which is now the medium of instruction, with the older children generally surpassing in fluency those of their fathers who can speak English but who were taught it as a second language and not as a medium of instruction. Other children of school age are likely to have attended previously but to have been obliged to drop out early, usually owing to a lack of school fees. A large number of them can speak English, yet though their general level of competence is likely to be slightly lower, they and others tend to exaggerate the difference grossly. We shall in due course see the significance of this perception of under-competence in English by school dropouts.

Use of either English, Swahili and the vernaculars generates a corresponding stereotype or set of stereotypes (Parkin, 1971; 1974; Scotton, 1976). When reasonably fluent English is spoken (i.e. by adults and adolescents) it connotes relatively high educational level and socioeconomic status (though not necessarily reflecting these in individual cases). Swahili has ambivalent connotations. On the other hand, people regard its indigenous African origins and its lack of association with any dominant ethnic group as facilitating the expression of national identity, a view taken long ago by the Tanzanian government (Whiteley, 1969; cf. Chapter 13). On the other hand, the informal contexts in which people come to know Swahili, and its secondary status to English as a curricular subject rather than medium of instruction in schools, can imply that those who use it in ethnically mixed situations cannot speak English and so lack education. The positive values attached to Swahili's capacity to transcend ethnicity and express national "brotherhood" is thus at variance with the negative value attached to the situational connotations it may have of low educational and, by implication, low socioeconomic status. We shall see how this ambivalence emanating from the use of Swahili, in contrast to the relatively unambivalent high status connotations of English affects children and adolescents. Finally, the four ethnic vernaculars generally connote ethnic inclusiveness and solidarity to native speakers, and, conversely, exclusion and opposition when used in ethnically mixed contexts.

Having provided a speech profile of the housing estate, I now describe the lifestyles (i.e. their culture) of its children and adolescents. The purpose of the description is to show the parts played by family, peer group and school as influences on attitudes to and use of English, Swahili and the four vernaculars.

The Process of Ethnic Polarisation among the Young: Case Material from Nairobi

A remarkable feature of young children in Kaloleni is their wide use of Swahili. It is characteristic that a group of brothers and sisters will speak their vernacular to their parents and to each other in the urban household. But, literally on leaving the threshold, they switch to Swahili both in talking to each other and to friends of other ethnic groups. Their play groups tend to be ethnically mixed and Swahili is used. From an early age, boys become avid and skilful soccer players and form teams which are organised in part imitation of the Kenya league teams. It is interesting to note that, whether or not the group of children playing soccer on a piece of spare land in Kaloleni is ethnically mixed, Swahili is the medium of communication, with English loan-words used only to refer to specific rules or properties of the game: e.g. goal, penalty, handball, corner, dodge, win, etc.[3] In other play contexts, Swahili is also frequently used between children of the same ethnic group, but with interference from the vernacular as well as from English.

A noticeable change occurs in the composition of playgroups as children approach puberty. Whereas the playgroups of young children comprise the four main ethnic groups of Luo, Luyia, Kikuyu and Kamba, the peer groups of older children gradually polarise into two types: Luo with Luyia on the one hand, and Kikuyu with Kamba on the other. Both represent proto-types of the two main adult political and/or cultural alliances. The use of Swahili diminishes slightly at the expense of Luo in the first case, and of Kikuyu in the second.

As they become adolescent, these groups harden into societies and gangs of the familiar juvenile type each consisting of between 30 and 50 members, not all of whom are likely to be interacting with each other on any one occasion but among whom is a regular core of 10 to 15. Thus, an adolescent is ethnically identified as belonging to either a Luo-Luyia or a

Table 2

Children ⟶		Adolescents ⟶		Adults
Ethnically mixed play groups (1) Swahili mainly used	(Luo) (Luyia) (Kikuyu) (Kamba)	*"Swahili-speaking" gangs* (2a) Luo-Luyia (Luo is main vernacular) (3a) Kikuyu-Kamba (Kikuyu is main vernacular)	*"English-speaking" societies* (2b) Luo-Luyia (Luo is main vernacular) (3b) Kikuyu-Kamba (Kikuyu is main vernacular)	(4) High rate of ethnic endogamy, resulting in even sharper lines of ethnic social differentiation and vernacular "loyalty"

Kikuyu-Kamba group. Within this group s/he is also identified as belonging either to a gang or a society (see Table 2 and explanation following in text).

First there are those which may actually call themselves student welfare "societies" and, in English, write their own constitutions, elect officers, attempt to collect subscriptions and closely imitate the ethnic and other voluntary associations of their elders, perhaps even becoming registered. They consist of boys and girls still at school but include a minority who, though they may be obliged to drop out, hope to return soon. Though they imitate their parents' ethnic associations, they are only loosely ethnically exclusive; Luo-Luyia on the one hand and Kikuyu-Kamba on the other but with some overlap and juveniles from other groups attached to either. Two such societies whose members I knew well in 1968–69 in Kaloleni were Benfica and Black Santos, the names of two prominent international football teams of the time. Members consciously link their personal educational status and aspirations to the formal aims of their societies and set up debates, dramatic performances, table tennis matches and profess themselves to be unconcerned with the ethnic background of their members, though there is the ethnic clustering I have mentioned. Members claim that they communicate with each other more in English than in Swahili. The claim holds good for formal activities of this kind, but is less consistently valid for informal leisure and recreational activities which provide the most important basis for regular interaction.

Second, there are what I call the "gangs", who call themselves by such names as Black Power, Biafra, Korea, The Henchmen, etc. They are not formally organised with elected officers nor do they attempt to collect subscriptions. Members regard themselves as having lost virtually all chance of returning to school, having dropped out early for lack of school fees, incompatible home conditions, or not having acquired the examination grades required for continuing. They play less soccer than the societies, claiming that this is because those still at school can be trained for the game with proper facilities, whereas they themselves are deprived of such facilities. In Swahili, which they claim to speak more frequently than English (though in fact no more frequently than members of societies in informal contexts), they jokingly refer to themselves as *wakora* (rogues) and contrast themselves with the *wazuri* (the good ones) of the societies, a self-designation which the societies light-heartedly echo. The gangs also claim to be always on the look-out for "war" and take pride in this facet of their philosophy in a way that is reminiscent of Anglo-American Hells Angels, or the recent "bovver boys" of South London, or the Rockers in Britain of the early sixties (themselves contrasted with another category called Mods). Most importantly, unlike the societies, these gangs are associated with particular areas of Kaloleni: thus, Black Power regards its area of recruitment as house lines U-Z (150 households), Korea recruits from the FQ houses (46), The Henchmen from A-G (148), and so on. There are no clear boundaries marking off neighbourhoods in Kaloleni and this facilitates the arbitrariness of areas and partly accounts for the fact that one aim in the rivalry between gangs is to enlarge their claimed territories. Certainly the areas arc uneven in size and constantly changing.

In other respects, the gangs and societies are similar and come together more frequently than they are apart. They almost take it in turns to stage dances every weekend in the Kaloleni social hall, to which all come, and there is little doubt that this is the activity which sustains most interest. As members of the gangs and societies themselves point out, these are the occasions also when each group tries to "raid" girls from the others and when most disputes and fights between them occur.

These Kaloleni dances involve more gangs and societies with Luo-Luyia membership than those with Kikuyu-Kamba. Kikuyu and Kamba teenagers tend to go outside Kaloleni for their entertainment. This has the consequence that, though Luo and Luyia "take" each others' girls, it is neither normally practicable nor expected that they will have much to do with Kikuyu and Kamba girls. The geographical separation of some Luo-Luyia and Kikuyu-Kamba leisure activities thus partly dictates the emerging pattern of courtship and pre-marital ties.

Two features affecting relationships with parents arise out of this development from childhood to adolescence. First, we see that by the time he or she is a teenager, a boy or girl in Kaloleni has already moved away from childhood leisure activities involving all four main ethnic groups, and is now beginning to fall into the ethnic polarisation of activities that characterises his/her parents' relations. The connectedness of Luo and Luyia in recreation (Luo and Luyia adult teams compete in the Kenya soccer league) and, to a lesser extent, marriage, is already implicit and contrasts with the separate development of relations among Kikuyu and

Kamba. Luo and Luyia boys and girls can mix freely and it is only in the years immediately before marriage that each is likely to be steered by parents firmly into choosing a wife from his or her own ethnic group, with the earlier likelihood of mixed Luo-Luyia marriages much reduced and those with Kikuyu or Kamba virtually eliminated.

Second, as well as depicting the trend to ethnic polarisation along these lines, the gangs and societies reveal how much education is valued by teenagers as a summary mark of their general worthwhileness. In fact, the actual levels of educational attainment, and English competence and usage, arc not very much higher in the societies than the gangs. The significant difference is one of hopes and expectations: between those who are able to continue and those obliged to finish their education below the point at which it is likely to help them get a job or at least one which satisfies earlier aspirations. Members of the societies associate their aspirations with a claimed continuing high usage of English. The gangs accept their "failure" to continue education with a claimed rejection of the use of English and its replacement with Swahili. Indirectly, then, the societies publicise the success of some parents in managing to continue their sons' and daughters' education, while the gangs publicise the failure of their members' parents to continue to pay school fees or to provide adequate studying facilities. In the minds of many of these adolescents in this highly competitive system, apparent parental responsibility or irresponsibility is a prime reason for educational success or failure.

Analysis

It is true that societies use mainly English in such formalised activities as debates. But how accurate is the mutually held claim that, even outside these formalised events, gangs speak more Swahili and societies more English, with no apparent difference between them in the use of vernaculars?

It is difficult to measure precisely the differential use of Swahili, English, and the vernaculars, since much switching distinguishes forms within utterances as well between whole utterances. But, taking broad parameters, there is only a slight tendency for gangs to use more Swahili and societies more English. But the claim has assumed exaggerated proportions and is insisted upon as a key distinguishing mark of the societies and gangs. The exaggerated and elaborated nature of the claim suggests that what is really at issue is the emergence of ideological differences regarding their respective statuses and prospects in the structure of urban opportunities.

One important generalisation may be permitted regarding actual rather than claimed or perceived language use. This is that the prepuberty children do use less English and their respective vernaculars than the adolescents and make correspondingly greater use of Swahili. There are two reasons for this. First, knowledge of English is only significantly acquired through school, for there has not yet developed a distinctive. East African form of English (so-called Creole or Pidgin) acquired independently of formal learning procedures.[4] Therefore, younger children whose attendance at school is as yet limited, rely upon Swahili, which in the housing estates is acquired informally outside school contexts and primarily in the polyethnic neighbourhood to which young children's playgroups are confined. A second reason for the greater use of Swahili by pre-puberty children is that their playgroups are much more likely to be drawn from all four main ethnic groups than are adolescent societies and gangs, which tend to bc either Luo/Luyia or Kikuyu/Kamba. Indeed, the younger the children's playgroup, the more likely it is to be quadri-ethnic and so to use Swahili as the common medium, in default of overall competence in English. Yet, within the purely domestic domain, in their houses with their parents, these children use their respective vernaculars. Then they switch to Swahili, even with full siblings, literally on leaving the home threshold to rejoin the peer group. Peer group and family here pull in divergent directions.

What does this pre-puberty pattern of language-use tell us about the way in which socialisation is occurring? First, the transethnic use of Swahili, and the suppression of the vernacular within the playgroup, corresponds with the positive value consciously placed on the use of Swahili in ethnically mixed situations by adults (and sometimes, in public pronouncements, by the government, even though its educational policy diverges from this). But, unlike adults, these children are not able to attach a negative value to the use of Swahili and a corresponding "snob" value to the use of English, for too few of them know English for it to be regarded as prestige-bearing. In other words, while adult use of Swahili is hedged around with status ambivalence and uncertainty by virtue of its opposed relationship to English, as I described above, use of Swahili among the pre-puberty children is not: indeed, it represents an "ideal" transcendence of ethnic alliances and oppositions, and casts the children in the role of ethnic melting-pot proto-types.

As children get older two developments occur. First, more of them acquire longer exposure to school influences, including the primacy placed on English as the key to educational success and employment opportunities. Taking puberty and the beginning of adolescence as the turning point, there develops the division between societies, which increasingly claim to use English in preference to Swahili, and gangs, which claim "defiant" use of Swahili rather than English as a conscious mark of their alienation. Second, both the societies and gangs undergo the process of ethnic polarisation, in which the Luo/Luyia alliance now shows itself in opposition to the increasing interaction with each other of Kikuyu and Kamba. Among both gangs and societies, adolescents confine the choice of girlfriends and boyfriends to within their alliances: the beginning of a tendency which narrows in adulthood to marriage preferences which are largely endogamous. Among these adolescents, actual and not simply claimed use of the Luo vernacular exceeds the use of Luyia in the one alliance relationship, while use of Kikuyu exceeds Kamba in the other. In this respect, too, a parental model is imitated. For, as mentioned above, a quarter of all Luyia household heads speak the vernacular Luo, while only 7% of Luo speak Luyia; and nearly a half of Kamba heads speak the Kikuyu vernacular, with only 27% of Kikuyu speaking Kamba (Parkin 1974).

Whether or not we regard these changing ethnic preferences and social composition of the adolescent societies and gangs as anticipatory socialisation prior to conformity with the adult model, it is clear that, in these respects, adolescent and parental expectations are mutually reinforcing. That is to say, peer group and family now converge in their assumptions of appropriate vernacular usage and choice of ethnic associates.

The socioeconomic basis of this convergence is that, though adolescents are less physically restrained to the local area and neighbourhood than their younger siblings, they are nevertheless subject to strong parental control; either because they are still at school and wish to stay there, or because, even though they have had to leave, they have no job or do not earn enough in a period of gross under- and un-employment to strike out independently. Over and above this socioeconomic basis, ideologies of ethnic exclusiveness and "purity", as held by adults, further reinforce it. In spite of the claimed differences between their use of Swahili and English by societies and gangs, adolescents in both are obliged by the wider political and economic situation to maximise their competence in English and Swahili and to retain use of their vernacular: English is needed for selection for white-collar or other "suitable" employment; Swahili for forging and maintaining extensive transethnic contacts as part of the quest for employment; and the vernacular for communication with those fellow ethnics who constitute the ultimate refuge and, alternatively, the most powerful political base.

At the level of adolescent perceptions, however, it is English and the school context which is by far the greatest divisive factor in relations (a) between peer groups, and (b) between peer groups and families:

(a) The division between societies and gangs, who otherwise recognise their common ethnic affiliations and preferences, is clearly based on such perceptions. It represents a remarkable case of status-consciousness based on a perceived link between educational success, competence in English and greater opportunities in employment, and, conversely, educational failure, incompetence in English, limited job prospects, and an associated use of Swahili.

(b) Similarly, parents' mismanagement of family resources is blamed by adolescents who have had to leave school early and who make up the membership of gangs. Here, the assumptions about the overriding worthwhileness of a school education set up a financially onerous notion of parental responsibility and so drive a wedge between family and peer group. But, because of the wider political and economic demands and constraints mentioned above (i.e. that Swahili and English continue to be needed), this conflict between peer group and family cannot be said significantly to affect actual use of language.

Summary and Conclusions

The actual use of language is principally governed by a process of city and nationwide ethnic polarisation. It works its way into the socialisation process and turns the neighbourhood playgroups of predominantly Swahili-speaking, ethnically transcendant pre-puberty children into trilingual (Swahili, English and home vernacular) adolescent peer groups, whose speech patterns and increasingly ethnocentric choice of peers and partners approach those of their parents. However, putative or believed use of language among these adolescents is not significantly affected by the process of ethnic polarisation *per se*. Rather, the mutually recognised claims of societies as being more English-speaking and of gangs as being more Swahili-speaking, derives from the high value placed on formal education and competence in English as the prerequisites of worthwhile employment.

The case described for Harlem by Labov is of school, standard English, and mainly White middle class norms converging to constitute a dominant and largely alienating factor which encourages solidarity among Black peer groups whose increasing use, from childhood through adolescence, of NNE, symbolises and substantiates this solidarity. Black/White ethnic polarisation largely corresponds with lower class/middle class differences of speech style.

In Nairobi, there is indeed also ethnic polarisation which largely coincides with the overall power situation, with Kikuyu in the ascendant. But the trilingualism of Swahili, English and any one of four vernaculars has had correspondingly complicated implications. Ethnic polarisation has undoubtedly sharpened the "vernacular loyalty" of the constituent ethnic groups. But the educational and socioeconomic basis of the value relationship of English to Swahili has produced an alternative process of linguistic alienation which cuts across vernacular differences separating allegedly dominant from subordinate ethnic groups. The gangs' putative rejection of English in preference for Swahili is, then, the development which most nearly corresponds with the Harlem peer groups' actual rejection of standard English in favour of NNE. But the economic realities of joblessness in Nairobi oblige gang members in fact to use English, as much as they can. Nor have they voluntarily rejected education. Rather, the system rejected them. They snap up any chance of returning to school.

It seems that we must distinguish two kinds of situation. One is that which I earlier called stabilised; where there is an unambiguous association between educational norms, standard speech style, and dominant ethnic group or class. In this kind of situation, ethnic/class polarisation is likely to be reflected, again unambiguously, in a polarisation of speech styles, as in Harlem.

The second kind of situation, emergent, is found in my description of an ethnically mixed area of Nairobi. Here, no one ethnic group nor class, nor even clearly defined elite, is unambiguously associated with a standard speech style or "High" diatype. Rather, English is a language of colonial origin spoken as a native tongue by almost none of the indigenous population of Kenya. There is no one reference group nor easily identifiable social category with which the language is exclusively associated. The lines of an association are emerging in the distinction drawn between themselves by the adolescent societies, as more English than Swahili-speaking, and gangs. But this exists mainly at the level of a perception.

Fox (1968) has usefully hypothesised that lexical penetration from an alien language may prepare the ground, so to speak, for a wider adoption of the contrasting culture represented by that language. Language here provides a preliminary "softening up" process. This would seem to fit the Harlem situation. There those Black children and adolescents, identified by Labov as peer group rejects, who voluntarily respond to school expectations regarding the desirability of speaking standard English thereby embrace the mainly White middle-class culture that is associated with it. The hypothesis also fits the situation described by Bernstein (1965) for working class children in Britain who, if they arc to perform successfully in the predominantly middle-class educational framework of school, are required to extend their competence in a restricted code appropriate to family (and peer group?) interaction to competence in an elaborated code deemed appropriate for school. The adoption of this elaborated code followed by school success effectively precipitates the child of working-class origins into middle class adulthood. In this way, adoption of the code in late childhood and adolescence softens up the process of adult entry into an "alien" subculture, which is almost inevitably a personally difficult process for the relatively few who undergo it.

Fox's hypothesis is thus likely to fit stabilised multilingualism in which acceptance of a High diatype or speech variety may also entail acceptance of the clearly delineated subculture of the group speaking it. But among the adolescent gangs and societies in Nairobi, who belong to an emergent multilingual speech community, two differences suggest a modification of the hypothesis. First, English and Swahili in Nairobi are not the preserve of clearly distinguishable cultural collectivities, which are at most embryonic. It is not therefore easy to speak of the adoption of either of them as softening up an ensuing process of cultural penetration and incorporation: for the cultures themselves are as yet inadequately defined. That is to say, the two languages may contrast the statuses of individuals and small groups but not of groupings larger than can be identified through face-to-face interaction. It is true that something approaching the coast culture of native Swahili-speaking peoples is found in Nairobi, but only among a small proportion of the residents of a very small area (called Pumwani; Bujra, 1974). It is true, too, that most European and other expatriates use English as a lingua franca in communication with the indigenous Kenyan elite: but a significant proportion of the Kenyan elite are often self-made business and political personnel of limited education, whose achievements originated before independence and have not required nor now need to be marked by fluent use of English. Fluent English speakers may still be found at all socioeconomic levels. There is, thus, not as yet any exclusive association between "elite" lifestyle and high competence in English.

Second, it will be remembered that, in fact, gangs and societies differ less in their actual use of either English or Swahili, but more in their claims regarding usage. As I have suggested, the gangs' claims to use Swahili correspond with their view of themselves as already educationally and occupationally disadvantaged-indeed, as already alienated from access to prime urban opportunities. By contrast, the societies' claim to use English reflects their continuing involvement in education and the assumption that this helps their occupational chances. In this kind of colonial or neo-colonial linguistic situation (cf. Polomé, 1971), (which is surely the most prevalent instance of emergent multilingualism), it is rather that people's ideas and claims as to how they use language soften up a growing consciousness that society is being increasingly organised along the lines of an inevitably imperfect educational meritocracy based on the Western model.

The distinctiveness of the various ethnic groups in Nairobi persists, however, and is likely to do so indefinitely, though particular ethnic boundaries will surely alter. With the continuing high rate of ethnic endogamy that this will entail, it is likely also that the vernaculars will continue to be used both within the family and within the peer group, with the latter's repertoire continuing to include also Swahili and English as pragmatic aides in the search for jobs and as indicators, almost symbols, of the emerging socioeconomic cleavage which will confront them.

Will the Nairobi language structure ever come to resemble that of Harlem, with ethnic, class and speech polarisation occurring together? For this to happen, one ethnic group would have to assume sufficient politicoeconomic dominance either to impose its own vernacular as the national and standard language, or to become clearly identified by the other ethnic groups as having inordinate mastery over a generally accepted High diatype, (e.g. English, in view of Kenya's favourable attitude to it as a medium of school instruction) as against a Low diatype (e.g. Swahili).

A more likely development is the emergence of a predominantly English-speaking elite which, though largely recruited from a dominant ethnic group (e.g. the Kikuyu), includes enough members of other ethnic groups to appear polyethnic. At present the Nairobi-based polyethnic national elite is loosely defined and consists of no more than a few hundred professional political, and commercial notables of mixed educational background. Few of the elite have English as their mother tongue. But a growing proportion use it as frequently as, if not more than, their respective vernaculars. Though small, this elite plays an inordinate role in Kenya's and Nairobi's political and economic organisation. As population growth, job scarcity, and educational disadvantage intensify, this elite may well become a culturally distinct focus around which notions of "correct" or "standard Kenyan English" crystallise. Depending on its status at that time in the national education and language structure, Swahili may well interpenetrate and complement the development of other kinds of non-elite English which come to be regarded as "non-standard" forms.

Why is this latter development more likely? Because, although English and Swahili are not yet unambiguously associated with ethnic groups or classes, the two languages already have the makings of High and Low diatypes. In interaction with the various vernaculars, they form an underlying template of language-use relationships which is waiting, so to speak, for socioculturally distinct groups to be built upon it. In spite of their differences, then, the Nairobi and Harlem situations have in common a system of opposed language-use relationships which provides the framework for an expression of ideological differences; established in the case of Harlem; and emergent in the case of Nairobi.

To conclude, stabilised multilingualism (or, more usually, bilingualism) refers to a situation in which a main ethnic group (or social stratum) not only has a distinctive language or speech variety, but is also fairly clearly distinguished by its own subculture and even ideology. In other words, language, subculture and ideology or worldview together define the group's boundaries. Familiar, if rather generalised, examples are the relationships of Black to White American English, Mexican/ Puerto Rican Spanish to varieties of American English, Quebecois French to Canadian English, Welsh to English, British "working class" English and/or regional varieties to "public school" English, Flemish to French and many others.

Emergent multilingualism (less commonly bilingualism) is a characteristic of colonial and recently excolonial societies. It involves the use of at least one important language which is not unambiguously regarded as the distinctive "property" of a particular group or stratum nor as its mother tongue. This language is, so to speak, waiting for an emergent group or stratum to "claim" it as its own and to be regarded unambiguously as the new group's distinctive property.

The notion of opposed language-use relationships can be applied to both stabilised and emergent multilingualism. It rests on the idea that each language or speech variety has weighted "value" in relation to the other(s), rather like pieces on a chess board at any stage of the game (see Ardener, 1971) on the Saussurian concept of value). To repeat, it is a characteristic of an emergent speech community of the kind which I have investigated in Nairobi, that a language has value deriving either from its position as a lingua franca of colonial administrative origin as opposed to one of pre-colonial origin, or from its position as exclusively the mother tongue of a specific ethnic group and therefore opposed to both kinds of lingua franca. But in both emergent and stabilised multilingualism there is a more fundamental dimension of value. For, in both, a language or variety has weighted value depriving from its relationship to all other languages or varieties as being of either High, Low or Middle diatype (see Ardener, 1971; Denison, 1971). This ranking is not fixed for all contexts and may sometimes alter. But an underlying consistency may be picked out.

Thus, (to take bilingual conversations first), when English and Swahili are the only two languages spoken in a conversation in Nairobi, then English is likely to be the High and Swahili the Low diatype. Similarly, English used alone with a vernacular is likely to be the High diatype. Swahili used alone with one vernacular is unlikely to achieve any particular diatypical rank. It is as if the two are complementary rather than opposed. They have neutral diatypical significance in relation to each other. Indeed, they fall into a speech zone of "affective neutrality" (cf. Parkin, 1971 on this Parsonian concept). Why is this? In spite of its superimposition in a few domains, Swahili is not seen as a serious threat to a main vernacular. For, with the possible partial exception of some Kenya coastal Bantu dialects, it is unlikely in the foreseeable future to supplant an ethnic group's mother tongue. Moreover, it has had low curricular status in schools, in spite of recommendations to the contrary (Hemphill, 1974; Gorman, 1974).

If English, Swahili and one of the four vernaculars are used in Nairobi making the conversation trilingual, Swahili is likely to emerge as a Middle diatype by seeming to transcend two kinds of social particularism: the localised particularism of a single ethnic group connoted by use of the vernacular: and non-localised particularism of high socioeconomic status connoted by use of English.

Quadri-lingual conversations are less amenable to generalisation. The Luo-Luyia and Kikuyu-Kamba adolescent groups (both gangs and societies) are potentially quadrilingual. Some members at least can speak English, Swahili and the two vernaculars. In their conversations, it is sometimes the dominant vernacular (i.e. either Luo or Kikuyu) which emerges as the Middle diatype in place of Swahili. It is here a Middle diatype because it can transcend the High and Low socioeconomic status connotations of English and Swahili, which are normally used to differentiate societies from gangs. The dominant vernacular transcends this socioeconomic polarisation by stressing instead an overriding loyalty towards the ethnic alliance (say, Luo-Luyia) in opposition to the rival one (Kikuyu-Kamba).

In neighbouring Tanzania, where Swahili has high educational, political and ideological status, numerous contexts make English the Low and Swahili the High diatype (Abdulaziz-Mkilifi, 1972). This may also occur in coastal Kenya, where Swahili is highly regarded, at least in connection with Islam, trade and the use of traditional medicine.

In Nairobi, these values attaching to the different combinations of language use[5] can alternatively be seen as general or high-level rules about their usage, which can be picked out from my description of the speech of adolescent peer groups, and, as I have shown elsewhere (1974), from adult speech. Presented schematically, they are:

> General Rule: lingua francas are opposed to vernaculars (lingua francas transcend the restrictions of localised ethnic vernaculars), yet may themselves be internally opposed (English to Swahili, and one vernacular to another).

In bilingual conversations the following arc derivative general rules:

> (a) English emerges as a H diatype in opposition to Swahili or to a vernacular (L diatypes). (Parkin, 1974).
>
> (b) (1) Luo emerges as a H diatype in opposition to Luyia (L diatype). (See references to the adolescent groups above, including Table 2, and also, for adults and Parkin, 1974.)
>
> (b) (2) Kikuyu emerges as a H diatype in opposition to Kamba (L diatype). (References as for (b) above.)

In trilingual conversations including English, Swahili and a vernacular, the following is a derivative rule:

> (c) Swahili mediates between the use of English as a H diatype and a vernacular (localised L diatype). (Whiteley 1971 and cases 1-3, 5-8 in Parkin 1974). Swahili is here a Middle diatype.

In multilingual conversations including English, Swahili and at least two vernaculars, Swahili is usually the Middle diatype. But Swahili may cede this intercalary status to one of the vernaculars, and may assume instead the status of Low diatype:

> (d) (1) Where Luo and Luyia speakers predominate, then the Luo vernacular may supersede Swahili as Middle diatype.
>
> (d) (2) Where Kikuyu and Kamba speakers predominate, then Kikuyu may supersede Swahili as Middle diatype.

Both (d) (1) and (2) may occur, respectively, in the Luo-Luyia and Kikuyu-Kamba adolescent gangs and societies, when the claimed socioeconomic status difference between gangs and societies are subordinated to an expression of common ethnic alliance-Luo-Luyia on the one hand and Kikuyu-Kamba on the other (see references under (b) (1) and (2)).

Now, this generally represents the actual use of language in Nairobi. The adolescent societies and gangs can, together, be said to follow this usage. But, as I have stressed throughout this chapter, the gangs and societies claim, respectively, to be more Swahili-speaking and more English-speaking. Their usage does not really differ as much as they claim. In other words, these adolescents have internalised the general rule stating an opposition between the lingua francas (English and Swahili) and the vernaculars, and have then moved on to its main derivative (i.e. that English is a High and Swahili a Low diatype), for creating the opposition among themselves between societies and gangs. At a verbal and linguistic level, this opposition is indeed putative. But, given the High status aspirations of the societies, and the acceptance of Low status by the gangs, the opposition both presages and makes intelligible an ultimate social reality, which we can only characterise as opposition by social class.

In this chapter, then, I have suggested that an emergent speech community's conceptualisation of its languages as being variously High, Low or Middle, may actually precede, and act as imitative models for, a ranking of groups in the speech community. In other words, a folk-classification of languages and speech varieties used by a community may provide the initial basis on which social groups become culturally distinguished.

This view has modern implications for the anthropological problem of whether the classification of and identification with flora and fauna ("totemism") is intellectually independent of (Lévi-Strauss, 1969 (1962)) or derives from (Durkheim, 1957) the differentiation of social groups within a community. Many contemporary communities consist of people drawn recently and rapidly from distant ethnic groups as a result of extensive colonial administration, labour migration, industrial urbanisation and political statehood. Within such polyethnic communities, diversity of speech rather than of flora and fauna provides the most readily available "raw" classificatory data for the differentiation of new social groups and the redefinition of old ones.

Notes

(1) It must be emphasised that polyethnicity in Africa, or "tribalism" as it is used to be called, has its direct origins in the colonial insistence on attributing distinct "tribal" identities to administrative areas, whose political boundaries were never so clear cut in the pre-colonial period but were rather shifting areas of great cultural and linguistic interchange (Southall, 1970).

(2) Although likely to be instructive, I do not deal with speech differences between male and female adolescents, except to say that there is not the same high discrepancy in English competence between them as among the parental generation and I treat this factor as constant in the analysis.

(3) It may be noted that English verbs incorporated in predominantly Swahili utterances normally (perhaps invariably) take Swahili pronominal and tense prefixes and English pronominal suffixes.
(4) Update 2020: it should be noted however that "Sheng", based on both English and Swahili, with ethnic vernacular borrowings, has become an important, largely young people's mainly urban vernacular identified as a distinctive diatype since the time of the fieldwork carried out for this chapter during the nineteen sixties.
(5) Unusual contexts may seem to produce "exceptions", which, at a more detailed level of investigation, may be seen as "inversions" of the general rules (see Ardener, 1971). This is because different levels of abstraction produce different levels of generalisation.

References

Abdulaziz-Mkilifi, M.H. (1972) Triglossia and Swahili-English Bilingualism in Tanzania. *Language in Society* l, 197–213.

Ardener, E. (1971) Introductory Essay. In "Social Anthropology and Language." (Ed. E. Ardener), pp. ix–cii. London: Tavistock Publications Ltd.

Bernstein, B. (1965) A socio-linguistic approach to social learning. In "Penguin Survey of the Social Sciences," pp. 144–168. Harmondsworth, Middlesex: Penguin.

Bujra, J. (1974) Language use in an urban muslim community. In "Language in Kenya." (Ed. W.H. Whiteley), pp. 217–252. Nairobi and London: Oxford University Press,

Calvet, M. (1971) The elaboration of basic Wolof. In "Language Use and Social Change." (Ed. W.H. Whiteley.) London: Oxford University Press.

Cole, D.T. 1964 (1953) Fanagalo and the Bantu languages in South Africa. In "Language in Culture and Society." (Ed. D. Hymes), pp. 547–554. New York: Harper and Row.

Denison, N. (1971) Some observations on language variety and plurilingualism. In "Social Anthropology and Language." (Ed. E. Ardener), pp. 157–184. London: Tavistock Publications Ltd.

Durkheim, E. (1957) "The Elementary Forms of the Religious Life." London: Allen and Unwin.

Ferguson, C.A. (1959) Diglossia. *Word* 15, 325–340.

Fishman, J.A. (1964) Language maintenance and language shift as fields of enquiry. *Linguistics* 9, 32–70.

Fishman, J.A. (1967) Bilingualism with and without diglossia; diglossia with and without bilingualism. *Journal of Social Issues* 23, 29–38.

Fox, R. (1968) Multilingualism in two communities. *Man* (N.S.) 3, 456–464.

Giles, H. (1977) Ed. Language, ethnicity and intergroup relations. London: Academic Press.

Gorman, T.P. (1974) The teaching of languages at secondary level: Some significant problems. In "Language in Kenya." (Ed. W.H. Whiteley), pp. 397–454. Nairobi and London: Oxford University Press.

Gumperz, J. and Hernandez, Ch.E. (1971) Cognitive aspects of bilingual communication. In "Language Use and Social Change." (Ed. W.H. Whiteley), pp. 111–125. London: Oxford University Press.

Hemphill, R.J. (1974) Language use and language teaching in the primary schools of Kenya. In "Language in Kenya." (Ed. W.H. Whiteley), pp. 455–480. Oxford University Press, Nairobi and London.

Labov, W. (1972) The logic of nonstandard English. In "Language and Social Context." (Ed. P.P. Giglioli), pp. 283–307. Penguin, Harmondsworth, Middlesex.

Levi-Strauss, C. (1969) [1962] "Totemism." Harmondsworth, Middlesex: Penguin.

Parkin, D.J. (1971) Language choice in two Kampala housing estates. In "Language Use and Social Change." (Ed. W.H. Whiteley), pp. 347–363. London: Oxford University Press.

Parkin, D.J. (1974) Language shift and ethnicity in Nairobi; Language switching in Nairobi. In "Language in Kenya." (Ed. W.H. Whiteley), pp. 167–216. Nairobi and London: Oxford University Press.

Polomé, E.G. (1971) Multilingualism in an African urban centre: The Lubumbashi case. In "Language Use and Social Change." (Ed. W.H. Whiteley), pp. 364–375. London: Oxford University Press.

Scotton, C. (1976) Strategies of neutrality: Language choice in uncertain situations. Language 52, in press.

Southall, A.W. (1970) The illusion of tribe. *Journal of Asian and African Studies* 5, 28–50.

Whiteley, W.H. (1969) "Swahili: The Rise of a National Language." London: Methuen.

Whiteley, W.H. (1971) (Ed.) "Language Use and Social Change." London: Oxford University Press.

Whiteley, W.H. (1974) (Ed.) "Language in Kenya." Nairobi and London: Oxford University Press.

Wioland, F. and Calvet, M. (1967) L'expansion du Wolof au Senegal. *Bulletin de l' Institute Fondamental d' Afrique Noire* 29, B, Nos 3–4. Dakar, Senegal.

3 Language Choice in Two Kampala Housing Estates

This chapter explores from a social anthropological viewpoint some problems of language choice in a multilingual urban community. The community is of 1,468 households in two municipal housing estates in Kampala East, Uganda. Kampala, the capital of Uganda, was extended in late 1967 to include Mengo municipality, until recently the capital of the former kingdom of Buganda. My data is based on the situation preceding this when Kampala and Mengo were administered separately yet were each part of a single urban complex. I refer especially to the situation as I observed it from the middle of 1962 until early 1964. During this period Uganda's independence was formally declared in October 1962.

I call the period shortly before and after independence the political context of situation. A second context is that of residential area or neighbourhood. A third is that of tribe or ethnic group. Though no relationship is set exclusively in one or other context, I shall try to show that, for certain interactions, norms deriving from one context have primacy as a determinant of language choice. My examples will be those of 'apt and isolated illustration' (Gluckman 1965) which, though obviously purposively selected, are most convenient for a short presentation. First, I describe each of the contexts.

The Political Context

Proportionally few of the local ethnic group, the Ganda, live in the housing estates, most preferring to live in Mengo. The non-Ganda who prefer to live in the estates, and out of the jurisdiction of Mengo, include townsmen from many different 'tribes', such as the Kenya Luo, Luhya, and Kisii, the northern Uganda Acholi, Lango, Alur, Jonam, and Lugbara, and small numbers of people from the former kingdoms of the Great Lakes and from elsewhere (Southall and Gutkind, 1956).

With the approach of Uganda's independence, Kenyans felt uneasy at what they believed were likely prospects of being dismissed from their jobs. Earlier fears were that Ganda would be most likely to cause this dismissal when Uganda became independent. Later many Kenyans feared that it would be not just Ganda but Ugandans generally who would seek to reduce the number of Kenyans employed in Kampala and other Ugandan towns. Kenyans were conspicuous because they constituted a relatively large proportion of the labour force and were active in trade unions. They felt exposed to any changes which independence might bring. A few constitutional developments and public announcements gave rise to this impression. These need not be dealt with here. In the end, Kenyans' fears that they would be dismissed from their jobs and sent back to their home country did not materialise (Parkin, 1969)[1]. The relevance of the widespread anxiety is its effect on language choice in a number of social situations.

The Residential and Neighbourhood Context

The transitionary period of Uganda's independence is thus the political context of situation. The housing estates of Kampala East have significance in this context because they include a large proportion of Kampala's expatriate Kenyan workers. But the estates also have distinct significance as dwelling areas *per se*.

The two estates are ranked according to the prestige of residence in them. Objectively, people with more secure and better-paid jobs live at Naguru, the higher-status estate, while less well-paid workers live in Nakawa, the lower-status estate. House rents at Naguru are higher than at Nakawa. Even within Nakawa one part of the estate has dearer houses than the other. People recognise that these geographical divisions coincide with socioeconomic ones. There is a steady movement by tenants from 'lower' to 'higher' areas. The situation is complicated by the long waiting list for a house of two or three years. A relatively prosperous and educated senior clerk may have to 'tolerate' residence in a cheaper house in a 'lower' area until a dearer one more befitting his status becomes available.

In conventional terms, therefore, Naguru can be said to be of higher status than Nakawa. But within Nakawa there is a similar ranking of its 'lower' and 'upper' areas. People who otherwise know no English refer to 'Upper' Nakawa (or the 'up groups') and 'Lower' Nakawa (or the 'down groups'). Tenants associate a different lingua franca with each area. Thus, Lower Nakawa is exclusively a Swahili area, Upper Nakawa more of an English one, and Naguru an English and Luganda area. These folk designations are, of course, no more than approximations to the truth. They are used also at the level of public meetings, such as those of the tenants' associations. Thus, Naguru tenants' association uses English and

Luganda at its meetings, while the Nakawa association uses English and Swahili. Ganda are, as mentioned above, few in the estates compared with their proportions in Kampala-Mengo. At Nakawa they provide only 4% of the household heads, though at Naguru they are the second largest group at 20%. Their higher proportion at Naguru explains the additional use of Luganda at public meetings there.

These three languages are lingua francas in a restricted and perhaps incorrect sense. English is the most widely spoken in the estates. The relatively high level of education and, again, the undeniably high prestige attached to a knowledge of this language make it the most widely used. A type of Swahili which ignores the grammars but is rich in vocabulary and expression is used mostly by Kenyans and Muslim Nubi, but over the years has come to be accepted by an increasing number of Ugandans, with the general exception of Ganda, many of whom feel that the use of Swahili would in some way undermine the nationally and culturally important position held by their vernacular. Luganda is itself understood and spoken at varying levels of fluency by a remarkably large number of nonGanda. Related peoples from the other Interlacustrine Bantu kingdoms obviously find little difficulty after even a few months in Kampala-Mengo in learning Luganda. But even a number of Nilotic Luo men, who have been in Kampala for some years, acquire a very useful smattering. Kenya Bantu, such as Luhya and Kisii, acquire even more. Only northern Ugandans, who include Nilotic and Sudanic speakers, seem not to have learned more than a few words of Luganda.

Each housing estate can be said to be made up of small neighbourhoods. Houses are allocated not according to tribal membership but according to socioeconomic status. Neighbourhoods are therefore multi-tribal and each set within a system of socioeconomic grading. A result of these factors, which lack of space prevents me from elaborating, is that the residential context emphasises the values of 'non-tribalism' and of individualistic competition for prestige and socioeconomic status (Parkin, 1969). Within this context English is associated with higher-status people of some education. Luganda is largely ethnically confined. Swahili is the lingua franca seemingly most used by socially distant socioeconomic and tribal categories, and so most likely to express their unity in the face of impending divisiveness.

The 'Tribal' and Ethnic Context

Nilotes form about 40% of the two estates' population. The most numerous are the Kenya Luo. Though there appears to be considerable dialectal variation, there is sufficient mutual intelligibility to allow some limited casual conversation. For townsmen from Nilotic tribes who have stayed for some years in Kampala any marked differences among them of vocabulary and expression are quickly learned. As well as Luo, the Nilotes in the housing estates include Acholi, Lango, Alur, Jonam (singular Janam), and Padhola, who are Ugandans. They are thus linked linguistically and culturally but split nationally.

The two main Bantu-speaking groups on the estates are, first, those of the Interlacustrine societies, such as Ganda, Nyoro, Taro, Soga, Ankole, and Kiga. Of these, Lunyoro and Lutoro are the most obviously mutually intelligible, as are Ruciga (Kiga) and Runyankore (Ankole). Secondly, there are those from Kenya, such as Luhya and Kisii, and from East Uganda, the Gisu, Gwe, and Samia. The Samia are usually regarded as a sub-tribe of Luhya. During the political transition period, however, many Kenya Samia claimed that they were Ugandans in an attempt to escape what they thought would be discrimination directed against Kenyans working in Uganda. Kenya Luhya are divided into a number of sub-tribal groups, sharing mutually intelligible dialects.

The Muslim Nubi are originally from different tribes in the Sudan. A small but significant proportion of them marry Ganda Muslim women. They speak a type of Arabic but also use Swahili for wider communication. Finally, there are small numbers of Para-Nilotic Teso and a larger number on the estates of Sudanic-speaking Lugbara and Madi.

This linguistic heterogeneity fosters the use of common media of communication. Whether a speaker uses Swahili, English, or Luganda as the common medium in any particular context obviously depends, firstly, on his linguistic competence in each of these languages. If he knows insufficient Luganda he can hardly communicate in it. It is worthwhile, therefore, to be selective and concentrate on speakers who have at least a smattering in all three languages and to see what social rather than linguistic factors influence their choice of language in particular relationships and situations.

The cases I now present are, I believe on impressionistic grounds, 'typical' enough on which to base generalisations, while being far from exhaustive of all possible cases.

Case 1. An example of instrumental aspects of language choice in the political context (partly observed and partly reported).

Jason is a Kenya Kisii living in Upper Nakawa. He is studying part-time in Kampala under the care and guidance of his elder full brother, with whom he lodges. Jason hopes to finish his course of typing and shorthand within another six months. He came to Kampala two years ago, but his course has been occasionally interrupted by various family crises which required him to return home to Kisii. Uganda's independence is due in a few weeks. Rumours have been circulating that Kenyans may have to leave Uganda in order to make way for the many young Ugandans who have no employment. During the preceding year the number of jobs declined considerably, and this and other factors have given rise to Kenyans' anxiety.

Jason was strolling by his house one evening when he met a young Luo, also in his early twenties, who lives a few doors from him. Jason is a Kisii whose vernacular is Bantu, while his Luo neighbour is a Nilotic speaker. But they use Swahili as their common language. Their conversation always starts with a greeting which includes the Swahili word 'ndugu', or brother. They have known each other well for a few months, during which time their conversation has revolved around the problem of Kenyans' future in Uganda. The Luo has recently lost his job, due, he claims, to his Ganda supervisor's prejudice against Luo. Together the Luo and Jason then blamed the Ganda for what they felt to be discrimination against Kenyans in employment in Uganda.

They bade farewell. Jason continued his stroll and later returned to his house in Upper Nakawa. He noticed that another neighbour, a Soga, had just come home from work, and decided to go and speak with him about a matter which had been on his mind for some time. The Soga is a senior clerk working for the head Post Office in Kampala city. He has School Certificate education, is now nearly thirty, and has been working in Jinja for a number of years before coming to Kampala. He is so obviously high status that it is widely assumed that he has applied for a house at Naguru. This is in fact the case. As a Soga he is also Bantu, or more specifically a member of the Interlacustrine Bantu group. All his life he has mixed with Ganda and speaks the language fluently. Nevertheless, he preserves a strong sense of Soga patriotism and is no blind admirer of Ganda institutions. He does, however, have a Ganda mistress, whom he met in Kampala and with whom he has established a good relationship.

Jason greeted him in Luganda and, for a little while, they spoke in this language. But Jason has not yet acquired great fluency in Luganda, and his Soga neighbour broke into English for easier communication. The Soga's English is, of course, excellent, while Jason's is certainly competent and better than his Luganda.

The purpose of Jason's visit was to ask the Soga to find him a job as an office messenger in the Post Office. With a job, he explained, he would be less of a burden to his brother and, with peace of mind, would pursue his studies more diligently. The request, which was granted, was actually made in Luganda, though by this time the two men were talking in English. The most remarkable aspect of the request was that Jason made an explicit appeal to the Soga: Jason claimed that because he himself was a Muntu (singular of Bantu) like the Soga, the Soga should regard this element of affinity as more important than his not being a Ugandan.

Analysis

Jason was in fact asking the Soga to overlook the difference in national origins or citizenship between them and to help Jason on the basis not of *cultural* but of general *linguistic* affinity.

There are many examples of men appealing to similarities of custom or culture, as distinct from language, as the basis of a relationship. The Kisii, and more particularly the Luhya, do so with the Luo. Both these groups in Kampala recognise that, compared to the Ganda, Soga and other people organised into kingdoms and possessing different customs, they have much in common. The Luo, like the Luhya and Kisii, are traditionally politically uncentralised. They all emphasise the significance of local descent groups in the allocation of land and property. They pay very high bridewealth for their wives and regard this bridewealth as giving them the rights over any children produced by the woman, even if begotten by another man. This cultural affinity is frequently the basis of relationships between Luo and Luhya or Kisii in spite of the fact that they are linguistically quite unconnected. The contrasting example of Jason and his Soga neighbour is of an appeal to disregard national and cultural difference and to consider only linguistic affinity of a general kind.

This is not to suggest that, simply because Jason and his Soga neighbour were both Bantu-speakers, Jason was given a job. Affinities of language, culture, or nationhood may separately be used simply as an idiom for confirming, strengthening, or utilising a relationship. The underlying strength of the relationship is based both on personal factors of compatibility and on reciprocal advantage. Jason and the Soga neighbour certainly got on well with each other. One might speculate that the Soga was gratified at the approach made to him and might even have seen personal advantage in securing a type of client relationship with the Kisii. Urban patron–client relationships in the sphere of job-getting and other aid are not uncommon in Kampala, though they do tend to be among persons of the same 'tribe'.

There are other sociolinguistically significant aspects of Jason's case. He used Swahili with his fellow-Kenyan, the Luo, even though they both knew English well and could easily have communicated in it. This they might have done in what I call a 'conversational arena of prestige competition', an example of which I shall give below. But they chose

Swahili, mainly, I suggest, because the relationship was situationally one of commiseration. The Luo had lost his job, and both expressed uneasiness as Kenyans regarding their futures in Uganda. They made frequent use of '*ndugu*' or 'brother' in addressing each other. Jason's relationship with his Soga neighbour was of status inferior to superior. English and Luganda, more formal languages from Jason's viewpoint, were used. But Jason's relationship with the Luo was of status equals in what seemed to them to be a common predicament as expatriates. The more 'brotherly' Swahili was used.

Jason's interactions with both the Luo and Soga were set in two of the three contexts described above, namely those of neighbourhood and political change. All three were neighbours. Both the Luo and Soga included in their conversations with Jason some discussion of the problems facing Kenyans. There can be little doubt that the choice of language used in each interaction was determined not by the norms of neighbourhood but by concern with these political problems. In other words, the prevailing political context had primacy in determining language choice in Jason's two interactions.

Politics involves a struggle for power or influence, or at least an attempt to make use of them. It is not surprising, therefore, that language choice in this case was manipulated almost deviously to forge cross-cutting alliances and divisions, e.g. Jason and the Luo expressed in Swahili their unity and common distrust of Ganda; but Jason and the Soga used Luganda and English in order to establish the beginnings of a patron-client relationship which explicitly repudiated the Kenyan 'brotherhood' and unity which Jason and the Luo had earlier communicated to each other in Swahili.

The political or instrumental aspects of language choice suggested by this case may be summarised as follows:

(1) An appeal to linguistic affinity may constitute the idiom through which a dyadic relationship may be manipulated for certain ends.
(2) Structurally there is no difference between the use of linguistic affinity as an idiom for manipulating relationships and the use of cultural, national, and, one might suggest, religious affinity as idioms for similar purposes.
(3) If this is so, then language is being used to convey much more than the conventional 'meaning' resulting from the actual conversation: it can be articulated to express either a difference or an equivalence of status between two (and perhaps more) persons (or groups), e.g. Jason and the Soga as incipient 'client' and 'patron', as against Jason and the Luo as 'brothers'.

(4) The use and potential use of Luganda, English, and Swahili in this case by persons for whom none were native languages suggests a special usefulness of a multiplicity of restricted lingua francas: they may be used selectively to bridge and manipulate the different role-relationships which an ego has with persons who are linked to him in varied and conflicting ways.

Case 2. An example of expressive aspects of language choice in the residential context (observed)

At one of the well-attended general meetings of the Nakawa tenants' association a well-dressed young Ugandan of the Teso 'tribe' (Para-Nilotic) stood up to speak on the problem under discussion, which was how to improve the poor condition of some of the Nakawa houses. He is a clerk with a good knowledge of English, which is required in his work. He has been in Kampala for four years, but has not yet acquired any more than a rough knowledge of Swahili, probably because most of his time has been spent in one of the Mengo suburbs where Swahili is used to a far lesser extent than in Kampala East, where there are many Kenyans. He certainly knows very little Luganda, which would not any way have been acceptable as a lingua franca at the Nakawa association's meetings, and so had little alternative but to use English.

Unfortunately for him, general meetings of the association are supposed to be conducted in Swahili, to enable a majority of tenants on the estate to follow and contribute to the discussion. On trivial issues English is occasionally used by a speaker from the floor, and its use is not challenged. On this occasion, however, the issue was an urgent one. The poor condition of a house had been responsible for the death of an unskilled Acholi's nephew. Poor and prosperous tenants alike shared a common concern in the matter, since many houses were in need of some kind of improvement. But, as explained, poorer people live in Lower Nakawa and, of the three lingua francas, tend to speak only Swahili. A number of these Swahili speakers from Lower Nakawa protested vehemently at the Teso's use of English, which they could not understand. They successfully demanded the arrangement of a running translation as the Teso spoke. More than this, they condemned the young Teso, who was obviously more educated and financially secure than themselves and who lived in Upper Nakawa, of acting "proudly", or of trying to exhibit his affluence and education through his use of English.

The association's chairman, a Nilote from northern Uganda, tried to reassure the Swahili speakers that the Teso had been unaware of the implications of speaking English at a general meeting of the association and had not intended to insult the Swahili speakers by 'showing them up'. After all, he said, the Teso had lived in Nakawa for barely more than a year and might be excused this ignorance of procedure. In time, no doubt, he would acquire a good knowledge of Swahili. The chairman recalled how he himself had come to Kampala many years before without any knowledge of Swahili, but that now here he was addressing a large gathering in the language.

In parenthesis, it should be noted that committee meetings of the association are held in English, a difference of usage which the association has written into its constitution and which is observed. Committee members, including the chairman, are almost all of Upper Nakawa and are all English speakers.

Analysis

In this case the use of English *expressed* or made known differences which were reflected in the special graded structure of the housing estate. I emphasise the word 'expressed' because there appeared to be no purposive manipulation of language by either the speaker, his accusers, or the mediator. That is to say, language was not an instrumental device for securing specific ends as it was in Case 1. Clearly, the distinction between instrumentality and expressiveness is not watertight. There are elements of both in many social interactions. But the general concern of people at this public meeting was that Swahili should replace English and be used to express the value of neighbourhood or residential harmony and that socioeconomic status differences and antagonism based on them should be suppressed.

The ideal norms of residence derive from the fact, firstly, that neighbourhoods are multi-tribal and that frequent disputes along tribal lines are simply inexpedient, and second, that socioeconomic differences among people are made more glaringly obvious as a basis for disputes by the graded housing system. While it is obvious that individuals occasionally depart from these ideal norms, the relevant point here is that the tenants' association is a forum in which the norms exhorting harmony may be publicised and that the use of language is determined by this factor.

Similar cases can be given for Naguru where a public concern with multi-tribal harmony is also expressed at tenants' association meetings. At Naguru, Luganda is additionally a lingua franca in public meetings, as the Ganda are the second largest group, and as there are more Interlacustrine Bantu than at Nakawa. But not all tenants know Luganda, though they may speak Swahili or English. Ganda people, as is well known, frequently oppose the use of Swahili, with the result that English emerges as the most commonly acceptable language at Naguru. But the choice may vary according to the issue under discussion, and all three languages are used from time to time. The main point is that, as with Nakawa, the choice of language in any situation is determined by a common need to override tribal and cultural differences among an ethnically heterogeneous community.

Returning to the case itself we may summarise some suggested findings thus:

(1) In the residential context of situation, with its emphasis on multi-tribal harmony, there is a tendency to select from the multiplicity of lingua francas that which has the highest common value as a medium of communication.
(This point may seem to be too obvious to warrant special mention. But it may at least be contrasted with the way in which a person may manipulate a number of languages to his advantage as Jason did in Case 1.)

(2) In this process of selecting a commonly acceptable lingua franca, convergent status differences are expressed: English-speaker and Swahili-speaker; rich and poor; educated and uneducated; clerk and unskilled worker; and Upper and Lower Nakawa, or Naguru and Nakawa.

(3) There is a loose structural parallel with the use made of religion: in small-scale, monolingual, rural societies public rituals may temporarily reconcile internal divisions by reference to commonly acknowledged symbols (Turner, 1957); in an urban, multi-tribal housing estate public meetings may temporarily reconcile internal status divisions by using the language which has greatest currency among both low and high status.
(This is not the same point as (1). In (1) I refer to the attempt to solve a problem of verbal communication. In (3) I refer to the attempt to play down publicly socioeconomic status divisions, which are nevertheless recognised by people as inevitable features of everyday life.)

The 'Tribal' or Ethnic Context and 'Affective Neutrality'

The preceding emphasis on 'non-tribalism' is not intended to suggest that 'tribal' disputes never occur. Indeed, they do. But, out of expedience, public 'leaders' discourage them and mark them out for special condemnation. Ordinary tenants share their condemnation of 'tribalist' behaviour and conflict. One or other of the three lingua francas is available to a person: to *express* a common interest with a person of another tribe, to bridge the social distance between them, or simply to initiate a dyadic relationship; or it may be used purposively or *instrumentally* to articulate a relationship for specific ends.

On the basis of two cases, I have suggested that in the residential or neighbourhood context the expressive aspects of the lingua francas are paramount, and that in the special political context their instrumental aspects are most significant. These are intended to be no more than very broad generalisations, and the converse may occur in other cases. I turn now away from the use made of lingua francas and describe very briefly one or two situations in which 'tribal exclusiveness' in the housing estates is acceptable, even though, in other situations, this conflicts with the value set on 'non-tribalism'.

A simple first proposition is that the use of a tribal vernacular by persons in conversation denotes their exclusiveness: those not of the tribe or unable to understand the language are excluded from the conversation, an exclusion which may or may not have been intended by the speakers. At this level of generality it is possible to distinguish a few observed social events at which tribal and vernacular exclusiveness is not condemned and arouses no resentment. That is to say, the speakers use their vernaculars with impunity because the activities fall into a zone of 'affective neutrality' as far as inter-tribal relations are concerned.

The events at which tribal exclusiveness is accepted are various family and individual urban rites of passage which mark the birth of a child, the welcoming of a new wife to her husband's house in town, and death. The events are celebrated or mourned by immediate kin in the early stages of the rite or ceremony, and by fellow tribesmen friends of the man or woman in its later stages. Intimate occasions such as these are most conveniently restricted to at least a core of relatives and friends who know the esoteric customs involved. The occasions tend, therefore, to be conducted in the vernacular. Those of the man or woman's friends who are of a different tribe and do not speak the vernacular are inevitably excluded from a central part in the activities and, I would suggest from observation, may discreetly and voluntarily withdraw to no more than peripheral participation in the event, especially if many of the subject's kin and fellow-tribesmen are present. In conventional terms they appreciate the intimacy of the occasion. Variables altering the degree of tribal privacy attaching to the event are the status and popularity of the subject, and the proportion of his friends from other tribes to his kin and friends from his own tribe.

Though the situation is nowhere near so clear-cut as this short summary suggests, there do seem to be these special events which are recognised by neighbours of other tribes to be 'morally' and 'ritually' private and at which exclusive use of a vernacular is permitted. Though the events are 'morally' private, they are physically public, in that beer parties or dances of celebration or mourning have to be conducted outside the small houses and in full view of the many nearby neighbours of different tribes.

In other social situations, as in a women's multi-tribal talk group or among a group of men drinking together at a local bar, use of the vernacular by a few of them may invite jocular and sometimes serious accusations of 'secrecy' and a demand that they speak Swahili, or, among a group of high-status men, English, and in a few cases, Luganda.

I have touched here on the use of vernaculars as distinct from the use of the three lingua francas. Falling between these two as media of communication are the respective dialects of persons of the same wider ethnic and linguistic group, an instance being those of the various Nilotes of Uganda and Kenya and, to a lesser extent, some of the Interlacustrine Bantu. It should not be assumed, however, that a group of, say, Luo and Alur, whose Nilotic dialects are very close, will necessarily use their respective dialects in conversation.

Case 3. An example of expressive aspects of language choice in a single ethnic context (reported)

In an interesting 'conversational arena of prestige competition' in a bar near to Nakawa, two Alur, two Jonam, and two Kenya Luo spent the evening drinking together but became involved in an argument which nearly came to blows. They were all residents of either Upper Nakawa or Naguru and had prestigeful clerical jobs in which they were required to use English. Most of their conversation had been inundated with banter and boasting about their individual statuses and achievements. This is not an unusual leisure pursuit among friends of relatively high status. The conversation was strictly in English, and indeed much of the jocular competition for prestige was to acquire credit for fluency and expression in this language. Towards the end of an otherwise pleasant evening one of the Luo was clearly emerging as the most articulate speaker of English. His jokes were witty and his light-hearted insults were always to the point. His main contender, one of the Jonam, was rapidly losing the game to him and began to suffer the also light-hearted derision of his other companions. Suddenly, without notice and to the surprise of all, the Janam took genuine offence and turned on the Luo. He accused Luo and other Kenyans of being 'so poor, and of having so little land that they have to come here to Uganda to work, but that really Kenyans are poor men'. It is the severest of insults to call a Luo a poor man and to refer to his home country in such disparaging terms, and the Luo was on the point of returning the insult with violence. The Luo's fellow-tribesman switched from English to their own dialect and succeeded in calming him. The Alur and remaining Janam did likewise with the inflamed Janam, again m the Alur/Janam dialect.

Analysis

English is a prestige lingua franca of the *élite*. A pastime among relatively high-status friends is to drink and joke, and to tease each other about their possessions, their jobs, their 'wealth' or lack of it, their girl-friends, and their places of residence. The banter usually involves nothing more than a verbal competition, even though, as in the case, the friends could have used, at least partially, their respective dialects, if straightforward, factual communication was their only aim. The respective dialects were only resorted to when the intended light-hearted level of communication broke down and constituted a crisis among the gathering.

Some suggested findings of this case and of the preceding discussion in this section are as follows:

(1) Vernaculars should not, if possible, be used in multitribal contexts, either public or private, except in crisis situations or structurally similar events, such as personal or family rites of passage.
(2) In normal everyday discourse the use of a vernacular in a multi-tribal context invokes mild or more serious accusations of exclusiveness, if the speaker is perfectly well able to use a lingua franca.
(3) Members of different tribes but of the same wider language group may use a lingua franca in preference to their respective mutually intelligible dialects. A lingua franca has a special quality in being linked to the status system (e.g. English), or in connoting 'brotherhood' (e.g. Swahili) or deference (e.g. sometimes Luganda when used by non-Ganda). A lingua franca may thus be used to communicate much more than the mere transmission of verbal statement. In this respect it shows yet another parallel with the communicative power of ritual symbolism.

Conclusion

This is a highly condensed attempt to suggest some factors behind language choice in a specific ethnographic situation. Many of the points touched on should, in a longer paper, have been illustrated by more case material. I believe that, as in intensive sociological research, problems of language choice may be analysed on the basis of considerable material of this type. My material was what has been called 'apt and isolated illustration'. Ideally it should include 'extended cases' also.

A second methodological suggestion is that the sociological use of language may be said to have parallels with the use of other social phenomena. Affinities of language may be manipulated in a way similar to that in which ties of common culture, nationality, and religion may be used. This is the instrumental aspect of language choice. The expressive aspect of language choice has, in my view, some parallels with the expressiveness of ritual symbolism in small-scale societies. Both fulfil a need to reconcile, if only temporarily, conflicts and divisions in the community.

To have this function, the language chosen must be at least a restricted lingua franca. A restricted lingua franca seems to be a contradiction in terms. But in a community which is ethnically and linguistically heterogeneous it is possible to have a number of restricted lingua francas, the usage of each of which varies quantitatively and overlaps, so that together they cover the whole community. While exposing oneself to the accusation of arguing falsely by analogy, one might venture the suggestion that in some respects ritual symbolism in the small-scale, monolingual community has 'functions' which in a complex, urban industrial, multilingual community are performed by public usage of lingua francas. Just as a process of ritual differentiation may be linked to a process of social differentiation, so the proliferation or delimitation of lingua francas may reflect the social shifts and movements of groups and persons. The central concern in this paper has certainly been the use made of lingua francas.

I have been unable in this paper to explore the implications of 'private' and 'public' languages, 'restricted' or 'elaborated' codes (Bernstein, 1965), which, in a multilingual community, are probably very complicated. I have looked at language choice, firstly, from the point of view of the individual in dyadic relations (Case 1), and secondly, as an expression of group activity (Cases 2 and 3). Though my particular cases dealt with the converse, it is, of course, possible to find the instrumental aspect of language choice in group activity, and the expressive aspect in dyadic relations. Dyadic and group relations, and instrumentality and expressiveness, are perhaps useful preliminary concepts in the study of language choice in a multilingual community. The additional Parsonian notion of affective neutrality may perhaps be used conveniently to refer to zones of social activity in which vernaculars are used with impunity in multi-tribal contexts. Otherwise the choice of language used in social interactions between people who live near each other but come from different tribes and sometimes, but not necessarily, from different linguistic groups, may be determined by norms deriving from the prevailing political context or from the residential context. These contexts, and others not discussed here, such as workplace, formally organised recreation, and others, are extremely arbitrarily defined and no more than conveniently abstracted spheres of social life, the boundaries of which are at best blurred. The norms of many or all of these contexts may be present in any interaction, group, or dyadic, but the cases suggest that the norms of one context emerge as dominant and so determine the choice of language in particular situations.

Note

(1) While true at the time of writing, Kenyans along with some other 'foreign' ethnic groups were later pressured by the Uganda government to leave the country, especially under president Idi Amin, from 1973.

References

Bernstein, B. (1965) A Socio-Linguistic Approach to Social Learning, in *Penguin Survey of the Social Sciences* 1965. Penguin Books, London.

Gluckman, M. (1955) *Politics, Law and Ritual in Tribal Society*. Blackwell, Oxford.

Parkin, D.J. (1969) *Neighbours and Nationals in an African City Ward*. Routledge and Kegan Paul, London, and California University Press.

Southall, A. and Gutkind, P. (1956) *Townsmen in the Making*. East African Studies No. 9. East African Institute of Social Research, Kampala.

Turner, V.W. (1957) *Schism and Continuity in an African Society*. Manchester University Press, Manchester.

4 Language Switching in Nairobi

Social Distance

Some interesting work on perceptions of 'social distance' among townsmen in the Zambian Copperbelt (Mitchell 1956) shows how ethnic labels denote group membership and are useful in providing a blueprint of relationships. The blueprint is a cognitive map enabling a townsman to place other people in the town in a category of closeness or distance according to their ethnic groups. Placing according to the ethnic map is necessary when the only information a person has is the 'tribe' of the person he encounters. It may still be necessary even when the person has other information, such as the occupation, income, education, and area of residence of the other person. In other words, we can use more than simply one referent for deciding how we should behave towards a person.

The work from the Copperbelt illustrated the importance of the two variables: ethnic group affiliation and socioeconomic status. Mitchell's study of the Kalela dance (1956) demonstrated the interplay of these two in a single activity. It should be pointed out that ethnic closeness or distance was, for Mitchell, based on cultural (including linguistic) factors. Putting the situation simply, I might act towards a person in a specific way because he is of a 'tribe' which is culturally close to my own. We understand each other's customs. But, additionally, I might also act in a specific way towards that man because I recognise that he is of the same socioeconomic status as myself. I may behave in a quite different way when I recognise that the man is neither of a 'tribe' like my own nor my socioeconomic equal. There is in both cases a compounding of cues for placing each other. Or there may be a divergence of cues. The cues for ethnic placing are the stereotypes we have of 'other tribes'. The cues for socioeconomic status are the stereotypes we have of poorer or richer men, men with less or more education, or men who have menial or prestigious occupations compared with our own. The almost constant competition for prestige, or honour, or esteem, and the desire to avoid shame, seem pronounced in many East and Central African towns of colonial creation (see Epstein 1959, and Parkin 1969). A concern with notions of prestige seems to be strongly associated with a 'constantly changing skyline of status' (Douglas 1962) such as typifies the rapidly changing social situations characteristic of such towns. The claims and counter-claims for prestige underlie much behaviour centring round differences of socioeconomic status.

The situation in Nairobi, Kenya, is in one respect more complicated than that reported for the Copperbelt of Zambia. In Nairobi, ethnic closeness has also to be seen in conjunction with the political processes at work. It is quite clear, for instance, that it is possible to talk in terms of at least putative political alliances between ethnic groups which do not always coincide with cultural closeness. Thus, shortly before and after Kenya's independence in 1963, Kikuyu and Luo provided most of the membership of the Kenya African National Union (KANU), the party which came to power at Kenya's independence. Though political allies at that time, they are linguistically quite unrelated (Bantu and Nilotic respectively) and differ markedly in terms of traditionally derived customs. By contrast, the Luo (Nilotic) and most Luyia (Bantu) are linguistically unrelated and were sharply divided between KANU and the Kenya African Democratic Union (KADU), the opposition party.. Within a few years, these alliances were reversed, with Kikuyu and Luo politically opposed and Luo and Luyia cooperating (both from western Kenya). Another important ethnic group, the Kamba (Bantu) were mostly KADU but with an apparently substantial minority in KANU. Their political party affiliations were thus not significantly affected by linguistic and cultural closeness to other ethnic groups and they were regarded as relatively neutral concerning the major political rivalry that later developed between Luo and Kikuyu. Although generally borne out by political voting patterns, these are folk definitions held by people in Nairobi abstracted from the more complex reality. They are the political stereotypes of ethnic groups. These are different from the cultural stereotypes dealt with by Mitchell for the Copperbelt, which were based on affinity of custom.

Our original ethnic variable should, therefore, be regarded as having two aspects, a cultural as well as a political one. In actual analysis It may not always be possible to demonstrate which aspect governs language or code switching in a conversation, but the possibility of an analytical distinction of this kind has to be noted (see chapter three; and Parkin 1971). The socioeconomic status variable is much easier to pick out in analysis.

When people interact they try to judge, consciously or unconsciously, what mode of behaviour best suits the interaction. In any role-relationship, even one occupying no more than a few minutes, there is a constant process of adjustment and counter-adjustment to each other's expectations by the role-players. The values, stereotypes, and symbols, of ethnic and socioeconomic status are just two of many basic contours on the general cognitive map within which these adjustments are made. In a total population of people who interact fairly frequently, there is inevitably something of a feed-back process between the basic values and individually replicated, interpersonal adjustments.

Following the lines of Barth's analysis (1966), we can say that the interpersonal adjustments take the form of 'transactions ' or 'prestations' between the role-partners. That is to say, the role-partners recognise certain basic postulates of the relationship (i.e. that a man is of X tribe and of A, B, C, education, job and income), yet make concessions, or challenges and counter-challenges to each other on the basis of qualities and skills which fall through the net of the necessarily loose definition of the role-relationship as made by the over-arching values or stereotypes.

Certain conversations include this transactional element. In them we can see clearly the influence of socio-economic status, particularly in the use of English and Swahili, and of ethnic status, particularly in the use of the vernaculars. But we can also perceive the speaker making use of a limited number of choices: how should s/he respond to the use of a particular language; is the use intended to connote 'solidarity' or assertiveness; at what stage in the conversation is it strategically sound for him to reveal a wider repertoire of languages known by him; what response may he expect in revealing a 'new' language? I emphasise now that these are not necessarily conscious choices nor are they randomly made. They represent a limited range of alternative ways of speaking which arise logically from a particular recurring situation.

In confining myself to the two variables, ethnic and socio-economic status, I see three ideal types of transactional conversation. One can be regarded as a type of language game, since an element of gamesmanship is present. The 'game' is to use language to resolve a contradiction between personal interests (here socioeconomic) and ethnic group loyalties. The second type of transactional conversation is distinguishable by the way in which putative relationships of alliance or opposition between ethnic groups affect language use. In the third type of conversation notions of socio-economic status affect language use or affect the interpretation of language choice. In practice these ideal types may partly overlap, and I have selected conversations in which the values of one type appear to predominate. In all types, paralinguistic features such as tone, gesture and, possibly, physical stance, are important, perhaps crucially so in the first type.

I regard these transactional conversations as critical 'speech events' (Hymes 1962). That is to say, they reveal certain fundamental ethnic and socioeconomic status values attaching to the use of languages in Nairobi. The language game is undoubtedly the most significant in this respect. From repeated transactional conversations flow the continually modified values, or non-verbal messages, of particular languages. In the much more common, non-transactional conversations of everyday life, these values or messages are assumed and incorporated frequently in the form of idiomatic usage and clichés. This modification of values has to be seen, or is most easily seen, in transactional conversations between persons of different ethnic groups, which thus constitute nearly all my examples.

Transactional Conversations 1. Joking and Gamesmanship: The Language Game

One of the most interesting aspects of conversations concerning ethnic and status relationships is that they are frequently jocular and accompanied by banter. This was the case in Kampala (Parkin 1971; Chapter three) and the Copperbelt (Epstein 1959) and is so in Nairobi. In other words, though people compete for prestige and status and may express their ethnic stereotypes in conversation and behaviour, they may refrain from doing so in a manner which is visibly hostile. It is hardly surprising that this is so. One does not normally score points over a rival by crude abuse or violence if public approval is one's aim. Approval has to be sought by manipulating subtly and skilfully norms of the existing social order, but not by breaking them. If abuse is used, it has to be wittily creative and socially insightful but not crude and unsophisticated (see Parkin 1980 and Chapter 5). In what I call (1971 and Chapter 3) a 'conversational arena of prestige competition', the game breaks down when a competitor runs out of witty abuse and resorts to violence.

In this example, men competed with each other in a taunting but jocular manner for the prestige of being regarded as the most articulate speaker of English. Each competitor acted here on the basis of personally achieved socioeconomic status. The break-up of the game occurred when the honour of a man's nation (a Kenyan) was impugned and he rose to defend it. From other cases it might well have been the honour of his ethnic group that be sought to defend. In other words, one of the two variables of interaction, that of ethnic or national status (group membership), intervenes and conflicts with the second variable, personal socioeconomic status.

This is, of course, a universal phenomenon. We may at one level seem to compete for prestige as individuals regardless of ethnic affiliation.

In Nairobi, a dire scarcity of jobs and housing is at the basis of much competition. Yet, at another level, we may be drawn to those who are closest to us ethnically and culturally. As members of a common group we may then blame the scarcity of jobs and housing on other ethnic groups who appear to us to have a monopoly. Personal status and ethnic group each has its own set of stereotypes, symbols and conventions of behaviour. For much of social life these are either kept apart or are mutually reinforcing. But sometimes, as in the example of a conversation I have just mentioned, they conflict.

This occasional conflict of expectations arises from what is ultimately a logical contradiction between the two variables of ethnic group membership and achieved personal status. There is a contradiction here because a man cannot maximise personal interests at all times without flouting the rules of group membership. Alternatively, he cannot fulfil the group's norms at all times without sacrificing at least some self-interest. In practice, speakers reach compromises. But, as an intellectual puzzle played out in actors' minds, a solution seems possible through a reversal of logic. For example, a Luo who initiates a conversation with a Kikuyu in the friendly atmosphere of a bar, may recognise that there is a stereotyped opposition between Luo and Kikuyu over certain issues. He may denote his recognition of this basic blueprint for behaviour by pointed jokes. Having expressed the putative state of hostility between them in the most friendly manner possible, i.e. having reversed the logic, he can then get on with the main task for which the particular relationship was established, namely the satisfaction of personal interests. This is stated simply here, but constitutes a basic strategy in many conversations which I have recorded between persons who are of different 'tribes'. As will become clear from my illustrations, language use and switching are convenient methods of succeeding in this strategy and of tempering conflicting role-expectations arising from this fundamental contradiction.

Following Bailey (1968, 1969), I have introduced such notions as 'strategy', 'game', 'scoring points', and 'competition', since I believe that these may be useful concepts in analysing certain day-to-day speech transactions or conversations of people who try to maximise personal interests yet are each members of groups which are putatively opposed in some contexts.

I have found it necessary to be selective and have concentrated on partconversations heard and afterwards written down[1] to the best of our memories by my assistant and myself in the market place of Shauri Moyo, or 'Barma' as it is called locally, which is across the Jogoo Road from Kaloleni. Its stallholders and customers are ethnically mixed and it is a good area for hearing language switching and 'mixing'. Marketplace transactions are additionally useful from the analytical viewpoint simply because they *are* transactional or contractual. That is to say, the transactional aspects of speech are thrown more clearly into relief because language is an important tool and symbol in the haggling which accompanies the economic transaction. I should emphasise that nearly all my examples in this chapter are of very short, casual encounters with very few words exchanged. The simplicity and brevity of these encounters makes them manageable for the limited analytical aims which I have set myself. I do not yet feel equipped to analyse an extended conversation of 'normal' dimensions.

In the following case of a Luo and Kikuyu speaking to each other the aim of my analysis will be to see the apparent effect on language use when individuals successfully joke off the contradiction between (a) what they want personally from the transaction and their use of numerous and novel techniques to satisfy this want, and (b) how they ought to behave on the basis of the limited information they have on each other as members of groups and categories laid out according to a blueprint.

Case 1: Kikuyu female stall-holder and Luo male customer. Parts of actual conversation as heard, with dashes denoting language switch.

1. KIKUYU STALL-HOLDER: Omera, nadi!
2. LUO CUSTOMER: Maber.
3. KIKUYU: Ati — nini?
4. LUO: Ya nini kusema lugha ambao huelewi mama?
5. KIKUYU: I know—kijaluo—very well!
6. LUO: Wapi!—You do not know it at all—Wacha haya, nipe mayai mbili.
7. KIKUYU: Unataka mayai—ariyo, omera,—haya ni—tongolo—tatu.

Languages used:

1. Luo
2. Luo
3. Kikuyu—Swahili
4. Swahili
5. English—Swahilised form—English
6. Swahili—English—Swahili
7. Swahili—Luo—Swahili—Luo—Swahili

Rough translation:

1. How are you, brother!
2. Fine.
3. What—what?
4. Why (try) to speak a language you don't know, Mum?
5. I know Luo very well!

6. Go on! You don't know it at all. Anyway, let's leave the matter, and give me a couple of eggs.
7. Two eggs, brother? O.K., that will be thirty cents.

We cannot be too adventurous about an analysis of this limited conversation. Even in so few words, switching is considerable. The paralinguistic data are important also, as I now show.

(1) The Kikuyu stall-holder opens up with a breezy, friendly and jocular Luo greeting, having recognised the customer to be a Luo. (In this case the two did not know each other and the Luo was recognised as such by certain distinctive features.) Here the Kikuyu stall-holder concedes to the Luo a claimed knowledge of the Luo vernacular, a customary way of attracting and holding the custom of Luo who are reputedly proud of their language. In making this language concession, we may speculate that the stall-holder hopes to profit from the economic transaction. Should she elicit a Luo response from the Luo, she may have pleased him. In terms of a language game, she will have scored a point.

(2) The Luo does answer the greeting in Luo and so awards her a point, but he answers her in an uncharacteristically (for Luo) brief and curt manner. We possibly see why in 3 and 4 below.

(3) The Kikuyu does not appear to have understood or to have heard even this simple Luo reply, thus seeming to betray immediately her very limited knowledge of the Luo vernacular. Thus, her gamble did not come off and she loses her point. The score is now even.

(4) With what is clearly a jocular mock indignation, the Luo lets the Kikuyu woman know that he realises that she has virtually no knowledge of his vernacular. To put it simply, he exposes her as having been using *his* language for her personal economic gain.

Significantly, the Luo here uses Swahili. It is pointless continuing to use Luo anyway, but the use of Swahili puts them back on neutral ground and denies the mock 'friendship' which the woman tried to create. The score is surely now in the Luo's favour.

(5) The Kikuyu tacitly admits that she does not really know the Luo vernacular by replying in English in even more jocular vein. Her switch to English after the Luo's previous use of Swahili may be regarded as a challenge to the Luo. Can he match her English and save his point?

(6) He successfully staves off the challenge and replies in English, now openly returning the banter. Having settled the challenge, he turns to the matter-of-fact business at hand and switches back to the neutral language of Swahili in order to purchase some eggs, which is for him the pragmatic purpose of the transaction.

He has won the language tussle, but the Kikuyu stallholder has won her custom. She seems to accept this and offers, as a final friendly gesture, some more words of Luo. including the word, 'omera', 'my brother'.

While there may be alternatives to this analysis, we at least have here an explanation for language switching which is consistent. Language use here is viewed as part of a contest. Admittedly, winning the language contest did not help the Luo buy his eggs more cheaply, which was not, anyway, his intention. But, at least, his 'honour' was maintained. More than this the 'honour' of his own vernacular, an undisputed source of pride, was maintained also. It could be argued fairly that it is in the interests of the stallholders to stimulate and then lose such language contests, provided that they win their custom. And this, of course, is perfectly true. Indeed, it is precisely by manipulating such systems of honour, and not just those concerning language, that such economic and thereby political interests are created and strengthened.

In this particular conversation, the use of English set up a challenge of a socio-economic nature. Because it is a prestigious lingua franca, English has normally to be used with caution. So, in some contexts, must Swahili. But English seems to have much less of the neutral emotional 'colour' that may sometimes characterise Swahili. If used incautiously with a man who is known by the speaker to know no English, the use of English is likely to cause offence. Sometimes, of course, it can be used in this situation as a deliberate snub.

It is important to observe how the vernacular, Luo, stimulates a different response from English and Swahili. Use of 'my' vernacular or mother tongue constitutes a form of borrowing and can please my sense of language loyalty or can offend it depending on the particular use to which the vernacular is put. This response is illustrated clearly in the Luo's reply (no. 4) in the case above. Here the Kikuyu's use of the Luo vernacular is too obviously out of enlightened self-interest. It 'offends', ostensibly at least, and requires a riposte. In contrasting situations, in a beer bar for instance, a Kikuyu, say, may greet and carry on a limited conversation with, say, a Luo across the table from him in the Luo vernacular for no other apparent reason than to express friendliness. This use of the vernacular is here more likely to please the Luo's sense of language loyalty and may elicit a concession, though not necessarily of a language or vernacular kind.

In general, the different responses to, on the one hand English and Swahili, the lingua francas, and on the other hand the vernacular, Luo, can be explained by the contradiction discussed above. That is to say, the response prompted by use of the vernacular derives from wider scale expectations of inter-ethnic group relations, which have their cultural and political aspects. By contrast, the response set up by use of English and Swahili has more to do with socioeconomic status relations of an interpersonal nature. The most obvious form of this contradiction in the case was the fact that, though both stall-holder and customer competed in the same language game, the stall-holder clearly had economic profit as her primary 'prize' (personal interest), while the customer saw the maintenance of ethnic honour as his 'prize' (the group interest). It is a contradiction for opposing sides in a game to compete for different prizes. The contradiction is resolved by being phrased in jocular terms. As Douglas says, following Freud, 'the essence of wit is neatly to span gulfs between different ideas' (Douglas 1968, p. 363). Regulated joking is a form of ritual behaviour, and like ritual it may reconcile, if only temporarily, conflicting and contradictory principles of social organisation and intellectual classification.

To repeat, language games phrased in a jocular idiom represent one way of resolving the contradiction of ethnic group loyalties and personal status considerations. In resolving the contradiction the language game throws into relief the basic behavioural stereotypes which use of each language conveys. In the next case, we see something of what may occur when the language game ceases to be phrased in a jocular idiom: the contradiction is openly expressed and language use may become an issue over which genuine hostility is voiced.

Case 2: Kamba stall-holder, neighbouring Kikuyu stall-holder, and Luo customer.

Parts of the conversation as heard:

1. LUO CUSTOMER: Bwana sikuweza kukulipa pesa zako za mwezi jana kwa sababu nilikuwa na haja zingine za haraka sana. Nisamehe, nitakulipa mwisho wa mwezi huu.
2. KAMBA STALL-HOLDER: And why did you not report this at the end of the month? Nyakati nyingine ninyi wanunuzi na hasa wale—employed—mnatuletea taabu nyingi sana katika biashara.
3. NEIGHBOURING KIKUYU STALL-HOLDER: Makiria aya—Jaluo—niandu acenji muno.
4. LUO CUSTOMER: Sasa ukisema—ati—sisi—joluo—tu washenzi, unafikiri sisikii lugha yako ya Kikuyu. Na ninyi wakikuyu si mwashenzi zaidi?—You n-----!
5. NEIGHBOURING KIKUYU STALL-HOLDER: Nenda zako mjinga wee!
6. KAMBA STALL-HOLDER: Go away and remember to bring this money at the end. And I am not supplying you with food this month until you pay the amount due.

Languages used:

1. Swahili
2. English—Swahili—English—Swahili
3. Kikuyu
4. Swahili—English
5. Swahili
6. English

Rough translation:

1. Mister, I wasn't able to pay my last month's account because of some other urgent expenses. I'm sorry but I'll pay at the end of this month.
2. Why didn't you let me know at the end of last month? You customers, especially those of you who have jobs, are always giving us businessmen trouble.
3. Sometimes these Luo have no sense.
4. So, by speaking in 'ati' (i.e. refers to the Kikuyu language) and calling us Luo barbarians, you think I can't understand your Kikuyu language. Well, aren't you Kikuyu even greater barbarians? You n-----! (a not uncommon form of abuse).
5. Go home, you fool.
6. (As the original.)

(1) The Luo opens up the conversation in the spirit of a frank request. He is not jocular about the debt. He uses the 'neutral' language of Swahili, chosen presumably because it is here the most efficient medium of communication in this business matter. He does not therefore initiate a language game. Note his 'standard' style of Swahili.

(2) But the Kamba does, it seems, initiate a language game by replying in English. He does so in a tone of mock haughtiness. His haughtiness is necessarily mock rather than real, since the Luo, for all his indebtedness, is a regular customer. If he genuinely offends the Luo, he may lose not only regular custom but also the debt. Retaining custom and eventually having his debt repaid may be regarded as the Kamba's primary 'prize' (compare the Kikuyu stall-bolder in Case 1).

By using English in what amounts to a jocular if taunting tone of voice, the Kamba has scored a point and has set up a challenge which the Luo may accept.

Having established his challenge the Kamba then switches to Swahili. In switching to Swahili he sheds the mock haughtiness and adopts a more ostensibly relaxed and friendly tone. He awaits the Luo's riposte.

We may note that in his switch from English to Swahili and from a mock haughtiness to a more openly friendly tone, he moves from a specific condemnation of the customer to a general condemnation of debtors. There is the suggestion here that not only is friction reduced by moving from use of the second person singular to the second person plural, but that this movement is best achieved by switching from English to Swahili. Swahili, it should be noted, frequently connotes equality or irrelevance of status and even connotes 'brotherhood' (see Parkin 1971), a point to which I return.

In parenthesis, we should note also that the Kamba uses the English word, 'employed', instead of, say, the Swahili 'wenye kazi' or 'wafanyakazi'. From other contexts, it seems that the English term tends to refer to office workers who, by definition, know English, while the Swahili terms refer to workers of all status levels in a more general context. The significance of the inclusion of the English term in an otherwise Swahili sentence seems to reinforce the general condemnation, i.e. they may be office workers, speak English, and wear suits, but they still don't pay their bills.

(3) At this juncture, the nearby Kikuyu stall-holder enters the arena. His entry was presumably not anticipated by the Kamba when he made his challenge to the Luo by replying in English. And now the Luo's acceptance of the challenge is forestalled. But, before seeing the effect the Kikuyu's entry has upon the game, let us ask what might have been the Luo's response to the challenge.

There might have been four possible alternatives open to the Luo.

(a) He could have continued to use Swahili. But he would not thereby have met the Kamba's challenge and so would have ceded the point.
(b) He could have used his own vernacular, Luo, but since the aim of the game is to exceed your opponent's expectations by disclosing an increasingly large repertoire of languages, this would hardly have achieved that aim and he would have ceded the point. Also, since few Kamba appear to know Luo, as we saw in the last chapter, this would have been tantamount to closing the lines of communication. It would have been literally pointless.
(c) He could have used English. This would have at least met the challenge and put the score at even.
(d) Finally, he could have used his opponent's own vernacular, Kamba. As we saw from the last chapter it is extremely rare for a Luo to know even a little of the Kamba vernacular. For the Luo customer to have done this, therefore, would probably have been

completely against the Kamba stall-holder's expectations and would have either cancelled out the Kamba's point and given the Luo one, or been seen by the Kamba as a new and very powerful counter-challenge (compare the initial use by the Kikuyu stallholder of her Luo customer's vernacular in Case 1).

Let us now return to the effect that the Kikuyu's entry into the arena has on the game. The Kamba had previously switched from English to Swahili and from mock haughtiness to open friendliness. This might well have been an invitation to bring more jocularity into the game.

The Kikuyu nearby stallholder does intervene in a jocular tone but does so in his own vernacular, in effect addressing himself to the Kamba. He seems to have broken some rule of the game by throwing his own vernacular uninvited into the arena. By speaking in Kikuyu to the Kamba (the two languages being closely related), he quite clearly closes the lines of communication with the Luo and creates a relationship of confidence with the Kamba which excludes the Luo.

(4) Even if the Luo could understand Kikuyu, this esoteric use of the vernacular is almost bound to offend him. Indeed, he claims to have understood the Kikuyu but takes the remark more as an insult than a joke and returns the insult. His final insult is traded in English, presumably as a final riposte. There is now little chance of bringing more jocularity into the game. As a result the game seems abandoned.
(5) The Kikuyu replies to the insults in the language of most efficient communication, Swahili. He seems also to regard the game as abandoned.
(6) The Kamba stallholder, presumably still anxious to retain the Luo's custom and/or to have his debt settled, reminds the Luo of this. He uses English. Is this a last attempt to restart the game and so reduce friction, or is it simply a means of asserting his demands in the language of highest authority? Either interpretation seems possible.

Again, as in Case 1, ethnic and status factors bring about conflicting expectations: competitors can make use of Swahili and English and the status associations that go with them; they might even have made use of each other's vernaculars; but when the esoteric use of a mother tongue is brought into the arena, ethnic stereotypes are connoted and ethnic loyalties are hurt. The language game and jocularity are then likely to be abandoned and hostility to be openly expressed in ethnic terms.

I do not wish to appear defensive about this approach to the analysis of conversations. But I cannot pretend that it is a panacea. There are many different ways of looking at the same data. I suggest that this is one of them. The problem before us is to discover factors prompting language switching. In everyday life, differences of status and of 'tribe' are frequently joked about and there is often a certain gamesmanship in competitions for prestige and status and in relations between people of d1fferent ethnic groups. This, as I have said, is a fact which has already been well demonstrated.

Given that the lingua francas, English and Swahili, invoke status stereotypes, and that the vernaculars, by definition, invoke ethnic stereotypes, it seems reasonable to assume that in conversations involving switching between these languages, we should sometimes find evidence of jocular gamesmanship.

I think I should emphasise again that people are not necessarily conscious that they are playing these language games. Sometimes they are (see Parkin 1971). Usually they are not. Whether or not the games are consciously played seems to me irrelevant, provided the same basic aims rules and techniques are employed.

The irrelevance of consciousness leads to another remark I would like to make about this mode of analysis. This is that it is not a psychological analysis. It is true that it makes use of such notions as 'stereotypes', which are essentially mental associations stimulated by symbols of a material or non-material nature, including words and languages. It is true, too, that it depends on observation of such paralinguistic phenomena as mood, stress, and even gesture (though I have not included the latter here). But the analysis is not concerned with how neuro-sensory processes give rise to, say, moods, or with how these processes are stimulated by stereotypes. The stereotypes and moods are deliberately loosely defined, are based on empirical observation, and are no more than descriptive labels. The essence of analysis is the limited number of language choices which a speaker has: he is limited by his personal repertoire as well as by that of his role-partner. The aim of the game is to expose the limits of his partner's repertoire before exposing the limits of his own. A game of this kind can be analysed without reference to psychology, though possibly psychology might be helpful.

Finally, one definitely has to be selective about the cases which may be analysed. The sort of conversations I have in mind are those in which there is a progressive unravelling of fresh languages by those conversing with each other. The simplest conversational set is between two people. The simplest unravelling is of the two lingua francas, Swahili and English, and each of the competitor's mother tongues. Each language is shown to have its own symbolic or communicative value in the conversation. These values seem highlighted when language use itself becomes a topic of conversation. It seems legitimate, therefore, to begin an analysis of language switching by selecting 'natural' examples of people actually talking about language, a topic which, except perhaps under the conditions of a simulated or controlled discussion, seems likely to invoke jocularity.

Transactional Conversations 2. Ethnic Relations

Even in some cases of language switching in which jocularity and gamesmanship are less easily discernible or absent altogether, it is possible to preserve the view that switching involves the granting of concessions as the following cases show.

The concessions in these cases are made on the basis of certain assumptions about the nature of ethnic group relations.

As shown in the first two cases, Luo-Kikuyu relations appear to be potentially sensitive over even a matter such as language. But it is possible for Kikuyu and Kamba in conversation, and for Luo and Luyia in conversation, to make certain assumptions about each other's likely language repertoire and not risk offence. These are assumptions which directly reflect the special sociolinguistic relations of these ethnic pairs, as based on self-reports and described elsewhere (Parkin 1974, i.e. chap 7 in Whiteley 1974).

(a) Kikuyu-Kamba

Case 3: Kikuyu stall-holder and Kamba customer.

1. KIKUYU: Hullo bwana—ukwenda kugura ki? (What do you want to buy?)
2. KAMBA: Ndienda maigu. (I want some bananas.)
3. KIKUYU: Ya pesa ngapi? (For how much?)
4. KAMBA: Ya—fifty cents.
5. KIKUYU: Unataka kitu gani kingine? (Anything else?)
6. KAMBA: Hakuna. Huwezi kunipatia—commission? (Nothing. Can you put it on account for me?)
7. KIKUYU: Kwa—commission—kuja kesho. (Come tomorrow for anything on account.)

Languages used:

1. Swahili—Kikuyu
2. Kikuyu
3. Swahili
4. Swahili—English
5. Swahili

6. Swahili—English
7. Swahili—English—Swahili

(1) Here, the Kikuyu stall-holder operates on the reasonable assumption that the customer (whom, he later told us, he knew to be either Kikuyu or Kamba but was not sure which) would understand and would not visibly resent being addressed in Kikuyu, even though he might happen to be Kamba (or Meru or Embu who also speak closly related languages).
(2) The assumption was correct. The Kamba customer seems to accept the legitimacy of the assumption and replies in Kikuyu. It would seem that, somehow, the Kamba's reply indicates that he is not Kikuyu and the stallholder switches to Swahili in 3. Thereafter, in 4-7 both stallholder and customer talk in Swahili, incorporating the English 'fifty cents' and 'commission'.

In the following interesting case, there is a similar indirect statement of Kikuyu-Kamba linguistic and cultural affinity. But here the Kikuyu stallholder actually knows the Kamba customer and makes the appropriate initial concession by speaking in her vernacular.

Case 4: Kikuyu stall-holder and female Kamba customer.

1. KIKUYU: Nata yu. (Now how are things then.)
2. KAMBA: Ni nesa kabisa. (I'm fine.)
3. KIKUYU: Ukwenda kungurira kii riu? (Now what do you want to buy?)
4. KAMBA: Nataka mandizi ya shimoni. Ni ngapi? (I want fifty cents' worth of bananas. How much are they?)
5. KIKUYU: Nauza moja kwa peni. (I'm selling one for ten cents.)
6. KAMBA: Nipatie basi na uniongezee moja. (O.K. but give me one extra.)
7. KIKUYU: Hapana siongezi ni—hathara. (No extras. I can't afford it.)
8. KAMBA: Asi! Naku mwikuyu uu.—Leta tu. (Ah! You Kikuyu (singular) —O.K. give me some.)

Languages used:

1. Kamba
2. Kamba
3. Kikuyu
4. Swahili
5. Swahili
6. Swahili
7. Swahili—Kikuyu
8. Kamba—Swahili

(1) The stallholder makes the concession of addressing the customer in her language.
(2) The customer accepts the concession by replying in her mother tongue. It should be noted here, however, that a greeting is likely to be continued in the language in which it is started since it most obviously constitutes a single linguistic set. Choice of language in a greeting is thus a very potent factor in establishing the 'tone' of a conversation.
(3) Here, the Kikuyu, having made his concession, reverts to Kikuyu. From 4-8, the conversation is most conveniently conducted in Swahili, with a possibly significant temporary reversion to her mother tongue by the Kamba as she jokingly condemns the Kikuyu stallholder.

(b) Luo-Luyia

As was shown in Parkin (1974 – ch 7 of Whiteley 1974), many more Luyia claim to know the Luo vernacular than do Luo make the reverse claim. From observation this claim is certainly borne out. In the following case, the Luo stallowner not only uses his mother tongue with a Luyia customer but actually elicits from her an agreement to incorporate Luo words in her Swahili. In other words, the Luyia concedes the frequent use of the Luo vernacular by her ethnic group and so confirms indirectly their special, what I have earlier called, alliance relationship.

Case 5: Luo stall-holder and Luyia female customer.

1. LUO: Nadi mama. (How are you, Mum.)
2. LUYIA: Maber ahinya. Adwaro—nunua—mana—unga. (Very fine. I want to buy some flour.)
3. LUO: Haya, unga—nitie.—Unataka ratili ngapi? (Yes, we have some flour. How much do you want?)
4. LUYIA: Adwar—ratili kumi. Ah! Unga hiyo haonekani kama nzuri. Endelea tu. (I want ten pounds. Ah! This flour doesn't look right. Never mind.)
5. LUO: Magi agolo mana e KFA—hiyo ni—first class—inashinda unga yote hapa Kaloleni. (I bought this from the KFA—it's first class and is the best flour in Kaloleni.)
6. LUYIA: Haya, nzuri, nitaona.—Oriti. (Well, we'll see.—Goodbye.)

Languages used:

1. Luo
2. Luo—Swahili—Luo—Swahili
3. Swahili—Luo—Swahili

4. Luo—Swahili
5. Luo—Swahili—English—Swahili
6. Swahili—Luo

Moving now from conversations between Luo and Luyia in the market place to those occurring in and around Kaloleni itself, we see the same mutual realisation of their alliance relationship reflected in the unquestioning way in which Luyia incorporate the Luo vernacular in their Swahili or respond positively to the Luo vernacular. Kaloleni housing estate is numerically and culturally predominantly Luo and so, in neighbourhood women's gossip sets and in children's playgroups, these factors are perhaps even more evident.

Case 6: A group of three women sitting together in Kaloleni (one Luo and two Luyia).

1. 1st LUYIA: Nitajaribu kumaliza yako sababu mpaka niende Uhuru. (I'll try and finish your (hair) because I have to go to Uhuru market.)
2. LUO: Kuleta nini? (To get what?)
3. lst LUYIA: Si chakula. (Food, of course.)
4. LUO: Jabwana olosi. (Your husband keeps you well.)
5. 2nd LUYIA: Ongere—sababu yeye bado mpya. (It's a well known thing-it's because she is still a new wife.)
   (The 2nd Luyia and the Luo here laugh.) Mpaka abembereze bwana. (And she has to please her husband in return.)
6. LUO: Siku hizi sisi wazee tunaweza kufanya wewe wote. We older women have been through it all and can tell you young wives all about it.)
7. 2nd LUYIA: Bwana siku hizi hatembei sababu wewe bado mpya. (Your husband isn't on the loose because you're still a new wife.)
8. 1st LUYIA: Alikuwa akitembea. (He was on the loose.)
9. LUO: Si ndiyo. (Of course.)
10. 1st LUYIA: Kama mimi iko hawezi. (But if I'm around he can't be.)
11. LUO: Manindo! (You really think that!) (Literally 'a sleeping matter', i.e. you are in a dream world.)

Languages used:

1. Swahili
2. Swahili
3. Swahili
4. Luo
5. Luo—Swahili
6. Swahili
7. Swahili

8. Swahili
9. Swahili
10. Swahili
11. Luo

These jocular teasing sessions at the expense of a newly married wife are very common, both in Nairobi and, as I have documented elsewhere (1969), in Kampala. The Luo woman and the 2nd Luyia woman are longer married and, one may assume, have spent more time in Nairobi in contexts such as this. They each use a word or two of Luo in their Swahili. The usage of Luo is very little but perhaps represents a recognition of the alliance relationship.

The following case illustrates this more strongly.

Case 7: A group of three Luyia women and two Luyia adolescent girls and a passing Luo male neighbour and his Luyia male friend (who does not figure in the conversation).

1. LUO: Habari ya wasichana akina bibi. (How are you, women and girls.)
2. LUYIA GIRL: Salama wote labda—in. (We're all well, and what about you.)
3. LUO: An—salama tu. (I'm just fine.)
4. LUYIA WOMAN: Ingima. (You are well.)
5. LUO: Angima. (O.K.)
6. LUYIA WOMAN: Maber ahinya (all laugh). (Very good.)
7. LUO: Mzuri tu. (Good enough.)
8. LUYIA WOMAN: Umepotea—kanye? (Where have you been?)
9. LUO: Niko tu. (I am just around.)
10. LUYIA WOMAN: Tinde—unataka kuwa mkora sana. (Nowadays you like to act the playboy/rascal.)
11. LUO: Kama ni mkora sasa—then—nilikuwa mkora zamani—If not I am not (a sentence here missed). (If I am a playboy now, then I have been so for a long time.)
12. LUO: Haya, asante. (O.K. thanks.)
13. LUYIA WOMAN: Udhi Kanye—sasa? (Where are you going now?)
14. LUO: Bayo. (For a stroll.)
15. LUYIA WOMAN: Wapi? (Where?)
16. LUO: Twende na sisi utaona. (Come with us and you'll see.)
17. LUYIA WOMAN: Ilikuwa yenu, ungeniambia kitambo ninge—prepare—tunge-accompany—nyinyi, sasa ni yenu. (This is your [plural] stroll. You should have let me know in good time and I would have got ourselves ready to accompany you [plural], but now it's your stroll alone.)

18. LUO: Haya, kwa heri. (O.K. Goodbye.)
19. LUYIA WOMAN: Oriti—uniletee vitu ya uko. (Goodbye—bring me something from where you're going.)

Languages used:

1. Swahili
2. Swahili—Luo
3. Luo-Swahili
4. Luo
5. Luo
6. Luo
7. Swahili
8. Swahili—Luo
9. Swahili
10. Luo—Swahili
11. Swahili—English—Swahili—English
12. Swahili
13. Luo—Swahili
14. Luo
15. Swahili
16. Swahili
17. Swahili with English verb roots
18. Swahili
19. Luo—Swahili

In this jokingly flirtatious encounter, there is something of a language game in the progressive unravelling of languages by the Luo man and the Luyia woman. The Luyia woman first greets in the Luo vernacular and gets a reply in the same vernacular. There is a general switch to Swahili but both Luo and, latterly, English are incorporated. Almost as if to challenge the pleasantly provocative Luyia woman, the Luo man introduces the few English words. The Luyia woman belatedly meets the challenge if only partly by incorporating English verb roots but preserving Swahili affixes. In parenthesis it should be noted that forms involving English roots and Swahili affixes occur commonly. I have no cases of the reverse.

Transactional Conversations 3. Socioeconomic Relations

When I say, with reference to Case 7, that the use of English here constitutes a challenge, I do not mean that only English can be used for this purpose. All languages can, depending on the person being spoken to and the situation in which the conversation is held and its topic. These are details which cannot be discussed here. I am simply referring to the socioeconomically prestigious stereotypes with which English is frequently associated. At other times, this stereotyping of English as socially exclusive is used as a weapon against the language. Swahili is then held up as the 'true' national language, freed of colonial implications and of the status divisions brought about by an urban, industrial and monetary complex, and alone likely to express the 'fraternity' of all ethnic groups in the nation and the dignity of their political independence. This powerfully emotive argument underlies many of the interesting debates in parliament and press regarding possible national language policy. Nevertheless, at the personal level in Kenya, the prestigious and socially exclusive stereotype of English remains the dominant one.

As well as Case 7, other cases in this chapter provide instances of English and Swahili possessing certain values which derive directly and indirectly from differences between people of socio-economic status. Having analytically isolated the use of vernaculars between people in 'special' ethnic relations of putative alliance or opposition, I can now outline very briefly the more general socio-economic factors prompting switching into English and Swahili. I shall not need to illustrate my comments with actual conversations.

In Whiteley (1974 Chapters 6 and 7) I showed that while the household heads who know English are likely to be younger and better educated than average, there is evidence that Swahili is used at all status levels, but most frequently used at the lowest rung of the occupational ladder. I showed further that Swahili may be learned informally in Nairobi, particularly through interaction at workplace. I then suggested that the relation to each other of Swahili and English is a dynamic one about which predictions may be attempted, arising from projections of an increasing imbalance in the ratio of 'educated' to employed.

Both English and Swahili are lingua francas in the sense that each provides an alternative to the use of vernaculars. Neither is associated with any particular cultural grouping as a mother tongue in Nairobi, with the special exception of the Muslim and possibly certain other residents of Pumwani (see Bujra in Whiteley 1974: 218). Swahili may be said to bridge both ethnic and status differences: it is a common medium of communication between ethnic groups as well as between men of different socio-economic status. Swahili thus stands in some contrast to English, which, though it can be said to bridge ethnic differences, nevertheless carries by its use an additional message defining the statuses of the persons talking to each other in it. These statements refer to 'normal' situations and constitute further stereotypes or symbols denoting modes of behaviour between status peers or unequals. In actual situations, people make use of these symbols in conversation.

Thus, in encountering someone for the first time, I may not know his ethnic group nor be able to guess it. I am not therefore likely to use a vernacular. The choice now is between English and Swahili. Do I want to establish a 'formal' relationship or an 'informal' one? If I am a government officer, use of English may affirm my authority and set a tone of formality. But if the man knows no English then, clearly, I must switch to Swahili. Alternatively, I may start on the assumption that the man knows no English and address him in Swahili. If the man does not know English then he is likely to welcome this 'fraternal' gesture, which is less humiliating to him than the step-down in status implied by the switch from English to Swahili. But he may resent it if he does know English, since he has thereby been classed as a non-speaker of English and therefore, according to the stereotype, as 'uneducated'. The whole course of the conversation may be affected by such initial choices. Tone and gesture do not always mitigate the effects of wrong choices, since they are themselves frequently ambiguous.

In most first-time encounters, the status of the speaker and his respondent cannot be demonstrated or guessed and, from an investigation of many such encounters, I suggest that Swahili is likely to be the initial choice, with adjustments being made to English or a vernacular as information about the role-partners becomes available in conversation. It is for this reason that I referred earlier to the sometimes 'neutral' standing of Swahili.

In encounters between people of different ethnic groups it is much more difficult to account for variation in the initial choice of language, and I would not attempt to do so here, though, as explained earlier, some choices can be seen as concessions or challenges sometimes giving rise to a language game.

A Non-transactional Case

Because my interest has been focused on ethnicity, I have dealt only with selected speech transactions between persons of different 'tribes'. I have not the space to illustrate the many examples of language switching occurring between speakers who are of the same ethnic and language group.

Why should such cases occur? Sometimes, of course, they occur as language games to the accompaniment of a variable degree of banter or jocularity. At other times, a specific topic of conversation or even physical or organisational setting may seem to prompt switching. Sometimes, switches may be marked by specific parts of speech, for example conjunctions. But perhaps more frequently, we can only speculate as to whether topic, context, the particular role-relationship, a particular part of speech, or a combination of all four variables, prompt switching.

These cases of switching between members of the same ethnic group who share a common mother tongue necessarily characterise studies of 'bilingualism' or 'multilingualism' focused on a single ethnic group (Fishman *et al.*, 1968). Though it is presumably a matter of degree and definition, many of Nairobi's African population can be said to be multilingual, and it would certainly be possible and profitable to concentrate analysis on one ethnic group. But I suggest that even if this were done, there would have to be a preliminary survey of language use between ethnic groups. They are, after all, involved together in a single urban system of relations and, as I have tried to show, need to forge relations across ethnic boundaries, sometimes at the cost of a conflict of personal and group interests. In this process of common interaction, common problems are coped with and similar solutions reached. Thus, even in relations between members of the same ethnic group language evaluations and choices are made on the basis of information received from a wide range of social interactions not confined to any one ethnic group.

As an illustration of this 'feedback' process and for the sake of completeness, I present a final case in which two men, of the same ethnic group, incorporate the use of Swahili and a little English in their speech, seemingly in response to a conversational topic involving speech forms likely to occur in all groups represented in Nairobi. The two men are Luo tailors who work together in the market already referred to.

Case 8:

1. 1st LUO: Onego ikendi. (You ought to marry.)
2. 2nd LUO: Kinyalo miya dhok. (If you can give me the cattle.)
3. 1st LUO: Dhi penj wuoru. (Go and ask your father.)
4. 2ndLUO: Baba bado anasema mimi niko—young. (My father still says I am too young.)
5. 1ST LUO: In—young—nadi? Itiyo—umetosa kuwa na mtoto—and everything. (How are you young? You are working. You've left being a child and (childish) things.)
6. 2nd LUO: Nyaka ayud nyako maber. (I have yet to get a good girl as a bride.)
7. 1ST LUO: Karango, masani to ichiegni bedo-mzee-ni. (But when? You are now swiftly becoming an old man.)

Languages used:

1. Luo
2. Luo
3. Luo
4. Swahili-English
5. Luo—English—Luo—Swahili—English
6. Luo
7. Luo—Swahili—Luo

In 4 there is a switch to Swahili and a word of English when the 2nd Luo has to confess that he is considered too young by his father to be given bridewealth for marriage. This switch may be caused by embarrassment. But it is interesting to note that in 4, 5 and 7 all references to youthfulness, age and to seniority (e.g. 'baba' for 'father') are in either English or Swahili.

More generally, certain basic kinship terms of reference and terms referring to seniority and juniority are indeed frequently in either Swahili or English among all ethnic groups in Nairobi. There are a number of explanations for this. An important general one is the need to place a possibly wide range of associates in categories denoting some degree of personal intimacy. To call a man 'baba' ('father' in Swahili) when he is not a relative and perhaps not even of your ethnic group, may indicate actual, potential or anticipated intimacy or friendliness. The use of Swahili or, as in some cases, English (e.g. 'brother ') rather than the vernacular may carry the additional information that this is an achieved, transferable and perhaps even negotiable rather than ascribed relationship.

This convention of sometimes using Swahili or English primary kin terms for non-ascribed relationships appears to 'feedback' into conversations between long settled townsmen of the same ethnic group even when they are referring to 'real' kin or to age or youth, for which they could use their own vernacular terms. This might explain the switch in Case 8, which may thus be said to be prompted by a specific element in the topic of conversation and not by any discernible transactions of speech between the two men.

The conventionalised use of these Swahili and English terms is made possible only by the 'value' constantly placed on each of the lingua francas in ordinary daily conversations: English is constantly emphasised as a language of high-status persons; Swahili is a common medium language, sometimes of 'neutrality' or 'fraternity', but sometimes connoting 'low' or 'ordinary' status. It is surely in the important if numerically limited cases in which these languages are used to make challenges or award concessions that these values are given their most poignant expression. Thus, the few cases of language switching which appear to be transactional may well have an inordinate influence on the vast majority of cases in which language does not set up challenges, counter-challenges, and concessions. This is at least a hypothesis worth testing.

Summary and Conclusions

I have suggested that we distinguish initially between transactional and non-transactional conversations. Transactional conversations are those in which there seems to be a progressive unravelling of a repertoire of different languages (or codes) by each of the two speakers. The two processes of unravelling are seen to be triggered off by each other in a to-and-fro fashion. This reciprocal stimulus-response mechanism may take the form of challenges, counter-challenges, and concessions.

In the particular ethnographic situation which I have described, these challenges and concessions are made on the basis of claims and assumptions concerned with two variables: ethnic group membership and personal socioeconomic status. Each of these involves a defence of or struggle for symbols of honour and esteem in all spheres of social life in Nairobi, not just in transactional conversations. In transactional conversations the competition can be played in two ways. One way involves defence of one's own mother tongue, concessionary or provocative use of one's opponent's, or 'neutral' usage of a vernacular which is not native to either speaker.[2] Or it may involve competitive use of either Swahili or English. English will tend to have high status connotations but must be used strategically to achieve this effect. Swahili can carry connotations which play down ethnic and status differences. It can thus connote 'humility', 'solidarity', or 'brotherhood', or simply 'neutrality'. But, because it is associated in much of Kenya with situations of socioeconomic disadvantage or deprivation, it can also mark off from each other persons of 'higher' and 'lower' status. All these connotations are dominant, in that they recur frequently in many situations.

These two ways of using language in prestige competitions are logically contradictory in that vernacular usage is likely to symbolise group interests and loyalties while usage of the lingua francas, English and Swahili, is more likely to symbolise individual interests. In actual conversations, people may 'joke off' the contradiction. Joking about ethnic and status differences is, indeed, a crucially important technique by which people of different 'tribes' and of different levels of education, income, and occupation cope with the sensitivity of these evaluated differences. This fact of everyday life is sometimes carried into a conversation with the result that the conversation becomes a language game, in which speakers of different 'tribes' and/or of different statuses display their knowledge of and skills in different languages.

The language game is one type of transactional conversation because it includes challenges and concessions which assume knowledge of the two major but logically contradictory principles of social organisation: ethnic group affiliation, and personal socioeconomic status ties.

Two other types of transactional conversation are each based on assumptions deriving from one rather than both principles. Thus, a conversation may consist predominantly of challenges and concessions made in vernaculars which assume knowledge of putative ethnic relations of alliance and opposition in Nairobi. Or, it may include challenges and concessions which turn on the socioeconomic status connotations of English and Swahili. In practice, transactional conversations are likely to include elements of all three types.

This said, it must be emphasised that transactional conversations as defined here are a minute proportion of all conversations. What, then, is their significance if any? Their significance is two-fold.

First, they highlight the normative value attaching to use of a particular vernacular or lingua franca in a particular situation. Thus, in a particular conversation English is seen to express, say, social exclusiveness, as against Swahili which may express social inclusiveness. In another conversation, this set of values may be reversed. Since English and Swahili may express other values, the number of value sets is numerous. When vernaculars are also included in the conversations, then the span and number of sets increases even more. Yet it is very likely that the number of different possible sets is logically limited even if, in practice, many elude our attention. Nevertheless, some sets seem to recur in more situations than others, e.g. English expressing social exclusiveness and Swahili expressing social inclusiveness. Frequency of occurrence is at least one criterion of dominance and so it should be possible eventually to construct a hierarchy of sets combining the same languages and, conversely, to isolate those contextual situations or 'domains' showing the greatest variation of sets.

The second significant aspect of transactional conversations is that they may well play an important part in generating new styles of language use. We know for a fact that there are many English and Swahili clichés, idioms and other recurrent forms in use among people of all ethnic groups in Nairobi. They do not appear overnight. What then is the process by which such forms are generated and diffused in the population? Common experience suggests that people do not sit down and rationally calculate the need for new forms and then create them. It is more likely that the forms arise in response to needs through the many separate but parallel experiences of persons in a single social system. The adoption of Swahili and English kinship terms in Nairobi is, I believe, an example of this process, which I have only touched on in this chapter. But there are probably many less obvious examples. Since transactional conversations require verbal inventiveness against a template of specific language values, it seems reasonable to hypothesise that they are important generators of the new forms.

I summarise the role of three chapters (5–7 in Whiteley (1974)) in reaching these conclusions. I noted in the first chapter the apparent dilemma confronting students of language use as to how they can bring together in a single, coherent analysis the investigation both of large-scale language shift among groups and of language switching between individuals in a single conversation. My own approach to this problem was to start from a consideration of the believed state of power relations among Nairobi's four major ethnic groups. I started from the fact that language is a cultural phenomenon and as such may be regarded as either demarcating ethnic boundaries, as with vernaculars, or transcending them, as with lingua francas. This use of lingua francas to transcend ethnic differences usually occurs when socioeconomic differences need to be expressed.

Language shift can therefore be regarded as reflecting the relations between ethnic groups in their adoption of each other's vernaculars. Or language shift can occur in response to an emerging but constantly changing division of the society into socioeconomic status categories.

Thus, in Whiteley (1974 Chapter 6) I showed how Swahili is increasingly fulfilling the main criteria of a lingua franca but is still associated with low status groups, yet English is potentially a long-term threat to Swahili because of the flood into Nairobi from rural districts of young, educated and English-speaking but unemployable migrants.

Extensive surveying of self-reports of competence in different languages provides a picture (in Whitely 1974 chapter 7) of the differential rates of vernacular adoption between pairs of ethnic groups. The types and rates of adoption correspond with putative political relations of alliance and opposition between Nairobi's four ethnic groups. Both simultaneously and over time it is clear that language shift tells us much about political and power relations between groups. This is perhaps an obvious fact but is nonetheless a crucially important background against which ordinary day-to-day relations and conversations occur.

It is facts of such magnitude which constitute the broad, even crude, stereotypes with which people in any system of relations deal. These stereotypes are among the most important in Nairobi of what Barth might call the 'over-arching, more general principles of evaluation' (1966, p. 14). A very few individual conversations, or, more likely, parts of conversations, appear to be conducted broadly on the basis of these principles. But people do not adhere rigidly to the stereotyped evaluations. They use the manifold behavioural connotations of different languages to compete with each other or to make concessions. I have called these transactional conversations. 'Bits' of different languages are transacted. This has two related effects. One is that the various 'values' attaching to any one language are publicised in distinct and regularly recurring situations. A second is that, because inventiveness is required in selecting and discerning the various values and in devising new ways to surprise an 'opponent', new contextual sets of 'meaning' are generated and also publicised. Common needs in similar situations produce similar sets which may eventually catch on in the population at large and may even affect the expression of group relations. Thus, the example touched on in this chapter of the development of a code of non-vernacular kinship and seniority terms could well constitute a 'bridge' between personal relations which might otherwise be more brittle in a society made increasingly more heterogeneous by socio-economic and ethnic distinctions. This approach is, as yet, at a beginning, but I believe it may continue to be fruitful because it is based on a consistent and comprehensive and yet manageable methodology, which I find lacking in other sociological approaches to the study of language use.[3]

Notes

(1) We have not tried to 'standardise' what we heard in order to make it conform to grammatically 'correct' forms. On the other hand, we cannot claim to have recorded conversations as accurately as a tape recorder, which, for various reasons, could not be used in this context. I have no evidence either way to determine whether my presence in the market place and elsewhere influenced the tone and course of conversations, but I should point out that I had become a regular and accepted figure in the area and believe that the cases I present are 'natural' instances of language use. The do not appear to differ significantly from those acquired independently by assistants.

(2) Luganda in Kampala is used in this way by some non-Ganda conversing with each other (see Case 2 in chapter three; and Parkin 1971). Nairobi does not seem to have a vernacular which is used in this way.

(3) I would like to acknowledge my gratitude to W.H. Whiteley for originally suggesting to me the usefulness of applying 'transactional analysis' to the study of language switching.

References

Bailey, F.G. (1968) Parapolitical Systems. In Marc Swartz (ed.) *Local Level Politics*. Aldine Publishing Co., Chicago, 1968.

Bailey, F.G. (1969) *Stratagems and Spoils*, Blackwell, Oxford.

Barth, F. (1966) *Models of Social Organization*, Occasional Paper 23, Royal Anthropological Institute, London.

Bujra, J. (1974) Pumwani: language usage in an urban Muslim community. In W.H. Whiteley (ed). *Language use and social change*. London. International African Institute. Oxford University Press.

Douglas, M. (1962) Lele Economy Compared with Bushong. In P. Bohannan and G. Dalton (eds) *Markets in Africa*, Northwestern University Press, Chicago, 1962.

Douglas, M. (1968) The Social Control of Cognition: some Factors in Joke Perception', Man (N.S.) 3, 3, 361–76.

Epstein, A.L. (1959) Linguistic Innovation and Culture on the Copperbelt, Northern Rhodesia', *Southwestern Journal of Anthropology* 3, 3, 235–53.

Fishman, J. (1968) *Bilingualism in the Barrio*, United States Department of Health, Education and Welfare.

Hymes, D.H. (1962) 'The Ethnography of Speaking' in T. Gladwin and W.C. Sturtevant (eds) *Anthropology and Human Behaviour*, Anthropological Society of Washington, Washington D.C.

Mitchell, J.C. (1956) *The Kalela Dance*, Rhodes-Livingstone Paper 27, Manchester University Press.

Parkin, D.J. (1969) *Neighbours and Nationals in an African City Ward*, Routledge & Kegan Paul, London.

Parkin, D.J. (1971) Language Choice in Two Kampala Housing Estates' in W.H. Whiteley (ed.) *Language Use and Social Change*, International African Institute, Oxford University Press, London.

Parkin, D.J. (1974) chs 6 and 7. In Whiteley qv.

Whiteley, W.H. (ed.) (1971) *Language Use and Social Change*, International African Institute, Oxford University Press, London.

5 The Creativity of Abuse[1]

While greetings, terms of address, jocular abuse, and other ritualised verbal exchanges, reflect and interpret social changes, they also contain within themselves an independent dynamic. This consists of a constant alternation of fixed and variant form and thereby throws up the opportunities for social comment and criticism. Exchanges of ritual and jocular abuse involve most linguistic awareness and, while retaining a formulaic shape, provide the most creative examples of semantic experimentation and social comment. The folk contrast between 'serious' politeness formulae and 'game-like' ritual insults reflects, at a meta-level, that within each kind of exchange between the use of 'proper' and 'improper' forms. The contrast more generally reflects the predictable and innovative aspects of language use.

Terms of address, greetings, farewells, and the verbal exchange contained in joking and insult relationships have a dual character. On the one hand, they can reinforce assumptions about the relative status and hierarchy of the speakers and listeners and so perpetuate the wider status-quo (Evans-Pritchard 1964: 221; Firth 1972: 7; Mitchell-Kernan & Kernan 1975; Sharman 1969: 115). This is to emphasise their fixed, enduring character. But they are also among those critical areas of language use which, simply because they are 'ritualised' (or at least conventional enough to trigger predictable responses), contain the potential for the starkest possible contrasts of meaning. The assumption of predictability makes the genuine element of surprise more dramatic. The recipient may well interpret such 'deviance' as abusive but is, for that reason, forced to re-consider the basis of the relationship.

This potential for contrastive meaning and subsequent re-definition of relationships is clearly evident in the use of pronominal and other address terms, on which much work has been done.

Address

Brown and Gilman's pioneering study showed how the development of egalitarian ideals in Europe limited the hierarchical exchange between individuals of the honorific second person plural pronoun (V) for the singular pronoun (T) of subordination (1972: 265–72). This 'non-reciprocal power semantic'[2] had been 'associated with relatively static society in which power is distributed by birthright and is not subject to much re-distribution' (1972: 265; and see also Haugen 1975: 334 on Gudmundsson 1972). The reciprocal solidarity semantic of either V or, more usually, T, became increasingly significant as feudalism gave way to early industrial and, especially, late industrial society. This partial decline of the pronominal power semantic has probably been complemented by a rise in social significance of other verbal and non-verbal modes of power and status definition and resulted in more complex modes of address. Scholars have recently analysed this complexity as systems of choices based on such cross-cutting criteria as age, sex, kinship position, as well as official rank and social class, the latter being seen as more remote controlling factors (Brown & Ford 1964; Ervin-Tripp 1972; Friedrich 1967; Lambert 1972; *et al.*).

While people are indeed often uncertain at first of others' social class membership or origins, this uncertainty also gives speakers the room to try to re-define statuses and roles by manipulating pronominal and other types of address. The revised formula may signify this intention yet thereafter continue to distinguish strata.

Paulston (1976) reports Swedes as claiming that nowadays only the reciprocal solidarity T (*du*) is exchanged by individuals between and within the classes. But she argues that each social class (upper, middle and lower) has informally and unbeknown to itself developed its own rules of personal address in ignorance of the other classes (1976: 385). We may speculate that, following a national shift from the egalitarian to an openly autocratic, class-based ideology, these hidden rules would become more explicit markers, such as appears to have been the case in rule-conscious feudal society.

In modern Italy, Bates and Benigni (1975) find that upper-class youth are no less politically radical than lower-class Italians, and indeed are in the vanguard of radicalism. But they are culturally so sharply differentiated from lower-class people that some have, quite unintentionally, fallen into the trap of reverse elitism: on the one hand, they have substituted the use of the *tu* intimacy for the *lei* of respect in addressing employers and professors, for example a switch which can be interpreted as a deliberate disrespect for the old authoritarian order; but, on the other hand, they use the form *lei* with lower class people (even superseding the old respect form, *voi*) in a new definition of respect for and solidarity with the proletariat (1975: 287). By using the inverted forms of address, radical youngsters thus unconsciously perpetuate what they otherwise consciously claim to destroy.

While speakers can in these ways communicate alternative views of status and hierarchy, the semantics of power and solidarity are preserved as each pronoun draws its sense by contrast with another: the one being 'proper' for a particular relationship and/or context, and the other(s) 'improper'. Moreover, such contrastive meaning can shift to or be complemented by other kinds of address: English does not now have separate forms for singular and plural second person pronouns, but use of first name (e.g. 'Joe') as against title plus last name (e.g. 'Mr Smith') and, sometimes third person address ('Would Sir require . . .'), can achieve comparable effects, as can other verbal and non-verbal formulae.

Greetings are a positionally fixed mode of address: you may use them to open a conversation rather than as an embedded feature of it. As with the use of pronouns, titles, and names, they may undergo yet retain a formulaic shape, and be used to affirm status or deny it. They may be powerful instruments of phatic communion (Malinowski 1948: 249), but may also be the creative tools of provocation and argument.

From Address to Greetings

One reason why I have so far refrained from referring to this genre of verbal exchanges as 'politeness formulas', as has been done by Fergusson (1976) and Esther Goody (1978), is that it is precisely their potential for *im*politeness and abuse that I see as most relevant to my discussion. Thus, just as the shift in pronominal usage from the power to solidarity semantic was an affront to diehards who demanded continued respect and who thereby unwittingly communicated the new view of class and status relations, so it is the provocative rather than affirmatory use of greetings and even of asking questions which we may regard as most likely to correspond with wider social transformations.

Using these two dimensions of politeness and abuse, it is possible to analyse the way in which individuals exploit the ambiguities inherent in greetings by seeing them as strategies by which persons minimise threats or, alternatively, gain influence, prestige or power, or secure deference appropriate to such new positions (see especially Brown & Levinson 1978). Irvine (1974: 175), who gives an intriguing analysis of greetings among West African Wolof speakers, stresses how individuals may even manipulate their greetings so that they come out as subordinate rather than dominant, in an attempt to avert a subsequent request for property or money, which can only be made by the speaker of inferior rank.

Wolof society is in fact stratified into caste-like groups and these provide the premise of inequality on which are based the hierarchical uses of greetings. These greetings draw on the asymmetry not only of caste origin but also the cross-cutting asymmetries of age, sex and achieved prestige. The greetings even limit to a minimum the expression of equality between partners in a joking relationship. The Wolof clearly recognise the hierarchical implications, or power semantic, inherent in their greetings, and my impression is that they would certainly be prepared to formulate relatively precise greetings performance rules.

The wide range of greetings formulae in Wolof, compared with the limited number of possible expressions of pronominal address, means that, even under the constraints of a stratified society, there exists enough potential for slight variation within the numerous forms of greetings for a speaker to turn encounters subtly to his advantage in defiance of the more enduring status hierarchy within the relationship. Thus, there exist the exterior limitations of a relatively perduring structure of rank, birthright, age, sex, or achievement. Yet, there also exists, within the semantics of the greetings themselves, the potential for speakers to move at least slightly beyond these structural constraints on status definition.

A diachronic study, for which the data are admittedly difficult to get, would enable us to view not just the internal strategies of status manipulation, but also the transformations in the wider structure of rules within which the strategies operate. We consider not just the different ways in which speakers compete for status through the use of greetings, but rather the possibilities offered by tacit assumptions behind the greeting forms to generate new meanings in existing relationships. By focusing on the unpredictable or 'surprise' element in greetings and associated formulae, we can discern their potential for making propositions about the state of society.

The key issue here is a concern with what I will call replicational semantics. By this I mean "the replication in different institutional contexts of core symbolic values and meanings" (Parkin 1978: 292 and cf. Ardener 1970: 155–6, & fn. 15).

Let me take a simple example of what I mean from the Giriama of Kenya. In Giriama society, the theme that generational predominates over genealogical seniority is replicated not only in the format of many greetings and exchanges but also in the order of phases of such events as weddings, funerals, dances, and occasions of worship. The theme of generational seniority is expressed by the spatial positions silently occupied by the participants, by the order of food and drink silently received, as well as by the sequence and content of speeches given. It is clear that in these different institutional contexts the theme is expressed non-verbally as well as verbally, just as the verbal component in greetings varies quantitatively across cultures, from often little more than a grunt, smile and/or handshake in some Western industrialised contexts, to long, drawn-out verbal formulae in, say, much of Africa (Firth 1972: 18–29). Questions of order or syntax, whether in the utterance, the acts of accompanying the utterance, or in the speech acts themselves, are thus a key dimension of semantics.

The concern with replicational semantics does not assume that greetings are necessarily pivotal in the dissemination of such a theme. I do assume, however, that where a greeting does take the form of a verbal exchange then its potential for articulating contrastive meaning by subverting the otherwise expected, predictable response, can make it a relatively clear social marker of change (or lack of it) in a cultural theme. The verbal greeting may then provide the earliest phase in the formal articulation of new propositions about social changes which have already been spreading throughout society through, for example, tacit alterations in the organisation of weddings or funerals, but which have not been consistently identified as such in speech.

The implication of this view is to regard greetings, address terms, and, as I later show, jocular exchanges of abuse, as *together* encompassing a range of propositions both within and across cultures, and over time. What some greetings systems, have, others may lack, but by looking cross-culturally at even a limited range of such formulae we get a reasonable idea of the overall stock of propositional possibilities.

While the movement from pre-industrial to industrial society appears to have lessened the element of predictability in address and greetings formulae, certain basic ideas about the individual and society persist, often by being transferred from one kind of routinised verbal exchange to another, one of which is jocular abuse or ritual insults.

Here, let me acknowledge that my view of proposition is unorthodox. The recent analytical emphasis on the illocutionary effect of such speech acts as here discussed must not blind us to the realisation (cf. Searle 1968) that even the strongest illocutionary frameworks contain propositions, however momentarily 'hidden' and weak, and that such weak propositions can, at particular points in history, assume special meaning. The weak and the implicit become strong and explicit. Thus, though we often initiate or respond to a greeting in stereotyped fashion, seemingly without thinking about it, the full implications of the greeting only become obvious when the stereotyped is threatened: it is precisely when someone does not play his expected part that the meanings of the greeting may become obvious and, often, discussed. This is its propositional force (e.g. that X is 'superior' to Y by *n* criteria), the truth or the falsehood of which is then decided by the social facts of a particular culture.

From a limited cross-cultural view, I discern four such culturally implicit propositions, each of which may contain elementary ones, may operate in combination, and may be ordered in the more complex proposition as follows: that personal autonomy depends on 'static' territorial autonomy; (but) that power external to the individual always flows unevenly; that (nevertheless) social changes are communicable through the exchange of verbal formulae before they are openly discussed; and that individuals have the creative capacity to debate and change their destinies. The four concepts of personal autonomy, extra-personal power, inter-personal communication and overall human creativity, are thus cognitively distinguished and, in this particular order, denote a progression outwards from a static or passive to active condition: from acceptance and/or subjection to the control over external forces. Let me now illustrate the four concepts.

Personal Autonomy

The first propositional characteristic of greetings reported in some societies is what I will call the static/moving contrast (cf. David 1977). It was first reported to me by a Giriama young man who, in explaining the logic of Giriama greetings, said, 'The one who is moving must greet the one who is stationary'. The key example is of a person entering a village and having to greet first, regardless of any of his other status characteristics of sex, kinship and generation. The principle extends to anyone approaching a person who is standing. If two persons approach each other along a long path, one must step aside and stand still, allowing the other to pass. The passer, even if he is an old man approaching a child, must greet first. Thus, he who approaches greets first; he who remains immobile receives this initial greeting, but is then under obligation to respond, sometimes, if approached in his home or village, to the extent of nominally offering a seat and even food.

Initially, then, the Giriama approacher is of supplicant or low status, a situation swiftly reversed in conversation thereafter if he or she is in fact a generational or kinship superior. Among the Wolof and Gonja of west Africa, both of whom are, unlike the Giriama, internally stratified into estates, the same principle applies but is seen by the people themselves to be determined by differences of estate between greeters. That is to say, for the Gonja (Goody 1972: 40, 44, 48–9) and Wolof (Irvine 1974: 173) a person known to be of inferior rank should approach and greet his superior who remains stationary. Irvine quotes Wolof as saying, 'A noble does not go to greet a *nyenyo* (a person of low caste) – it is the *nyenyo* who must come to greet him' (1974: 173). The static/moving contrast here is used to express pre-existing and enduring status differences. For the Giriama the relationship is the other way round. The person who is physically moving into a situation, whether a village or gathered group, or towards a stationary individual, greets first regardless of his rank, a rule about which the Giriama are fiercely adamant and which *is* observed. The static/moving contrast is in itself fundamental and, in the Giriama greeting exchange, is expressed if need be through a momentary reversal of status difference. It is interesting that the Giriama roundly condemn the Muslim Swahili, with whom they have lived for generations, for making status and extreme age differences rather than the static/moving contrast the overriding criterion for opening greetings. In fact, this largely applies among the Swahili to non-kinsmen of superior religious rank, e.g. a *sheikh* or *sharif*, who are persons of high 'caste' called *waungwana* ('free-born', and 'civilised'), a *sharif* also being able to claim descent from the Prophet. Very old men and women entering a village may also be greeted first by younger persons already in it.

Though they are hardly everyday occurrences, these Swahili cases are significantly different from the Giriama pattern and reveal the somewhat blurred stratification of Swahili-speaking peoples, some of the lower echelons of whom may actually be descended from a Giriama forebear (or related group) or have converted to Islam from that group. In this limited sense, then, the Swahili parallel the more clearly stratified Gonja and Wolof in regarding non-kinship rank differences as more important than physical movement against non-movement in determining who should greet first. Putting this more obviously, non-kinship rank and the static/moving idea are logically opposed to each other as determinants of who should greet first. Non-kinship rank is dominant in stratified society, and the static/moving idea is dominant in non-stratified society. The data on these societies are here very clear.

It must be admitted that, otherwise, in the few unstratified or weakly stratified societies for which we have data, the static/moving contrast may also apply in reverse, with the stationary person initiating the greeting. This *may* be the case among the Tikopia and Kelantan Malays among whom passers-by receive but do not initiate greetings (Firth 1972: 12). Similarly, among the Maori, who were traditionally unstratified, the ritual encounter called *hui* comprises a greeting which is initiated by those who were stationary in their village, though in fact the approachers do speak first, by way of incantation rather than greeting (Salmond 1974: 194). It is not clear how general this is, or whether, in other kinds of greeting, those who approach (or pass by) do in fact greet first. The exceptions do suggest, however, that in some unstratified or weakly stratified societies there is an inherent flexibility as to how the static/moving contrast might be applied and whether, in the absence of non-kinship rank, differences of kinship, generational, or sexual status may take precedence. I would suggest, however, that a cultural emphasis on the idea that the visitor must greet first regardless of kinship or non-kinship rank, as among the egalitarian Giriama, is the highest possible expression of personal autonomy, for it presupposes that the territory occupied by the person visited, ideally his own village, is inviolable to all claims on it, a proposition about a person or group's inalienable rights of territorial possession. The reverse proposition denies inalienable rights to landed property and is implicit when non-kinship status is held to be the main determinant of who should greet first. These underlying propositions, the second being the negation of the first, are of course perfectly consistent with both the ethos of land-holding ascribed by kinship in unstratified society and the contrasting one of its achievement, and possible loss, in stratified society. So, a shift in the incidence of greeting type within a society, such that the static/moving idea becomes subordinated to that of enduring status differences, suggests a change in rights to land and thereby in the overall economic structure.

Thus, among the still largely unstratified Giriama, the person who neglects the rule that visitors must greet first, may be regarded as a witch. In some Giriama contexts the witch is also a thief: he kills people for their land and property. In recent years there has in fact been much sale of property among Giriama, and a growing number of people are becoming landless. The misfortunes causing their bankruptcy are attributed to witchcraft which may then be construed as theft. We see how under such a situation of change, disrespect for the static/moving idea, in being a kind of witchcraft, can become even more poignantly associated with appropriation of a person's territory and loss of his autonomy. We may speculate that in due course the idea will become less and less important and merely come to express non-kinship status differences of occupation, education, and income, as in much of modern class-based society.

Extra-personal Power

The second characteristic of some greetings formulae is that they actually incorporate the use of plural and singular second person pronouns to denote power or respect, and solidarity or intimacy, or similarly use kinship terms of address and titles. As well as the many European languages normally associated with such pronominal usage, there is Wolof and Giriama, (including related peoples) in west and east Africa, and Gujerati, Hindi, and Assamese in south Asia.

Replicational semantics is concerned with 'meaning' arising not just from the intrinsic signification of 'the word', but from its possible syntactic arrangements with other words. Thus, it is not just the intrinsic meaning of V as a plural form of personal address that may give it a power semantic but rather its use as an alternative pronominal arrangement to T (and in some languages to a third person pronoun as well).

Among some young Giriama men a third possibility is to use *neither* pronoun and to drop them altogether from the greeting, a technique also reported in modern Swedish (Paulston 1976: 380, 382–4). Among the Giriama this usage has developed recently, certainly within the 12-year period during which I have studied them. It still occurs in only a few cases, notably by a younger to a half-brother or full brother. A couple of speakers confided that the omission is deliberate. Though we cannot know whether this is always so, I was given the following explanation of the new usage.

Brothers should exchange singular pronouns (e.g. *(u)dzalamukadze*, have you woken well?/*(ni)dzalamuka (si)manya(uwe)* etc., I have woken well. I don't know about you?), rather than the plural exchange of persons of adjacent generations (e.g. *(mu)dzalamukadze*/*(hu)dzalamuka, ka(hu) manya (ninwi)* etc.). To initiate with the plural is offensive, for it is like denying brotherhood. So, by omitting any pronoun of address in the greeting, you create an uncertainty which can be interpreted in any one of two ways: either that the brother opening the greeting would like to respect his brother as an older person to whom he feels more like a son but does not wish to risk public disapproval by proffering the plural pronoun of respect; or that he despises the older brother for having, say, unlawfully appropriated property held in trust for him, and so withholds the normal singular pronoun of solidarity. The emergence of the new usage does in fact correspond with recent land adjudication and settlement schemes, which have, in many cases, divided extended families at an earlier stage of their developmental cycle than before, and provide a new focus of jealousy and conflict between brothers. I was myself sometimes addressed without the use of a second pronoun by men who were, as I was later told, unsure as to whether I should be regarded as of their own or of an adjacent generation, or, putting it another way, whether the relationship would be one of solidarity or power. Omission of the pronoun of address thus suspends judgement as to the status definition of the relationship.

It follows from all this that greetings which make use, however variable, of these pronominal semantics are really commenting on the nature of power and its uneven distribution between categories of persons and social strata of the kind I discussed earlier.

The use of titles in address, sometimes with third person pronouns, can be viewed in the same light, as Brown and Ford have shown (1964). The use of kinship terms of address in greetings may also make statements about existing, putative, or changing power relations, but need not do so, being used instead as statements recognising an ascribed authority which may, in reality, lack the power of enforcement. For societies rapidly undergoing stratification but still essentially egalitarian in ethic, kinship terms of address in greetings seem indeed to have far greater capacity than non-kinship titles of rank and pronouns to 'mask' or at least publicly deny the real distribution of power in relationships. Thus, wealthy Giriama entrepreneurs and poor people may continue to greet each other with classificatory kin terms. The significant feature here is not kinship terms *per se* but rather their use as alternative and transitional to non-kinship forms in greetings.

Esther Goody notes that while the centralised Gonja rarely use kinship terms in their greetings, even though their total repertoire is wide, the uncentralised LoDagaa use *only* kin terms (1972: 64–5). These contrasting tendencies can be supported by cases from elsewhere (e.g. the centralised Interlacustrine Bantu of east Africa use terms meaning 'Sir' or 'Madam' (*Ssebo* and *Nyabo* – *ssebo* sometimes has an extended meaning of 'father' for which the 'real' kinship term is *tata*) which have specific connotational terms of hierarchical respect, while the uncentralised Nilotes and Giriama use kin terms). The presence or absence of a cultural model of enduring unambiguous strata here governs the extent to which kinship is or is not an appropriate meta-language of power.

The exchange of rank titles in greetings on the one hand, and of kinship terms on the other, each tends therefore to occupy opposite ends of a continuum denoting the degree of centralisation and stratification in society. But, again, these are only tendencies and the terms can cover any area of the continuum, though to a lesser extent than the variable use of pronouns. Though different from each other by virtue of these tendencies, titles and kinship and pronominal terms of address exchanged in greetings all disclose a view of an uneven ebb and flow of power.

Interpersonal Communication of Change

The third characteristic of greetings which may acquire propositional force is their tendency within a culture to polarise in the direction either of those greetings that stimulate a stereotyped response or of those that vary in initiator and response. We can call this the variant-invariant contrast.

With regard to Syrian Arabic, Ferguson explains that a number of politeness formulae, including greetings, occur as stereotyped initiator-and-response sequences. Many formulae 'come in pairs where a specific initiator formula is followed automatically by its appropriate response formula' (1967: 37). Ferguson identifies four such types of stereotyped greeting in Syrian Arabic. In other cultures the number and types may vary. To take one of the Syrian examples, which is a type found more widely, the initiator and response is linked by reference to a single word. For example, the automatic response to greeting *ssalam alekum* is *wa'alekum ssalam* which echoes the root word *slm* (meaning 'peace).

Ferguson insists, however, that this linking of root-echo response to greeting opening is not dependent on the intrinsic meaning of the root term, *slm*, 'peace' (a view later taken, quite independently, by Firth 1972: 17), but that the linking is of a special grammatical rather than semantic kind. But we can take a syntacto-semantic view of these stereotyped greetings as drawing meaning from their contrast with others which do not consist of stereotyped initiator and response.

Thus, because these kind of stereotyped greeting openings and responses are generally confined to a limited range of situations, they effectively confirm the unchanging nature of these situations. At the least, their predictability does not suggest change. However, the use in these same situations of greetings which do not carry an obligatory response but rather allow for many, and even new ones created on the spot, presuppose a different semantic implying uncertainty of outcome and the possibility of redefining the dyad. Taken together, then, stereotyped and variable greetings formulae may be said, respectively, to make initial propositions about the preservation of the *status quo* or its possible alteration.

This is not to say that once a stereotyped greeting has been exchanged the greeters cannot thereafter redefine their relationship (sometimes prompted by a voice tone or stress in the greeting itself). But use of a stereotyped greeting, even when its status implications are reversed as when, among the Wolof, a superior intentionally greets an inferior as if he were a superior, tends to be a statement in support rather than in defiance of the overall status system. Any questioning of the status system has, so to speak, to be renegotiated anew after and independently of the greeting. Similarly, a reverse status greeting merely enables the one individual on that one occasion to switch statuses. It does not, by itself, question the overall status hierarchy. By contrast, variable and unpredictable openings and responses in greetings immediately propose a situation of uncertainty, which any information exchanged after the greeting may or may not reduce.

The distinction between stereotyped and variable greetings is not always absolute. But pre-industrial societies appear to have proportionally more of the former, as is suggested by the well-documented cases of Syrian Arabic (Ferguson 1967), Wolof (Irvine 1974), Gonja and LoDagaa (Goody 1972), and from my own work on Giriama and Swahili society, while industrial society does, as Firth notes (1972: 17), appear to have relaxed certain conventions in correspondence with changes in class structure.

Something of a transition is noted by Firth for the Tikopia who 'have converted an invariant style to a variant style: the traditional greeting could be used unaltered at any time of day, whereas the modern greeting modulates as the day proceeds' through forms corresponding to 'good morning', 'good midday', 'good afternoon', etc. (1972: 14). The new Tikopia greeting forms appear to have been adopted smoothly and without strain. But it was school children who used the new greeting forms first, probably encouraged by the Anglican mission. Perhaps the transition from the invariant to variant styles of greeting also gave expression to a mutually reinforcing emergent social division between uneducated, non-Christian, and elderly folk on the one hand, who used traditional stereotyped forms, and educated, Christian, and young people on the other hand, who used the new forms, thereby presenting people who straddle this social division with some uncertainty as to which set of greetings to use and when.

If this is so, it would modify the view, held by Firth himself among others (1972: 31, though see also 1972: 17–18 and fn. 5), that an important function of greetings is to reduce uncertainty in social contact. As a general rule this is perfectly acceptable, but it is precisely the converse potential of greeting exchanges also to *create* uncertainty that makes them semantically significant. For to create uncertainty in social interaction is effectively to question the *status quo* without openly discussing emergent changes in it.

Taking another example from Ferguson (1976: 148), we may speculate that the shortening over the past forty years of the American English greeting *How are you* to *Hi*, via the intermediate *Hiya*, articulates the increasingly egalitarian view of relations in a range of contexts not just between men but, most significantly, between men and women. Since the shortened greeting appears to have carried a greater semantic load when exchanged between a woman and a man rather than just between men (with age an intervening variable), it thus presaged, in its own small way, the later, specifically egalitarian demands of the women's movement.

Similarly, in the growing number of trading centres of coastal Kenya, which attract Giriama immigrants not previously known to each other, a set of highly shortened, semi-jocular greetings, devoid of pronominal and tense affixes, has developed between young men and between young men and young women in place of greetings whose elaborate forms were structured by and in turn reinforced generation, kinship and sex differences. The lack of pronouns in the new greetings not only represents a denial of the relevance of classificatory kinship and generational relations for these new contexts, it replicates what has been occurring nearby at the dances accompanying weddings and funerals where temporary liaisons between young and women have been initiated which are in strict defiance of the rules of the clan exogamy and which may well result in demands by young people to marry in the teeth of such rules. In other relationships, however, longer but predictable greetings continue to be exchanged which preserve the distinctions of generation, sex, and kinship.

We move here to the process noted by Ferguson (1976: 147–9) by which while some verbal greetings undergo shortening or weakening, others within the same language remain particularly resistant. Those identified by Ferguson as governed by a root-echo response are a good example of the latter. Still other greetings may undergo some weakening yet preserve archaic constructions, as is often the case with politeness formulae generally.

Weakened and archaic greetings tend to be associated respectively with informality and formality and so roughly parallel the solidarity and power semantics of T and V usage. As with the more extensive use of T, weakened, shortened, and variable greetings seem especially to characterise industrial society. Weakened greetings may in fact merge with deliberately inventive modes of address, sometimes formed on the spot by greeters. The merged forms may take on a ritualised style and content characteristic of a particular culture or sub-culture and still be used to express lexical and conceptual creativity. This appears to characterise the development of ritual insults among the Harlem adolescents studied by Labov (1972), which I shortly discuss. Whether some of these elaborate exchanges become stereotyped initiators and responses, i.e. effectively greetings, so completing a cyclical development, is an open question. What we can say is that the variant-invariant contrast in greetings is sufficiently dynamic that speakers can use it to hint at emergent social changes.

From Greetings to Jocular Abuse: Recognising Creativity

The fourth characteristic of greetings, which may assume propositional force, is its potential for locating relationships of negotiable exchange by contrast with those in which the means and the ends of exchange are fixed. Classically this can be seen in the contrast between joking relationships, which hint at flexibility in social rules and their possible re-negotiation, and respect (and avoidance) relationships, which presuppose the maintenance of a set social distance. Both kinds of relationship may express alliance or consociation, but, within each distinctive forms of address are exchanged. Thus, among the Giriama the rule is that second person plural pronouns of address and plural verb forms be exchanged in greetings between speakers 'respecting' (*ku-ogoha*) each other and defined as being of adjacent generations (e.g. 'fathers/mothers' and 'sons/daughters'), and that singular pronoun and verb forms be exchanged between speakers identified as being of the same or alternate generations who joke with each other (*ku-tseyana*) (e.g. 'friends', 'siblings', and 'grandparents' and 'grandchildren'). The two must not be confused and it is as abusive to address a brother by the respect plural pronoun and verb as to address a father by the singular.

Note that speakers are *defined* as being of adjacent or alternate generations. For, as Radcliffe-Brown observed, in some societies in which privileged familiarity is permitted between mother's brother and sister's son, the mother's brother is actually called by the term for the grandfather in logical conformity with the fundamental rule of classification by generation (Radcliffe-Brown 1972: 181–2). The Giriama do not do this, however. Mother's brother and sister's son call each other by the term *ahu*, which is not used for any other relationship. They reciprocate the respect plural forms of verb and pronominal address. The Giriama say that the mother's brother is a kind of father, whom one must respect (*ku-ogoha*) and not joke with (*ku-tseyana*). Yet, address forms apart, the behaviour towards him may be very playful, identified by a third verb, *ku-umiria*, and is much like the behaviour in mother's brother relationships reported in patrilineal societies elsewhere. The Giriama inherit patrilineally but have shallow lineages, and this *formal* classification of the mother's brother/sister's son relationship as one of respect rather than familiarity points up the ambivalence and transformational quality of their kinship system, in which patriliny 'becomes' matriliny in some of the various sub-groups which make up the wider cultural grouping of whom the Giriama are one. Whereas among a 'strongly patrilineal' Nilotic people like the Padhola, a sister's son and mother's brother 'can abuse each other in the worst possible way' (Sharman 1969: 107), the Giriama permit only limited familiarity with the mother's brother, certainly allowing nothing on the scale of abuse and sometimes obscenity occurring in relationships between persons of the same or alternate generations. The relationship is in fact seen as intermediary between those of 'pure' respect and those of 'pure' joking. The greeting formula in the mother's brother relationship thus posits a set pattern of interaction through the exchange of predictable respect forms, but the exchanges thereafter are more variable. For instance the two may haggle in a very jocular fashion over whether the nephew should claim his customary right to some of the uncle's property, and whether he should take a mere chicken, a goat, some clothes, or even some money.

In Giriama culture, then, joking and respectful greetings are sharply contrasted, but the possibility of a third kind of behaviour is expressed by the term *ku-umiria*, which is not a type of greeting, but can be a way of behaving after greeting. Less formally, and more generally, unintended humour and even jokes threaten to break out in even the most serious of relationships, once the greeting stage has been passed (cf. Brukman 1974: 239). In ignoring the definition of the relationship as prescribed by the formal greeting, such jocular exchanges can go some way towards redefining the relationship. They smudge the boundaries of relationships defined by formal contrasts, and can be used instead of formal, predictable greetings.

The main feature of respect greetings, like the use of the power semantic of pronominal address, is that, by themselves, they do not predispose to a questioning of the *status quo*. They observe the structure and demands of hierarchy or distanced equality. In so far as they predispose at all to negotiation, it is through means and ends which must be expressed as already acceptable to that culture.

Much more exciting and potentially innovative are joking relationship greetings. At first, we might regard joking relationships themselves as no more than temporarily subversive of the social order, as Mary Douglas notes (1968: 372), and so, by the predictability of their structure, just as supportive of the long-term *status quo* as respect relationships. But this is to take a static view of the society. In a changing one, joking relationships which are established and perpetuated by jocular verbal openings or greetings are receptive to new ideas and able to disseminate them. By disclosing the 'hidden meanings' (1968: 371) behind the everyday social façade, jocular exchanges present opportunities to those who are creative enough to articulate such meanings in new combinations, and so, through what is culturally interpreted as licensed abuse, to defy the existing restraints. Douglas is right to emphasise that jokes do indeed depend on social consensus for their efficacy, while obscenity and unrestricted abuse genuinely threaten to destroy current social categories (1968: 372). But this also means that the jokes that may lead to obscenity transform the power of social acceptance into that of criticism and confrontation. The obscenity or abuse that retains its jocular content and idiom may cause overlap between established and emergent social paradigms and so draw attention to the latter under the social protection of the former. The jester does more than reinforce social hierarchy by reminding its incumbents of the values that put them there. Under the cover of his license to abuse, he can also slip new cards into the pack and slightly change the rules of the game.

From fieldwork and the extensive literature it appears that in traditional, pre-industrial society the teasing in joking relationships covers three domains of discourse which can be read as three further, elementary propositions: that sex entails marriage; that senility and death entail succession and re-creation; and that unreciprocated but limited appropriation of food and goods may be socially permitted.

Many examples could be given but it is sufficient to provide an apt, early statement by Radcliffe-Brown:

> A very common form of joke … is for the grandchild to pretend that he wishes to marry the grandfather's wife, or that he intends to do so when his grandfather dies, or to treat her as already being his wife. Alternatively the grandfather may pretend that the wife of his grandchild is, or might be, his wife. The point of the joke is pretence at ignoring the difference of age between the grandparents and the grandchild.
>
> In various parts of the world … the nephew may take his uncle's property but not vice versa; or, as among the Nama Hottentots, the nephew may take a fine beast from his uncle's herd and the uncle in return takes a wretched beast from that of the nephew (1977: 180).

As my own Giriama data also show, joking relationships in such societies between persons of the same or alternate generations (e.g. 'grandparent' to 'grandchild', (cross) 'cousin' to 'cousin', 'affine' to 'affine', 'friend' to 'friend', or (mock) 'enemy' to 'enemy') frequently include sexual obscenities but, equally frequently, presuppose the possibility that the girl(s) or woman (women) joked with or about may be taken in marriage. Secondly, jokes about, say, a 'grandfather's' age and/or sexual impotence turn subtly on the inevitability of his eventual death, at which his wives and position may be inherited by the teaser or someone of the teaser's generational status. And even between generation peers, mutual joking about each other's physical 'frailties' may hint at the passing years and/or the possibility of sudden death. Third, the customary acceptable appropriation of property such as chicken or livestock by a nephew does not extend to items of considerable value nor is it carried out too frequently.

Where they are conventional and therefore predictable, the greeting formulae preceding such familiarity state in advance, that reasonable limits of licence will not be exceeded. But what do we say of those greetings which, while preceding jocular prestations, are unfamiliar in form, or recognised as of recent origin, or significantly removed from an original, conventional greeting? It would seem that these greetings propose a new definition of the limits of licence. Thus, to return to a Giriama example, over a twelve-year period at least, it has become increasingly common for young men in or near rural trading centres to greet each other and girls in a wide variety of ways. These new greetings do not lose sight of the notion that sex and marriage may go together, but they do offer choice, a) of where to draw the limits of clan exogamy, and b) of sex without marriage.

In the rapidly growing small urban centres young men and young women are drawn from diverse areas and new, often explicitly temporary, liaisons between distantly related people of the same clan can occur. Some become serious affairs and the couples concerned try to rebel, usually unsuccessfully, against the elders' prohibitions on such 'incest', as it is perceived. One greeting typical with this new context opens with *She* (or *sheshe*), to which the response is also *she*. The word *she* here derives from the Swahili word *Shemeji*, which means brother- or sister-in-law, for which the normal Giriama term is *mulamu*. *She* may be exchanged between men who know nothing of each other's kinship status. It may also be exchanged between a married or unmarried man, as initiator, and a woman, usually unmarried but not always, who may or may not respond and whose clan membership may not be known to the man until the exchange has occurred on several occasions. In spite of the ignorance of clanship, the greeting may be followed by increasingly daring pleasantries and mock insults and is frequently an attempted prelude to a sexual liaison without the obligation of subsequent marriage, though sometimes leading to it albeit beyond the control of the respective families. To greet a person as a prospective mate by exchanging a 'foreign' Swahili term when neither knows the other's clanship, is a reversal of the Giriama custom, which is here precisely its propositional force. That is to say, it negates the 'traditional' proposition that sex entails marriage, or at least that full sexual partners should be eligible to marry each other.

As yet, rural Giriama greetings do not seem to question generational succession, nor claims on the maternal uncle's property; but these are early days in their contact with industrial society.

The joking greeting among the stratified Wolof mediates the wide gulfs of status and the premiss of open competition by allowing individuals, provided that they are not too far apart in status, to engage in mock insults which produce a temporary equality between them (Irvine 1974: 180–3). We would therefore expect that in fully industrialised, urban society, with its ideology of class mobility and shifting boundaries of strata, to stress even more in its joking greetings the premiss of equality through open rivalry and competition. This openness and tendency for free negotiability in the form and content of joking greetings in industrial urban society accounts for their frequent dissocation of sex from marriage, and of age and death from any obligation to replace or recreate the person socially. However, even in industrial society, the proposition still holds in joking that one does not 'borrow' too much of one's fellow's property nor too often.

The free negotiability in joking greetings in industrial society may also so alter the range of possible forms that the greeting is no longer discernible as a discrete opening to a conversation and merges imperceptibly with the subsequent, newly created jocular exchanges. Yet the three propositional themes still underlie these exchanges.

Thus, in Labov's study of ritual insults among urban Black American young male[3] peer groups (1972), sex, ageing, and poverty are central themes. The sexual and sometimes obscene jibes usually refer to a joking opponent's mother (and may start with the claim to have slept with her), but may refer to his other relatives as well as to the opponent himself. The sexual innuendos hint at the existence of matrifocal households with peripheral fathers. Since the joking partners show a brotherly solidarity in their peer groups, such insults thereby neatly bridge a vague notion of 'incest' with jocular and therefore acceptable sexuality but without the possibility of marriage. Other insults refer to a sometimes premature ageing process which, were the jibes taken to a logical conclusion, would surely hint at the inevitability of death itself. Yet another kind of insult is for A to say that B's family is poor and hungry, to which B ripostes by saying that it was A who ate all their provisions (1972: 317, 333–4).

These themes parallel those reported in traditional, pre-industrial joking relationships, except that, as among the 'new' generation of Giriama young men and women, sex is not thematically constructed as leading to marriage, nor are ageing and death concerned with the principle of social continuity. The theme of privileged but limited property claims, such as exists between the mother's brother and sister's son in pre-industrial society, is inverted in Harlem between peers as illicit appropriation or 'theft' of food and, by further extension, as associated with the precipitating poverty.

These joking themes appear to refer to universal concerns which speakers here make logically consistent with their own distinctive Black American culture and environment. Thus, as well as being reflexive, and thereby positive assertions about the richness and creativity of such Black speech events (called 'sounding' and other names, cf. Abrahams

1974) and of Black culture, these ritual insults reveal an awareness of the class structure by which the speakers are distinguished. Labov, for instance, explains that the reason speakers evaluate many obscene ritual insults so highly is precisely because they are so repellent to those people, including other Blacks, who are committed to the 'good' standards of a predominantly White middle-class society (1972: 324, cf. also Parkin 1977: 194–200). The exchange of ritual insults, then, is indeed freely negotiated among Black peers who compete to out-insult each other and win approval, but occurs within a framework of social class consciousness expressed in the confrontational language of urban industrialised society. That is to say, the negotiability of ritual insults is seen to be relevant to class as well as ethnic differences.

In contesting established authority in this way, the exchange of ritual insults breaks free from some linguistic constraints, yet retains a formulaic shape recognised by speakers as distinctive of their class and sub-culture. The 'ungrammaticality' by middle-class standards of the insults facilitates new kinds of syntactic complexity which heighten the 'outrageous' nature of the propositions contained in the utterances. Syntactic creativity thus engages heightened attention and becomes both the instrument of argument, and part of its content.

It is probably the case that in industrial society there are relatively few joking relationships marked by specific greetings. But there are many sets of relations especially between peers where the exchange of jocular greetings is expected. From common observation we know also that youthful peer groups and face-to-face work groups in industrial society sometimes substitute jocular insults for greetings, often prolonging them far beyond the bounds of the conventional greeting. Labov gives one case of this in New York (1972: 350–1) but, otherwise, in Harlem the most elaborate jocular insults neither accompany nor substitute for greetings but are rather exchanged spontaneously (prompted by a random remark or event) at different times during an interaction.

These culturally elaborate ritual insults thus share basic themes with the jocular greetings among, say, the Giriama, but are positionally the opposite because they normally punctuate conversations rather than open them. Therefore, jocular greetings and such ritualised exchanges of jocular insults differ less in what they 'say' but more by the positions they have in discourse. That is to say, they are subject to different rules of discourse syntax, a difference, we shall see, which does nevertheless have semantic significance.

This possibility of either the formal merging of greeting and ritual insult or of their separation and transposition in discourse – what we might call the floating nature of ritualised exchange – would seem to be especially (though not exclusively) associated with the blurring in industrial society of the line between institutionalised joking and all other forms of joking. That is to say, institutionalised joking, by definition, follows fixed rules of discourse syntax while 'ordinary' joking does not, so that a weak distinction between them creates rule uncertainty: one is uncertain in which relationship to initiate a jocular greeting or whether, or at what point in the ensuing conversation, to proffer a jocular insult.

Similarly, because urban industrial society is likely to be highly differentiated socio-economically and ethnically (and I acknowledge that my notion of 'industrial society' is, albeit necessarily, broad), there may be little agreement among the different social sectors as to which relationships need to be marked by respect and which by jocularity, a fact which is consistent with the highly negotiable and thereby creative nature of jocular exchanges.

The negotiated nature of the forms and occasions of jocular exchanges also makes people more aware of the language they use: they are conscious of the gamesmanship involved and of the inventiveness required in seeking semantic anomalies with which to create new constructions and ideas within a formulaic or ritual structure.

The areas of semantic anomaly or ambiguity in a particular culture are those from which words of abuse are normally taken (Leach 1964). Serious abuse attacks social categories unambiguously. But abuse transacted in a jocular manner takes on the capacity of the joke to suspend consideration of whether the proposition contained in the utterance is true or false. The implication of this is three-fold. First, suspending the truth or falsity of a proposition through joking usually relieves the speakers of personal, direct responsibility for the attack on cherished social categories carried by the abuse. Jokes that fall flat or 'go too far' do not provide this protection. Their management therefore requires creative skills. Second, by suspending truth and falsity in this way speakers can experiment with alternative propositions in prolonged or separate exchanges of jocular abuse. Finally, though the truth or falsity of propositions may initially be unverifiable during the jocular exchange itself, listeners will eventually check them out and, if they are shown to be true, take them seriously. In these ways, abuse can use jocularity experimentally to establish new social facts, by making the implicit explicit.

Through their ritual insults the Harlem groups experiment creatively with such frequently 'tabooed' subjects as sex and death, and theft and poverty, and in doing so bring to light such social developments and possibilities as strong matrifocal families or the effects of labelling poverty as shameful, which are otherwise hardly recognised as worthy of discussion by the wider society. Though I have no space to discuss them, I suggest that many ‘working class’ speech events in Britain are also used experimentally to this effect.

I noted earlier than conceptual creativity in greetings turns on the use of such contrastive semantic features as the static/moving idea, power versus solidarity, and variant versus invariant forms. Ritual insults may certainly use these contrastive features to make verifiable statements about their social environment. But they also make use of gradable evaluations of society around them, for the Harlem joking partners are judged not just in terms of whether a jibe is empirically correct or false but in terms of whether it is syntactically complex and/or whether it is grammatically, semantically, and aesthetically outrageous, and therefore attractive. Verbal skills and ‘new’ ideas are thereby applauded and ranked. With new rounds of ritual insults, new rankings are set up. The potential for creativity in jocular abuse thus derives from this licence to go beyond a respect for binary discriminations of what is socially recognised as true or false and of syntactic and grammatical correctness and incorrectness, and from the preparedness to blur the relative positions in discourse of the formulaic exchanges themselves. Converting polar opposites of ‘truth’/‘falsity’ and ‘correctness’/‘incorrectness’ into gradable ‘more’ or ‘less’ opposites widens the interpretive potential of these words and helps create new perspectives. At a later stage these new perspectives may become lexicalised as new polar semantic opposites, and the process continues.[4]

Conclusion

We can view the exchange of terms of address and greetings, and probably other such everyday formulae, from two main perspectives. First, these formulaic exchanges may interpret emergent social changes. Second, they are a cultural sphere of activities in which ritualised conformity generates non-conformity which then eventually conforms to a type, and so on.

The interpretive aspect draws on four partially overlapping questions of performance: whether whoever approaches a stationary person greets or addresses first, regardless of who is socially superior; whether the power or solidarity semantic is used in pronouns or titles; whether greetings are opened and/or replied to with invariant or variant forms; and whether a greeting form denoting familiarity rather than respect may further denote a possible redefinition of the relationship. Though very basic, these offer alternative interpretations of personal autonomy, power, and change in society.

It is often regarded as abusive to address or greet someone 'improperly'. But this dramatic repudiation of the politeness formula can in some circumstances draw on such alternative interpretations and provoke comment and even argument about alterations in status, both between persons and between strata.

Ritual insults also make social statements. All formulaic exchanges entail definitions of power relations, so that those in authority tend to maintain the orthodox verbal presentations, while those debarred or distant from such authority tend to subvert it through alternative ones. The special facility of ritual insults, as in the case of Harlem discussed here, or in the ritualised jocular abuse characteristic of many societies, is that their 'outrages' against conformity free speakers to experiment with alternative, normally hidden, views of personal worth and power relations.

Ritual insults are also distinctive in that they repudiate the very idea of politeness formulae. In this sense they are the most reflexive kind of formulaic exchange. They go beyond the inversion of 'proper' forms and meanings and constantly create new ones.

However, ritual abuse and politeness formulae are two sides of the same coin, and it is the clarity of this formal contrast which makes each effective: the use of one throws the other into sharp relief. Just as they are opposed in this way, so in each of them we find an inner struggle between conformity to a preconceived pattern of language use and a contrastive propensity to linguistic innovation. This struggle often has a gamelike quality and does not simply reflect the 'external' struggles of competing social groups. Quite independently, in the ritual exchange of set forms, *homo ludens* works new variations which may or may not thereafter be interpreted as social statements.

This view of creativity through formulaic regeneration puts an extra gloss on the Saussurian idea of an unchanging *langue* comprising the unique, individual utterances of *parole*, an idea recast several times over in the Chomskyan contrast between underlying competence and surface performance, that between paradigmatic and syntagmatic structures (cf. Ardener 1971: lxxvi) and that of some linguists between categorical and variable rules of discourse (e.g. Sankoff 1974: 42 sq.)

Verbal formulae of this kind discussed in this article are a limited instance of the more general formulaic element which we call idiom. Semantic creativity in speech is said to depend not on idiomatic and ritualised expressions but on novel syntactic, lexical, and phonological combinations. But novel combinations, even though they may later become idiomatic or ritualised, achieve their initial effect by juxtaposition with fixed expressions (cf. Friedrich 1975: 206–7). 'Formalised' speech may stifle conceptual creativity at a particular point in time (Bloch 1975: 17), but it also provides the fixed forms against which speakers test their wit and create new ones.

Notes

(1) Curl Lecture, 1979.

(2) Given the fact that the feudal clergy had status but not necessarily power, unlike the nobility who had both, this form of address might better be called a non-reciprocal power-status semantic. I acknowledge this point, but, for purposes of consistency, reproduce Brown and Gillman's own, original usage to cover both power and status, differentiating only when necessary, and thank Audrey Hayley for drawing it to my attention.

(3) Shortly after the presentation of this lecture Prudence W. Berger kindly informed me that girls in Black speech also exchange ritual insults, with boys as well as each other, a fact which might strengthen analytical comparison with the joking greetings of modern Giriama youth. See her 'Ceremonials in obscenity', an unpublished paper presented in 1970 to the Department of Social Anthropology, University of Stockholm.

(4) For Leech (1974: 108–110) and Lyons (1977: 278) examples of such evaluative polar oppositions are 'good/bad', 'beautiful/ugly', and 'kind/unkind'. If, however, we accept that ritual insults sometimes set new sub-cultural linguistic standards by *deliberate* grammatical and semantic abuse, then perhaps the opportunities for converting polar into gradable opposites are greater and result in more than temporarily modifying the language system (Lyons 1977: 279).

References

Abrahams, R.D. (1974) Black talking on the streets. In *Explorations in the ethnography of speaking* (eds) R. Bauman & J. Scherzer. Cambridge: Univ. Press.

Ardener, E. (1970) Witchcraft, economics and the continuity of belief. In Witchcraft confessions and accusations (Ass. Social Anthrop Monogr. 9). London: Tavistock.

——(1971) Introduction. In *Social anthropology and language* (ed.) E.Ardener (Ass. Anthrop Monogr. 10). London: Tavistock.

Bates, E. and Benigni, L. (1975) Rules of address in Italy: a sociological survey. *Language in Society* 4, 271–88.

Bloch, M. (1975) Introduction. In Political language and oratory in traditional society. London: Academic Press.

Brown, P. and Levinson, S. (1978) Universals in language use: Politeness phenomena. In *Questions and politeness: strategies in social interaction* (ed.) E. Goody (Camb. Pap. Social Anthrop 8). Cambridge: Univ. Press

Brown, R. and Ford, M. (1964) [1961] Address in American English. In *Language in culture and society* (ed.) D. Hymes. New York: Harper & Row.

——and A. Gilman (1972) [1960] The pronouns of power and solidarity. In *Language & Social context* (ed.) A. Giglio. Harmondsworth: Penguin.

Burckman, J. (1974) Tongue play: constitutive and interpretive properties of sexual joking encounters among the Kaya of south India. In *Socio-cultural dimensions of language use* (eds) M. Sanches & B. Blount. New York: Academic Press.

Douglas, M. (1968) The social control of cognition: some factors in joke perception. *Man* (N.S.) 3, 361–76.

Ervin-Tripp, S. (1972) [1969] Sociolinguistic rules of address. In *Sociolinguistics* (eds) J. Pride & J. Holmes. Harmondsworth: Penguin.

Ferguson, C. (1967) Root-echo responses in Syrian Arabic politeness formulas. In *Linguistic studies in memory of Richard Slade Harrell* (ed.) D.S. Stuart. Georgetown: Univ. Press.

——(1976) The structure and use of politeness formulas. *Language in Society* 5, 137–52.

Firth, R. (1972) Verbal and bodily rituals of greeting and parting. In *The interpretation of ritual* (ed.) J.S. La Fontaine. London: Tavistock.

Friedrich, P. (1967) Structural implications of Russian pronominal usage. In *Sociolinguistics* (ed.) W. Bright. The Hague: Mouton.

——(1975) The lexical symbol and its relative non-arbitrariness. In *Linguistics and anthropology* (eds) M.D. Kincade *et al*. Lisse: Peter de Ridder Press.

Goody, E. (1972) 'Greeting', 'begging' and the presentation of respect. In *The interpretation of ritual* (ed.) J.S. La Fontaine. London: Tavistock.

——(ed.) (1978) Questions and politeness: strategies in social interaction (Camb. Pap. Social Anthrop. 8). Cambridge: Univ Press.

Gudmundsson, H. (1972) *The pronominal dual in Icelandic*. Reykjavik: Institute of Nordic Linguistics.

Haugen, E. (1975) Pronominal address in Icelandic: from you-two to you-all. *Language in Society* 4, 323–40.

Irvine, J. (1974) Strategies of status manipulation in the Wolof greeting. In *Explorations in the ethnography of speaking* (eds) R. Bauman & J. Sherzer. Cambridge: Univ Press.

Labov, W. (1977) [1972] Rules for ritual insults. In *Language in the inner city*. Oxford: Blackwell.

Lambert, W.E. (1972) The use of 'tu' and 'vous' as forms of address in French Canada: A pilot study. In *Language, psychology and culture*. Stanford: Univ Press.

Leach, E.R. (1974) [1964] Anthropological aspects of language: Animal categories and verbal abuse. In *Mythology* (ed.) P. Maranda. Harmondsworth: Penguin.

Leech, G. (1974) *Semantics*. Harmondsworth: Penguin.

Lyons, J. (1977) *Semantics*, 1. Cambridge: Univ Press.

Malinowski, B. (1948) *Magic, science and religion*. Glencoe: Ill.: Free Press.

Mitchell-Kernan, C. and Kernan, K.T. (1975) Children's insults: America and Samoa. In Sociocultural dimensions of language use (eds) M. Sanches & B. Blount. New York: Academic Press.

Parkin, D. (1977) Emergent and stabilized multilingualism: polyethnic peer groups in Kenya. In *Language, ethnicity, and inter-group relations* (ed.) H. Giles. London: Academic Press.

——(1978) *The cultural definition of political response*. London: Academic Press.

Paulston, C.B. (1976) Pronouns of address in Swedish: social class semantics and a changing system. *Language in Society* 5, 359–86.

Radcliffe-Brown, A.R. (1977) [1940] On joking relationships. In *The social anthropology of Radcliffe-Brown* (ed.) A. Kuper. London: Routledge & Kegan Paul.

Salmond, A. (1974) Rituals of encounter among the Maori. In *Explorations in the ethnography of speaking* (eds) R. Bauman & J. Sherzer. Cambridge: Univ Press.

Sankoff, G. (1974) A quantitative paradigm. In *Explorations in the ethnography of speaking* (eds) R. Bauman & J. Sherzer. Cambridge: Univ Press.

Searle, J.R. (1968) Austin on locutionary and illocutionary acts. *Phil Rev* 77, 405–34.

Sharman, A. (1969) Joking in Padhola: categorical relationships, choice and social control. *Man* (N.S.) 4, 103–17.

6 Exchanging Words

The Aim

The concept of exchange has two broad referents in anthropology. On the one hand the reference is to a universal and fundamental principle by which society and culture are organised. The principle is expressed in Malinowski's identification of the binding obligations of reciprocity, in Mauss's notion of the gift, and, at its most comprehensive, in Lévi-Strauss's view of the systems of cultural exchange involving women (and, one should add, men), goods and services, and messages, and in his view of the underlying rules regulating the interrelationships of these "surface" exchange systems (Lévi-Strauss 1963: 296).

On the other hand, the concept of social exchange may refer microscopically to a process by which individuals' actions, beyond and apart from normative constraints, are governed by their personal perceptions of the most rewarding ends of relationships and the means by which such ends may be attained. The two partners to the relationship are engaged in a constant process of exchanging or withholding deference, affection, information, or material goods, of making concessions or securing recognition, all of which may alter their positions of dominance or power with regard to each other. Such processes are frequently referred to as transactions and, for consistency, I refer to their study as transactional analysis.

Transactional analysis draws its metaphors from familiar economic concepts and from game theory. Here it is interesting to note that, in a paper presented in 1952, Lévi-Strauss conceptually links together the rules underlying his systems of exchange and communication and those underlying the economic maximising game theory of Von Neuman and Morgenstern (1944). The latter are quoted approvingly as contributing to a consolidation of social anthropology, economics, and linguistics into one great field (Lévi-Strauss 1963: 297–300). In referring to their work Lévi-Strauss uses such terms as "maximizing ... to advantage" and "play, move, choice, and strategy" (*ibid.*, 298). He claims that the "formal" rules of marriage and the rules underlying individual or group strategies aimed at acquiring, for instance, the most or the best wives are susceptible to the same methods of investigation and, indeed, we dare interpret, are fundamentally of the same order.

And yet, in spite of this early conceptualisation, the spirit of intellectual unity can hardly be said to be reflected in the influential transactional analyses of such scholars as Bailey (1969), Barth (1966), Blau (1964), Homans (1958 and 1961), Kapferer (1972), Paine (1967 and elsewhere), and others, to say nothing of the numerous mathematically minded game theorists usually labelled as economists, sociologists, or political scientists.

To confine ourselves to anthropology colleagues, why have they rejected the search for common factors linking the two kinds of rules? Is it because they believe that the two kinds are simply not of the same explanatory order? Or because their intensive focus on the individual, or on the group acting as an individual, technically precludes a more comprehensive analysis of socially more extensive rule systems? Though rarely explicit, both of these may be found as reasons.

Bailey, it is true, does formulate an important distinction between normative and pragmatic rules (1969: 4ff.), which has echoes of Firth's normative asymmetry of ideals, expectations, and action (1951), as well as of Lévi-Strauss's mechanical and statistical models (1963: 283–289). But Bailey's rules are, as he frankly points out (p. 17f.), at a more "concrete" level of abstraction than those mathematically formulated by Von Neuman and Morgenstern, and, it is reasonable to assume, than those more general rules of communication proposed by Lévi-Strauss.

On the one hand, then, Lévi-Strauss and, in his own view, Von Neuman and Morgenstern deal with rules of exchange which are products (or "ends") of logical systems, whether the system be mathematics, marriage, mythology, or language. On the other hand, the transactional analysts are dealing with rules which indicate means to ends and arise from the condition of man as a maximising and economising animal able to choose for himself independent courses of action. This chapter is an attempt to relate the latter to the former: I want to show that individual strategising does indeed operate within areas of choice and "rational" means-toend relationships but that, at a more inclusive level, the choices are set in ordered categories of social and personal meaning over which the individual per se has little if any control. These larger categories are themselves governed systematically by rules. The distinction is essentially (and not merely analogously) the classical Saussurian one between *parole*, by which individual creativeness is manifested in unique utterances, and *langue*, which paradoxically directs this creativeness by requiring it to be expressed by reference to, though not necessarily in slavish imitation of, an existing body of grammatical rules. In short, the constraints on choice are the limitations of any grammar of communication, in both its positive and negative aspects.

My starting point is to consider the methodological assumptions of transactional analysis. I go on to suggest that while transactional analysis looks for the points of disjunction in human relations, that related branch of anthropology also focused on interpersonal relationships, symbolic interactionism, tends to emphasise the points of conjunction, mutual satisfaction, and harmony. From this I then argue that, both in the anthropologists' methodological assumptions and in the cultures of the people they study, we can distinguish the operation of two conceptually opposed ideologies: of negotiable (i.e. disjunctive) and altruistic (i.e. conjunctive) exchange. The ideologies are examples of the ordered sets of social and personal meaning mentioned above whose logical relationship to each other is governed by more general rules of communication. These in tum provide a kind of underlying cultural blueprint for the specific (e.g. normative and pragmatic) rules of interaction obtaining within a particular culture.

The Methodological Assumptions of Transactional Analysis

Enough has been written about transactional analysis for us to agree on a number of immediately obvious defining characteristics. The field is concerned with actors consciously or non-consciously taking decisions and making choices. These decisions and choices are based on a notion of rationality in the terms of the particular culture. The notion of rationality assumes the existence of material and nonmaterial objects of value. It further assumes that men are generally impelled to possess or have access to these valued objects and that they do so at what they perceive to be the minimum cost to themselves. But the very existence of valued objects implies that the objects are technically limited in quantity, or conversely that they are relatively scarce, and that, therefore, men are engaged in a zero-sum game necessarily predicating competition.

These are some of the distinctive properties of the approach. They are assumptions about human behaviour and cognitive orientation. Provided that you start with the notion of actor, any of the other four or five assumptions can follow and the explanatory paradigm falls logically into order. For example, the actor is capable of selecting between alternative courses of action; he does so while playing a zero-sum game; this assumes that he is competing for valued objects; the game further implies consensus among the combatants about the rules of competition; the agreement about rules implies a common conception of rationality within the terms of the game (i.e. within the terms of a given culture); rationality, as a cultural conception of the most *efficient* organisation of means to ends in social action, assumes that men are likely to maximise their chances of attaining desired goals at least cost, or certainly not at greatest cost, to themselves and so on.

Leaving aside the question of whether this kind of tautology is justified if it can be used as a heuristic device (see Kapferer 1972: 5 on Blau 1964), I wish to consider three issues arising from it: the concepts of value and of rationality, and the extent to which individuals can operate freely beyond and apart from the wider institutional and normative constraints of society.

Regarding the first issue, I think that Kapferer puts his finger on what is important when he asks us to discover 'the circumstances which may lead individuals to value the activity in which they are engaged for the intrinsic qualities of the activity itself rather than for the benefits it may typically bring' (1972: 6). I regard this as referring to the process by which certain kinds of activities may achieve a state of unquestionable legitimacy or sanctity, and so become imbued with symbolic justification. We move closer here to the familiar view that all kinds of transaction, material and nonmaterial, are to be understood as a process of symbolic communication.

With regard to the second issue, Kapferer also asks us to discover "the conditions under which an individual or group may display one kind of rationality rather than another" (1972: 6). Though the jargon is clumsy, I think it may be preferable to refer to the different kinds of rationality as different emic *sets* of classification and explanation within a culture. That is to say, I am interested in the way in which people within a culture may "switch" from one mode to another of classifying, explaining, and justifying events and behaviour as "rational." The etic rationality of the external observer – for example, the view that man is fundamentally an economising animal – is assumed to be over and above these folk rationalities and to be based on universal rather than particular cultural rules, an assumption which ignores ethnocentric intellectual bias. The distinction between emic and etic modes of explanation suffers the stigma of once fashionable concepts. But the distinction does enable us to ask whether, for example, the "values," "roles," and "statuses" being newly generated by social interaction fit logically into the actor's views of his culture (emic), or whether they can be identified as part of "our," the outside observer's, analytic categories (etic).

The third issue, the extent to which individuals may manipulate social relationships independently of normative and institutional constraints, is complex. Kapferer approvingly contrasts Blau with Homans and Barth: Blau "does not view individuals as independent social actors and he attempts to avoid the dangers of psychological reductionism"; through his concept of "emergent property," Blau "recognizes that wider structural and institutional processes influence individual action" (Kapferer 1972: 6–7).

Barth and Homans certainly suggest a kind of individualistic reductionism. Homans announces himself frankly as an "ultimate psychological reductionist" (1958: 597); and Barth suggests that though roles (i.e. actual performance) may be generated by statuses (i.e., sets of rules of interaction) we can only understand the ways in which these latter are generated by starting "on a more elementary level" (1966: 3). It is true that Barth explicitly excludes a "psychological" explanation (p. 5) of this elementary level, which he sees as based on transactional or reciprocal evaluations of behaviour. But when we look at the one empirical context in which his ideas are applied, that of a fishing vessel off the coast of Norway , we find him claiming that a consistent pattern of the fishermen's behaviour "can only be explained in terms of *their* transactional obligation, involving prestations of willingness or eagerness and constant readiness to work, as well as their interest in observing , evaluating , and controlling the dispositions of the skipper" (p. 8). Not quite a psychological explanation perhaps, but one that leaves us in no doubt as to the emphasis placed on the individual in the explanation. Nevertheless, Barth has constant need of the concept of role in the section of his paper that deals with this one empirical context, a point of some significance as I shall indicate below.

That said, I do not really see a significant difference between Blau's concept of emergent property and Barth's notion of a generative model, or even between these and Homans ' description of an exchange paradigm in his 1958 essay (pp. 598–599). Perhaps the difference for Kapferer is one of intention, for Blau does "attempt to bridge the gap between abstract institutional and normative explanations of social behaviour and the psychological reductionism exemplified in Homans' theory of social exchange" (Kapferer 1972: 7). More generally, this relates to the now rather worn debate about the relative merits of methodological individualism and holism (for recent examples see Boissevain 1968, Cohen 1969, Gluckman 1968, Kennedy 1967, and Paine 1967). Mitchell states succinctly that the analysis of social relationships in terms of social networks anchored on individuals is not a substitute for an analysis in terms of social institutions, that the two involve different levels of abstraction, and that they in fact complement one another (1969: 14–15, 48–49). At first sight this would seem to imply that the debate referred to above centres on a false problem – that there is in fact nothing to debate, since both analytical dimensions are necessary and we cannot therefore prefer one to the other.

This invites two comments. First, the two dimensions are indeed complementary, in the way that any social analysis must comprehend the organisation of interpersonal as well as collective relationships and activities. But there is still considerable room for debate as to (a) how much emphasis may be placed on either in the interpretation of data and, most important, (b) how much "change" (however this is defined) in either dimension is determined by change in the other. The answer to (a) may indeed be a matter of preference between micro and macro: wife beating may be explained as a product of a particular correlation of personal networks and conjugal expectations, but may also be explained as a product of a combination of institutional and historical factors characterising the development of specific social and economic strata. The answer to (b) is commonly that the idea of a feedback mechanism ensures that both institutional and personal influences can be accommodated within a single analysis. But this is something of a blind, since it is clear that the feedback is not seen as evenly flowing; moreover , the very *raison d'être* of transactional analysis, with its concepts of "emergent property" and "generative model," is to demonstrate the creation of new social forms ("institutional change") out of the processes of personal interaction-with historical, institutional, and wider economic and political forces as little more than environments exercising short-term restraint and offering manipulable resources. There remains much to debate.

The second comment, however, is that Mitchell himself, while repudiating an exclusively structural-functional holistic approach, is not by any means an individual reductionist. Whatever the varying views of his fellow contributors to *Social Networks in Urban Situations*, Mitchell turns to the concept of role to link the explanations of institutional normative processes on the one hand and processes of personal interaction on the other (1969: 45–46). The concept of role is given only a few paragraphs' attention (and, of the three orders of relationships identified by Mitchell, the structural, categorical, and egocentric, relates very closely to the structural), but they are illuminating and important. From different theoretical standpoints, then, both Barth and Mitchell make use of the concept of role.

Let me do some recapping. I have reconsidered three issues, arising from methodological assumptions in transactional analysis, which may now be stated as simple propositions. First, the most familiar one: material and nonmaterial transactions can be regarded as aspects of a more general process of symbolic communication. Second, we may usefully incorporate in our analyses the distinction between emic and etic categories and explanations of social process. And third, the concept of role, and by implication role theory generally, emerges as an important descriptive and analytical "bridge" linking institutional and ego-centred explanations of social process.

These three propositions overlap. (1) Symbolic communication by definition has its own grammar or system of rules which (2) can be analysed (phon)emically as well as (phon)etically, while (3) the concept of role itself refers to a main component of symbolic communication which can be explored at a "subjective" level, in terms of a culture's emic categories, or at an "objective" level, in terms of an inferred universal or etic set of categories . In either case, role is ultimately a verbal symbol. I do not want to become bogged down in this chapter in the emic/etic distinction, and do no more than use it as a piece of shorthand methodological notation.

Bearing in mind the overlap, I shall deal with these three propositions. After that I shall attempt to show that, whatever else it may involve, social interaction must be understood as the transaction of symbols and that what we conventionally call social change can be viewed as the transaction of those kinds of verbal symbol which we call roles.

Material and Non-material Exchange as Symbolic Communication

Rewards of Exchange

Analytically we can distinguish between (a) the rewards, goals, or ends of exchange and (b) the items or media of exchange-that is, what is actually transacted. Empirically these are sometimes, though not always, the same. The focus on rewards puts the emphasis on the actor and on economising or maximising behaviour aimed at the acquisition of material and nonmaterial "goods." As Burling puts it, in opposition to the view that economic anthropology is primarily and even exclusively concerned with material goods, "we must repeatedly economize between material and non-material ends. We must make repeated choices between goals, some of which are material while some are not. We must decide whether added leisure is more important to us than the extra money we could earn by working overtime. Would I rather have a new car or a trip to Europe?" (1962: 803).

A logical extension of this view, as all transactional analysts seem to agree, is that it is the satisfaction of cultural "values" which is the reward of all successful transactions, whether the value is in the possession of a material good or in some intangible item like "the symbols of approval or prestige" (Homans, 1958: 606). But of course a cultural value is itself symbolic: whatever the personal intentions of the new-car buyer, his choice of car, and his own genuine protestations that the car is for purely "practical" rather than, say, prestige purposes, he is by his very purchase of the vehicle slotted into one of a number of categories of car owners and so is, to a lesser or greater degree, likely to be accredited with particular social characteristics. Apart from being distinguished from persons who do not own cars, he is distinguished by year, size, condition, colour, and make of car. That is not to say that, like turbans on "chiefly" Kachin, these distinctions necessarily make statements about his status, as car insurance firms feel obliged to assume. They may indeed do so, though frequently wrongly and inconsistently. They constitute some of the forms of the everyday cosmology of an industrial society, in which persons are identified by and with consumer goods and thus classified. The totemic parallel may be spurious, but it is clear that many people do have crude stereotypes of a Volkswagen owner as distinct from a Morris Minor or Jaguar owner. Their stereotypes are constructed no doubt out of the more specific exegesis of the car dealer and mass media experts, but are also formed by currents of public opinion arising from observation and rumour. Whether we intend or like it or not, then, the material rewards of exchange locate us in a system of social classification and "stand for" or symbolise popular conceptions (or, if you like, misconceptions) of social and personality types pertinent to our particular culture or subculture.

The example is extreme, but it demonstrates an analytical shift from the actor to the environment in which he acts. The parties to a relationship may indeed control much of the way in which transactions are conducted between them, but settlement of the deal and due apportionment of the rewards of exchange place them in a classificatory frame over which they have little, if any, control. In this respect it is irrelevant whether the rewards of exchange are material cars or the nonmaterial "symbols of approval or prestige" to which Homans refers, since both place the actor controlling the transaction in a more general cultural scheme of symbolic classification. The nonmaterial is by definition conceptual and so subsumes the material, the value of which can only be interpreted by the actor within a scheme of intellectual and verbal classification.

Gift Exchange

When we turn to the items and not just the rewards of exchange, we encounter an analytical distinction which is difficult to substantiate empirically. A strict interpretation of the distinction would imply that some transactional media (material and nonmaterial) are unambiguously means to ends. Transactional analysis, in its emphasis on the rationality of actors, and implicitly on a distinction between means and ends, takes a subjective starting point: the means and ends of an exchange relationship are what the analyst interprets as its costs and rewards in the minds of the actors. Moreover, what may be a reward of exchange now (say, the acquisition of wealth or some "symbols of approval") may at a later stage be bartered in a "new" (or continuation of the "old") relationship. Or, the means of exchange may be ends in themselves at one point in time (i.e. they are "expressive" in that they produce short-term gratification, as Parsons would say) but may be means to further ends at a later point in time (i.e. they are "instrumental" in that they produce long-term gratification). Goods which are transacted therefore may be either means or ends of exchange, depending on the actor's perception of the use to which they are being put within a specific time sequence. This is itself open to the analyst's interpretation.

It follows that the only transactional medium which can be identified in the actor's mind as unambiguously both a means and end of exchange is Malinowski's "pure" gift. Like true love, with all its pains and pleasures, the "pure" gift is both cost and reward. Now, as outside analysts we know well that the "expressive" exchange of gifts can have the unintended consequence of eventually securing non-altruistic interests. Looked at from the outside, the expressive is thus seen to be instrumentally effective. But the very use of the word "gift," the meaning of which I assume to have universal semantic identification of one kind or another indicates that we see the actor as concerned primarily with the altruistic interpretation. However, culturally approved altruistic exchange, when carried on in more than simply ephemeral contexts, frequently and perhaps always establishes accumulated and even corporately held material and nonmaterial interests. This being the case, the actor who voluntarily engages in altruistic exchange, yet is unaware of the growing web of utilitarian interests enveloping him, thereby subscribes unquestioningly to whatever moral dictates buttress the altruism.

Put in a more familiar vein, then, institutionalised gift exchange is loaded with moral content: the morality proclaims altruism, or such similar ethoses as egalitarianism, while concealing the development of a range of personal and group interests which are unlikely, in "reality," to be distributed equally. But we know that a system of morality is rarely communicated to an interacting population in the form of rational argument. Symbols do the job more effectively. What are the symbols in institutionalised gift exchange? Do they emanate from the gift itself or from the relationship in which the transactions occur? In fact, they come from both. To argue that it is the social relationship alone out of which the symbolism arises is tautological, for this is tantamount to saying that a morally binding relationship is symbolised only by itself. The communicative power of a symbol has its initial locus in either a concrete object, a gesture, or a word, and ultimately in an abstract idea. What better in gift exchange than that the initial locus be the gift itself? The gift may assume a variety of forms, material and nonmaterial, and may be said to release symbolic "meaning" in the context of the relationship. The symbol itself may be regarded as de Saussure's "sign," which can be broken down into two components: the "signifying," in other words the locus or gift itself; and the "signified," or the social relationship. The general "meaning" of the symbol is then the social implications and consequences of the perpetuation of this particular culturally recognised relationship of gift exchange as distinct from other such relationships.

If the gift can be regarded as the signifying component of the sign, then we are attributing an active rather than passive role to it: we are claiming that, like the form of a word, it is an inanimate material object, yet that, in conjunction with whatever is signified, it can exert sufficient force to stimulate our perceptions and evoke an intellectual response. I find this view close to the first part of Mauss's largely intuitive belief that "The thing given is not inert. It is alive and often personified, and strives to bring to its original clan and homeland some equivalent to take its place" (Mauss 1970: 8). And if we accept the likelihood, as anthropologists seem to, that a gift triggers reciprocal obligations to repay, then we surely accept the second part of the statement. I do not mean that we accept it literally in its form as an ethnographic metaphor, any more than we accept that a gift among Maori necessarily has a "magical and religious hold over the recipient" (*ibid.*). May I speculate that Mauss was here expressing his intuition through what he regarded as correct ethnography – or perhaps he unintentionally fitted the ethnography to his intuition?

On the basis of his own extensive field work in the area, Firth has questioned the validity of Mauss's ethnography (1967: 9–10), and we must accept his objection. But even if the ethnographic examples were correct, they would still be no more than particular cultural realisations of a presumably universal mutual responsiveness of the consciences of donors and receivers which keeps the exchange of gifts going until honour is satisfied or enmity expressed and conscience therefore made redundant. In short, not only the process of transacting gifts, but the very choice of which gift to transact, locates the donor and receiver in a wider scheme of symbolic classification. I once witnessed an anthropologist of upper-class origin commenting on the alleged tendency of working-class people to give each other sweet (rather than dry or medium) sherry for Christmas. Whether or not this is true, it is clear that here the "thing," sweet as opposed to medium or dry sherry, had classified not only working-class gift exchange but, by its negative innuendo, a perception by the upper class of its own rules of gift exchange. I instance this genuine if trivial case concerning an anthropologist to illustrate how all of us are frequently unaware of how, in our choices, we are ourselves classified by the objects of our evaluation. Examples abound in everyday speech.

Negotiable and Altruistic Ideologies of Exchange

I have examined the analytical distinction between the means and ends of exchange. Transactional analysts impute rationality to actors who strive to ensure that the rewards of exchange (the ends) are worth more than the costs (the means). The attainment of the reward goes beyond satisfying the actor's drive toward maximisation of self-interest. Whether material or nonmaterial, it locates him in a symbolic system which, at its most significant, classifies whole social categories, and at its most trivial invokes elementary personal stereotypes. Taking culturally recognised gift exchange as the one example in which the actor minimises his perception of differences between costs and rewards, we find that here too the choice and nature of the gift (whether material or nonmaterial) locate the donor and receiver in the same overall symbolic system of classification.

Transactional analysts have concentrated on the more "rational" kind of transactions rather than on gift exchange, because they have seen the former as fundamental in generating new forms of social organisation. But I would hypothesise that patterns of gift exchange can be at least as potent, if not more potent, forces for change. Their high moral content facilitates the symbolic and therefore unquestioned ideal of altruism which may act as an unintended cover for the development of utilitarian interests between donor and receiver. Where the development of these interests becomes increasingly biased in favour of one of the two parties, then the discrepancy between the altruistic ideal and the utilitarian content of the relationship is particularly marked. As a general process characterising exchange spheres other than that of gifts, this is at the heart of many examples of emerging social inequality: in a recent publication (1972) I showed how two custom-hallowed exchange spheres centring respectively on bridewealth and funerary expenditure symbolised a supposedly "egalitarian" order of relations, yet in the long term actually facilitated the economic differentiation of social categories in an African farming community.

The two types of exchange, altruistic and non-altruistic, are of course familiar anthropological fodder. To take a recent and important example, Sahlins has proposed a spectrum of reciprocities which extends from altruistic ("pure gift") generalised reciprocity at one end, through balanced reciprocity in the middle (nonexploitative and overlapping with gift exchange), to negative reciprocity at the other end. Negative reciprocity includes "transactions opened and conducted toward net utilitarian advantage. ... The participants confront each other as opposed interests, each looking to maximize utility at the other's expense" (1965: 148).

The spectrum can be reduced to the two poles of altruistic and negotiable (or exploitative) exchange to correspond with the distinction with which I have been dealing. Sahlins associates movements along the spectrum with large-scale, morphological, and partially evolutionary developments of society. This is the level of abstraction and generalisation at which he has chosen to operate and, as far as I can judge, it is both legitimate and borne out by the admirably detailed evidence he presents. But Sahlins obviously does not deny the coexistence of the different modes of exchange in a society at one point in time, and indeed I think his findings can be used to suggest a range of possible combinations of this coexistence.

In an essay concerned with interpersonal exchange, I am clearly dealing with a level of abstraction which is much more limited in time and space and in its range of types of society. I am concerned with the coexistence of the two idioms of exchange and their covariant relationship, a matter to which Davis (1973: 166) draws our attention. Transactional analysts, by focusing on the rationality and the maximisation of self-interest of actors, have obliged themselves to consider negotiable exchange as a fundamental fact of all human behaviour rather than as one of two principal modes by which actors may interpret the forms of exchange in interaction. I argue, however, that as ideologies the two modes can be treated as independent, covariant social facts.

Let me try to elaborate on this. Transactional analysts require that the most significant social relationships be regarded as transactions between parties. So far, so good. They impute rationality and the maximisation of self-interest to the actors. That is to say, they climb into the minds of the actors and see them managing their relationship according to a personal, but socially universal, program which urges them to achieve profit at minimal cost. But, unlike what is implicit in Sahlins' scheme, the transactional approach does not appear to be concerned with whether or not this is a culturally valued process. The maximisation of self-interest can be recognised by a part or the whole of a society, as a cultural ideology. As examples we have the Dionysian ethos, the "get-ahead-quick" ideals in many Western commercial career contexts, and the local acceptance of the institution of *chakari* and other forms of institutional exchange as "bribery" in Nepal (Caplan 1971). In a complementary but opposite manner, institutionalised gift exchange is based on an ideology of altruism. In referring to "ideologies," anthropologists have tended to focus their analyses on those which emphasise the altruistic "goodness" of man; and when they focus on negative ideologies, like beliefs in witchcraft, they frequently place them apart from altruism. But, of course, an ideology of witchcraft is of the same analytical order as an ideology of altruism or ennobling morality.

There are, then, ideologies of negotiation just as there are altruistic ones; they may coexist in the same social situation and, in variable combinations, in the same society.

The central tenet of transactional analysis, however, appears to be that the maximisation of self-interest is an axiomatic and universal feature of the human condition that underlies the exchange nature of social relations. Transactional analysis does not attempt to identify and analyse those social circumstances in which this supposed axiom of human behaviour is raised to a level of cultural consciousness and identification. This is surely incomplete: it is like recognising as an axiom the human propensity to symbolise and impose intellectual order on man's physical environment but neglecting to consider also the recognisable cultural manifestations of this propensity.

In summary I suggest that the transactional nature of relationships obliges us to take into account not only the actor's view of means and ends as costs and profits, but also the fact that these means and ends, as "goods" transacted and acquired, are "things" which because they fall into cultural systems of classification, locate the actor in these systems. Where the perceived relationship between the "thing" and the actor is very close and even "intimate," as in Mauss's view of the gift, then the "thing" may be said to provide the primary locus for the symbolic expression of the social relationship. This is most obvious in institutionalised gift exchange but is surely embryonic in all individual cases of "pure gift" giving.

Similarly, there can be a perceived close relationship between the actor and the goals or rewards of an exchange relationship: goals and rewards valued by the actor are also culturally valued; and so the actor's social fortunes are tied up with the more general cultural evaluations of these "things." To my mind, the most important contribution of Barth is his emphasis on changing ecological conditions as constituting variable environments of opportunity. Ultimately it is ecological (and we might also add, technological) conditions which govern the availability of valued goods; and, though cultural evaluations of the rewards of exchange are not strictly determined by techno-ecological conditions, these conditions impose limits on the intensity of such cultural evaluations. If diamonds were discovered and produced in uncontrollable abundance, or if an unprecedentedly large number of persons in a society assumed saintly dispositions, there would surely follow some cultural redefinition of the places of these "things" in the system of values. Diamonds might even cease to be regarded as rewards of negotiable exchange relationships; they might assume the status of "cheap" and therefore more frequently transacted gifts. Saintliness might cease to be bestowed through an ideologically "pure gift" relationship with a god, spirit, or prophet, and instead be legitimately regarded as the prize of successful bargain and negotiation with these agencies. Thus the two ideologies of negotiable and altruistic exchange would be preserved as coexisting spheres of cultural evaluation, but with some transposition of the "goods" transacted in them.

Role Terms as Symbols of Exchange

To say that actors' choices of rewards and gifts locate them in a wider environment of cultural and symbolic classification is to raise again the issue of the relationship between the micro and macro levels of analysis-between individuals making strategic choices in interaction and normatively defined institutional frameworks. I repeat that I agree with Mitchell, whom I do not regard as a transactional analyst, in viewing these two levels of analytical abstraction as complementary rather than as alternatives, though I think also that one may be emphasised much more than the other, to the latter's possible detriment. The concept which seems to lock these two levels in flexible but balanced complementarity is that of "role."

Have we really recognised Nadel's contribution here? As well as viewing role as an intermediary between society and the individual, he recognised it as operating "in that strategic area where individual behaviour becomes social conduct."[1] Even more importantly, he argued that the concept of role was based as much on systems of "linguistic" (meaning "verbal") classification as on observation of "constancies of behaviour" (1956: 20). In other words, "roles" are more than consistent ways in which people carry out tasks; they are above all verbally identifiable. The distinction is akin to the etic/emic one. The question is: With whose verbal identifications do we start our analysis of other societies? With our own semantic labels or with those of the society under study?

This is not quite the simple methodological question it seems. Though in our distinction between "society" and "culture" we always attempt not to confuse our "subjective" with our "objective" criteria, we tend to use the concept of role "objectively," superimposing a seemingly agreed set of terms for distinct types of social conduct. At the most general level we talk of ritual experts, political representatives, jural spokesmen, economic managers, homestead heads, and so on; and at the most specific we identify witches, doctors, priests, warriors, elders, chiefs, plaintiffs, defendants, litigants, entrepreneurs, and others. Such concepts as role differentiation, role reinforcement, role conflict, and role deviance are also used in this "objective" manner.

Now it is precisely through the use of such agreed "etic" concepts that social anthropology and sociology are able to formulate hypotheses and test them cross-culturally. They are part of our common language of discourse without which communication becomes impossible. They may sometimes reflect the dispositions and prejudices of centuries of Judeo-Christian thought, but they are all we have.

Nevertheless, though with Berreman (1966) I balk at the extreme formalism of much ethnoscience, I share the concern expressed by Sturtevant (1964) and others at the continuing tendency in much anthropology to omit any systematic discussion of how these imposed classifications relate to classifications of the same activities in the particular culture (see Whiteley, 1966). Does the culture have a specific term for plaintiff, for defendant, or for witness? Does it have many such terms for what we would identify as one role? Or are some of our roles expressed only by phrases (i.e., paroles) in the culture's language, phrases which have to be created anew every time the person's activity is described? There is, in other words, an emic as well as an etic classification of forms of social conduct, and the relationship between them is essentially that between what we commonly call "subjective" and "objective" criteria. But whereas the description "subjective" suggests "ideal" or "imagined" phenomena, supposedly observed by us in the minds of our informants and distinct from the "factual objectivity" solely dependent on our own observations and judgments, the emic/etic distinction places both views of culture within a verbal and ultimately linguistic framework. Is this an advantage? It supposedly is, for that kind of study in which one wishes on the one hand to place systematic emphasis upon the cultural meanings which actors attach to events and on the other hand to avoid exaggerating the uniqueness of a particular culture. The etic, if the linguistic analogy is correct, represents a theoretically limited range of "roles," only some of which are socially significant in a particular culture and only some of which are given consistent semantic identification.

In practice it is neither possible nor necessarily fruitful to attempt an etic classification of all the roles (even assuming agreement on the definition of this concept) identified in human cultures. For American society alone,

Klapp (1962) is reported to have identified a folk classification of over 800 roles (Sturtevant 1964). It may be here that the analogy with phonetics, concerned as it is with a technically limited human physical capacity for making communicable sounds, breaks down. For role, as a concept, cannot be reduced to physical features. Moreover, it is an element of man's symbolic creativity which, by definition, is unlimited. Our "etic" classification of roles is, in the end, no more than the somewhat arbitrary collection of concepts which we use in sociological discourse.

So, to return to my question, do we start our field work by fitting this collection of concepts to our observations? Or do we start with a folk classification of "social types" – that is, roles operated by members of the particular society in which we are working? Though the two must constantly be kept in mind and seen against each other, I find persuasive the case for explicitly and systematically starting with the people's own classification. Indeed, I suspect that, less systematically, this is what we always do, but then we slip from the vernacular terms and phrases to our neater analytical ones. In the process of translation from folk concepts to "scientific" ones, we not only distort emic features to fit them to our own way of thinking (cf. Douglas 1973: 27), we also miss the opportunity of tracing changes going on within the folk classifications. Consider, for example, the gradual adoption of loan words in place of an earlier variety of phrases, many formed on the spot, to describe "new" or innovatory roles and objects. This movement from the use of a wide and potentially infinite variety of phrases to the use of a single word or limited number of words represents not only a transition to phonemic economy and specificity, but also the development of formal terminological categories out of more wordy functional ones (Bruner *et al.*, 1956, in Spradley 1972: 173). From a psychological perspective, Bruner illustrates the development thus: "From 'things I can drive this tent stake with' we move to the concept 'hammer' and from there to mechanical force.'"

The Giriama of Kenya, among whom I worked, seem not to have a single vernacular term for "entrepreneur." Since World War II, entrepreneurs in their current, "capitalist" form (defined in Parkin 1972: 8) have emerged in numbers in the area in which I worked. The "traditional" term *shaha*[2], which refers to a person of wealth and authority, could conveniently be used to refer to entrepreneurs. Elders do use it, but less often than such phrases as *atumia enye mali* (literally, "elders having property") or simply *enye mali* ("having property") and other, less common phrases. The Swahili-Arabic loan term *mtajiri* ("rich merchant") and sometimes even the abstract term *utajiri* ("wealth") tend to be used by younger men, though all age categories of men (not women) appear to be equally competent in Swahili. The apparent partial eclipse of the more traditional term *shaha* by the

Swahili root term *-tajiri*, conceptually mediated by intervening phrases, tells us something of the ideological conflict going on in Giriama. Elders by no means fully accept the customary legitimacy of modem capitalistic entrepreneurship and, it may be speculated, are reluctant to attach the term *shaha*, with its sense of wealth incurred through legitimate authority, to this new phenomenon.

It is almost inevitable that, as in other languages, both types of reference, the variable phrase (the "functional" or descriptive category) and the invariable word (the formal category), will continue to coexist, the former perhaps increasingly the euphemism or circumlocution for the latter. It is precisely this coexistence of the two types of signification that permits the fitting of new concepts to existing lexicons, for varying phrases can smuggle in modifications of "meaning" beneath the single term to which the phrases are perceived to be attached. We can speculate that the changes in connotation of such well-known anthropological terms as "native," "primitive," and "tribe" have been mediated through innumerable attached phrases of this kind. The loan word, by contrast, may represent a terminological abridgment of concepts which challenge too fundamentally and rapidly some key cultural rules and ideologies. This goes counter to the conventional view that loan terms are adopted because they already depict a particular practice. Sometimes this is indeed the case. But often the borrowed term by no means replicates the original "meaning"; consider the famous pan-Indian and African example of *hoteli*, which refers to a cafe/eating house/shop rather than to a place offering accommodation – for what sense would there be in paying for accommodation when there are likely to be "relatives" nearby to provide it? In the Giriama example, the Swahili-Arabic root term *-tajiri*, insofar as it is used more by young than by older men, parallels a growing cleavage in the society between young farmers who are accumulating property and those who are losing it (the latter conceptualised as "elders"). In other words, this "drastic" adoption of a loan word corresponds with a recent economic cleavage which is itself associated with cognitive dissonance – in the sense that disputes about appropriate and inappropriate behaviour centre on a perceived conflict between what I earlier called altruistic and negotiable ideologies, associated respectively with property-losing elders and entrepreneurial younger men. I shall return to this ethnography later.

It is not the adoption of loanwords with which I am specially concerned. I used the loan word as an extreme example of the formalisation of diffuse modes of classification in single words rather than phrases. A folk concept of "role" or "social type" (like that of "policeman" or the *Nuer kuaar muon/kuaar twac*, meaning "leopard-skin chief") is of course a formalised abridgment of the same kind: like Turner's symbol it condenses a fan of meanings around a core within a single acoustic form. Put simply, then, the verbal concept of a role is a symbol. This is hardly surprising for, as Sapir noted long ago, the word is the symbol of all symbols. But the verbalisation of social type, which we call a culturally recognised role, contains within its particular symbolic configuration specific information about the expectations, aims, and qualities of actors, and even about some of the rules for interaction.

The wheel is coming full circle and we can talk again about the analysis of exchange. The idea that verbalised roles are symbols, the information from which is constantly and selectively exchanged by persons in interaction, is surely central to that general field which, after Blumer 's original coining of the term we call symbolic interactionism. Consider, for example, Blumer's and Mead's discussion of role taking (Blumer 1969, in Spradley 1972: 76). The overlap between symbolic interactionism and the work of Homans, Barth, Kapferer, Blau, and other transactional analysts has become increasingly obvious to anthropologists. The difference can be crudely stated thus: Symbolic interactionism focuses on the exchange of ideas or concepts, on the assumption that the individual in interaction uses them to direct his behaviour in such a way that the result will be what he interprets as a harmonic fit between his own and other people's views of his role[3]. There is no explicit use of the notions of maximisation and rationality. Transactional analysis is centred on such notions and is concerned with the exchange of "values" (both conceptual and material) without respect to and commonly in the face of any consideration of a harmonic fit between the actor's and other persons' perceptions of his role. Transactional analysis emphasises the points of disjunction and negotiation in a relationship, while symbolic interactionism emphasises the areas of common, even if newly interpreted, conceptual understanding. Both are concerned with the generation of new social forms; these forms are seen on the one hand as resulting from negotiated exchange in which the two partners compete for dominance, and on the other hand as arising from mutual adjustment to a shared interpretation of the meaning of the relationship. My contrast ignores the partial overlap and is of course highly simplified; it might be argued that Blau and Kapferer have at least half a foot in the field of symbolic interactionism. But I believe that the contrast represents the tendencies inherent in the two approaches.

I think that by analysing interaction (a) as the exchange of verbalised roles and (b) in the context of altruistic and negotiable ideologies as I defined them. we go some way toward accommodating the two approaches within the same analysis. The distinctive feature of my approach, I think, is that I emphasise not just the general exchange of concepts or "values" but more particularly the exchange of folk conceptualisations of roles, expressed in the language of the culture concerned. My methodological starting point is the axiom that in all cultures altruistic and negotiable ideologies coexist, but their respective degrees of legitimacy as normative rules of social conduct covary both with situation or "domain" and with time. I turn now to apply these ideas to my own field data. As always in social anthropology, we begin less by asking our informants preselected questions (for we lack the categories to do so) than by listening to them asking each other, usually through an interpreter. Ideally at least, mastery of the language will eventually enable us to move from the position of an audience to that of a participant.

An Ethnography

An early vivid introduction to the Giriama of Kenya was a meeting at a local trading centre in mid-1966, two and a half years after that country's independence, between government and political party officials and local people, including men and women of all ages and also children. The meeting was conducted almost entirely in Swahili and I had no difficulty in following it, though most later meetings of a more localised kind were conducted in the closely related Giriama vernacular, which I had to learn. From this linguistic point of view, the field work situation was not typical, though I did what most field workers would do and simply listened.

As at many such meetings in this immediate post-independence era, the call was for communal unity and cooperative economic progress. Older men stated that, though economic development was desirable, many men who had achieved great personal wealth returned insufficient wealth to such cooperative enterprises as new school buildings, communal commercial ventures, scholarship funds for bright pupils and so on. They referred to such entrepreneurial men as *wafanya maendeleo* (swahili for "makers of progress"), clearly and publicly indicating respect for the principle of economic development. They also reminded the gathering that the men were nevertheless no more than *watoto wetu* (Swahili for "our children"), with a style and emphasis that suggested that this alone gave the moral weight to their accusation.

The counter to this accusation came not from anyone identified, either by himself or others as an enterprising farmer/trader, but from the officials who, after first paying deferential tribute to the wisdom of these elders (*wazee* in Swahili), urged them not to impose their "old ways" on the "young and educated" lest economic development be jeopardised.

Two examples given of such old ways were (a) allowing relatives and family and close friends (summarised by the Swahili *jamaa*) to "consume" individually acquired wealth and (b) "spending" time, labour and money on "medicines," "curing" (*dawa* and *uganga*), sorcery (*uchawi*), and ceremonial festivities (the officials used the term *matanga*, "funerals," but seemingly referred to other ceremonies as well).

This is a tight abridgment of many hours of talking. From it we can discern a perceived opposition between "elders" and the "young and educated. There is also the suggestion of an alliance between the latter and government officials. Though both sides ostensibly agreed on the value of economic development, the two were spoken of as opposed on the question of which set of normative rules should be followed in distributing the acquired wealth. Reduced still further, the debate concerned the respective moralities of an ideology of individualistic enterprise. only ultimately and indirectly benefiting the wider community. and an ideology of communal contributions. The first justifies the negotiable, entrepreneurial roles of individuals as both the means and end of economic development. The second justifies these features only insofar as they are subsumed in an overriding altruistic obligation.

This familiar twofold division of moral claims occurred at just about every meeting that I attended and was expressed in both the Giriama vernacular and Swahili. It is presumably universal and occurs in a variety of forms and emphases. It was stressed among Giriama as a result of recent changes which have been compressed within living memories.

The particular cultural emphasis (as illustrated, for example, by the elders' categorisation of wealthy, entrepreneurial men as "our children") takes the form of a belief, widely held by all age groups and largely but not completely documented by figures (Parkin 1972: 3), that contemporary Giriama society has seen the emergence of rich young men and poor older men. This situation is stated to be a reversal of the customary expectation that control over such resources as patrimony should be the prerogative of biologically senior men. By drawing on existing cultural terms of address and reference which stress generational distinctiveness, including the use of teknonymy, the speakers can discuss the economic cleavage as an intergenerational one. In other words, the same issue can be talked about in two culturally alternative ways.

We can return at this point to my distinction between the variable phrase (the functional category) and the invariable word (the formal category). When Giriama explain a dispute between the rich young and the poor old as caused by intergenerational conflict, they tend to draw on condensed word formulas for describing such familiar events-that is, they use a kind of ethno-jargon.

A witness to the dispute may condemn a young man 's "insolence" simply by declaring, "I call that elder my brother, yet I am called father by X," implying that X (possibly a man in his forties) is therefore son to the elder and should heed the rules of generational seniority. A switch in the classification-"I call that elder my brother, yet I am also called brother (or brother-in-law) by X"-implies that in the speaker's view the rules of generational seniority have been misapplied and that perhaps a moot between elders who are "equals" should be held to decide the issue. And so on.

But when Giriama explain the dispute in bald, "exploitative" economic terms, they are much more likely to use variable phrases created more or less on the spot, and such familiar "secondary" elaborations as "He achieved his wealth by ensorcelling/poisoning his kin/neighbours/rivals." More recently, they might say that wealth was achieved by "bribing" (using the Swahili word *ku-honga*) government officials.

Giriama society has always had its wealthy men who could be seen by the outside observer to be every bit as "exploitative" as any contemporary entrepreneur. But the Giriama distinguish between what I translate as the "redistributional" economy and the modern "capitalist" economy. According to the Giriama, the former men of wealth (*shaha*) did not permanently alienate the property but channelled it back into a community of supporters; in the "capitalist" economy, on the other hand, as a result of cash cropping and external market factors, property (i.e. land and trees) is seen as permanently alienated, with no compensatory redistribution. These are, I repeat, folk conceptualisations; as in any other society, "redistributional" and "capitalist" exchange spheres continue to coexist, though the larger economic transactions occur in the latter at present.

The terms "redistributional" and "capitalist" are actually inadequate translations for the two contrasting sets of Giriama concepts or ideologies. The first refers to set terms indicating rules for holding, allocating, and acquiring property on the basis of generational and agnatic seniority. Giriama justify such rules as being at the heart of Giriama "traditional" notions of property. They frequently link the concept of redistribution to specific customs, in particular the agreement among neighboring palm-tree owners not to sell their palm wine to each other at significant profit: a mental tally is kept of such "sales" with a view to ironing out any undue profits made by a neighbour, though large producers may sell with moral impunity at a distance from their neighbourhood. This profitless exchange sphere shades into "pure" gift giving among kin, affines, and neighbours, as evidenced by the expectation that people will contribute amply to collective drinking and eating ceremonies and by the demand, described above, that successful entrepreneurial men contribute some of their wealth to communal enterprises. It is this set of "traditional" concepts which is constantly attacked by government officers as a drain on economic development.

The second set of concepts, that of "capitalism," is manifested in the disapproval of *permanent* sales of land to non-agnates for the benefit of young men; this disapproval is expressed particularly by those who are dispossessed yet have some kind of political voice-in other words, poor elders. That is its "negative" side. Its "positive" side is, as we saw from the account of the meeting, the encouragement given it by government officials, who reward successful entrepreneurship with loans and who condemn communal restrictions on individual enterprise. Bearing in mind my earlier definitions, I think we can identify these two respectively as overarching altruistic and negotiable ideologies.

Let me link up much of the foregoing discussion and suggest that the three broad categories of "social types," the poor elders, the entrepreneurial young men, and the government officials, are verbally associated with these two ideologies as shown in Table 6.1. This schema depicts two contrasting sets of claims not just about how political authority and economic privilege should be exercised but also about how it should be discussed.

Let me focus on the left-hand part of the table and look at the key vernacular terms which denote, in a symbolically condensed way, an altruistic authority system. We start with a Giriama taxonomy of social types (i.e., roles) of authority. In a number of unprompted conversations with Giriama elders the following blueprint emerged: The Giriama "government" is headed by *autumia a kaya* (singular: *mutumia wa kaya*), meaning elders of the kaya. The kaya is a kind of traditional capital occupied nowadays only by a handful of senior elders and their wives, but it is a symbolic rallying point in anti-government demonstrations. As well as agreeing that these elders

Table 6.1 Two Ideologies and the Support Expressed for Them by Various "Social Types" Among the Giriama of Kenya

Altruistic Ideology	**Negotiable Ideology**	
Poor Elders	**Rich Young Men**	**Government Officials**
Support for the ideology is expressed mainly in the vernacular through the use of key "customary" words, each a symbolic condensation of cultural rules and concepts about the acquisition of property according to generational and agnatic seniority.	Support for the ideology is expressed both in Swahili (mainly loan words) and in the vernacular, mainly through variable phrases, themselves reflecting the still half-defined and partially accepted concepts about acquiring property in the face of generational and agnatic seniority.	Support for the ideology is expressed in Swahili through a possibly equal mixture of formal and functional terms (set words and variable phrases).

head the "government," Giriama of all ages speak of them as the foremost experts on traditional lore and ritual. In addition, they are supposed to have some legitimate supervisory powers not only over local ritual activities but also over a number of secret societies of male elders which were apparently strong 60 years ago (see Champion 1967). They are said to belong to the most senior living age-grade (*rika*). They are contrasted with other elders who are not members of the *kaya* and who are assumed to be of less senior age-grades. The term for such an elder is simply *mutumia*.

Any man beyond the age of about 50 will be called *mutumia*, but only an elder who is a homestead head will be called *mwenye mudzi* (literally, "owner of the homestead/village"). In the contemporary period of rapid economic change involving much dispute over rights to land and trees, neighbourhood and lineage/clan moots, called kambi, are as active as ever. To sit on them as a regular witnesscum-mediator (*mugiriama* or *chodherwa*) – not just as a witness called to give evidence for the occasion only – a man must be not merely a *mutumia* but also a *mwenye mudzi*. In practice the jural sphere overlaps the ritual one, for most local moots use mystical oaths (*viraho*) and, less frequently, a shaman (*muganga wa mburuga*; literally, "doctor of the oracle"). Of all these roles, that of the shaman is the only one filled almost exclusively by either women or young men, not by elders. Giriama also say that most senior elders who regularly attend moots are medicine doctors (singular: *muganga wa mukoba/kombo*).

One term, *mwenyetsi*, which once meant "territorial section head," has lost this meaning nowadays and refers to a Kenya citizen generally (cf. Swahili *mwenyeji*); it is not used to distinguish Giriama from each other. Other terms are *muhongohi* (literally, "the main pole supporting the beams of a house"), applied to the most senior member of the six main kaya elders, and *dzumbe*, applied to a government chief or sub-chief. (Interestingly, *shaha*, with its meaning of authority with wealth, was rarely mentioned in discussing authority per se but would sometimes come into other discussions about past or "traditional" men of property.)

I did not carry out word-frequency tests to check the degree of lexical predictability of these terms, but I believe from actual accounts that there is a high probability that most will occur when Giriama elders explain or discuss their "own" authority system. I stress that these are not terms which I have had to dig out, so to speak, from the language; rather, they encountered me frequently and I had to use them in turn. If one were to investigate a particular item of conversation including these terms, one would discover a number of organisational principles by which the terms were related to each other, for instance, neighbourhood, kinship, friendship, and religion. As it is, two main principles are apparent from my abstract: authority is dependent on divisions of age and generation, including both agnatic and non-agnatic seniority; and jural authority shades over into ritual authority. Lumping these together in a single summary statement, one might say that elders rule through their command over ritual resources and the redistribution (but not monopolisation) of economic resources. This is a familiar sociological definition of authority in subsistence societies with limited movable property, simple technologies, and low rates of role differentiation and specialisation. And it is no accident that, by this process of abstraction, we find that the "emic" Giriama and the "etic" sociological definitions of authority converge. For Giriama as much as for the sociologist, the definition represents an ideal type. The cultural expressions of the definition may differ, but within their repetitive codes these definitions depend on formal terminological categories – that is, invariable words. The words are *mutumia*, *mwenye mudzi*, *rika*, *muganga*, and so on, on the one hand, and "multiplex," "undifferentiated," "unspecialised roles," and so on, on the other hand.

For the reasons I have already given, relating to the use of ascriptive generational rules for acquiring property, the Giriama definition of customary authority does seem to presuppose an altruistic ethic. The ideal that elders, in contrast to government magistrates and doctors, provide their jural and ritual expertise not for personal gain but simply because it is "the custom" actually receives some empirical support. As I have explained elsewhere (1972), proportionately few entrepreneurial men are elders, and of those eiders who are ritual specialists few earn incomes which approximate those of enterprising farmers. Most significantly, it is in the name of "custom" that such elders continue to dispose of land and trees, selling them to raise cash for sons' bridewealth, lavish ceremonies, and medicines even in the face of genuine poverty.

I tum now to consider how the negotiable ideology is expressed by predominantly young, entrepreneurial men who are encouraged by government officials in their policy of economic development based on the individualistic expansion of productive capital. The question now is: what conceptual channel enables enterprising young Giriama farmers to "smuggle in" their own perception of the local-level authority system? After the preceding analysis of economic changes in Giriama society, it should not be surprising to find these young farmers legitimising their new roles by "qualifying" and elaborating on the normally less variable connotations of such authority terms as those listed above. That is to say, by implicit reference they verbally redefine these key role terms. An alternative though probably less frequently used channel is to employ such loan words as *mtajiri* to provide a focus for a new or modified concept.

The modification of a key role term's meaning is achieved by juxtaposing it with a phrase, the meaning of which is actually at variance with that connoted by the role term when used by, say, an important elder. The result is to introduce an ambivalence or even a semantic contradiction within the key role term. Should the altered meaning catch on, one may then find elders themselves moving toward a usage of the word with this new meaning.

To take an example, it is frequently asserted by both elders and young men (a) that *mutumia* can only be used to refer to an aged man or a man of a senior *rika* (age-grade), and (b) that a *mwenye mudzi* (homestead head) must be a *mutumia*. But on other occasions *mutumia* is used as a term of address and sometimes of reference to the relatively few men who are homestead heads but are not otherwise biologically or genealogically senior. In other words, the explicit rule is that a *mutumia* is necessarily an aged person and that only a *mutumia* may be a *mwenye mudzi*; it is qualified in practice by an implicit rule that a *mwenye mudzi* must be a *mutumia*, even when his age and genealogical status suggest otherwise. This semantic ambiguity of *mutumia* was noted as long ago as 1891 when Taylor (p. 37) pointed out that as "a title of respect" for an old man (or woman) *mutumia* was also "sometimes applied to a young person in a position of authority." We do not know the proportion of such young men or the nature of their authority. Homesteads were very much larger then, but it may have been possible in a few instances for a young man to become head, in the absence of father's brothers or close agnates able or willing to take on the position. The meaning of *mutumia* would here be ambiguous with regard to the man's age but not, as nowadays, with regard to his genealogical seniority and his wealth. Now the few young men (in their thirties and forties) who are homestead heads tend to be well above the average in wealth and entrepreneurial achievements, and they constitute a relatively recent status category resulting from the economic changes described earlier. Their designation as *mwenye mudzi* and therefore as "respected" *mutumia* legitimates not only their status but also the negotiable ideology by which they achieved it, the ideology which is seen to flout an altruistic idealisation of custom. That is to say, their designation by these role terms legitimises their permanent purchase of trees and land and their alienation of this property from agnatic descent groups; their necessarily selective refusals to contribute "generously" to communal enterprises or "needy" individuals, perhaps agnates, other kinsmen, or affines; and their increasing use of government courts and legal facilities in preference to the local-level moots. The old ambiguity contained in the role term *mutumia* which Taylor indicated seems therefore to have undergone a shift which is to the ideological benefit of entrepreneurial young men.

The conferment of legitimacy is not all one way, however. The redistributional-cum-altruistic ideology continues to be legitimised by the recognition of elders' mediatory and ritual roles, which do remain vitally important in a society in which land disputation and a common belief in the mystical cause of such misfortune require these informal sources of adjudication and cure to supplement those of the government courts and hospital. To give an example, it seems very likely, on the basis of an analysis of life histories (cf. Taylor 1891: 82), that 25 or 30 years ago the roles of diviner-shaman (*muganga wa mburuga/kitswa/pepo*) and medical doctor (*muganga wa mukoba/kombo*) could and often would be performed by one male elder, with some elders emphasising one or the other as a specialty. The formal verbal distinction now regularly made between the two roles would not have been expressed so frequently, if at all; a ritual specialist would be called simply *muganga*, with further contextual elaboration needed to indicate which of his special skills was being referred to. Nowadays the two main functions of divination and therapy are performed by separate persons who are thereby designated as distinct social types. More than this, medical doctors are exclusively male elders (genuinely senior) while shamans are either young males (usually under 30) or women (whose position warrants more discussion than can be attempted here). In the jargon this is what we might call a simple case of role differentiation and specialisation. It has paralleled, within the same time period, the development of an economic cleavage, conceptualised as an opposition between a minority of wealthy young homestead heads and the majority of more senior ones. During this period the role of medical doctor appears to have become more profitable while that of diviner-shaman has become relatively much less advantageous (though even the doctors are poor by comparison with the young entrepreneurial farmers, to whom they continue to sell land and trees).

It is striking that this precise differentiation into the two types of *muganga*, the one older and earning more than the other, corresponds inversely with the appearance of a number of young homestead heads who are often much wealthier than their more numerous older counterparts. In noting this inverse homology, I have interpreted it as one of a number of customary concessions non-consciously given by entrepreneurial young men to elders in exchange for the jural protection and freedom from customary constraints which they need in order to pursue their expansionist aims (1972: 15, 38). That is to say, the young men acknowledge the superior ritual powers of elders not only by paying them medical fees but also by using the precise terminological distinction between the two types of *muganga*. In exchange, their anti-customary entrepreneurial activities are implicitly legitimised by the elders, whose expertise they have sought, under the cover of the elders' "agreement" to redefine such terms as *mutumia* and *mwenye mudzi* in the way I have described. Over the long term, of course, the exchange is unfairly balanced, because few medical doctors enjoy a consistently high rate of success; moreover, doctors can easily, through repeated failure, become subject to accusations that they are against rather than for humanity – in other words, that they practice sorcery. Entrepreneurial farmers, on the other hand, continue to amass the1r holdings of land and trees. Indeed, it can legitimately be argued that the young homestead heads cede ritual potency for economic freedom and that, in doing so, they secure a bargain.

But we must also place equal emphasis on the taxonomy and semantic interrelatedness of role terms, through which this process of bargain and differentiation is identified in the culture. The system of exchange here described is not only that of individuals formulating strategies to maximise personal benefit by transacting ritual for economic "goods." Each individual exchange relationship runs along the lines of a wider exchange of new, modified, or existing concepts of role, which are made cognitively salient in the culture by being transacted in verbal form. Speakers shift back and forth from formal verbal categories of the conceptually condensed and lexically predictable kind to functionally descriptive ones which are conceptually more diffuse and lexically less predictable. But they do so within channels largely outlined by an underlying homology of ideas.

This homology may be regarded as a kind of "pristine" set of ideal correlations as the preceding material has demonstrated:

(1) Age:youth :: (politico-jural) seniority:juniority
(2) Age:youth :: wealth:poverty
(3) Age:youth :: ritual power:ritual impotence

The homology could be picked out from just about any "traditional" African ethnography, and possibly from other ethnographies, on the basis of the words and phrases which people in the culture use to compare and contrast and thereby to evaluate social conduct. This chapter provides an example in which the first and third sets remain unchanged: elders are still sought as the most important witnesses and mediators; and supreme ritual power remains a vested attribute of age. But there is also a partial inversion of the second set through the tendency for young homestead heads to be wealthier than older ones. It is also worth noting that a short-lived inversion of the third set occurred among Giriama in 1966 in an anti-sorcery movement in which young men temporarily dispossessed elders of their ritual medicines and in some cases proclaimed their own better methods of cure (Parkin 1968). The more enduring, but by no means permanent, inversion of the second set described in this chapter can be seen in Giriama contemporary modes of explaining disputes and misfortunes; I believe it to be associated with a threatened shift from a primarily altruistic to a negotiable ideology of exchange relations, and with a movement from a primarily redistributional to a capitalist economy.

The attempt to relate an underlying explanatory logic to observable behaviour invites the familiar charge of mystifying the analysis. But the analysis does have an empirical starting point, namely the words people use to identify social conduct. The homology of underlying ideas and their partial inversion do seem to reflect a "shadow"[4] in the way in which people speak of social conduct: new "meanings" are attached to role terms, or new role terms are affixed to old "meanings." It is not Simply that new relationships are generated by this process; a reordering of concepts and signs is also given legitimation.

Conclusion

An analytic and theoretical concern with exchange as the basis of communication is implicit in all anthropology. If we regard one broad category of the theory as focused on actors then the antithesis is the type of theory that sees actors themselves as also, at a different remove, objects of exchange. The first has as its basic postulate that man's maximisation of gains over costs is a fundamental motivating principle in social interaction. The second can be illustrated by a quotation from Ardener (1971: xlv): "The terminology of semiotics can be expressed more mechanistically through communication theory. We have to visualize that the message on one channel becomes itself the channel for meta-messages. Lévi-Strauss (1963: 61) implicitly states the general case, from the particular case of women: *human beings speak, but they are themselves also symbolic elements in a communication system.*"

The second comprises the first. The actors transact valued goods in a zero-sum game; but the valued nature of such goods (both material and nonmaterial) locates the actor himself in a wider system of classification. These systems of classification are themselves not static: the signs and meanings of which they are made up may be transposed; or new concepts may be given meaning through existing signs.

Two such systems of classification which appear universal in human cultures are what I simply call altruistic and negotiable ideologies. That is to say, I see actors legitimising their social conduct by reference to these two ideologies. An altruistic ideology may be regarded as the cultural expression, writ large, of a notion of the "pure" gift; a negotiable ideology holds, in Calvinist fashion, that everything has its price and must be paid for. A strong tendency in transactional analysis is to view both as manifestations of "maximising man" and to argue that, in the end, even altruistic ideals may be given or taken as concessions in social relations according to the free play of market forces of supply and demand-in other words, that even the "pure" gift is either a cost, an investment, or a reward. But, as well as being tautologous, this view ignores the extent to which an altruistic ideology, including the notion of the "pure" gift, achieves conceptual and semantic distinctiveness only by standing in an opposed relationship to a negotiable/exploitative ideology. We have to understand the process by which there is a shift in emphasis in a society from one kind of ideology to the other for the legitimation of particular events and activities. To include the actor in this process, we have to look at the culturally designated roles which he is regarded as playing, for folk concepts of roles are crucial elements in any ideology of legitimation. Just as we may say that a system of classification "changes" by transpositions of its constituent signs and meanings, so we may say that an ideology "changes" by transpositions of the cultural meanings of roles and the verbal forms in which they are expressed.

A folk taxonomy of authority roles which achieves a high degree of lexical predictability through the regular use of one or two "words" for each role (e.g. the familiar *kuaar muon/twac* for the Nuer leopard-skin chief) expresses an ideology in a conceptually abridged and condensed form. Changes in a taxonomy may come about by the incorporation of a loan word; but most changes in meaning of the individual "words" regularly used to describe roles seem to result from repeated qualifications or elaborations expressed in accompanying phrases. Thus, through the medium of *paroles* of infinite verbal variety but similar conceptual thrust, the most formalised elements of the taxonomy are altered. To take one example, I have suggested that a partial shift in the meaning of *mwenye mudzi* among Giriama (from "one who rules by dint of age" to "one who rules by virtue of economic self-sufficiency") has come about in this way, in correspondence with an increase in the legitimation of a negotiable rather than altruistic ideology of authority roles.

But I have also suggested that this change of meaning of a key role term within the taxonomy has in tum modified the meaning of some other role terms by virtue of contrastive or homologous relationships to them. Pocock (1961:76; cited in Ardener 1971: lix) provides a superbly crisp quotation from Adam Ferguson (1767) which illustrates this phonemic character of role terms: "The titles of fellow citizen and countryman unopposed to those of alien and foreigner, to which they refer, would fall into disuse and lose their meaning." The exchange of role terms is therefore not random; it generally follows an underlying cultural template of ideas, a kind of *langue*, which is also recognisable in other cultures.

It must be individuals whom we observe in verbal exchanges of role terms, the result of which at one level of abstraction is to affirm a switch in emphasis from one to the other set of legitimising claims. At the more fundamental level of abstraction is the much more difficult task of finding the principles by which one key role term and not another has been subjected to significant alteration of meaning; or has been supplemented by a loanword; or has been dropped altogether from the folk taxonomy. To do this we need to discover how the concepts behind the taxonomy relate systematically both to each other and to the constituent role terms making up the taxonomy.

Notes

(1) Cf. Nadel's "governing property" of a role (1956: 34ff.).

(2) Although this term is in fact of Swahili and Arabic origin, Taylor (1891: 24–83) regarded it as unquestionably Giriama at the time of his writing.

(3) The following is one of the many passages in Blumer's work which aptly summarise these features: "[Symbolic interactionism recognises that] one has to fit one's own line of action in some manner to the actions of others. The actions of others have to be taken into account and cannot be regarded as merely an arena for the expression of what one is disposed to do or sets out to do" (Blumer 1969: 72).

(4) E. Ardener (1978) introduces the concept of the language-shadow. I acknowledge the danger of allowing an attractive metaphor to delude us into crediting it with analytical usefulness. But I do think that this one provides a way to apprehend the relationship between cultural "thought", speech and action.

References

Ardener, E. (ed.) (1971) *Social Anthropology and Language*. ASA Monograph No. 10. London: Tavistock.

——(1978) Some outstanding problems in the analysis of events. In E. Schwimmer (ed.) *Yearbook of Symbolic Anthropology. London: Hurst* pp. 103–120.

Bailey, F.G. (1969) *Stratagems and Spoils*. Oxford. Blackwell.

Barth, F. (1966) Models of Social Organization. Royal Anthropological Institute Occasional Paper No. 23. London.

Berreman, G.D. (1966) Anemic and emetic analyses in social anthropology. *American Anthropologist* 68 (2), 346–354. Reprinted in Spradley 1972.

Blau, P.M. (1964) *Exchange and Power in Social Life*. New York: John Wiley.

Blumer, H. (1969) *Symbolic Interactionism: Perspective and Method*. Engelwood Cliffs, N.J.: Prentice-Hall. Abstracted in Spradley 1972.

Boissevain, J. (1968) The place of non-groups in the social sciences. *Man*. N.S. 3 (4), 542–556.

Bruner, J.S., *et al*. (1956) *A Study of Thinking*. London: John Wiley. Abstracted in Spradley 1972.

Burling, R. (1962) Maximization theories and the study of economic anthropology. *American Anthropologist* 64 (4), 802–821.

Caplan, L. (1971) Cash and kind: two media of bribery in Nepal. *Man*, N.S. 6 (4), 266–278.

Champion, A.M. (1967) *The Agiryama of Kenya*. Royal Anthropological Institute Occasional Paper No. 25. London.

Cohen, A. (1969) Political Anthropology: The analysis of the symbolism of power relations. *Man*. N.S. 4 (2), 215–235.

Davis, J. (1973) Forms and norms: The economy of social relations. *Man*. N.S. 8 (2), 159–176.

Douglas, M. (1973) Self-evidence. In Royal Anthropological Institute, *Proceedings* 1972. London.

Ferguson, A. (1767) *An Essay in the History of Civil Society*.

Firth, R. (1951) *Elements of Social Organization*. London: Watts.

——(ed.) (1967) *Themes in Economic Anthropology*. ASA Monograph No. 6. London: Tavistock.

Gluckman, M. (1968) Psychological, sociological and anthropological explanations of witchcraft and gossip: a clarification. *Man*. N.S. 3 (1), 20–34.

Homans, G. Social behaviour as exchange. *American Journal of Sociology* 63, 597–606.

——(1961) *Social Behaviour: Its Elementary Forms*. London: Routledge and Kegan Paul.

Kapferer, B. (1972) *Strategy and Transaction in an African Factory*. Manchester: Manchester University Press.

Kennedy, J.G. (1967) Psychological and social explanations of witchcraft: a comparison of Clyde Kluckhohn and Evans Pritchard. *Man*. N.S. 2 (4), 216–225.

Klapp, O.E. (1962) *Heroes, Villains and Fools: The Changing American Character*. Engelwood Cliffs, N.J.: Prentice-Hall.

Lévi-Strauss, C. (1963) *Structural Anthropology*. Trans. C. Jacobson and B.G. Shoepf. New York: Basic Books.

Mauss, M. (1970) *The Gift*. Trans. I. Cunnison. London: Routledge and Kegan Paul.

Mitchell, C. (ed.) (1969) *Social Networks in Urban Situations*. Manchester: Manchester University Press.

Nadel, S.F. (1956) *The Theory of Social Structure*. London: Cohen and West.

Paine, R. (1967) What is gossip about? An alternative hypothesis. *Man*. N.S. 2 (4), 278–285.

Parkin, D. Medicines and Men of Influence. *Man*. N.S. 3 (3), 424–439.

——(1972) *Palms, Wine and Witnesses*. Scranton, Pa.: Chandler. London: Intertext.

Pocock, D.F. (1961) *Social Anthropology*. London and New York: Sheed and Ward.

Sahlins, M.D. (1965) On the sociology of primitive exchange. In M. Banton, ed., *The Relevance of Models for Social Anthropology*. ASA Monograph No. 1. London: Tavistock.

Spradley, J.P. (ed.) (1972) *Culture and Cognition: Rules, Maps and Plans*. Scranton, Pa.: Chandler.

Sturtevant, W.C. (1964) Studies in ethnoscience. *American Anthropologist* 66 (2), 99–131. Reprinted in Spradley 1972.

Taylor, W.E. (1891) *Giriama Vocabulary and Collections*. London: Society for Promoting Christian Knowledge.

Von Neuman, J. and Morgenstern, O. (1944) *Theory of Games and Economic Behaviour*. Princeton: Princeton University Press.

Whiteley, W.H. (1966) Social anthropology, meaning, and linguistics. *Man*. N.S. 1 (2), 139–157.

Part 2

Political and Formulaic Communication

Chapter 7. As noted by Stasch (2011: 160), there have been few overall reviews since Parkin (1984) of anthropological analyses of political language and rhetoric. This review, reproduced as Chapter 7, examines the argument made by Bloch (1975) and contested by Paine (1981) among others as to whether the rhetoric of political language does not just persuade its audience to believe in its propositions, but actually stifles the possibility of audience response and challenge through its grammatically and lexically governed formalism. *De facto,* such political language seeks unquestioning proto-physical compliance. However, it was suggested *pace* Bloch that, alongside their use of formulaic language, the political rhetorician has to anticipate audience reaction and therefore be ready in effect to shift stance and creatively negotiate the terms of appeal. It is this very variability inherent in live political language, as against written, static political tracts, that in fact characterises it. Formalism is thus one presentational mode and, as in religious language, may be unquestioned enough to induce listeners to comply with what is demanded of them. But formulaic language can generate its opposite such that listeners do not comply. This can happen if rhetoricians use tropes, especially metaphor and metonymy, to embellish their otherwise formulaic speech and persuade listeners. The very use of tropes can introduce new perspectives which an audience can adopt and interpret differently from and in opposition to the speaker. Thus, in its aim to persuade listeners to a point of view, political rhetoric may inadvertently draw the audience's attention to a contrary viewpoint. In other words, messages from the pulpit, so to speak, may sometimes persuade but may sometimes backfire as listeners pick up on the wider vision created by tropes and challenge the speaker who may even lose control of their dialogue. A political speaker has therefore to weigh their rhetorical 'performativity' against the possibility that this diverts audience response from the central message of the speech. Key cultural phrases or terms, including 'buzzwords' and enthymemes (i.e. packed-in syllogisms; Paine, 1981), sit between performative and formulaic pronouncements in that they are propositions packaged for special stylistic effect. Successful rhetorical strategy has to balance their usage: buzzwords and the like can easily be overdone and lose their effect and so require calculated restraint and timing.

Chapter 8. Nevertheless, as described in Chapter 8, formal and formulaic language remains an ideal in the minds of many educators and government authorities as the basis of the ideologically 'correct' national standard (Blommaert, 2009), with deviations from it seen by them as 'impure' language and therefore needing rectification. The chapter (Parkin, 1994) demonstrates this demand for rhetorical and general language 'purity' on the part of both religious and political authorities. In the case presented of a Muslim community, this insistence percolates down to local-level mosque leaders, or maalims, who regard everyday language purity as the hallmark of politeness and as therefore pleasing to God, which in effect equates civil with divine respectability. The rationale is evident in an explicit chain of associations according to the maalims: the 'purest' form of Swahili includes much Arabic-derived vocabulary; Arabic is the sanctified and ideal language of the Qur'an which Muslims should aim to know, with translations into other languages at best of secondary importance and sometimes rejected as unacceptable; the Arabic verses of the Qur'an are the words of God transmitted to Mohammed and therefore sacred; the injunction to speak the 'pure' Arabised form of Swahili is therefore to participate in divine inspiration. Alongside this Islamic perspective on the nature of Swahili and its relationship to other languages is that of secular, government educators who strive to teach standard Swahili in schools. They are concerned more with a different notion of language 'purity' than its religious instantiation, namely the 'correctness' of the formal, syntactical and grammatical features of the language. However, while religious language is thus presented as differing from its non-religious counterpart (Bowen, 1993; Keane, 1997a), both can use the hortatory techniques and strategies of rhetoric aimed at persuasion, admonition or enlightenment.

Chapter 9. A key component of religious rhetoric takes the form of sermons delivered on regular or special occasions. Chapter 9 (Parkin, 1985a) presents a case of the celebration of the Prophet's birthday called in Swahili *maulidi* (from the Arabic: مَولِد النَّبِيّ, romanised as *mawlidu n-nabiyyi*). In it, the maalim deviates from his prepared words to take the opportunity of a dispute occurring disruptively in the congregation among youths by referring to is as an example of their unacceptable and irreligious behaviour in modern times. He launches into a catalogue of the morally good qualities that should ideally constitute a Muslim and the evils that may otherwise define them, switching to heavily metaphorical language. This is rhetoric which moves from condemning human actions to identifying human frailties as a condition which only Islamic piety and worship can hope to overcome. Of note is how the youthful physical disruption of the religious occasion colours the language of the maalim who switches from praise of God and divinely inspired morality to condemnation of mortals and their moral depravity. The material or physical here becomes a defining feature of the discourse, thus echoing more widely how competing and sometimes violent religious factions (e.g. Sunni versus Shi'a) are commonly premised on the textual and linguistically material embeddedness of their respective self-justifications.

Chapter 10 (Parkin, 1985b) explores this case further by raising the question of what it is for listeners not only to accept such admonition but to believe in the validity of the maalim's moral claims as indicating the true path of (divine) knowledge. After all, and consistent with the observations above that listeners do not unthinkingly and unreflectively conform to what is being told them, they may question and challenge it, if not during the sermon itself but in the talk that follows it. The case reveals a paradox: formal sermons presuppose rhetoric premised on a generally universal public stereotype of people making up the congregation; yet unintended and unexpected interruptions of the prepared sermon (i.e. the youths' dispute and noise) make possible a deeper excavation of private and waywardly diverse human motivations and failings and its use in justifying the sermon's universal moral theme. The particular instance thus challenges and yet reinforces the maalim's general argument. Of relevance here is Keane's (1997b) reference to 'the relationship between the exteriority of language and its implications for the interiority of speakers … language can seem both deeply subjective (as an apparent medium of inner thought), and eminently social (as a preexisting system and a medium of communication)' and, we may add, as eminently able therefore to effect physical changes in the world and on such 'inner thought'.

The communicative struggle to define desirable personhood may, as in the case of the maalim, sometimes have to face and incorporate random challenges. But linguistically defined institutional checks sometimes play a role in stabilising notions of the moral person. The use of personal names is one such, as shown in chapter eleven.

Chapter 11 (Parkin, 1989) describes the Giriama of coastal Kenya, who are neighbours of first-language Swahili speakers and are historically mutually involved with them over the generations. The Giriama have a traditional naming system that, certainly until recently and probably still today, is very precise in its identification of persons as belonging to particular kinship, affinal, clanship and generational categories. The naming system is a cognitive map by which even complete strangers can locate each other in the wider knowledge of relatedness. They can use this map to build up more information about each other and so define each other as morally 'true' Giriama persons. This mutual knowledge is also micro-political in that it leads to details about Giriama-wide events and the part played in them by persons identified through their names as Giriama and their affiliations: for instance, are they of a rival clan or extended family with whom, say, on-going land disputes occur? The micro-political and inter-personal thus shade into each other through this particular naming system. More than this, named persons are always potentially political persons through the objectification that arises from being identified by a name or names and thence interpellated by, say, the state or religious organisation or other institution. Extending this point, names bring people and things into being: the nameless cannot really exist in any sustainable way. Being named as an identifiable person is thus double-edged: s/he has identity and being and possibly agency, but may lose that agency through the very fact of having been identified as, for example, a social deviant and therefore incarcerated as a prisoner or political undesirable.

Personal naming systems vary considerably across societies in the extent to which they provide such parameters of personhood. Some names are for life, some are of fleeting duration, others change at different stages of the lifecycle, the use of some is prohibited by certain categories of people or used only in certain contexts, and so on. The western nursery rhyme ditty arguing confidently that 'sticks and stones may break my bones, but names will never hurt me' clearly falls far short of the longer term and sometimes immediate material consequences of naming persons, some of them negative.

7 Political Language

The Development of a Field

It is curious that the classical and postclassical views of political oratory or rhetoric (Perelman 1974) were not the subjects of much study by the early generations of sociocultural anthropologists. Narratives, including myths, legends, fairy tales, and incantatory spells and chants, were recorded of course, but they were seen as charters for authority, or were sufficiently different and interesting to be explained in their own right as embedded cultural features. Malinowski's views have been regarded as typical; each Trobriand folktale is "owned" by a member of the community, to be recited only by him, while myths belong to clans and justify their claims to territory and autochthony. Yet Malinowski himself notes that "not all the 'owners' know how to thrill and to raise a hearty laugh, which is one of the main ends of such stories. A good raconteur has to change his voice in the dialogue, chant the ditties with due temperament, gesticulate, and in general play to the gallery" (Malinowski 1948: 80).

Malinowski usually has been attributed with the view that formulaic narratives do little more than validate political and property claims, a view most evident in his concept of phatic communion (in which the polite exchange of words has no intrinsic "meaning" beyond the tie which it establishes between speakers) (Malinowski 1948: 249). But it is clear from the above that he was both well aware of and interested in the creativity and ingenuity of individual speakers in reciting myths and stories, as well as in the exchange of greetings. It was only in later years, largely as a result of the programmatic work of Dell Hymes and followers on the ethnography of speaking, that there developed a systematic interest in the performative rather than validating aspects of such speech.

Leach, at least, recognised the delicate balance between the performative-innovative on the one hand and the functional and confirmatory on the other, and regarded both as political (Leach 1954) though this was not immediately pursued as a special field of interest until the 1960s.

There is a strange paradox in the contrast between anthropologists of the generation immediately preceding and following World War II and those of the late 1960s and onward. Those earlier anthropologists ordinarily would spend at least two years in the field and would expect to learn the vernacular with tolerable fluency. The language of informants, however, was seen primarily as the route to underlying principles about which the natives were assuredly ignorant. Language was a tool of discovery but not part of the discovery itself (Ardener 1971: xiii–xxx). By contrast, modern anthropologists rarely spend two years in the field in the first instance, and even more rarely return to the same area on a subsequent occasion. Shortage of research money and time, and an unjustified professional push into new geographical areas, has produced too many anthropologists with limited skills in the vernacular, with few of them daring to acknowledge their limitations in the preface to their books. Yet the few among them who have had the opportunity to learn their informants' tongues have turned their attentions very firmly to problems of speech, style, and performance. It is as if they are making up for the opportunities lost by an earlier generation who really did speak the vernacular well.

While the ethnographers of speaking have cultivated a rich and satisfying field, they are not the ones from whom the main impetus for work on political language has come. In fact, the interest in oratory arises out of recent changes in ideas of the political itself, rather than of the uses of language. One scholar, F.G. Bailey, is often cited as having had direct influence.

It was Bailey's initial study of committees that inspired a large number of field studies and analyses, first of committees (e.g. Richards and Kuper 1971) and then of formal political speech-making (Bloch 1975; see also Bailey 1969). Bailey's experience of the cut and thrust of university committee politics and his attempt to explain its surface unpredictability in terms of rules governing individual strategies, and later the calculated display of emotions (Bailey 1983), could only be done through an analysis of the language used by combatants. This is, of course, what anthropologists had always done. But their observations of language use recorded in notebooks rarely became the "data" of the polished publications of political structures and processes. The ways in which people talked about politics and the way their talk could influence an audience politically had become lost. The contributors to Bloch (1975) made good that loss, not through any sophisticated display of linguistic skills of the kind often shown by the ethnographers of speaking, but by careful analyses of speech events and styles in a range of different cultures.

Before the development of this interest in language as a specifically political phenomenon, ethnographers of speaking had produced a few notable studies of rhetoric or oratory whose political implications were but one of several. Ethel Albert's remarkable paper of 1964 [republished in 1972 (2)] entitled " 'Rhetoric', 'logic', and 'poetics' in Burundi: Cultural patterning of speech behaviour," remains one of the most sensitive accounts of the way in which the socialisation and use of different speech styles in a community can serve to perpetuate the existing social hierarchy. Much later came the studies of Ilongot oratory by Rosaldo (1973) and of Malagasy oratory by Keenan (1975), and of Thai village rhetoric by Bilmes (1975). Of these only Rosaldo sees her analysis of oratory as an aspect of specifically "political encounters" (1973: 194), with the term "political" not used at all by the others. Bilmes sees his work partly as that of an "interpretive theorist" (1975: 45), while Keenan's, as well as that of Rosaldo, are cited by Bauman as illustrating some of the communicative means making up verbal art as performance (Bauman 1975).

It is clear that all these papers were dealing with activities which we can legitimately call the local-level politics of language. On the other hand, however, we have them portrayed as examples of language use as performative art. This contrast between political language and performative-artistic language nicely summarises the differences in inclination between the American ethnographers of speaking and the mainly British political anthropologists whose interest in language is motivated by a desire to reduce the opacity of political processes (see Borgstrom 1982; Moeran 1984; Paine 1981; Parkin 1978, and contributors to Bloch 1975 and Paine 1981). The Americans take a broader view and do not emphasise the political effects over any other; if anything, Americans play them down. The British see their work as a continuation of traditional concerns at the heart of political anthropology itself.

Yet, in spite of this division, which itself reproduces American anthropological eclecticism and British institutional specialisation, the more recent British studies of political language have borrowed heavily from the American interests in two areas of linguistic philosophy, the relevance for cognition of metaphor and other tropes, and speech act theory. From Rosaldo (1973: 206), through Sapir & Crocker (Sapir and Crocker 1977), to Paine (1981: 11–17 and passim), there is the direct influence of Burke (1969) in studies of the role of tropes in defining and creating political types and situations. More generally, there has been a veritable academic industry founded on tropes [e.g. from Black 1962 to Ricoeur (1978), Ortony (1979), Lakoff & Johnson (1980), Brandes (1980), to, most recently, Fernandez (1977)], with, however, the specifically political dimension becoming increasingly subsumed in questions of the metaphoric objectification of persons. I shall examine in more detail below this tendency of the political to become "lost" in other aspects of culture.

Speech act theory is the second area of interest which in recent years has been developed, more in the United States than in Britain, since Austin's seminal study (1962). Though Finnegan (1969) and Tambiah (1968) produced early innovative papers in Britain, it is the work of the linguistic philosopher Searle (1969, and many subsequent papers) which mainly carried on that of Austin and itself spawned many analyses of the different effects of illocutionary speech and of intentionality. Bloch's introduction to the volume on traditional oratory (1975: 1–28) and a number of papers in British journals (e.g. Ahern 1979: 1–17) have drawn heavily on these twin features of speech act theory.

It is already clear how much scholars explicitly concerned with political language will continue to benefit from the work of those ethnographers of speaking who emphasise the performative, artistic, and metaphorical attributes of language use. One can go so far as to claim that it is to the benefit of both camps that each maintains its distinctiveness, with the performativists, if I may generalise thus, repaid through constant reminders that ultimately even the most culturally elaborate sociolinguistic artistry is mediated by people's changing constructions of the nature and distribution of power.

On the one hand, then, we must concede that any anthropological discussion of political language can be recast in terms of, for example, the definition of personhood arising out of metaphorical play, changing views on the relation between subject or agency and object, or on the description of folk rules governing speech events. All these are implicitly political as are all social relationships and the rules applying to them: no relationship remains equal for more than an instant, and reciprocal imbalance and normative asymmetry provide the differences which motivate human behaviour. It would, however, be a barren reductionism which insisted that these political underpinnings should provide the starting point and conclusion of such analyses. The value of the work of the performativists is precisely because it leaves relatively undigested such considerations of power.

On the other hand, then, are those political anthropologists who, quite arbitrarily, carve out domains of social behaviour, dub them political, and proceed to analyse the ways in which people talk about and within them. They draw on some of the ideas of the performativists and linguistic philosophers but are held together by a specific interest in the creation and distribution of power. This is, of course, deliberate epistemological naivete. Yet, in following the debate created by the publication first of Bloch (1975) and then of Paine (1981), together with associated papers, we can hardly deny the intellectual stimulation arising from it. More than this, the issues covered by it are being relocated in a wider anthropology which, following Foucault and Habermas in particular, sees society itself as a discourse within which speech both liberates and enslaves (e.g. Turton 1984, and contributions to Fardon 1985 and to Parkin 1982). Let me now focus on this recent debate and on its further implications.

Formalisation and Creativity

With characteristic boldness, Bloch's introduction to the 1975 volume of essays on traditional oratory (1975: 1–28) so severely overstated his case that barely a paper on the subject misses the opportunity to correct him. That said, the reservations of a more qualified statement would not have appealed to the circus element in anthropology and would have been ignored or, at best, taken for equivocation. Bloch's argument, broadly that of an earlier paper (Bloch 1974), is that traditional political language or oratory is so formalised as to show little variation of vocabulary, syntax, and style. It is the oratory of those already in established positions of authority. Through the predictability of its forms, it confirms the speaker's authority, validates his right to impose demands on an audience, blocks dissident replies, and in general stifles creativity in speech. In outline, the argument is reminiscent both of Malinowski's concept of phatic communion and, even more so, of Plato's attack on the supporters of Homer's poetry. While the latter claimed that from poetry people could get all they needed to know of reality, from making a chariot wheel to conducting military campaigns, Plato insisted that only living dialectic could reveal reality, and that poetry, like representational art and metaphor itself, could only deceive (Plato 1948: 314–29).

Moreover, the thesis continues Bloch's own dichotomous worldview, which itself follows an earlier generally held distinction between mystification or false consciousness and "true" consciousness. Thus,

> Formalisation (of speech, songs, dance, and ritual : creativity
> (Bloch 1974; 1975: 1–28),
> :: ritual communication : practical communication (Bloch 1977)
> :: ideology : cognition (Bloch 1985).

Illuminating though such re-castings of the same basic dichotomy may be (and there are others), Bloch himself faces the danger of his own interpretive reductionism. It is essential to recognise that such dichotomous phenomena are complementary aspects of a single "reality" and not simply opposed as ideological "misrepresentation" and "reality." Such a view is actually closer to that of a dialogue or dialectic operating in discourse (whether verbal or nonverbal). I shall return to this criticism. It does not, however, figure among those which have been directed at Bloch's argument, and it is necessary here to outline these.

The most serious is that of Werbner (1977), who remarks that none of the contributors to the volume edited by Bloch provide evidence for the thesis of the introduction. In all cases, oratory combines elements of both formalisation and creativity. Orators are shown as having to adapt very quickly to the changing demands and responses of audiences, alternating between set and innovative speech. Sometimes it is distinct occasions which require the one or the other. In either case, some idea exists in the cultures themselves as to when a style of speech is or is not appropriate. The speaker is less in control than Bloch's argument allowed.

For example, Comaroff, writing on the Tshidi, remarks that formal speech codes used by politicians may indeed be characterised by linguistic rigidity (1975: 160), but that people evaluate rival politicians who must therefore counter the judgments made of them by using a different style emphasising their own personal qualities rather than those of the office they hold or wish to hold. Parkin similarly distinguishes between different assumptions made of an audience by speakers: that of a docile audience elicits a kind of speech called ideology, which conforms to Bloch's formalised speech, but when the audience shows itself to be critical and unlikely to conform so passively, the same speakers have to switch to a style of rational discussion, which openly invites questioning and follows no predictable forms (1984). Seidel shows how political discourse in Paris during the events of 1968 alternated in the use of semantically ambiguous pronouns (*nous*, *vous*, or *on*) depending on whether speakers identified themselves and their audience as either left or right-wing (Seidel 1975: 205–26).

Here we may note that in comparing Wolof (Senegal), Mursi (Ethiopia), and IIongot (Philippines) political meetings, Judith Irvine shows that the very concept of formality refers not to one but to many aspects of speech and behaviour which can co-vary in their interrelationship. Wolof political speech might appear to be despotic compared with, say, Mursi, who are publicly egalitarian, but Wolof leaders still have to lobby privately for the consensus they need to enforce decisions, as do the Ilongot "soldiers" who are otherwise mute in political meetings (Irvine 1979: 773–90).

It is not only the outside analyst who observes these adaptive variations. Peoples themselves may have their own sophisticated vocabulary to describe them. Rosaldo describes how the Ilongot distinguish between "crooked" speech, a traditional oratory which emphasises the creative individuality of speakers, and "straight" speech, which has become the modem oratory of recent, wider ideas of an authoritarian hierarchy (1973). Keenan (1975: 93–112), likewise, lays out the Malagasy distinctions between ceremonial *kabary* oratory and ordinary *resaka*. An allusive style called "winding speech" is obligatory in the first but optional in the second. But while it is true that both kinds of speech are said to be governed by rules, this does not preclude rule-governed creativity in either.

Moreover, elders do not agree as to what the rules are (Keenan 1975: 98), nor do the elders in the audience all agree in their evaluations of a particular orator's *kabary* skill. If there is no such audience consensus, then how can a *kabary* produce the unquestioning response of which Bloch writes? Indeed, a *kabary* which stifles answers is regarded as the speech of a dictator and "it is the partial unpredictability of the oratory that stimulates most of the talk which occurs" (*ibid*: 112). The impression we have of *kabary* is of a broadly defined notion of ceremonial speech, the "rules" for which are made up and negotiated as orators speak. Among the Maori, too, Salmond notes a distinction between two types of oratory. One is formulaic and prestigious and the other is less formal and more informative. But even within the formulaic type a speaker can be creative: he can choose to use or omit a text, proverb, or genealogical recitation, and can vary the manner of his delivery, knowing full well that his audience wants innovative oratory which both entertains and informs (Salmond 1975: 53–55).

Again, of the three named speech levels in Bali described by Hobart, only one approximates that of formalised speech, while oratorical skill consists of manipulating existing speech elements if not of innovation, a procedure that certainly allows for debate (Hobart 1975: 78). Since the skill of individual orators shapes to a large extent the success of one faction against another, there is clearly in this situation no one-to-one correspondence between traditional authority and formalised speech having predictable effects. Firth also sees Tikopia *fono* oratory as sometimes formalised but notes also that speakers can experiment within the rules defining it and can communicate new information which can be contested by the audience (Firth 1975: 40–42). David Turton stresses the skills required of the Mursi orator in timing his speeches as to when they should begin and end, how long they should last, and to capitalise on the fact that it is elders alone who are privileged to speak (Turton 1975: 177). In his contrast in Mount Hagen between "veiled speech" and "war talk," Strathern readily notes how closely the latter parallels Bloch's characterisation of formalised speech. But "veiled speech" is full of subtle metaphorical usage and, while those who control it most successfully have commensurate influence, its use is open to all those who become "big" enough. While the figures of speech are generally conventional, its openness as a speech style enables new usages constantly to be fed into it (Strathern 1975: 190).

It is only fair to say that Bloch was able to capture a critical aspect of traditional oratory, namely the fixed forms by which it is ordinarily defined. But, as is clear from the above examples, it is the idea of fixity rather than its practice that most typifies oratory among most peoples. Or if there does exist a fixed style, then there is inevitably an alternative oratorical style which allows for more flexible and creative interpretive exchange between speaker and audience (Parkin 1980: 63). To remain with the hypothesis that traditional political language stifles creativity and reinforces control comes dangerously close to a tautology: any speech style that deviates from this, or any audience response which is of a questioning nature, can so easily cause us to assume that the form of oratory is non-traditional, perhaps no more than an innovation.

We can suggest more fruitfully either that there is often a belief by a people that a form of oratory is formalised and predictable, or that we are dealing with the appearance, say for ceremonial purposes, of such oratory. Repetitive formulae do not necessarily evoke the same responses. Speakers, audiences, contexts, and the implicit issues constantly change. What one oft-repeated phrase meant on one occasion or at a particular point in the speech need not convey the same meaning later. The repetition of phrase or loudness or tone of voice is only acoustical, not conceptual. The shifts may be slight but, as with Derrida's endless signification and dissemination (Derrida 1972), or with Ricoeur's surplus meaning (1981: 169–170), the evocations are not constant. There is a continual dialogue in the way speaker and audience relate acoustic image to sense in new combinations. There may be a limited period when listeners do indeed appear to respond, like Ardener's mute categories (1975), to formulaic admonitions. But, paradoxically, the speaker himself may fall prey to his own rhetorical fixity. Among the Luo of Kenya, elders constantly harangued women and young men to observe traditional custom. But their own idea of custom and the terms they used to describe it were so fixed that they could not see that the majority of the population by then understood something else by them. Under the cover of set terms and vocabulary, the rebellious and disadvantaged had smuggled in new meanings (1978: 284–85). The riposte to Bloch represented by Paine (1981) has not raised these latter suggestions but has focused on other issues which I now consider.

Rhetorical Exchange and Negotiation

Bailey's chapter and Paine's own contributions to his 1981 volume bring together elegantly their own and many of the ideas that have been expressed by other writers on political language. Indeed, after reading them it is possible to feel that, apart from further ethnographic illustration of their points, no further major steps are likely to be made in the field. I think that within what we might call the positivistic episteme there probably is little more to be said. Nevertheless, the concern with political language can be said to have metamorphosed into a still-developing interest in the idea of society as discourse. I shall deal with this development in due course, but first let me outline the responses of Paine (1981a; 1981b: 9–23; 1981c: 187–200) to Bloch and the contribution generally. My point is to show both the richness of the conclusions and the limits which they appear to have reached.

The first obvious difference between the contributions to Bloch (1975) and Paine (1981) is that none of the latter are taken from Third World countries; even Bermuda comes across as a Western offshoot (Manning 1981: 165–86). This means that Paine's colleagues have no obvious problems of verbal translation, though Gold (Gold 1981: 143–64) gives a number of vernacular terms of importance among the French-speaking Cajuns of Louisiana. Thus, whereas many of Bloch's colleagues start out by explaining folk descriptions of speech styles in the particular societies they have studied and the significance of such distinctions to the peoples themselves, this is inevitably a less important concern for Paine's contributors. We get some idea from Bloch (1975) of how, across disparate cultures, types of speech are thought about: the Malagasy *resaka* is opposed to the *kabary* but both may be enhanced by "winding speech"; the Mount Hagen *el ik* contrasts with *ik ek* and distinguishes men, roles, and events, as in Madagascar; the Tikopia "political" *fono* inverts the "poetic" *oriori*; the Maori *whaikoorero* encompasses the whole of Maori culture in a way that the European *pakeha* speech cannot; the Bali speech levels of *alus*. *biasa*. and *kasaronly* make sense when placed within the diarchy of patron and orator; while among the Mursi, another diarchy, that of the notable/orator *jalabai* and the priest *komoru* convey a sense of Mursi "other worldly" cosmology, for the former term is rarely heard, and the *komoru* priest must transcend the conflicts expressed in speech at public meetings.

These and other examples requiring translation from other cultures could take the reader away from the explicit concern with political language into epistemological issues. The focus on Western (mainly English-speaking) cases in Paine (1981) does not cause the effect of cultural differences to be totally ignored. We are, for instance, given excellent insight into the lives of Durham miners (Rodger 1981: 41–64), Burmudan co-worshippers (Manning 1981), and Louisiana Cajuns (Gold 1981). But the virtual absence of any discussion of various folk classifications of speech styles does not encourage the reader to think of the definition of rhetoric and other ways of speaking as itself problematic. On the other hand, this unicultural focus enables both Paine and Bailey to construct interesting logical formulations of the nature, conditions of utterance, and effects of a kind of pan-cultural political language.

Paine's starting point, as might be expected from his other work, is to privilege the creative capacities of the speaker and his audience over and above the culture or political system in which they are operating. While for Bloch the political culture determines who is in authority and how he speaks, for Paine these are matters to be negotiated. Sometimes speakers produce formalised speech, but sometimes they must switch to another mode. Sometimes the switch is relatively easy, but on other occasions it requires a struggle. The best speakers, like the most successful politicians, must be quick with their minds and tongues as well as on their feet. Paine's point is that persuasion, to which rhetoric is devoted, is arrived at by a speaker through experimentation and exchanges with his audience. If, therefore, rhetoric is equated with formalised language, then the latter cannot be regarded as stereotypically evoking an unvarying response. It will in fact be noted that the re-examination above of the cases in Bloch (1975) illustrate how speakers do expect audience responses to vary, and how much political speeches are indeed seen as exchanges, a feature to which Comaroff (1975), Hobart (1975), Salmond (1975), and Keenan (1975) draw our attention. In this respect Paine's introductory remarks might almost be applied to the contributions in Bloch, although he makes no specific reference to them.

An important task for the rhetorician, Paine notes (1981: 10), is to organise the experiences of his listeners such that they see their interests as reflected in the words of the speaker. Since all audiences are to some degree heterogeneous, this means that the speaker must discover or create a limited number of "lowest common communication factors" (see also Richards and Kuper 1971 and Parkin 1975), perhaps by acting as a cultural broker, as among the Kpelle of West Africa (Murphy 1981). The further task is not simply to convince listeners but to persuade them to act or to let the speaker act on their behalf. Thus, rhetoric, like performative utterances and illocutionary speech, is intended to have practical effects in altering an existing state of affairs or at least preserving them in the interests of the speaker or those whom he represents.

Although rhetoric is indeed illocutionary in stylistic effect, it is also actually constructed of propositions, however inconsistent or contradictory they may appear to be if ranged alongside each other. Here, an important Aristotelian concept introduced by Paine is that of the enthymeme, which is an abbreviated syllogism, often reduced to a single word, e.g. " 'democracy' = 'democracy as practiced in Western societies is parliamentary; democracy in communist societies is not; therefore, the only 'true' democracy is Western and must be protected against contamination by the other." To unpack the enthymemes (which are more commonly short phrases) of a political text is a salutary exercise.

By shortening the syllogism, the enthymeme can leave things implied, to be understood tacitly and even to be interpreted in more than one way. All manner of assumptions can be smuggled into the rhetoric and, in their innocuous guise as single word or expression, can slip past an audience's critical guard. Discussions by Lloyd-Jones (1981: 97–112) and Wallman (1981: 113–42) of "immigration" and "race" in Britain provide good examples. There is here a similarity in the use of key verbal concepts (Moeran 1984: 252–66); Parkin 1978: 286–311), with the idea of enthymeme forcibly reminding us that even the pithiest slogans may contain complex arguments (Paine 1981: 3–18).

Propaganda may consist of much enthymemic argument, but for Paine, propaganda is rejected rhetoric. That is to say, while propaganda may be propositional, the sincerity of the speaker's intentions is doubted by the audience. This is a fair contrast to be drawn for Western societies. But could such a contrast be drawn for all other cultures? Thinking of the African societies in which I have worked, a more immediate contrast might seem to be that between "truthful" and "false" speech. The same word would be used for both "lies" and "propaganda". This is not as simplistic as it might seem. For the very concepts of "truth" and "falsehood" in these same societies cover an area of great semantic complexity involving ideas not only of empirical verifiability but also of (a) partiality (if the moot's verdict is in my favour, then it confirms my belief in it as true) and (b) efficacy (if the diviner's prescription works, then it is true regardless of whether the same prescription failed elsewhere (Parkin 1984).

A similar epistemological problem concerns Paine's identification of the underlying notion of rhetoric as action (1981: 20–21). Again, this is a reasonable assumption to draw from Western definitions of rhetoric. But there are many speech events in other cultures where, inexplicably to the Western observer, nothing seems to be accomplished nor does the audience seem to expect action. The lengthy speaking becomes an end in itself, falling into Bauman's category (1975) of artistic performance as much as anything, and yet seemingly cast in the idiom of persuasion.

In other words, persuasion may itself sometimes be an aesthetic device, having no other end than its own satisfactory performance. Parliamentary debates are often of this kind, the results having been decided beforehand in the lobbies. We are then left with rhetoric as speech that is cast in the idiom of persuasion but behind which the intention actually is to spur listeners into action. Note here how the whole definition devolves on the question of speaker's intention. Yet we know from our own observations and from the cases presented that audiences do not always know the speaker's intention. Indeed, this is a point which Paine and such colleagues as Bailey (1983), Park (1981), and Rodger (1981) emphasise. It is surely true that listeners sometimes misread the speaker's intention. Like a theatrical tragedy so badly written or performed that it is heralded as a farce, audiences may misinterpret yet make sense of the event. Between speaker's intention and the manifold possible interpretations of his addressees, we have, perhaps more than anything else, a gulf of uncertainty. It is making sense of the uncertainty that confronts the rhetorician as much as his audience. This fact is a main plank in Bailey's argument.

Bailey recognises that rhetoric aims to persuade and that one way in which this can be done is through deliberation of ideas, with figures of speech used to highlight an argument. But an alternative rhetoric is that which seeks devices that inhibit questioning and stifle the consideration of more than the speaker's viewpoint (Bailey 1981: 26–27). In this kind of hortatory rhetoric the skilled speaker has his set ideas right from the beginning and is alert only to the different possible techniques by which he can foist them upon an approving audience, such that it acts upon them.

He can appeal directly to the emotions, or through language that masquerades as reason, or through reasoned argument itself. Commonly all three devices are used within a single speech. The style of the appeal will in each case either be grandiloquent, with symbols and tropes appealing to sentiments which preclude discussion, or tempered such that discussion is allowed, or so plain and direct that discussion is an inevitable part of the whole discourse. Bailey raises this question: should there not be some predictable logic in the choice by the speaker of these modes? After all, the effects look predictable enough and, if the issues and audience are known, there should be no difficulty in making the right choice. But there's the rub. The speaker may be quite clear in his intentions. But does he really know his audience? And do they really know him? This is where uncertainty begins, and with it calculation and compromise.

Uncertainty becomes reduced through broad and often unquestioned agreement as to "basic principles." Indeed, these are most effective as ultimate references when left undiscussed. Such fundamental values concerning matters of life, death, or the perpetuation of the group are most easily affirmed through emotional, hortatory rhetoric expressed grandiloquently. But when such axioms are secure, a speaker may shift to a more deliberative, tempered, and reasoning kind of rhetoric. Bailey notes that since neither rhetoric is more "true" than the other, it is curious that people allow themselves to be persuaded through it into making decisions. Why not just toss a coin instead? The answer is that we aspire to decision making through what we perceive to be calculated reason because it seems to us to be the best way to control our own destinies. Magic, God, or reason can be believed in for similar effect. This is an intriguing answer. Once again, however, we can point to the difficulties arising from a cross-cultural comparison of different epistemologies. We in the Western world privilege reason over magic and religion. Yet in many societies of the world those activities which we judge to be religious or magical are, for the people who practice them, the most reasonable courses available to them, perhaps the only ones. We distinguish intellect from emotion, head from heart, but elsewhere in the world bodily parts are as often the seat of reasoning wills as of sentiment, a distinction that in any case may not be made (Heelas and Lock 1981; Lienhardt 1980).

If an audience drawn from a particular culture does not draw a distinction between what we call deliberative and hortatory rhetoric, then how would a speaker be able to make use of it? The distinction is based on Western assumptions, and its further fruitfulness will now need to be discovered through intensive study in other cultures whose languages are well known by the investigator.

The debate between Paine and Bloch may now be summarised as posing the view of rhetoric as negotiated political persuasion against that which sees it as reinforcing traditional authority. The role of tropes in this negotiation is explicit in Paine's own contribution, but less so in those of Bloch's colleagues. The difference indicates the increasing interest in figurative speech now shown by anthropologists, to which I now tum.

Figuring Power

Bailey's notion of structural metonymy (1981: 29), by which a speaker's focus on a small part of an issue deflects his listeners' attention away from the greater issue, is itself analogical. Paine, however, addresses himself to the uses of metaphor and metonymy in language itself (1981: 87–200). He argues that metaphor extends concrete notions into abstract ideas: "George is a lion" converts an animal into courage and attributes this quality to a man. Metaphor thus enables a politician to explore, with his audience, new ways of looking at things. He can change his line of argument or his audience's view of it. It is experimental and flexible and is good for attacking established positions by bringing together as whole ideas those notions which were previously set apart. By contrast, metonymy is conservative. It moves in the opposite direction and converts ideas into tangible phenomena: we shift from a discussion of "emotions" and speak instead of "the heart," thereby closing off the possibility that, for instance, emotions may actually be good for thinking with, and indeed may actually take the place in other cultures of what we call "reason." Metonymy can therefore be used for defending a political stance by placing it beyond discussion. It narrows conceptual options. It inclines towards Bloch's formalised language.

Such tropes thus become instruments used by the speaker in both identifying and hiding the gaps and possibilities in his argument. But what is a metaphor for one section of the audience may be a metonym for 'another (Paine's example is that "Bastille" is metonym for the Bourbons who see it as an aspect of the Crown, while it is metaphor for Jacobins whose wish to storm the building is associated with overthrow of the royals). Therefore the speaker may gain but may also risk a loss of face and of power in switching between the two tropes. We are back to uncertainty, though more on the part of the speaker than of the audience.

The variability of tropic interpretation also raises the interesting question of how culturally universal are the recognition and use of tropes in the political languages of other cultures. The contributors to Sapir & Crocker (1977) do deal with this problem, not always explicitly, but as a result of interpreting cultures and languages quite distinct from their own, a feature generally absent, it may be remembered, from the Paine volume, though present in that edited by Bloch.

While Bailey's early work may be said to have given rise to the recent concern with political language per se, it was the contributors to the Sapir & Crocker volume who seem first to have highlighted in anthropology the crucial role of metaphor in rhetoric. The preface and two introductory chapters by the editors illuminate the development. Thus, from Bailey we inherited the idea of speech as a strategy of control, while from Sapir and Crocker we have the cross-cultural excavation of metaphor as the hitherto hidden power behind the capacity of speech to define and so place persons and events. That there was seen to be a difference of perspective on the part of the latter may be evident from the fact that neither Bailey's work on councils and political statements nor that of Bloch and his colleagues are mentioned, though this may alternatively be traced to a lack of acquaintance with the studies.

In any event, the case studies of tropes prove to inform all approaches to the study of political language. Howe's discussion of Cuna chiefs is, perhaps, the only one of the studies which presents political language of the kind and in the contexts discussed by Bloch and Paine. Cuna chiefs and their interpreters use words, tales, and grammar which are different from everyday language, and do so through song. Chiefs are likened to animals, different kinds of trees, to enlightenment, families, and family-like units. In controlling access to the use of metaphors, such authorities produce discourse which can be viewed as conforming to Bloch's criteria. At first, Fernandez's analysis from Gabon promises to follow the same line. But it then addresses itself to the manner in which key metaphoric statements uttered in a religious cult bring together and re-order disparate experiences. There is no reference to political language as such, but the Bwiti cult links individuals first socially and then spiritually by way of a number of metaphors, four of which are examined. Metaphoric "shadows" alternate with metonymic specificity and so reconstruct reality.

Even less with Sapir (1977) is there reference to political contexts, as conventionally defined. But we learn that the telling of folk tales is normally the prerogative of the young. Being a public act, it dramatises social and ontological puzzles through successive phases of explication, temporary resolution, and critical deconstruction. The problem explored is that while natural childbirth gives women and children their legitimacy, it is nevertheless dangerous and results in imperfect offspring, indeed the constant imperfections of humanity itself. A supernaturally produced child is both perfect and brings no danger to the mother. On the other hand, since such a child has no recognisable consanguines, how is he legitimised? The tale, told by or with regard to bastards, orphans, or the adopted, can be said to point to hurtful gaps in the Kujamaat system of inheritance, succession, kinship, and residence, though this "political" implication is not suggested by Sapir himself, and, indeed, we would need to know the normal social context in which tellings occur for its confirmation.

Crocker (1977) does mention clan ceremonials as the contexts which assert Bororo political identity. But it is an identity that refers intraculturally to men's dependence, as they see it, on women, in a society which is matrilineal and uxorilocal and in which men distrust women. The key aphorism "we men are red macaws" equates the bird, kept as a pet, with men, kept by women, but goes further and sets off chains of other associations that constitute Bororo thought and action. The metaphor both motivates and seals off men's existential dilemma. Finally, Seitel's study of Haya proverbs reveals the strategies entailed in a distinction that operates at all levels, though more so in the micropolitics of everyday life. Some proverbs are directed at a listener such that he is in no doubt that he is being accused of wrongdoing or idiocy; others are uttered indirectly or through reported example in order to retain the hearer's cooperation. What is particularly interesting is that the Haya themselves have words for distinguishing these two usages of proverbs (Seitel 1977).

These compressed remarks are an injustice to the richness of the case material, but serve to show how, in most cases, there is little notion of a specifically political language. The latter is, of course, something of a Western analytical artifice, and it is the persuasive effects in the usage of tropes that is really being considered. In much of the material the persuasion amounts to an attempt to cultivate a collective belief in either the rightness or unfairness of a cosmology. The trope is effective to the extent that people accept the conceptual links it makes. It thus operates as much in the field of folk philosophy as in "politics."

However, the generalisations drawn from the exercises can usefully be applied to what we ethnocentrically call political language. Crocker's notion (after Burke) of "entitlement," by which a trope makes sense of and therefore makes manageable ideas and actions which are diffuse, puzzling, or difficult, must surely be found among the skills of public oratory. Similarly, his distinction between "shifters" and "nonshifters" points to other devices. Proverbs can be shifters in that they remark aptly on particular situations and disregard the existence of other, quite contradictory proverbs: we shift from "Look before you leap" to "He who hesitates is lost" according to situational need, as does the political speaker. Nonshifters, like most usages of folk tales, refer to "global truths" which are supposed to transcend the situation in which the tale is told. Third, the characterisation of external metaphors as requiring conscious, intellectual thinking about (as in analogically differentiating clans A and B through bear and eagle, and vice versa), suggests a technique of political rhetoric akin to Bailey's cerebral or pseudo-cerebral modes. Conversely, the effect of internal metaphor (Sapir's "George is a lion"), being "felt" more than "thought" and so a form of hidden persuasion, is surely a more common feature of hortatory political address. Finally, the ambivalence in our sense of "identification," first raised by Burke, enables a clever speaker alternately to join or distance himself from his audience: I identify with you such that we become as one; or I identify you as of a particular type, different from myself (Crocker 1977: 43–66). Seidel (1975) had earlier described something of this process in the use of "nous," "vous," and "on" pronouns in the political speeches in Paris in 1968.

The four main tropes, namely metaphor, metonymy, synechdoche, and irony, can, again following Burke (1969), be seen as perspective, reduction, representation, and dialectic. Or, following Hobart (1975: 55), they may be viewed as resemblance, relationship, classification, and contrast. No doubt other glosses are possible. As Sapir explains (1977: 3–32), there is continual interplay between tropes, which may "turn" from one kind into another. If all language is metaphorical (Lakoff and Johnson 1980; Ricoeur 1978), and if political-cum-ritual language has an especially large proportion of "live" to "dead" metaphors, then we may expect the use of tropes in rhetoric to be a most efficacious means of redefining an audience: first through disaggregation and then through various kinds of internal reclassification, e.g. contrasting and opposing those sections, suggesting affinities between these, creating overlap with yet others, and marking out for isolation another, and so on. Just as tropes may turn one into the other, so people being addressed or talked about may figuratively be converted from, say, humans into animals, or into objects. Like the interpretive perspectives, the possibilities seem endless.

These many particular uses of tropes point, nevertheless, in one direction: it is people who retain the power to name, entitle, and objectify others, who determine the terms of discourse.

Political Language and Society as Discourse

Out of the recent work showing how ordinary English language use subordinates women to men (e.g. Lakoff, R. 1973; Spender 1980), or how professional jargon, for example legal language, renders powerless the ordinary language of the uninformed (O'Barr 1982), there has been raised the question: is it ever enough to change the linguistic forms of domination without also changing the social? More than this, is it even futile to regard the linguistic as any more than epiphenomenal and as dependent on the political and economic? No doubt a compromise answer is to attack the problem on both fronts. The purpose in raising this issue here is to indicate the mutual irreducibility of the linguistic and the social. Further to this, the view of language as discourse then becomes part of the broader equation of society itself as discourse. The metaphor, having served this purpose of pointing up the inseparability of language and society, then takes on a life of its own. In Pêcheux's terms the discourse in question refers not to a semantics that leads to knowledge, which is what "science" promised us, but to a socially embedded rhetoric, the art of which is "to convince by use of the verisimilitudinous" (Pêcheux 1982: 40).

It is clear that all discourse embodies hegemonic aspects, in the combined sense of shaping and dominating others' will. Though somewhat redundant, then, hegemonic or ideological discourse may be substituted as a term for that of rhetoric. It means more than just speech or language but includes, for example, as in Foucault's discussion of architecture, the use-meanings of buildings: we are taught to recognise a prison or a mental hospital when we see one (Foucault 1973; 1978; Hirst 1984). It brings in history, not as the linear development of "scientific" theory out of rhetoric but, up to now, as the one retracing the steps of the other, at least according to Pêcheux and many contemporary radical French philosophers. Habermas of Frankfurt perhaps more optimistically sees our gradual enlightenment as arising from our exposure of the different prejudices and presuppositions underlying what we say and interpret (1972). Insofar as this requires the tearing down of metaphoric screens, the anthropological studies of tropes have direct relevance. But, as those same studies have noted, the social uses of tropes can be highly creative. The problem, then, facing the analysis of ideological discourse is not whether it is matched by, or reducible to, some kind of literal and scientifically true language. It is rather that, within itself, so-called ideological discourse provides creative insights as well as repressive directives, a quality well understood by commercial advertisers, and that our problem is how to distinguish these. This will in turn depend on the particular standpoint taken. An initial standpoint or standpoints are those of the peoples whom we observe and write about.

We are back to questions of entitlement, naming, and the objectification of other humans, and of the extent to which human wills are ignored or resisted in actions of this kind. The point is that none of these acts, such as naming and entitling, ever occur without shaping, determining, or subordinating someone else's will. Baptising a baby, declaring someone insane and then hospitalising them, sentencing a man and then imprisoning or executing him, and even awarding an honorific title, are all examples. Even the apparently positive act of proffering an award tests the will of the potential recipient: many opponents of the establishment are deemed to have "sold out" to it in accepting the innocuous-seeming title.

In being able to provide detailed microhistorical cases of ideological discourse in action, anthropologists can contribute much to the discipline. Andrew Turton integrates a theoretical discussion of the ideas of Althusser (1971) and Therborn (1980) and many others with his own Thai ethnography, suggesting that "ideology operates as discourse, addressing, or as Althusser puts it, interpellating human beings as subjects" (Turton 1984: 41). The important concept of interpellation stresses the mandatory and one-sided nature of the discourse in which people participate. The term has the sense of interrupting in order to exact an explanation, or of delivering an irrefutable appeal: the round of everyday village communication and activity can never for long remain an uninterrupted harmonious exchange, for the state or a neighbouring or colonising people will at some point cut in. With this sense of interpellation, it is small wonder that Sheridan feels justified in equating Foucault's concept of discourse with violence (Sheridan 1980: 128).

Turton asks what do young, poor Thai peasants make of being addressed by the radio as "ladies and gentlemen, most respected listeners," etc (Turton 1984: 43)? To deny people their own consciousness of their depredation is to impugn their right to speak and act on it. Juxtaposed with such strategic terms as "farmer," "the people," "the community," the possibility of protest becomes framed as inappropriate rather than simply illegitimate: their sense of "poverty" and "alienation" simply do not fit in with the more widely articulated view of an integrated nation.

Much has been made by anthropologists and others of the mystificatory effects of certain official uses of ideological discourse. A more complex phenomenon is where metaphorical associations linking national and locallevel "evils" feed on each other and impose themselves on the people. Thus, Walter Irvine (1982) shows how village Thai associate what we might call capitalist economic madness (growth for growth's sake) with the madness sustained supernaturally by young men. The wider economic irrationality is thus talked about only in an oblique fashion which in no way ameliorates peoples' conditions.

Here we may note that the use of strategic terms, to which Turton refers, has echoes in the idea of "key words" (Leach 1954; Moeran 1984; Parkin 1978; Quinn 1982), "key metaphors" (Crocker 1977: 65–66), and even "key cultural ideas" (Murphy 1981) and "key symbols" (Herzfeld 1982), and no doubt other comparable formulations. Behind all these is the assumption of a power of appropriateness or aptness in the use of certain relatively fixed terms and phrases, some of which are enthymemes in Paine's sense. They can constitute taxonomies and, as such, make up the text of a whole culture or subculture. But, as argued elsewhere (Parkin 1978), such relatively predictable taxonomies do no more than represent the dominant view of the culture. Counter-posed to these fixed terms of the elite are the more variable expressions which question established assumptions. They are the murmurings of a shadowy counterimage. They are the property of the mute categories, to use Ardener's concept (1975), which strive to attain the articulateness of those who dominate them. Luo elders speak authoritatively in the firm taxonomy of segmentary lineages, but young men and women seek more modern, and also much more variable, ways of opposing such tradition. Young men become elders themselves, but women remain subordinate, and so it was predicted that it would have to be the latter who would introduce new vocabulary into the ideological discourse of Luo society. The notion of internal cultural debate, as it concerned discussion of the forces for change in cultural as well as political identity, has also proved useful in descriptions of Greek rhetoric (Herzfeld 1982) and of Japanese reactions to "Westernization" (Moeran 1984).

The use by elites of firm taxonomies, much akin to formalised language, is often premised on strong binary discriminations. Thus, for a political speaker to argue a case for Western democracy is, at some point, to oppose this term or a substitute such as "capitalism" to "socialism" or "communism" or, from a leftist perspective, to "fascism." The "-isms" of academic theory, no less than those of political language, are a result of segmentary discriminations originating from a single opposition. Derrida's and other poststructuralists' attempts to deconstruct the meaninglessness of such abstract theoretical language could usefully be turned on ideological discourse as a whole. Yet while some "reactionary" views expressed in Lerner (Lerner 1983) see Derrida as a radical sabotaging the possibility of independent value judgments, a radical sympathiser, Terry Eagleton, has also criticised Derrida's work as overconcerned with minutiae and as a defeatist reaction to left-wing disappointments after the events of Paris in May 1968 (Eagleton 1983: 143).

Surely the solution to this dilemma is not to reject deconstructionism, for its corrective value in exposing the falsity of axioms is immense. A viable alternative is to recognise the inevitably strong explanatory power of binary oppositions, dualisms, and dichotomies, but constantly to recast them in the gradable and qualified language of the unprivileged, and then, as new polarities emerge, to question them all over again. Such rotating deconstructionism is hardly a conservative enterprise, as some might think. It recognises that it is not formalism in language which represses people and their thoughts, but rather the degree to which speakers impose such discourse on others. It also recognises that these others have the means to reply but may need the freedom to do so. We may even be optimistic, for, as Borgstrom (1982) notes in his analysis of the Nepalese king's rhetoric, a political speaker may attempt to anticipate the rising expectations of his subjects by talking to them about, say, "democracy," "development," "education," etc. But the very use of these new terms enables listeners to assess their existing conditions in the light of these promises.

In conclusion, there is a dimension of discourse in which the speaker is assumed to control knowledge. There is a second in which the discourse is scrutinised and its assumptions criticised and even negotiated between speaker and audience. But there is also a third in which, as with the Nepalese king, unintended and accidental events have somehow to be accommodated in the discourse (Parkin 1985). Whether these are really accidents of history rather than its logical unfolding does not matter. They should add up to a widening of historical perspectives, or, to put the point another way, to an increasing awareness of social inequalities.

References

Ahern, E.M. (1979) The problem of efficacy: strong and weak illocutionary acts. *Man* 14, 1–17.

Albert, E. (1964) [1972] Cultural patterning of speech behaviour in Burundi. In *Directions in Sociolinguistics* (ed.) 1. Gumperz. D. Hymes pp. 75–102. New York: Holt. Rinehart & Winston.

Althusser, L. (1971) Ideology and ideological state apparatuses (Notes towards an investigation). *In Lenin and Philosophy and Other Essays*. London: New Left Books.

Ardener, E.W. (1971) Introductory essay. In *Social Anthropology and Language* (ed.) E.W. Ardener. London: Tavistock.

Ardener, E.W. (1972) [1975] Belief and the problem of women. And The Problem revisited. In *Perceiving Women* (ed.) S. Ardener. London: Malaby.

Austin, J.L. (1962) *How To Do Things With Words*. London: Oxford Univ. Press.

Bailey, F.G. (1965) Decisions by consensus in councils and committees. In *Political Systems and the Distribution of' Power* (ed.) M. Banton. London: Tavistock.

Bailey, F.G. (1969) Political statements. *Contrib Indian Sociol* 3, 1–16.

Bailey, F.G. (1981) Dimensions of rhetoric in conditions of uncertainty. In R. Paine: 25–40 qv.

Bailey, F.G. (1983) *The Tactical Uses of Passion*. Ithaca/London: Cornell Univ. Press.

Bauman, R. (1975) Verbal art as performance. *Am Anthropol* 77, 290–311.

Bilmes, J. (1976) Rules and rhetoric: Negotiating the social order in a Thai village. *J Anthropol Res* 32 (1), 44–57.

Black, M. (1962) *Models and Metaphors*. Ithaca: Cornell Univ. Press.

Bloch, M. (1974) Symbols. song. dance and features of articulation. Is religion an extreme form of traditional authority? *Eur J Sociol* 15, 55–81.

Bloch, M. (ed.) (1975) *Political Language and Oratory in Traditional Society*. London: Academic.

Bloch, M. (1975) Introduction. In Bloch: 1–28 qv.

Bloch, M. (1977) The past and the present in the present. *Man* 12, 278–92.

Bloch, M. (1985) From cognition to ideology. In Fardon qv.

Borgstrom, B.-E. (1982) Power structure and political speech. *Man* 17, 313–27.

Brandes, S. (1980) *Metaphors of Masculinity*. Philadelphia: Univ. Penn. Press.

Burke, K. (1969) *A Rhetoric of Motives*. Berkeley: Univ. Calif. Press.

Comaroff, J. (1975) Talking politics: oratory in a Tswana chiefdom. See Ref. 15. pp. 141–62.

Crocker, J.C. (1977) The social functions of rhetorical forms. In *The Social Use of Metaphor: Essays on the Anthropology of Rhetoric* (ed.) J.D. Sapir. J.C. Crocker: 33–66. Philadelphia: Univ. Penn. Press.

Crocker, J.C. (1977) My brother the parrot. In Sapir and Crocker: 164–92 qv.

Derrida, J. (1972) Structure. sign and play in the discourse of the human sciences. In *The Structuralist Controversy* (ed.) R. Macksey. and E. Donato. Baltimore: Johns Hopkins Press

Eagleton, T. (1983) *Literary Theory*. Oxford: Blackwell.

Fardon, R. (ed.) (1985) *Power and Knowledge*. Edinburgh: Scottish Academic Press.

Fernandez, J.W. (1977) The performance of ritual metaphors. In Sapir and Crocker: 100–131 qv.

Fernandez, J.W. (1982) *Bwiti: An Ethnography of the Religious Imagination in Africa*. Princeton: Princeton Univ. Press.

Finnegan, R. (1969) How to do things with words: Performative utterances among the Limba of Sierra Leone. *Man* 4, 59–69.

Firth, R. (1975) Speech-making and authority in Tikopia. In Bloch: 29–44 qv.

Foucault, M. (1973) *The Birth of the Clinic*. London: Tavistock.

Foucault, M. (1978) *Discipline and Punish*. London: Lane.

Gold, G.L. (1981) Cousin and the 'Gros chiens': The limits of Cajun political rhetoric. In Paine 1981a: 143–64 qv.

Habermas, J. (1968) [1972] *Knowledge and Human Interests*. London: Heinemann.

Heelas, P., Lock, A. (eds) (1981) *Indigenous Philosophies*. London/New York: Academic.

Herzfeld, M. (1982) The etymology of excuses: Aspects of rhetorical performance in Greece. *Am Ethnol* 9, 644–63.

Hirst, P. (1984) Foucault and architecture. In Fardon qv.

Hobart, M. (1975) Orators and patrons: two types of political leader in Balinese village society. In Bloch: 65–92 qv.

Hobart, M. (1982) Meaning or moaning? An ethnographical note on a little understood tribe. In Parkin 1982: 39–64 qv.

Howe, J. (1977) Carrying the village: Cuna political metaphors. In Sapir and Crocker: 132–63 qv.

Irvine, J. (1979) Formality and informality in communicative events. *Am Anthropol* 81, 773–90.

Irvine, W. (1982) The Thai-Yuan 'Mad-man', and the Modernising, Developing Thai Nation, as Bounded Entities under Threat: A Study in the Replication of a Single Image. PhD thesis. Univ. London, London, England.

Keenan, E. (1973) [1975] A sliding sense of obligatoriness: The polystructure of Malagasy oratory. In Bloch 1975: 93–112 qv.

Lakoff, G. and Johnson, M. (1980) *Metaphors We Live By*. Chicago/London: Chicago Univ. Press.

Lakoff, R. (1973) Language and women's place. *Lang Soc* 2, 45–80.

Leach, E.R. (1954) *Political Systems of Highland Burma*. London: Bell.

Lerner, L. (ed.) (1983) *Reconstructing Literature*. Oxford: Blackwell.

Lienhardt, G. (1980) Self: public and private. Some African representations. *J Anthropol Soc* Oxford II: 69–82.

Lloyd-Jones, D. (1981) The art of Enoch Powell: The rhetorical structure of a speech on immigration. In Paine 1981(a): 87–112 qv.

Malinowski, B. (1948) Myth in primitive psychology. In *Magic, Science and Religion*. Glencoe, III: Free Press.

Manning, F.E. (1981) Campaign rhetoric in Bermuda: The politics of race and religion. In Paine 1981a: 165–86 qv.

Moeran, B. (1984) Individual. group, and *seishin* – Japan's internal cultural debate. *Man* 19: 252–66.

Murphy, W.P. (1981) The rhetorical management of dangerous knowledge in Kpelle society. *Am Ethnol* 8, 667–85.

O' Barr, W.M. (1982) *Linguistic evidence: Language, power and strategy in the Courtroom*. New York: Academic.

Ortony, A. (ed.) (1979) *Metaphor and Thought*. Cambridge: Cambridge Univ. Press.

Paine, R. (ed.) (1981a) *Politically Speaking: Cross-Cultural Studies of Rhetoric*. Newfoundland *Inst Soc Econ Res*. Philadelphia: ISHI.

Paine, R. (1981b) When saying is doing. In Paine 1981a: 9–23 qv.

Paine, R. (1981c) The political uses of metaphor and metonym: An exploratory statement. In Paine 1981a: 187–200 qv.

Park, G. (1981) 'Weaklings wax biggest with words': U.S. and Norwegian populists. In Paine 1981a: 65–86 qv.

Parkin, D. (1975) The rhetoric of responsibility: Bureaucratic communications in a Kenya fanning centre. In Bloch 1975 qv.

Parkin, D. (1978) *The Cultural Definition of Political Response*. London/New York: Academic.

Parkin, D. (1980) The creativity of abuse. *Man* 15: 45–64.

Parkin, D. (ed.) (1982) *Semantic Anthropology*. London/New York: Academic.

Parkin, D. (1985) Controlling the U-turn of knowledge. In Fardon 1985 qv.

Pêcheux, M. (1982) *Language, Semantics and Ideology*. New York: St. Martin 's.

Perelman, C. (1974) Rhetoric in philosophy: The new rhetoric. In *Encyclopaedia Britannica*. XVth ed. Vol. 15. s.v. Rhetoric.

Plato (1948) Trans. F.M. Conford. *The Republic*. Oxford: Clarendon.

Quinn, N. (1982) 'Commitment' in American marriage: A cultural analysis. *Am Ethnol* 9, 775–98.

Richards, A.I. and Kuper, A. (eds) (1971) *Councils in Action*. Cambridge: Cambridge Univ. Press.
Ricoeur, P. (1975) [1978] *The Rule of Metaphor*. London: Routledge & Kegan Paul.
Ricoeur, P. (1981) *Hermeneutics and the Human Sciences*. Cambridge: Cambridge Univ. Press.
Rodger, I. (1981) Rhetoric and ritual politics: The Durham miners' gala. In Paine 1981a: 41–64 qv.
Rosaldo, M.Z. (1973) I have nothing to hide: The language of Ilongot oratory. *Lang Soc* 2, 193–224
Salmond, A. (1975) Mana makes the man: A look at Maori oratory and politics. In Bloch 1975: 45–64 qv.
Sapir, J.D. (1977) The anatomy of metaphor. In Sapir and Crocker 1977: 3–32 qv.
Sapir, J.D. (1977) The fabricated child. In Sapir and Crocker 1977: 193–224 qv.
Sapir, J.D., Crocker, J. (eds) (1977) *The Social Use of Metaphor: Essays on the Anthropology of Rhetoric*. Philadelphia: Univ. Penn. Press.
Searle, J.R. (1969) *Speech Acts*. London/New York: Cambridge Univ. Press.
Seidel, G. (1975) Ambiguity in political discourse. In Bloch 1975: 205–26 qv.
Seitel, P. (1977) Saying Haya sayings: Two categories of proverb use. In Sapir and Crocker 1977: 75–99 qv.
Sheridan, A. (1980) *Michel Foucault: The Will to Truth*. London: Tavistock.
Spender, D. (1980) *Man Made Language*. London: Routledge & Kegan Paul.
Strathern, A. (1975) Veiled speech in Mount Hagen. In Bloch 1975: 185–204 qv.
Tambiah, S.J. (1968) The magical power of words. *Man* 3, 175–208.
Therborn, G. (1980) *The Ideology of Power and the Power of Ideology*. London: Verso Editions.
Turton, A. (1984) Limits of ideological domination and the formation of social consciousness. In A. Turton and Shigeharu Tanabe. (Eds) *History and Peasant Consciousness in South East Asia*. Senri Ethnol. Stud. No. 13. Osaka: Natl Mus Ethnol.
Turton, D. (1975) The relationship between oratory and the exercise of influence among the Mursi. In Bloch 1975: 163–84 qv.
Wallman, S. (1981) Refractions of rhetoric: Evidence for the meaning of 'race' in England. In Paine 1981a: 113–42
Werbner, R. (1977) The argument in and about oratory. *Afr Stud* 36, 141–44. Annual Review of Anthropology Volume 13, 1984.

8 Language, Government and the Play on Purity and Impurity: Arabic, Swahili and the Vernaculars in Kenya

The Theoretical Basis

Among current tensions in anthropological theory (see Ulin 1991), there is one that appears to be acting as a prolegomenon to a new synthesis. On the one hand, there is the now rapidly fading postmodernist position, dating especially from Lyotard (1984), that technological specialisation and compartmentalisation in the modern world have shattered the universalist illusions of grand theory and have broken it up into an infinitely expanding number of relativised discourses. On the other hand, there is the continuing influence of political economy, emanating from Taussig (1980), Habermas (1981), Wolf (1982) and Mintz (1985), with its insistence on global interconnectedness as the overall determining context of human action, development and history. With regard to the synthesis, it might be argued that the current experimentation with such conceptual metaphors as global 'creolisation' and 'post-pluralism' (meaning, in effect, old-type oppositional pluralism, but with the constituent elements now in communication with each other) is a blending of the postmodernist concern with fragmentation and the universalist premise of political economists that social formations are grounded historically in the irreducible reality of human labour and the exchange of its products. In this new synthesis, the products are, of course, seen as commodities, whose principal feature is not that they have become alienated from their producers in the classical Marxist sense (which is taken for granted), but that they have become embedded in endless chains of consumerism, whose proliferation is stimulated by the promise that they will return to satisfy the equally endless desires of the producers-turned-consumers (cf. Baudrillard 1972).

Language has also nowadays become commoditised to the extent that it is commonly held up as the property of an ethnic or national group, class and even caste, often regardless of how many members of the group speak it and whether they do so fluently. Thus, to take obvious examples from Europe, there are many Basques, Bretons, Welsh and Poles of German extraction whose identification with their purported ethnic languages is more in their promise to speak it than in their current proficiency but who are imperceptibly merged with those for whom these are indeed first languages. There is, then, here an overall premise of identification with the object, language, which is ontologically central to some persons but only peripheral to others, even if desired by them. The distinction between linguistic haves and have-nots reproduces the motivating force in consumerism as all-pervasive or global and yet highlights the fragmentary and fragmenting reality of uneven linguistic distribution.

The point here is that language proficiency is only ever partial and never evenly distributed. Among a close community of, say, native English or Swahili speakers, there is always at some moment or other a recognition that someone speaks the language more 'fluently' (or 'elegantly', 'expressively', 'correctly', or whatever is chosen as the relevant criterion) than someone else. In direct comparison with other purported speakers of the same language from another community, however, the differences are dissolved in favour of an unambiguous distinction between the different characteristics of each speech community: 'they speak a purer/less pure form than us'. Further comparisons move from those of mutually intelligible dialects to allegedly unintelligible 'foreign' languages, sometimes acknowledged as related and sometimes as totally unconnected historically.

This segmentary feature of comparison underlines one of the problems in a concept like 'creolisation' which, by presupposing the continuing interchangeability and recombination of new and old elements within a growing synthesis, imposes a panchrony or globalisation over and above the fragmentary aspects of language use. Language is commoditised but, like commodities in capitalist consumerism, is held out at one level as potentially available to all who desire it but at another level is in practice accessible in different forms to separate and often specialised and privileged sectors of a community.

Government policies on language diffusion and development commonly presuppose an egalitarian distribution of the desired language. We could hardly expect otherwise. Yet we are never surprised that purported proficiency is in fact unevenly spread, as a result of unequal educational opportunities, regional remoteness from the sources of diffusion, and differential access incurred through differences of status, gender, age and ethnic origin. This is one side of the problem of linguistic engineering that confronts any government, particularly one in Africa and Asia.

The other side is that which stems from the fact that, like a commodity, a language can be believed to develop a life of its own. In other words, there are processes of language dispersion which may exist independently of government policy and even in defiance of it.

The Argument with Reference to Kenya

I describe such a case on the Kenya coast with reference to the role of Arabic both as a religious register and as having practical significance for those who seek work in the Middle East. My aim is to show that language viewed as a commodity may be 'produced' in schools according to formal government programmes and yet may also flourish independently of such factors, as if self-determining. I suggest that this is the same tension implicit in the metaphor of global sociocultural 'creolisation', which blends the idea of fragments of supposedly autonomous or specialised knowledge with that of a universal interconnectedness of knowledge. I further suggest that this obliges us to reconsider the linguistic concept of diglossia as concerned not with discrete diatypes but as resting on the idea of unattainable linguistic desire.

First, by way of general introduction, I describe the formal distribution of languages in Kenya and the government's broad policy with regard to them. English is Kenya's official language, while Swahili is its national one. The official language, English, is prescribed as the medium of instruction in schools, the state central bureaucracy and in parliament. Although Swahili is much used informally in these contexts, and sometimes formally, there is considerable use of English, reflecting more generally the high competence in the language nationally compared with the neighbouring countries of Tanzania, Uganda (where more English is spoken than in Tanzania) and Ethiopia. Swahili is a compulsory taught subject in schools but not a medium of instruction. There are Swahili and English radio stations and newspapers. Swahili radio is listened to much more than English, while English newspapers sell more than Swahili ones. Television is mainly broadcast in English. Most people use more Swahili for everyday issues in towns and in ethnically mixed contexts than English. The ethnic vernaculars are not taught in schools and are not used in any governmental context. They are exclusively ethnic and domestic languages whose significance for expressions of regional and local identity remain strong. They are 'mother tongues' while, for the vast majority of people, Swahili and English are acquired second languages.

On the Kenya coast are people for whom Swahili is their first or 'mother tongue'. Although now a numerical minority, the Swahili-speaking peoples and their rich, textualised culture have shaped coastal society indelibly. Among these Swahili-speaking peoples are some who regard themselves and are regarded by others as 'Arabs', and who can to various degrees trace ancestry from the Middle East, principally either the Hadhramaut (the so-called Hadhrami) or Oman (the Omani). Since these 'Arabs' have migrated to East Africa in different waves over many centuries, the concept of 'Arab' is a contestable one, shaped nevertheless by the recognition that the most recent arrivals are likely to be the most 'Arab'.

Coastal East Africa up to a depth of ten miles inland was in fact a British Protectorate ruled by the Sultan of Zanzibar, an Omani Arab, from 1895 to 1963. The hinterland of Kenya, but not its coastal strip, was a British colony. In 1963 the coastal strip of Kenya and the hinterland, that is to say the Kenya part of the Protectorate and the colony, became the single, unitary republic of Kenya. Before 1963, Arabs and some non-Arab Kenya coastal Muslims had campaigned for the political autonomy and even independence of the coastal strip. They failed in their attempt and, under the new African Government, became politically less active, especially after the Zanzibar revolution in 1964 in which large numbers of alleged 'Arab' landowners were massacred.

Their demands for regional autonomy were echoed by other so-called minority peoples, and resulted, before 1963, in the formation of a political party, the Kenya African Democratic Union (KADU), which wanted a federal Kenya in which all regions would be represented. The opposition party, the Kenya African National Union (KANU), in fact came to power. It was dominated by the two large ethnic groups, the Kikuyu and the Luo, and was opposed to federation. KADU disbanded itself shortly afterwards, allegedly in the interests of national unity. Still later, in 1969, another opposition party, the Kenya Peoples Union (KPU), was banned and some years later, Kenya was declared a one-party state.

Under the Kenya Government of KANU and Jomo Kenyatta from 1963 until 1978, the small minority of Arabs and Muslims received no special privileges and, nowadays, will often claim that their coastal area, religious institutions and schools suffered privations.

In 1978 Daniel arap Moi became president. Although chosen as head of the KANU Government, he had previously been a prominent member of the now disbanded federalist party, KADU. He was himself a member of the minority group, the Kalenjin. He survived an abortive coup d'état in 1982, and it was widely reported that he and his government had been saved by the commander of the Kenya armed forces, a Somali and Muslim, both minority categories. Whether Moi had already embarked on a policy of covert federalism, or at least of appointing members of minority groups to key positions, is speculative. After 1982, however, a rapidly increasing number of such appointments were made. By 1990, Moi was resisting calls for multi-party democracy on the grounds that this would simply make it possible for the two large groups, the Kikuyu and Luo, to regain control of the state and usher in 'tribal' (*sic*) conflict. Coupled with his dispersal of political, fiscal, administrative and military appointments, this was almost a formal acknowledgement that a kind of federalism through adequate minority representation was being practised.

As a result of this quiet policy under Moi, Muslims saw themselves as benefitting from a more equitable distribution of school places at all levels of the system and of resources for the coast. Whereas under Kenyatta, Muslims had felt insecure regarding their religion, they did not do so under Moi. Money for mosques, *madrasa*, and bursaries to study at mosque colleges in Kenya or the Middle East flowed in freely from individuals resident in or linked to Saudi Arabia, Kuwait and the Gulf Emirates, and Iran and Pakistan. Under Kenyatta, these inflows of money had been questioned while under Moi there was little interference, despite his own Christian beliefs. The general verdict both of Muslims and the Arabs among them was that Moi valued them, as members of a minority group like himself, for their political support, an assumption that was borne out by later events, including an amendment in 1991 to the Kenya inheritance law which respected and took full account of the Islamic *sharia* by exempting Muslims from the 1981 uniform legislation on intestate succession.

During the late 1980s, an increasing number of Kenya coastal Muslims returned from courses at Middle East theological, or heavily theological, universities and mosque colleges. Schooled in a profound knowledge of Islamic *sharia*, texts and the Arabic language, but uninstructed in the secular subjects taught in Kenyan schools, such returnees had little alternative but to teach in the proliferating rural and urban *madrasa* (Islamic schools) which were being sponsored by benefactors, many from or connected with the Middle East, Iran and Pakistan. A consequence was not only an acceleration in the number of young persons able to receive Islamic instruction, but also a revitalisation of the Arabic language. Previously in the *madrasa*, pupils had only ever learned to recite the Qur'an, without understanding the language itself. The recent revival changed all that, and Arabic became a language usable for religious but also non-religious purposes. Accompanying this development was the propensity of many young men of Hadhrami origin to seek work in Saudi Arabia and other

Gulf countries, many of whom also returned with a spoken, if not literary, knowledge of Arabic.

Traditionally, a notion of 'Arabisation' had always been regarded as a desirable feature of high Muslim status in coastal Kenya and other parts of the former Protectorate. But few people could do more than recite memorised passages from the Qur'an. From the early and, especially, the mid-1980s onwards, 'Arabisation' took on new meaning as enabling creative communication in the language and not merely a phatic religious communication.

Although still confined to a minority of Muslims, this new Arab articulateness accentuated the phatic and religious value of the language among the mass of other Muslims. These latter aspired to competence, however limited, in a language which, for them, has sacred value as the 'true' language of Islam. There has always been this reverence for Arabic among Muslims who could not speak it. Now, however, their reverence was reinforced by the value placed on it by the increasing number of young Muslims learning it as a full language.

In this development, Arabic took on the ambivalent qualities of a commodity as I have described it. At the level of the new teachers of the madrasa it was purveyed as a universal good which can be deployed in a fuller understanding of Islamic texts and in communication with other Islamic scholars, as well as for practical work purposes. At the continuing level of the mass of Muslims, it existed in the fragments of memorised Qur'an and in the desire on the part of individuals to know more of the language and Islamic texts as sacred sources.

Arabic thus developed a kind of internal diglossia which is not however that of a formal versus informal kind, but rather that of universalising assumptions and productive efficacy, on the one hand, and of individual, relativised, and incomplete linguistic knowledge on the other hand. The difference is indeed reminiscent of that distinguishing political economy and postmodernism.

Arabic is, however, inscribed in the values and uses of other elements that make up its linguistic environment, principally Swahili. For, just as the two sides of Arabic have a distinctive relationship to each other, so do Arabic as a whole and Swahili. Arabic and Swahili are thus also diglossic in the sense of the former being set apart as a diatype from the latter. In addition, however, Swahili is also seen as at the beginning of a desirable route to competence in Arabic: one desires in Swahili the sacredness and 'civilising' qualities ascribed to a full knowledge of Arabic.

However, and this is where the logic of commodity consumerism shows its falsity. While a full, 'proper' and perfect command of Arabic is the desired goal of Muslims, they commonly acknowledge that this is in practice never attainable. There is always a better version, phrase or speaker, an unattainability which reinforces the sacred status of the language. Moreover, Swahili becomes regarded in the same light: there is always a more 'Arabised' and therefore more desirable form of Swahili one can speak. Diglossia is, then, not concerned only with the delineation of linguistic diatypes on the basis of formal communication contexts and status, as was Ferguson's original suggestion (1964) and as has become an accepted basis of the concept. It arises out of a pursuit of linguistic forms which, as in the desire for the endless proliferation of commodities in modern capitalist consumerism, can never be satisfied.

Arabic and Sacredness

In embarking on this argument, let me take as my starting point the relation between the Qur'an and the Arabic language. I begin with the early and bold assertion by Guillaume that the Qur'an has a different holy status from the Christian and Jewish Bibles. He claims that "textual criticism and modern study have made it impossible for modem scholars", apart from a minority of fundamentalists, to hold the belief that God inspired every word contained in the Bible. By contrast, he says:

> in Islam the doctrine of the infallible word of God is an article of faith, and the few who have questioned it have for the most part expressed their doubts in enigmatic language, so as to leave themselves a way of retreat from a dangerous position. (Guillaume 1956: 55)

For Guillaume, these believed qualities of the Qur'an can only truly be appreciated in its Arabic form or version. Since Guillaume wrote, fundamentalism may have become a more marked feature of both Christianity and Judaism, as it has also of Islam. Nevertheless, the difference is one with which most researchers working in Islamic communities will be familiar. The Qur'an in its Arabic form is held to be unquestionably sacred or holy, and exegetical disagreements about it among Muslim scholars appear to be relatively few.

Guillaume also mentions that the Qur'an must never rest beneath other books, but always on top of them, that, when it is being read aloud, listeners must never drink or smoke and must remain silent, and that it is used to counter disease and disaster (Guillaume 1956: 74). It is admired by many Arabic speakers not only for its religious import, but also as a literary work of poetry and prose and a source of wisdom through parables as well as through assertion and command.

This is the Qur'an basking in the idealism surrounding it. By contrast, Gilsenan also emphasises the authoritative element in the designation in Islam of the Qur'an as the holiest of holy texts. Produced as it was during a period when the masses were illiterate, any exegeses of the Holy Book were the sole preserve of the few who could read it. As time went on, more and more textual specialists would add their own, distinctive commentaries on the Qur'an, piling sub-text upon sub-text and so making it ever more difficult for the religious non-specialist, even if literate, to dare to assume the right to a personal interpretation of the original version. At the same time, as Gilsenan notes, any Muslim can in theory be accepted into religious training and so, in due course, join the ranks of those deemed qualified to comment on the Qur'an and on the texts it has spawned (1982: 31). The process of exclusion from, and of achieving the right to be included among the scholarly ranks serves to perpetuate the hierarchy of and respect for learning.

For those who do not reach this position of being able to offer such textual commentary, particularly the illiterate, the holiness of the Qur'an as text is metonymically re-cast as the sacredness of its Arabic script and of the Arabic language, especially for those who don't know it. Set down by the Prophet Himself as the proper language of the Qur'an and of Islam (Chapter 12, verse 2; Chapter 41, verse 3, see Akinnaso and Ogunbiyi 1990: 1), the sanctity of Arabic is of course a view shared by many Muslims. It may become the basis of a political protest movement, as when the Salafiya movement in Algeria based itself in the Arabic language of the Qur'an, itself regarded as a miraculous creation, and fought French cultural and linguistic hegemony (Gilsenan 1982: 153).

In many parts of Africa today, the sacred status of Arabic may be unquestioned, and its associated administrative and judicial functions much valued, but this by itself does not always qualify it for inclusion in school language education. As in Akinnaso and Ogunbiyi's study of language planning in Nigeria (1990), the secular educational position of Arabic may be under constant threat despite its high religious standing.

Arabic and Swahili in East Africa: A Story of Hegemony, Absorption and Alternating Fortunes

In the Kenya coast area, where I have worked, as elsewhere in African and other Muslim communities, we meet some of the same general characteristics, although, at the same time, there are also locally distinctive aspects.

The East African coast, from Mogadishu in Somalia to northern Mozambique and mainly comprising the Kenya and Tanzania shorelines, has experienced extensive Arab settlement over a period of centuries, mainly from the Hadhramaut (now south Yemen) and Oman. Arab influence on the language of the Swahili-speaking peoples of the east African coast primarily takes the form of religious and legal idioms, those concerned with courtly etiquette and behaviour and with evaluations of personal morality, and with medical therapy allegedly derived from the Qur'an. Amazingly, however, the Swahili language has remained resolutely Bantu in most of its vocabulary, and in all its syntax and grammar. Wave after wave of new Hadhrami and Omani Arab visitors settled at the coast. The most recent tended to assume overall power. These new arrivals would, for a generation or so, speak Arabic as their first tongue. However, after some few generations, sometimes through intermarriage with Swahili women, these Arabs would speak Swahili as their first language, gradually forgetting their Arabic. Thus, the Arabic language remained the preserve of whatever Arab élite was in power, while other, earlier groups would call themselves Arab and recall Arab genealogies, sometimes recruiting a wife from the Hadhramaut or Oman, but would themselves become Swahili-speaking.

It is for this reason that I.A. Salim prefers to refer to such peoples of the coast, of both Arab and African descent, as Swahili-speaking (1973). At any point in time, there would always be a small minority of East African coastal people who spoke Arabic, but they and their descendants were parties to a more general process of assimilation into Swahili language and culture.

Indeed, two inverse processes of assimilation occurred and continue to occur. One is the absorption into Swahili language and culture of peoples of Arab origins; and the other is the assimilation of coastal peoples of African and mixed descent into the various versions of Islam. These varieties of Islam were, and still are, carried and propagated by Muslim arrivals, who come, not just from the Hadhramaut and Oman but from other areas of the Middle East, and also from Pakistan and India. Despite such variations, most by far of East Africa's Muslims are Sunni.

Islamic and Arabic identities have had oscillating fortunes in recent generations. As mentioned above, in 1895 the British agreed with the Omani Sultan of Zanzibar to recognise his sovereignty over the whole East African coast up to a distance of sixteen kilometres inland (ten miles). This ensured Muslim dominance over the coastal area with respect to *sharia* law and land and property holdings. At about the same time, the British curtailment of the slave trade ruined the productivity of Arab plantations in the area, as agricultural labour became scarce. Tensions between so-called 'Arab' landlords and 'African' plantation workers (including ex-slaves) became severe, especially when the latter preferred no longer to work for the landlords and simply to use the land as their own, and were joined by new African migrants doing the same. Many of the ex-workers had themselves adopted Islam, and so the Arab-African division cut into the wider Islamic community.

If I may focus now on Kenya, Afro-Arab Muslim solidarity was regained for a while in the years immediately preceding Kenya's independence in 1963. The various political movements seeking coastal autonomy, principally that called *Mwambao*, emphasised coastal interests over and above internal differences. They sought to counter the growing influence of non-Muslim migrants from up-country Kenya. In census and other population returns, the numbers of respondents prepared to call themselves Arab and Swahili was considerable. They were seemingly prepared to announce such ethnic and Muslim identities unambiguously and with confidence.

Coastal autonomy was never achieved, however, and the area fell under the political control of the new, independent non-Muslim Government of President Jomo Kenyatta. Thereafter, the numbers of people referring to themselves in official censuses as either Arab or Swahili dropped markedly. Arabs might call themselves Swahili, and Swahili who could trace non-Swahili African descent, e.g. Digo, would refer to themselves as being of that African ethnic group.

Fortunes were, from the local viewpoint, reversed yet again from 1973 onwards, the year of the Arab-Israeli war. The war prompted a huge increase in the price of Arab-produced oil. Large amounts of money from the Middle East were poured into East African Islamic communities, as part of the more general Arab attempt to proselytise and expand Arab Muslim influence. The money was for new or refurbished mosques, scholarships for studying religious and other subjects in Saudi Arabia, Kuwait, or elsewhere in the Middle East, and for building schools in which Islamic as well as secular subjects would be taught.

In one area in which I worked, the southern coastal area of Kilifi district, several new mosques were built. They were rapidly followed by new Pentecostal churches constructed with North American funds. Visiting Arab Muslim scholars and American Christian missionaries and teachers proselytised in open competition with each other. Swahili, the language common to all communities, whether Muslim, Christian or drawn from traditional African pantheistic religion, became the medium of such proselytisation.

At the same time, the new Arab money encouraged young men of Sunni persuasion to study in Saudi Arabia, Kuwait, or, if they had Shi'ite links or were prepared to convert, in Iran. Paralleling this was the new desire on the part of men of Hadhrami Arab origin to try to seek work in Saudi Arabia and to go there as migrant workers. Both influences led to an increased knowledge of the Arabic language among people who, as second and even first-generation Kenyan residents, had largely forgotten it.

We may take, as an example, a Hadhrami family known to me (called Bawazir) who live in Mombasa. They consist of three brothers, two sisters, various cousins, and an aged father and mother. Two brothers run their own businesses independently of each other. They are ship chandlers, with one of them also trading to and from Uganda, where his wife lives nearly all the time and where he also spends long periods. Their father arrived in Mombasa from the Hadhramaut in the 1920s, where he immediately began work as a water carrier. He built up a small business of water-selling from this humble base, employing local people. He married a woman from a local Hadhrami family, whose children, including the man's wife, now spoke only Swahili. As the couple produced children, these latter, too, learned Swahili rather than Arabic, which their father himself had less and less occasion to use. But the wheel has come full circle. While the sons and daughter in the 1980s had Swahili as their mother tongue, the sons had taken a renewed interest in converting their rudimentary knowledge of Arabic into fluency. They saw this as another possible benefit of working in Saudi Arabia. They also listened to Egyptian-produced videos of Arabic-speaking stars of song and dance. They saw themselves as becoming re-Arabised. An entailed part of this process was to attend the mosque and pray five times a day, and to observe all other ritual demands. They were conscious of themselves becoming integrated within the strengthening stream of Islamic fundamentalism.

On the face of it, then, this process of re-Arabisation among Hadhrami families has a religious dimension. It entails greater commitment to Islam. But what about those other Muslims, the vast majority, who do go to Saudi Arabia, and for whom Swahili continues to be the language with which they will continue for the rest of their lives? How are they affected by the processes of reArabisation and Islamic fundamentalism?

We can begin to answer this question by tracing the ties of the same Hadhrami family, the Bawazir, to their locus among these other, nonArab, Swahili-speaking Muslims. Thus, the Bawazir Arabs, while having their main residence and businesses in Mombasa, also run shops in rural, or semi-urban, areas outside Mombasa. They run them through other members of the family, namely a brother or cousin. The brother, whom I first knew well, not only ran a shop in a rural centre (called Majengo), he also attended the local Friday mosque, which had itself been set up with funds donated by a prominent Muslim of South Asian origin, who had been to Mecca and was versed in Islamic learning.

This man, let us call him Mohammed, did not himself claim to be an Islamic scholar nor yet to know much Arabic, but he was commonly spoken of by local people as closer to God through his rudimentary knowledge of Arabic and his intention to go to Saudi Arabia, both to visit Mecca and to seek work. At local *maulidi* celebrations in honour of the Prophet's birth, he could explain to those who didn't know them, the meanings of portions of holy Arabic script taken from verses of the Qur'an and imprinted on the large cloths used to create an enclosure, or *riyadha*, round the men participating in the ceremony and between the men inside and the women outside.

The same veneration is accorded to those *maalims* and Muslim healers who take paper containing verses of the Qur'an written in Arabic and use it for both preventive and curative medicine. A piece of paper containing the requisite verse may be wrapped securely in a piece of cloth or leather and worn as an amulet. Or, Arabic verse may be written on, say, a slate or piece of glass, and then washed off with water, which is then drunk by the client seeking cure, good fortune, or an end to illness or misfortune. This use of the Qur'an to make talismans is well known throughout the Muslim world.

Here, in the coastal area of Kenya in which I worked, southern Kilifi district, these practices serve as a device to illustrate the extraordinary value given both to the utility and grandeur of a speaking knowledge of Arabic, and to the language's mystical powers. The people in the area do not on the whole themselves speak Arabic, although certain of their *maalims* may have anything from a smattering to a good command. Let us call them the Swahili, an appellation which is a crude, but useful, shorthand label. To repeat, the number of permanent residents in Kenya who speak Arabic is very small, but they represent the possibilities that are available to any pious Muslim scholar, Arab or Swahili, to study Islam and the Arabic language.

There are many other ways in which I could show the local people's view of the sacredness both of the Qur'an and of the Arabic script, especially when taken from the Qur'an. This veneration of the Holy Book and its script percolates down and takes the form also of a pre-eminence accorded to Arabic itself, as a whole language. It further serves to denote the life-style of high-status Muslims, including Arabs originating from or having spent time in the Middle East. There is in fact a Swahili verb, *ku-staarabu* or *ku-staarabika*, which means to acquire understanding, wisdom and civilisation, and which is locally sometimes taken (mistakenly in fact) to be derived etymologically from the idea of becoming Arabised.

None of this is to say that, as individuals, persons designated as Arabs are unconditionally accorded respect. They, like anyone else, must demonstrate good manners (*adabu*), humility and piety, in order to earn respect. It is rather that such people are potential carriers of a line that reaches back to the heart and origins of Islam. This is an idea most explicit in the designation of certain Hadhrami agnatic lines as containing Sharifs, or Sayyids, who claim descent from the Prophet. The idea of Arabness, as fused with the sanctity of the Arabic language, thus provides a model to be aimed at. Some Swahili aim to marry their daughters to men regarded as 'Arab', while the high-status form of Swahili marriage is itself said to be of Arabic origin.

Institutions and roles may also be characterised by local people as either 'Arabic' or 'Swahili'. Thus, people distinguish between Arabic and Swahili *maulidi*, diviners, marriages, and life-styles. For example, an Arabic *maulidi* opens up with Arabic prayers. Its verses, also called *maulidi* (i.e. as well as the overall ceremony) are long-established ones originally composed in Arabic, and in at least one case still untranslated into Swahili. In some cases they are verses on the life of the Prophet taken from the Qur'an. Such *maulidi* are relatively formal. By contrast, the so-called Swahili *maulidi* begin with prayers said in Swahili, while Arabic may not be used at all in the proceedings. The sung *maulidi* verses are not only in Swahili but are commonly made up specially for the occasion, and even created spontaneously on the spot, rather than being of ancient origin. Moreover, the Arabic *maulidi* ceremonies are said also to be larger than the Swahili ones, a claim confirmed by my own observation.

The larger and more important *maulidi* sermons contain a much higher proportion of Swahili words of Arabic origin than the smaller ones. On one occasion, at the prominent *maulidi* ceremony held at Takaungu in 1978, not only I but also some of the Swahili speakers who accompanied me, were baffled by certain highly Arabised passages as presented by the sermon giver, namely the then Chief Kadhi of Kenya, Sheikh A. S. AI-Farsy. Ironically, it was Al-Farsy who had produced one of the best Swahili translations of the Qur'an. The irony to which I refer is that AI-Farsy could, on the one hand, provide the non-Arabic speaking masses with a Swahili version of the Qur'an which they could read, and yet could also present a sermon before thousands of the same people which not all could fully understand. An authoritative Muslim response, which I heard once or twice from *maalims*, was that this was a deliberate and wise ploy on his part to underline how necessary it was to have children and adults learn to read, write and understand Arabic, for then they would have direct and full access to the wisdom and purity of Islam. Did not the Prophet describe the Qur'an as "A book whereof the verses are explained in detail – a Qur'an in Arabic for a people who understand" (chapter 41, verse 3 of the Qur'an. Cited from Akinnaso and Ogunbiyi 1990: 1)?

The linking of wisdom and understanding with purity, and of these with piety, is, of course, common in Islamic pronouncements. To be pious is to achieve understanding, and this is to achieve purity. But how widespread among Kenya Muslims is the view that this is in practice only fully possible through a knowledge of the Qur'an in Arabic, and that those who do not possess this knowledge suffer a definite handicap? Is in fact the purity that leads to Godly understanding linguistic as well as based on prayer and righteous observances?

Justo Lacunza (1991) considers this question in comparing the pronouncements of three religious writers, one of whom is Sheikh Al-Farsy mentioned above. The earliest writer, Sheikh Al-Amin bin Aly Al-Mazrui, 1875–1949, takes a hard, pro-Arabic line. Writing in 1939, he claims that 'Arabic is the language of the Qur'an, Almighty God has commanded us that we think about the meaning of the Qur'an every time we read it, and how will we know its meaning if we do not know the Arabic language?' (cited by Justo Lacunza, 1991, from Sh. Al-Amin b. Aly (1939) *Uwongozi*, Mombasa: EAMWS, 21). Much later, in 1976, Sheikh Al-Farsy (1912–82), the *maulidi* preacher referred to above, sees an insistence on the knowledge of Arabic as tantamount to the colonisation of religion. He does not dispute the supreme importance of the language among the Muslim scholarly elite of the East African coast, but, in the words of Lacunza, he 'realised that Kiswahili had become de facto the language of Islam in the context of East Africa ... (and wished) to harmonise, from the point of view of Islam, the coast and the interior, the Arab and the non-Arab, the Swahili and the non-Swahili' (Lacunza 1991 in which he cites Sh. A. S. Al-Farsy (1976) *Tunda la Qur'an*, Mombasa: Adam Traders, 4–5). In 1987 the most recent of the three writers, Sheikh Saidi Musa (born 1944), expresses unambiguously his support for the Islamic revolution of Iran and Khomeini's leadership, seeing it as a model which East Africa should emulate, and finds no need at all to tie Islam to the Arabic language, since, in East Africa, Kiswahili is for him now the indispensable medium for teaching and propagating the religion and organising Muslim society.

It may well be, as these examples intimate, that among the East African literati and scholars, the Swahili language is beginning to take precedence over Arabic as the medium by which Islam should be communicated and discussed. There is no doubting the impact of Al-Farsy's Swahili translation of the Qur'an, which, heavily subsidised by Middle East benefactors, is available to all Muslims at a low price. But how far has this relative dismissal of Arabic percolated down to the vast majority of ordinary Muslims? I would argue that, among such people, little has changed with regard to the sacred and purificatory healing potentialities offered by the Arabic Qur'an and its scriptural text, as I have outlined above. I would also suggest that, as a result of the proliferation of new *madrasa* headed by Islamic teachers trained in the Middle East or local mosque college in Arabic and in the religion, the sanctity of Arabic has been further boosted.

Indeed, as we move down the social hierarchy, we see that the notion of purity takes on even greater significance as a route to understanding and self-improvement. Here, too, this purity is given linguistic essence.

A Muslim Fishing Community in Mtwapa, Coastal Kenya

More microscopically, let me move at this point to consider a small community of Muslim fishermen inhabiting the shoreland of an area north of Mombasa, called Mtwapa. These are poor Muslims. They use Swahili as their first language in conversation with each other, both publicly and privately, but the older ones among them can understand surrounding dialects of peoples related to the Swahili but, until recently, non-Muslim, from whom the community of fishermen derives. These dialects are in fact the vernacular varieties of a people called the Mijikenda. Thus, we may call the fishermen intermediary Swahili, for they no longer speak a Mijikenda language, but instead speak Swahili, and have the appearance of being transitional between their non-Muslim Mijikenda origins and the full Swahili status to which they aspire. Most other Mijikenda both continue to speak their Mijikenda dialects and remain non-Muslim.

Taking a broad view, then, people will speak of there being three language groups, each associated with one of three, roughly defined, groups of people standing at different distances from Islam: Arabs, Swahili, and the non-Muslim Mijikenda. Those fishermen I am calling intermediary Swahili thus stand between the latter two groups.

Kiswahili comprises the vocabulary both of Arabic and the Mijikenda vernacular. It is often itself seen as intermediary in religious terms between Arabic, which has high diglossic status, and the non-Muslim Mijikenda vernacular which has low status in the eyes of Muslims.

But these Swahili-speaking fishermen see themselves, also, as intermediary in a cultural and ethnic sense. This is a theme that comes out often in sermons, divinations, and conversation. A *maalim* speaking at a *maulidi* ceremony will denounce palm-wine tapping and, of course, drinking, and will link such activities to neglect of Islamic prayer, ritual and attendance at mosques (see Chapters 9 and 10). He will also link the origin of such behaviour to the origin of the people themselves, namely their non-Muslim Mijikenda 'cousins' (*wenzetu*). He argues that such misconduct is sin or negligence bordering on sinfulness.

Outside of the context of ceremonies and sermons, *maalims* combine ideas about proper religious conduct with those of proper social behaviour. The use of language commonly features in such ideas. From an early age, children are scolded if they reciprocate the non-Muslim forms of greeting. Such training is easy in a totally Muslim home. It also occurs, though with greater difficulty, in homes of mixed religion. For example, a non-Muslim Mijikenda/Giriama[1] friend and I entered a Giriama homestead, in which one of the women had converted to Islam as a result of spirit possession. My friend greeted the woman's six-year-old daughter in Giriama, but the child did not answer. This is normally unheard of, but was explained as necessary, since both mother and child would suffer severe sickness if they were not to obey the dictates of their possessory Islamic spirit, which is in fact called an 'Arab' spirit (*pepo* or *nyama ya kiarabu*) and which refuses to be addressed by a non-Muslim and in an 'impure' (*chafu*) language like Giriama. The mother and her daughter would only speak to and answer members of her homestead in Swahili. Moreover, this was neither opposed nor discouraged by the homestead members, who well recognised the power of Islamic spirits to determine people's destinies in this way.

Among the fishermen I have been describing, not only is Swahili the only acceptable language of communication, but also its members will not normally respond to any of the non-Muslim Mijikenda dialects, despite the fact that some have a passive knowledge of them. They explain this by claiming that to speak and respond to such non-Muslim Mijikenda dialects is to lay oneself open to the contaminating practices associated with the non-Muslim speakers, namely their production and drinking of alcohol, their heavy reliance on non-Qur'anic divination and therapy, their lengthy funerals involving dance and drink, and the fact that their diets may include pork and other foodstuffs forbidden to Muslims. To speak and know a non-Muslim language is to become consubstantial with the character and practices of its speakers.

The Swahili word that is used most succinctly to define these nonIslamic practices is *ushirikina*, which, deriving from the Arabic, *shirk*, refers to the worship of many gods, or polytheism. Certainly, the traditional religion of the non-Muslim Mijikenda can reasonably be called pantheism or animism involving the veneration of spirits in addition to or instead of the single Allah, although its sophisticated complexity is lost in the translation as *shirk* or *ushirikina*. Such polytheistic veneration is described by Muslim *maalims* and their followers as the root cause of impurity, for they see it as opposed to the idea of a single God and as therefore liable to re-contaminate those whose conversion to Islam is historically only recent. They say that speaking the language of those who practise *ushirikina* is like communicating with, and in the tongues of, the Devil (Al-Shaitan), who manifests himself in the form of countless possessory spirits or demons, which, unlike the jinns identified in the Qur'an, have no legitimate religious status.

At the other end of the diglossic spectrum, children and adults in this fishing community are encouraged by their local *maalim* to incorporate as many Arabic words as possible into their Swahili vocabulary, and children are urged to emulate the few African *maalims* in the district who have studied Arabic at one of the prominent mosque colleges in either Lamu, Kenya, or the Middle East. The Arabic terms denote concepts of a religious and legal nature, but also prescribe and evaluate so-called 'civilised' behaviour. The effect is that people become aware not only of their distinctive Muslim status but of a putatively Arabised life-style and manner of speaking. Religious, linguistic and behavioural socialisation here go together. The purity of Arabic language and conduct becomes an inseparable part of the unquestioned purity of Islam.

Thus, the non-Muslim Mijikenda dialects are shunned as contaminating, while Arabic vocabulary, language, text and script are embraced as providing the purest communicative access to Islam.

Lacking the possibility of almost any of them ever learning Arabic, we might at this point imagine that the members of this fishing community would be happy, therefore, to settle on Swahili, albeit as Arabised as possible, as the language most appropriate to the social and religious demands made of them by their *maalim*.

Incredibly, however, the process of differentiation and of proliferation does not end here. The *maalim* not only specifies the use of Swahili over and against the Mijikenda dialects, he also insists on a distinctive form of Swahili pronunciation, which we may gloss as Ki-Mvita or, as some put it more specifically, Ki-Jomvu, which is broadly associated with the long-established elite of Mombasa Old Town. The *maalim* rebukes children and young people who use the standard Swahili forms as heard, for instance, on the radio and as spoken by non-Muslim Mijikenda or up-country people as a second language.

For example, the standard Swahili form, *njoo* (come!) is rendered as *ndo-oo*. As one young girl put it, 'If any of us were to say *njoo*, our *maalim* Hassan would get very angry and ask, "Whoever taught you to speak like that? That is modem Swahili (*ya siku hizi*), but it is not of any importance (*si ya maana*) and is not polite (*si ya adabu*)."' According to this *maalim*, Hassan, one should also say *mwiche*, 'call him', and not the standard form, *mwite*, and so on. For *maalim* Hassan, such standard Swahili forms are not sources of impurity, as is the use of the non-Muslim Mijikenda vernaculars, but they are debased or fallen forms. This is an ironic judgement, in that standard Swahili is in fact founded on an older form of Zanzibari Swahili (Ki-Unguja). Even when one thinks one has mastered the distinctive consonantal changes and nasal sounds, one may then be told by the *maalim* to use an Arabic word rather than a Bantu one. 'Say, "taib", not "nzuri" (good), and say "ku-arifu" and not "ku-ambia" (to tell) whenever possible', he will declare.

Some contrasts between standard and Kimvita Swahili are as follows:

	Kimvita	***Standard Kiswahili***
(to) take	*tukua*	*chukua*
play	*teza*	*cheza*
slaughter	*tinda*	*chinja*
throw	*tupa* (explosive, tongue forward)	*tupa*
bottle	*tupa* (implosive, tongue back a little)	*chupa*
uncooked rice	*mtele*	*mchele*
leave!	*ata*	*acha*
hunger	*ndaa*	*njaa*
outside	*nde*	*nje*

Conclusion

At issue in this drive by this and other *maalims* are two contradictory tendencies. On the one hand, the *maalim* attempts to differentiate ever more finely the Islamic distinctiveness of his group of Muslim fishermen. In seeking increasingly refined concepts of religious purity, he focusses on language and, in doing so, identifies people with these language differences. Alleged speech differences are the most salient identity tag and come to summarise other differences, some desired as in the case of

Arabic and high forms of Swahili, and some unacceptable and impure as in the case of the non-Muslim Mijikenda dialects. On the other hand, the *maalim* evidently believes in some kind of core Islamic purity, an ideal that can be attained through both speech and behaviour. But in seeking this ideal, he sets up one line of differentiation after another: speak Arabic and not Mijikenda; speak this Swahili variety and not that; incorporate Arabic words rather than Bantu words in Swahili vocabulary; use only phonemes judged to be most distant from non-Muslim usage. Since the *maalim* has constantly to admonish speakers for falling short of such expectations, he clearly never completely gets his community to reach this core of Islamic purity. All he can do is to attempt always to move away from what he regards as the contaminating effects of non-Muslim life and language. But this constant escape, so vividly captured in *maulidi* sermons given by himself and others (see Parkin 1985 and Chapters 9 and 10), becomes a ceaseless struggle to attain the purity he advocates. Like Zeno's arrow which, in distancing itself further and further from its point of origin, nevertheless has to move through an infinity of mid-points, this and other *maalims* seem never to reach the puritanical destination. The play on language is, after all, a play on the endlessness of signification. Diglossia comprising high and low diatypes is one such play, which, having a life of its own, may fall through the net of government policy.

Note

(1) The Mijikenda are regarded as comprising nine sub-groups, the dominant one of which is that of the Giriama.

References

Akinnaso, F.N. and Ogunbiyi, I.A (1990) 'The place of Arabic in language planning in Nigeria', *Language Problems and Language Planning* 14, 1, 1–20.

Baudrillard, J. (1972) *Pour une critique de l'économie politique du signe*, Paris: Gallimard.

Ferguson, C. (1964) 'Diglossia', in D. Hymes (ed.) *Language in Culture and Society*, New York, Evanston and London: Harper and Row.

Gilsenan, M. (1982) *Recognizing Islam: an Anthropologist's Introduction*, London and Sydney: Croom Helm.

Guillaume, A. (1954) *Islam*, Harmondsworth, Middlesex: Penguin.

Habermas, J. (1983) [1981] 'Modernity- an incomplete project', in H. Foster (ed.) *Postmodern Culture*, London and Sydney: Pluto Press.

Lacunza Balda, J. (1991) 'Tendances de la litterature islamique swahili', in Francoise Le Guennec-Coppens and Pat Caplan (eds) *Les Swahili entre Afrique et Arabie*, Paris and Nairobi: Credu Karthala.

Lyotard, J.F. (1984) [1979] *The Postmodern Condition: a Report on Knowledge*, Manchester: Manchester University Press.

Mintz, S. (1985) *Sweetness and Power*, London and New York: Penguin.

Parkin, D. (1985) 'Being and selfhood among intermediary Swahili', in J. Maw and D. Parkin (eds) *Swahili Language and Society*, Vienna: Institut für Afrikanistik und Agyptologie der Universität Wien.

Salim, A.I. (1973) *The Swahili-Speaking Peoples of the Kenya Coast 1895–1965*, Nairobi: East African Publishing House.

Taussig, M. (1980) *The Devil and Commodity Fetishism in South America*, Chapel Hill: University of North Carolina Press.

Ulin, R.C. (1991) 'Critical anthropology twenty years later', *Critique of Anthropology* 11, 1, 63–90.

Wolf, E. (1982) *Europe and the People without History*, Berkeley: University of California Press.

9 Being and Selfhood among Intermediary Swahili

There is a Mijikenda (Giriama)[1] verb, *ku-ingiriria*, which can be translated as "to infiltrate" an ethnic, cultural, religious grouping other than one's own.[2] It is widely used along the coastal strip north of Mombasa in Kenya. In this area, Mijikenda homesteads are interspersed with Muslim variously designated 'Arab', 'Gunya', and 'Digo'. Only a few Mijikenda homesteads bear this label and are also called Muslim. Until independence in 1963 the non-Muslim peoples in this area were dubbed "squatters". Various developments since then, including the conversion of previously Muslim-held land into settlement schemes, have removed this label.

Before working in this rural area, and in particular in a village called Mwando wa Panya and its environs, just north of Mtwapa, I had had a working experience in both Swahili and Giriama. My intention, indeed, was to capitalise on this knowledge of the two cognate languages and do a bi-lingual, bi-cultural study of both Muslim and non-Muslim peoples. I had been unhappy with the tendency in previous studies known to me, to treat either the Swahili (however they might be defined) or the Mijikenda (or their sub-groups) as separable and discrete ethnic units (see Salim 1985 and Swartz 1985 for related discussions). For it is clear that the Swahili have constantly increased their stock from intermarriage or miscegenation with the Mijikenda and from the conversion to Islam of Mijikenda individuals, as I have shown (Parkin 1970); that certain key cosmological ideas are held in common (Parkin 1979a); and that the marriage systems of both peoples, so different on the surface, may be seen as variations on a basic pattern (Parkin 1980).

The surface features of marriage, dress, residence, diet, occupation, speech, and style, might indeed persuade the casual observer that the Mijikenda and Swahili are indeed discrete entities. More than that, I sometimes had the curious experience of introducing to, say, a Swahili rural homestead a Mijikenda acquaintance of mine who would express genuine amazement at the differences of custom between the two groups, even though he might have come from the same area of interspersed homesteads, in which his own neighbours of a few hundred metres distance might themselves be Muslim. Similar 'hidden' differences of custom among peoples who live near to each other have been reported from village India among peoples separated on the basis of *jati*.

Yet, as well as the underlying similarities in, say, processes of divination, in spirit possession seances, in methods of cure and therapy, and in proverbs, the use of the term *mwangiriri*, an infiltrator, indicates that Mijikenda are perfectly well aware that there is, and for a long time has been, a voluntary movement by individuals not just from one Mijikenda ethnic group to another, but from the non-Muslim Mijikenda to groups carrying various designations, one of which is 'Swahili'.

The key appellation in this transition is that of 'Digo'. Digo principally refers to the now wholly Muslim Mijikenda group of Kwale district, (see Gerlach 1963, Gomm 1972, *et al.*). There are also, however, a number of village groupings distributed along the coastal strip north of Mombasa at least as far as Kilifi who both sometimes go under the name of 'Digo' and, moreover, include members who claim relatedness to people in Kwale Digoland and visit them frequently.

In other words, these northern villages include a core of 'genuine' Digo, to whom are added others of diverse origins, including some from such Mijikenda sub-groups as Duruma, Chonyi, Jibana, Ribe, Rabai, Kambe, Kauma and even, though to a much lesser extent, Giriama, as well as some from Tanzania and Central Africa. With the exception of the few latter, it does not appear to be the case that these village peoples are descended from slaves. They appear to have migrated within the last hundred years or so from Digoland itself or other Mijikenda areas. The fishing village of Mwando wa Panya, in which I lived for over a year, has very strong ties with certain homesteads in Digoland, yet its members speak only Swahili. They, together with a community of Muslims numbering many hundreds in an area of a couple of square miles, are frequently referred to as Swahili, especially on collective religious occasions such as the Maulidi celebrations, when sermons are delivered by religious leaders from near and far. Over the generations, nonMuslim Mijikenda women have been taken in marriage or concubinage into this mainly Digo Muslim group. Also, however, the Muslim women of this Digo group have themselves been taken by another local grouping, regarded by Digo as being of higher religious status, called Gunya (sometimes Bajuni by outsiders). Gunya claim and are accorded connections and origins with the similarly prestigious Arabo-Swahili traditional town of Lamu. These lines of infiltration may not always be discussed openly, indeed they rarely are, but they are occasionally referred to positively and are clearly not forgotten. Moreover, they are recognised as a common thread running through the diversity we call coastal society.

This is the underlying similarity of essence about which all people express hinted knowledge, even if, more openly, they sometimes deny it.

I venture to suggest that this unusual imposition of nominal difference on essential resemblance and equivalence creates the distinctive features of the ontology, or theory of being, characteristic of these particular non-urban Swahili. I emphasise the non-urban aspect of their definition, for it is to sea or, marginally, to the land that they look for their livelihood, with an aspiring number moving, as one might except, into shops, stalls, and trade in the small centres and towns growing along the line of road from Mombasa to Malindi.

These rural Swahili, if I may call them such, are thus distinctive in two main ways. First, they are clearly not products of the top echelons of coastal society. It is, indeed, doubtful whether high-placed families in, say, Mombasa, Lamu, or even Takaungu, would even accept them as 'Swahili' in any sense of the term, (cf. Salim 1973). Yet, these same high-placed urban-based Swahili are frequently consulted by rural Swahili for religious and other advice and are brought in as religious leaders and preachers to Islamic festivals, especially those of the Maulidi celebrations. Observationally, then, we are obliged to think of the whole Sunni Muslim community of the coast in terms of a single canvas: there are festive occasions and there are courts and systems of patronage which create enduring linkages, however, much there may also be internal sub-group distinctiveness and exclusiveness.

Second, these lower-order Swahili, as we may further call them, are thus intermediary as a social category between those who would regard themselves as *waungwana* (elite) Swahili of the twelve 'tribes' and the non-Muslim Mijikenda (formerly the infamously called Wanyika – 'people of the bush') who exist in large numbers both in the hinterland and along the coast. Yet, though the lower-order Swahili are an intermediary category, I would argue that, in their activities and in their private and public discussions about selfhood and destiny, they express most poignantly issues that affect higher-order Swahili as much as themselves. They are, so to speak, that much closer to the question of how origins shape destiny and how much the individual and his God are constrained by those origins in the search for ultimate 'purity' and 'truth'.

Exhortations, rhetorical questioning and evaluative commentary on behaviour make up much of the *maulidi* sermons. They implicitly turn on ontological issues. *Maulidi* celebrations are not the only occasions on which these issues are discussed. But they have a special significance in that they involve: (a) an extensive network of the same people attending different *maulidi* at different times along the coastal strip; and

(b) prominent as well as local-level religious leaders. The impact of a single *maulidi* is not, therefore, to be seen in isolation. Rather, it is part of a chain of communications which is spread geographically as well as over time, and which connects the views of higher and lowerorder Swahili.

We can see this spatial, temporal and communicative spread in a list, with dates, of the *maulidi* attended by at least some of the members of my village and myself. Not all village-centred *maulidi* networks will be the same, of course but there is sufficient overlap for issues discussed in sermons to reach across large areas of coastal society. Here, it must be emphasised that sermons are listened to by many in the congregation and thereafter discussed in some context or other. Preachers take pride in their oratorical skills and in the subtlety and impact of argument, and try to ensure the memorability of sermons.

The following are *maulidi* celebrations known and attended by myself and some other members of the village of Mwando wa Panya, with 'owners' or sponsors indicated where applicable. I tape-recorded a number of these *maulidi,* which were transcribed in the Swahili in which they were delivered and later translated into English.

***Maulidi* sites and 'owners' within Mtwapa-Junju locations:**

9 February 1978.	*Barani*. Maalim Hamisi bin Swaleh
11 Feb.	*Barani*. Maalim Ali Haji
16 Feb.	*Kikambala*. Maalim Juma Zahoro
18 Feb.	*Mwando wa Panya*. Maalim Hassan bin Idi
19 Feb. (morning)	*Mtwapa*. Maalim Hassan bin Mdigo
19 Feb. (afternoon)	*Jeuri*. Maalim Salim Mwaidani
4 March	*Majengo*. Maal im Hassan bin Idi/ Sharifu Ahmed Bedui

In addition, there were a number of smaller *maulidi* in the area, the last one occurring on 19 May 1978.

***Maulidi* Outside Mtwapa-Junju locations:**

22 February	*Takaungu*
9 March	*Mambrui*
9 March (also)	*Lamu*
25 March	*Kibokoni* (Old Mombasa). Mohamed Ahmed Hussein (see also below)
25 May	*Ngombeni* (in Digoland). Maalim Mwinyi Hamisi
27 May	*Sidiriya* (Mombasa). Musa Yusuf Boto and Mohamed Ahmed Hussein

People claimed (as of 1978) that there had in recent years been a proliferation of *maulidi*, and that this was the reason that the month in which the prophet was born (*mfunguo wa sita*) was simply not long enough to accommodate them all. The motives for sponsorship of individual *maulidi* celebrations were mixed: prestige, recognition, acceptance on the part of newcomers, and religious devotion. Local-level political factors were important, too, for, as is often pointed out, the *maulidi* are inherited from one *maalim* to another and so, over the years, validate a community's claim to land. After Kenya's independence in 1963, land rights were under much scrutiny and new claims and counterclaims were made with great rapidity.

Religious connections, marriage alliances between religious leaders, and mutual participation in each other's Maulidi, are reflected in the spatial dispersal of different *maulidi*. For example, Maalim Mohamed Ahmed Hussein, who cosponsored and sang at two important Mombasa *maulidi* (Kibokoni and Sidiriya) was the then recent (1975) son-in-law of Maalim Hassan bin Idi who sponsored two *maulidi* in the local area of Mtwapa-Junju (Mwando wa Panya and Majengo). Maalim Mohamed was called and called himself an "Arab" (in fact Hadhrami/Yemeni) whose former Yemeni wife was divorced after nine years of marriage, and Maalim Hassan was referred to as "Digo"/"Swahili" and was recognised as the area's senior religious leader by Arab patrons who provided money to improve local mosques.

As the texts below show, territorial and factional claims are inevitably brought into sermons, though in such a subtle way that only the informed could detect them. But running through these subtle differences are the common themes of human selfhood, destiny, and the problem of personal control. The most important single premise on which these themes are based is precisely that of 'infiltrations' i.e. of a potentially 'pure' Islamic way of life being tainted and hindered by lapses of morality associated with pre- or non-Islamic barbarity. In other words, the 'infiltration' by persons into other groups which is joked about by non-Muslim Mijikenda and denoted by the verb *ku-ingiriria*, is an aspect of the same channel through which come ideas and practices which threaten the purity of Islam. Phrased still more starkly, the opposition between Muslim and non-Muslim, between Mijikenda ('Wagiriama/ Wanyika') and Swahili ('Waswahili'/ Waislamu/Wajomba'), and between 'the enlightened' ('Waungwana') and 'the barbarians' ('Washenzi'), provides a basic framework in which ideas and practice can be placed and evaluated. The point of the sermons is not to emphasise these as distinctions of peoples or 'races', but of alternative personhoods.

It is important to stress this aspect: it is so easy to misinterpret these folkdistinctions as in some way examples of 'racial' or 'ethnic' prejudice on the part of the preachers of sermons. Nothing could be further from the truth. It is well recognised by the preachers, *maulidi* sponsors, and congregations of the *maulidi* attended by my villagers that they are all, or mostly, genealogically related to non-Muslim Mijikenda. In making such distinctions of worth, such speakers simply indicate the alternative moral possibilities open to any individual; not only in making the conversion from non-Muslim to Muslim, but also, among Muslims themselves, in fulfilling as much as possible the demands of a 'true' Islam.

I illustrate the various aspects of this ontology by selecting passages from *maulidi* sermons. These abstracts are minute fractions of the full texts but point up salient features. They are taken from the tape-recordings made by myself with the permission of the preachers. I have attempted to keep to the original and have ignored grammatical standardisation.

An important skill of preachers is their ability to turn an incident during the *maulidi* into an opportunity for moral comment. Thus, during the sermon of the Maulidi of Mwando wa Panya (my own village) a fight between youths broke out. It was soon quelled. But the preacher, Maalim Omari, uses the incident to illustrate the dangers of allowing disorderliness into Islam:

> Haya vipi, tutakuwa watu bora? Mwenyezi Mungu atatupaka rangi ... na rangi yenyewe nituwe tutakuwa. tukiamrishana sisi wenyewe mambo mema ... na tuwe tukikatazana mambo maehafu, mambo maovu, mambo yasiyopendeza kabisa, mambo yatatufanya sisi kutafuta katika rangi ile tuliyopakwa. Sasa katika dhana hizi tulizo sisi rangi hii imetutoka kabisa. Rangi hii tuliyopewa na Mwenyezi Mungu .... imetutoka. Hatuamrishi tena mema, hatutakasi tena maovu. Na dalili tutaieleza, tutaionyesha wazi, Mwenyezi Mungu .... katika kutuweka katika ulimwengu huu alituwekea vitu kadhaa, ili sisi tunufaike kwa vitu hivyo na akatuwekea mipaka kwa vitu kadhaa, kuwa tusijinufaishe sisi kwa vitu hivyo. Angalia maasia makubwa ulirmJenguni ambayo yajulikana tangu mwanzo hakujatokea binadamu ilikuwa hakuna kama tembo .... Mama wa maasia ni tembo. Tuangalie zana zetu hizi za sasa tembo latoka kwa kina nani? Tembo la gemwa na kina nani? Waislamu, waislamu walipewa miti hiyo wanufaike kwa miti hiyo. Leo watoa maji katika miti ile ikawa akili ya watu zitapotea zikawa katika ghafula kama hizi zitaharibu.

Translation. *So how can we be better people? God paints us (i.e.gives good character). This paint means we shall and should demand of each other to do good deeds, and to disallow ourselves from doing dirty things (machafu) or rotten things (mabovu), things which will cause the colour*

> *we were painted to be wiped away. Nowadays the colour has faded (i.e. we have no faith). The colour that God gave us has come out from us. The Almighty God does not command us to do good anymore, He no longer cleanses us our evil deeds. And this we can explain it, we can clearly show it: God, in placing us in this world, he placed before us certain things for us to use for our benefit, but he also placed boundaries (mipaka) around certain other things which we are not to use (i.e. the permissible and the forbidden). Since the beginning of mankind there has been no greater source of trouble known to the world than liquor. The mother of this evil is liquor. And these days let us see from whom the liquor comes? The palm pine is tapped by whom? Muslims! Muslims were given these trees (by God) for their beneficial use. Today they produce water (i.e. liquor) from those trees which makes people lose their minds and, unawares, destroy them.*
>
> Na yote haya ni sababu ya kukosekana shariti hakuna kamwe, yaonyesha hivi kwa kukosekana. shariti hata swala zetu zaonyesha pia hazina shariti .... Na laula kama zingekuwa zina shariti haingewezekana kabisa ama ingekuwa si adabu kabisa kuwa ati sisi tumealikana kuwa tuje katikati mkutano huu wa Mtume ... Leo mmoja yuko Makaburini, mmoja yuko Mbirani, mmoja yuko Magengeni ...
>
> *All this is because of a lack of rules (sharti). There are none at all. It shows in this way that even our prayers show no respect for rules. And if there were rules it would not have been possible or would have been seen as unseemly conduct for us to invite ourselves here today to this meeting in honour of the Prophet and yet to find someone in the cemetery, another watching football, and another in clubs (e.g. playing cards or gossiping) (i.e. not everyone attends maulidi but should).*

There is further reference to the disorderly nature of the youths who fought in the *riyadha*, which is then followed by other contrasts with the ideal state of Islam:

> Mtoto wa fulani leo amefanya kosa kwa sababu huyu ni mtoto wa fulani ni basi tunyamazeni. Mtoto wa fulani leo akifanya kosa basi tulinyamazeni kwa sababu ni mtoto wa fulani. Mtu fulani leo amefanya kosa kama hilo haliwezekani kufanywa, kwa sababu ya makosa kama haya walilaniwa. Katika hawo wako ambao Mwenyezi Mungu aliwadodomeza katika haki, katika hao wako ambao waliangamizwa katika bahari na katika hawo wako ambao waliangamizwa kwa ukelele.
>
> *Today, (if) someone's son (child) has done something wrong, because he is the child of someone (whom we know or who is important), we keep quiet. (Repeated to indicate that the offender is the child of someone*

important). Someone today has done something wrong which it's impossible to do (unheard of). Because of such wrongs they (the people of old) were cursed. Among these were those who the Almighty God justly sank, among whom were those who were destroyed at sea and those who were destroyed by thunder (i.e. a noise from god?).

Na sisi tukifuata nyayo walizopita watu hawo itatupata kilicho wapata wao. Na dalili twayiona imebakia kugeuka sura kama nguruwe. Imebaki hii lakini hali nyingi tushaziingia sasa tulikuwa twapenda sasa kuigiza. Basi sasa imebaki ije sura ya nguruwe nasi tujifanananishe. Nayayo tuwe tumeshakwisha tena umeshaondoka ule uso wetu. Ajabu kabisa, sifa mbaya tulizo nazo hazipendezi kabisa. Hivi lau(la) kama mimi ndimi mamulaka wa maulidi haya ningewataka kwa lazim wale (i.e. the fighting youths), maanake mtoto asema ... sentence Lost ... ikiwa wewe utaogopa kulea mtoto kwa sababu nikimchapa atalia au labda kutakuja na nyanyake atanitolea jicho nawe uligope, au maanake atakuja nitolea jicho, basi utalia wewe.

And if we follow the ways (footsteps) of the people who did such things, we will experience what they experienced. And the indication can be seen, what remains is for our faces to change to that of pigs. We have immersed ourselves in most of their ways because we like imitating them. So now, what is next is the face of pigs to come so that we look like them. Then we shall be finished, and our face shall have disappeared. Astonishingly, our bad reputation does not please anybody at all. If I could be the one with authority over these Maulidi festivals I would have compelled those (fighting youths), because the child says ... ... if you will fear to bring up a child because you say 'if I beat him he will cry or maybe the grandmother may come and scold me and I fear that, or his mother, will come and scold me, then you will end up crying yourself. (a Swahili proverb: "If you don't want your child to cry, then you will cry yourself").

Na dalili twaziona watoto wetu, kwa sababu ya kuogopa kitu kama hiki wamekuwa hawatuajali sisi baba zao.

And we see the signs in our own children, Because of our fearing (to be firm) they no longer take notice of us, their fathers.

The interconnected themes of allowing liquor to enter the lives of good Muslims, of thereby falling into evil ways and being cursed forever by God (like Christians and Israelites, as others put it afterwards), and of losing control over one's young, are repeated in different ways. The key culprit is liquor and, though it is not explicit in this sermon, it is always made clear in other contexts that most tappers of palm wine and most consumers are the non-Muslim Mijikenda, from whom much of the congregation has direct ancestry. The expunging of the evil effects of the palm wine and of the disorderly characteristics of a people allegedly without a 'true' sense of order, become interchangeable idioms.

The use of the term 'rangi' (paint, colour, or dye) introduces the idea of the changeability of character. We may be born with a character, yet we are also given a character by God. That is to say, God gives us the potential for good and honourable living, yet we have it within our intrinsic nature to reject that character and paint ourselves in a different, evil shade. We may even, as the sermon later tells us, assume the facial characteristics of the unholy pig. Given that pigs may be, and sometimes are, both eaten and, nowadays, kept by Mijikenda non-Muslims, the equation between this kind of cultural culinary preference and unholy personal characteristics is clear. But, more than this, there is an equation between non-Muslim lifestyle and intrinsically evil human characteristics on the one hand, and a lifestyle according to Muslim law and a personal control of our Godgiven characteristics on the other. Bearing in mind, again, that all or most of the congregation are well aware of their non-Muslim ancestry and, in some cases, of non-Muslim relatives actually living nearby, it is easy to see why God is seen as inspiring men and women with the knowledge that they can *choose* to suppress those intrinsic 'natural' characteristics. The contrast between, on the one hand, pigs and animality, raw palm wine which is tapped straight from the tree, wild, abandoned youth and the prayerlessness and rule-lessness of the people associated with these heinously regarded characteristics, and, on the other, the "enlightenment" of proper Muslims, reminds one of the analytical contrast often made between 'nature' and 'culture'. It is, perhaps, no accident that the Mijikenda used to be known, and privately often still are, as the Wanyika, literally people of the 'bush' or 'wilderness', and so are contrasted with the 'enlightened' *Waungwana* Swahili of the towns. To call a man Mnyika nowadays would swiftly bring a violent riposte, at least if insult was intended, and it is clear that the general contrast is not lost on the non-Muslim Mijikenda, some of whom have their own unfavourable image of Islam and its adherents. What is particularly poignant about this contrast as expressed in the sermon I have referred to, is that the preacher and his congregation are unlikely to be accepted as *waungwana* by the 'elite' Swahili who are able to demonstrate satisfactorily some connection with the twelve tribes. The people of Mwando wa Panya are clearly among those who Salim has called "poor Swahili" (1973), and who are intermediary in many respects.

I am interested here, however, in the implicit contrast made in this and other sermons between what we may translate as innate human characteristics which are ignorant of distinctions between good and evil, and those human characteristics which are man's gift from God and which he himself may choose to nurture or reject. Though this contrast is often alluded to metaphorically in the contrast between nonMuslim Mijikenda practices and beliefs, and ideal Muslim Swahili ones, it is also, at a more general level, one that pervades more orthodox Islamic and, it must be said, Christian theology. In Christianity the general contrast is, for example, evident in the pre-Fall state of the world when Adam and Eve were ignorant of the differences between them, and the post-Fall when they were knowledgeable of the choices between good and evil before them but were given useful divine advice.

The contrast comes out in the same sermon in the telling of the story of the two angels, Harutha and Marutha: (from the *maulidi* of Mwando wa Panya, Maalim Omari).

> Harutha na Marutha walipewa habari na Mwenyezi Mungu kuwa "Mimi nitaumba kiumbe kitukufu nikiweke katika ulimwengu kwa pia kitafanya kazi katika uliimwengu ..."
>
> *Harutha and Marutha were informed by God that "I will create a holy creature whom I place in the world and who will also do works in the world ..."*
>
> Harutha na Marutha kwa kuwa walijua ndiwo wanaomtukuza sana Mwenyezi Mungu na wanamthabiti kwa kila hali, waliambia "Ya nini kuwapeleka watu hawo wafanye kazi hiyo, tuate tutazifanya kazi hizo, hapo Mwenyezi Mungu". Akawaambia "Mkiwa mwakitaka cheo hichi haya nendani, ...". Hapo ikawa viko viumbe fulani katika ardhi waje wavihofishe. Hapo katika kushuka kwao malaika hawa waliposhuka Mwenyezi Mungu akaigeuza nyota moja inayoitwa Zuhura, ikawa ni mwanamke.
>
> *Harutha and Marutha, because they knew that they are the ones who glorified the Almighty God the most and who confirmed Him in every way, told Almighty God, "Why send those people to do that work? Leave us to do those works". Then the Almighty God said, "If you want this responsibility then go ...". There were some certain creatures on earth which were supposed to be scared by them. While these angels were descending the Almighty God changed one star, called Zuhura (Venus?), into a woman.*
>
> Hapo malaika wakashuka mmoja kwa mmoja wakija wakipambana na yule mwanamke, wakamwambia sisi viumbe vya Mwenyezi na tuko kati utimwengu huu kwa kumwahukumu ninyi. Zuhura akamwambia basi ninyi mkiwa ni mahakim basi mimi namwatafuta sana. Na mume wangu

> mimi yu ni mtesa sana, kwa hivyo nataka mfanye sababu yo yote ya kuweza kunipambanua baina ya mimi na mume wangu. Hapo, malaika Mwenyezi Mungu aiikuwa amewatia kitu cha mathamani ambacho kitu hicho kimewekewa sisi binadamu, wao hawana.
>
> *The angels then descended one by one and got together with the woman, telling her that we are creatures of the Almighty God and we are in this earth to judge you (dwellers of the earth). Zuhura told them if you are judges then I really need you. I have my husband who mistreats me a lot, so I want you to do everything possible to separate me from my husband. The angels of the Almighty God had been given something (lust) which has been the preserve of mankind, the angels don't have it.*
>
> Wamejiepusha na mambo mengi lakini kwa kuwa walitaka kazi hizi za binadamu wakatiwa kitu hichi cha mathamani hapo wakamthamani bibi yule, wakamwambia ikiwa wewe wataka tukuepushe baina ya wewe na mumeo basi tuko tayari lakini uturidhie tunayoyataka.
>
> *The angels restricted themselves from many things but because they wanted to do the work of men. the Almighty God imbued them with this lust, thus they lusted for the woman, telling her: if you want us to separate you from your husband then we are ready, but in return give us what we want.*

The text continues in this vein with the woman agreeing to grant the two angels her favours provided they harm and kill a person and also drink liquor. They agree only to the liquor, recognising that even this apparently lesser evil is bad enough. They drink heavily, the husband returns, is set upon by them and beaten to death. Liquor, the lesser of the evils has in fact made possible the greater, namely the assault and murder of a man. The woman also extracts from them the secret (literally the 'name' *jina*) by which they make their descent from and ascent to the place of God, and ascends herself.

God's punishment was to immobilise them, telling them: "Did I not tell you that I understand things which you do not, and that you cannot do the work of human beings?"

The clear message here is that God concedes, indeed encourages, humankind to be responsible for its own creations. God intercedes through beautiful things including the prophets, but it is intercession through advice and example. Men and women must choose for themselves: spiritual agents, like angels and God Himself, cannot do their work and their choosing for them.

This expectation that humankind should control its own destiny and not be controlled even by God's own angels is paralleled by the disapproval shown towards control by malevolent spirits (*mashetani*). As the same preacher concludes in his Barani sermon:

> "Basi binadamu tujisitiri wenyewe, tusitake kusitiriwa na mashetani ama kusitiriwa na wo wote ..." (*So, let us humans provide our own atonement/ cover, don't let us want to be protected from our immodesties by others, spirits or whoever* – i.e. let us govern our own destiny).
>
> God's angels and Satan's devils stand in a parallel and complementary relationship: the former carry good messages to humanity from God, and the latter evil ones from Satan. But neither is expected actually to control us. That is our own job.

* * *

It is somewhat unfashionable in the humanities at present to suggest that non-Western modes of explanation and epistemologies might conform to the Cartesian duality of mind and body. The Swahili Islamic duality which I am discussing here, however, has traces of this. Liquor, animality, and nonMuslim forms of behaviour represent ourselves as uncontrolled by the enlightened knowledge of Islam: without that mental consciousness we are reduced to harming and even killing our fellow-men. But the metaphoric extensions of this opposition (which is itself metaphorical) go far beyond an opposition of mind to body or materiality.

Both in sermons generally and in other ordinary contexts, three key concepts become the interconnected themes of discourse: *dini*, *elimu*, and *uganga* (religion, learning and healing). These are not exhaustive of a single discourse, but are often critical. Thus, the purity of Islam demands that we not forget that a Qur'anic education is just as important as a secular one, which was originally associated with Christian missions and is now organised by government. Secular education is valued but not, of course, to the exclusion of an Islamic one. *Uganga* is treated with some ambivalence. *Uganga wa koma* (ancestral spirit healing) is, of course, that associated with and seen as originating from non-Muslim Mijikenda, among whom it is regarded as central rather than peripheral in their systems of belief and cure. But there is the recognition that the Qur'an contains curative advice which can be regarded as a form of acceptable *uganga*. *Uganga wa koma* (sometimes referred to simply as *uganga*) is rejected as no more than *ushirikina* (addicted beliefs). The view therefore is that addicted beliefs (*ushirikina*) can only be overcome through education (*elimu*), which must include the Qur'anic form, which requires complete commitment to the 'true' religion (*dini ya kiislamu*).

Man's capacity for acquiring knowledge through education is thus both a route to salvation and the possible means of his own destruction. This capacity actually places him above the angels. This is a point brought out by Maalim Omari in his Barani sermon:

> ... Mwenyezi Mungu alipokuwa anawakusanya malaika akawaambia huko ulimwenguni mimi nitamweka mtu ambaye atazitoa amri zangu ambaye si katika nyinyi malaika ...
>
> *"When God gathered the angels, He said to them here on earth I will appoint a man who will give my command to you who is not among the angels ...*

The angels, as in the other version of this story, ask God to let them perform his work on earth, rather than this other person:

> ... (malaika) walikuwa na hamu zaidi kuletwa huku wawe ndio mitume, wawe ndio walimu, wawe ndio mashehe. Mwenyezi Mungu akawaambia, nyinyi msitake mambo hayo, mimi maana ya kufanya hivi najua, mambo msioyajua nyinyi ...
>
> *... (the angels) were more eager to be brought as apostles, to be teachers, to be leaders. God said to them, "Do not covet those things, I know how to do this, things you do not know ...*

Following his refusal of the angel's request, God then creates Adam and gives him the capacity for knowledge. God tests the angels and asks them to name everyday items of human use: a pressure lamp (sic), a cooking pot, a pestle and mortar, a tree (i.e. the coconut palm) which could provide good things but also wine. But the angels did not drink nor could know any of these things. How, then, could they ever be good teachers? Better that a human comes and teaches (presumably a reference to God's eventual appointment of Mohammed for the task).

It is for this reason, as a result of this special quality bestowed on them, that men must continue to send children to Qur'anic school. To do otherwise is to follow the alternative educational route which, if taken alone, leads to self-destruction

> (from the sermon at Majengo by Sharifu Ahmed Bedui):
> ... Mababa wataulizwa na watoto wao, Je wale mnawaacha tu hamtawafundisha chochote katika dini , hamu yao ni kuwafundisha katika maskuli basi, Aaah! Lazima tuwafundishe yote mawili, tuwafundishe dunia na dini sababu twaishi duniani lazima tuwafundishe namna gani ya kuishi katika ulimwengu ...

> *The fathers will be asked by their children, why are you leaving those children like that, not teaching them religious education but just secular education in schools? Aaah! We must teach them both, we should teach them about the world and religion because we live in this world and we must teach them how to live in this world ...*

The claim made here is that failure to give children their Qur'anic education will mean that they will not be able to read the Qur'an and to pray, so how will they answer before God?

The opposition between *dunia* and *ulimwengu* here nicely parallels that between secular and Islamic education and knowledge, and so returns us to our original duality: non-Muslim 'infiltration' or channels of communication on the one hand; and Muslim entirety and purity of knowledge on the other.

Conclusion

Those whom I have called intermediary Swahili are closest to Mijikenda non-Muslim ancestry. They might therefore be expected, through idiom, allusion and metaphor, to wish to emphasise their Islamic distinctiveness and propriety of belief and behaviour. But, in doing this, they reveal also a theory of being and selfhood, which I suspect is shared by more orthodox Islamic pronouncements and by higher-order Swahili. The theory is that humankind not only does, but should, control its own destiny. What is revealed to humans, positively through angels and prophets and negatively through malevolent spirits, are the two dimensions of good and evil behaviour. Non-Muslim habits and activities are conveniently close for illustration of the latter. The freedom open to individuals to choose between the two dimensions is complemented by a remarkable openness to accept converts by this particular group of intermediary Swahili. Theirs is by no means an ethnically exclusive Islam. And it is this which may well partly explain the emphasis on selfhood as constructed more by the individual than by God Himself. God provides guidelines, but the individual is free to create within or beyond them, for his betterment or at his peril.

Notes

(1) Mijikenda is the term, coined in the 1940's to refer to nine closely related groups who share mutually intelligible dialects and a common culture with minor variations, and the principal of which are the Giriama. I worked among the Giriama in 1967–77, 1977–78 and for various periods of a few months during and after these times, and

also among a mixed group of Mijikenda and 'Intermediary' Swahili in 1977–78, thanks to research grants from the School of Oriental and African Studies and the SSRC (UK).

(2) It can also mean to enter other people's arguments and, as the personal noun mwangi-riri, can also refer to a man who creeps into another's house at night, not to steal, but in order to force a woman there to have sexual intercourse with him.

References

Gerlach, L.P. (1963) Traders on a bicycle: A study of entrepreneurship and culture change among the Digo and Duruma of Kenya, in: *Sociologus* 13, 32–49.

Gomm, R. (1972) Harlots and bachelors: Marital instability among the Coastal Digo of Kenya, in: *Man* 7, 95–113.

Parkin, D. (1970) The Politics of Ritual Syncretism: Non-Muslim Giriama of Kenya. *Africa* 40.3., 217–233.

——(1979a) Straightening the Paths from Wilderness: of Divinatory Speech. *Journal Anthropological Society of Oxford*, Vol. X, No. 3, 147–60.

——(1979b) Along the Line of Road: Expanding Centres in Kenya's Coast Province, in: *Africa* 49, 3., 272–282.

——(1980) Kind Bridewealth and Hard Cash: Eventing a Structure, in: *The Meaning of Marriage Payments* (J. Comaroff ed.). London and New York. Academic Press.

Salim, A.I. (1973) *Swahili-Speaking Peoples of Kenya's African Coast*. Nairobi: East Africa Publishing House.

10 Controlling the U-turn of Knowledge

Knowledge is not always power. People may be wise but may lack the means to implement their knowledge. If they are ignored, their private wisdom will have no effect on the world. In popular Western thought this apparent separability of knowledge and power, and the various ways in which the two may be combined, has long fostered a reified view of them. We speak of knowledge and power in both quantifiable terms ('increase your knowledge', 'reduce their power'), and as distributable (evenly or unequally). Yet, though we see them as 'concrete things', we do not regard them as limited in time, place, and overall amount. Power and knowledge are, in popular Western epistemology, both seen as potentially limitless. This is not always the case in other cultures. Salmond describes how knowledge and power among the Maori are both limited and inseparably fused (1982). Knowledge is of genealogies, ritual chants, incantations, and folklore. It is what makes elders powerful through the respect held for them. Their ultimate task is to transmit the knowledge, and the power that it constitutes, intact to successive generations. The knowledge/power should remain neither more nor less than when it was originally constituted at the beginning of time. It is to that extent beyond quantification. It simply is.

The Western propensity to regard knowledge and power as separate 'things' is, in Western discourse, a governing epistemological assumption. It enables people to aim to expand or improve knowledge without necessarily worrying about how much power is thereby put into whose hands. As in the famous yet still relevant case of the atomic physicists in C.P. Snow's *The New Men*, rare are the scientists who are prepared to fully confront such implications.

Yet this separability of knowledge and power is more semantic than 'real'. We commonly assume that language contains concepts, rather than the two being mutually constituted (Reddy 1979). Similarly, we assume that the semantic separation of knowledge and power implies that they are independent entities, sometimes mutually reinforcing but sometimes relatively unaffected by each other.

However, whatever might be the case at a particular moment, it is difficult to deny that knowledge and power are always *potentially* part of each other. A person may keep their wisdom private forever; but that same wisdom is still there eventually for others to experience and act upon independently. This potentiality may be realised in two ways. The semantic positivising of Western theorising has, often to great effect, enabled scholars, scientists, politicians, and many lay people, to *plan* alterations in amounts of knowledge and power. But they may also come to 'know' things 'accidentally' through *unplanned* experiences, often unaware of how simultaneously their new knowledge re-defines relations of power between themselves and others. Speech embodies knowledge and presupposes differences of power between speaker and hearer, however fleetingly. It is in speech that we find this alteration of assumption: that differences of knowledge and power can be planned and unplanned.

I take as a general point that, in describing what speech does, I am also showing how its use is interpreted – by scholars and by other speakers and hearers. That is to say, speech may legitimately be regarded as having functions, both intended and unintended. But, since different ways of speaking are recognised as appropriate for particular purposes and occasions, distinguishing modes of speech is a matter of assumption, beliefs and truths.

I begin the argument with an ethnographic illustration from my own fieldwork in coastal Kenya during 1977–78 and documented in the preceding chapter (*Being and Selfhood*).

There is a puzzle in Muslim Swahili society. Do the religious maalims have power? This is my puzzle not theirs. None of their words which we might translate as power quite convey the English sense. They are best translated as 'ability', 'capacity', 'efficacy', (e.g. *uwezo*), and semantically shade over in actual use into words referring to 'wisdom' (*busara*) and thence to 'moral dignity' and 'religious worth' (e.g. *utukufu*). The Swahili language is made up of Bantu and Arabic vocabulary, and this shading of attributes from those denoting practical ability to those indicating religious worth corresponds in Swahili speech with a shift from Bantu to Arabic words.

To refer back to the maalims described in the preceding chapter, they are expected to have oratorical ability (*hotuba*-oratory, formal speech) and also to be religiously worthy. Religious worthiness in Swahili society, however, rests upon some degree of asceticism and renunciation of earthly treasures, and a humble, passive character. Given the competitive territorial framework within which maalims work, maalims can only really communicate their religious worthiness through effective oratory:

they will not become known through silent prayer and invisible good deeds. Yet, oratorical ability casts them in the potential role of community leaders. They must therefore struggle to keep at bay the pressures of ordinary Muslims to represent them politically over local issues. A good maalim loses his worthiness once he becomes a man of politics (*mtu wa siasa*). He then loses the esteem required for effective oratory, and even the right to preach.

In other words, once interpreted as a political power, his oratorical success can lead to a political dissolution.

East Africa has had virtually no Muslim prophetic leaders such as exist in other parts of the world, who, clearly, have transcended this problem. They tend to transcend it by becoming in some way possessed by spirit: in other words, they become freed of the restraints normally placed on their discourse, as among Dervishes. Spirit, or God, speaks through them and so they need not observe the delicate balance between effective oratory and religious worthiness. It is God's and not their responsibility.

Why do Swahili maalims not achieve this transcendence? There is a division is East African coastal Islam between (a) the higher status 'Arabo-Swahili' of Wahabi persuasion who denounce celebrations (*maulidi*) in honour of the Prophet Mohammed, regarding them as *biida* and debasing; and (b) so-called "African" Swahili who hold massive celebrations in different parts of the coast and, together, prolong them over many months, far beyond the month in which the Prophet was born.[1] An important part of the celebrations are maalims' sermons.

The 'Arabo-Swahili' are the channels through which wealth and patronage come, and the 'African' Swahili are to that extent restrained by their dependency on their patrons, who also provide religious legitimation in other spheres. This dependency is, however, often resented. Yet, the 'African' Swahili *maulidi* celebrations never quite become a vehicle of political protest. They explicitly remain 'religious'. Likewise, their maalims' sermons never quite turn to political problems of landlessness, unemployment, poverty, and marginal status. The ideas of religious worthiness which restrain them from becoming political leaders reflect their wider restraint under 'Arabo-Swahili' and other non-Swahili domination.

Given this overall system of restraint, maalims and their congregation have to stifle their own enlightenment. That is to say, during the sermons maalims inevitably touch on sensitive, potentially political themes, yet must refrain from elaborating on them. They hit upon such self-knowledge accidentally or unintendedly and must control their own discourse. They must, in other words, control the U-turns of knowledge which confront them in their sermons. Yet their oratorical success depends on imagination and creativity in speech.[2] While the problem in other studies has been to show how speakers control their audience through their rhetoric (Bloch and contributors (1975)), the problem of the Swahili maalims is how to control themselves.

Stepping back from the question of how legitimate it is to talk of speakers' intentions, this situation of speaker restraint results in the maalims' rhetoric operating on three levels relating speech and knowing things.

The first level, let us call it *A*, can be characterised simply as *control over the means of communication*. Thus, the maalim starts his sermon by praising God and the Prophet, and explaining why the congregation is celebrating the latter's birthday. This leads to explanations of why they must pray five times a day and observe Islamic rules and prohibitions, and why Islam is superior to other religions. There is considerable use of Arabic religious vocabulary, punctuated by devotional statements, and the level is to some extent a formalised element running right through the sermon.

But it is intertwined with a second level. At certain points in the sermon, the maalim elaborates on particular words and phrases. He unpacks and explains what he sees as their wider implications. Thus, God and the Prophet are associated with a number of words connoting 'light', 'brightness', and 'brilliance'. The maalim plays with this association and raises such questions as: is it that the light (i.e. enlightenment) penetrated the Prophet, or was it some quality in the Prophet himself which 'glowed ', producing the light that enabled him to overcome his earlier ungodly ways and reach out to God? For some local scholars, the questions come close to raising the awkward theological one of who is the more responsible for the glory that is Islam: God, by first sending out the light or inspiration? Or Mohammed, by having the human compassion and intelligence to make contact with God? Phrased ontologically does God or does man himself control his own destiny? The maalim is here raising a potentially heretical question which arises in response to his own questioning of basic terms and assumptions. In view of the more established and formalised position of the 'Arabo-Swahili ' religious clergy, the maalim would be well advised to control such self-questioning which threatens to divert him from his more formal, conformist message.

This second level of the discourse is less a case of the maalim controlling how and what is being communicated. It is more that the presuppositions of key terms and phrases come back at him and cause him to reveal certain paradoxes in the implications and senses in which they are used.

Let us call this second level *B*, and refer to it as (attempted) *control over the implicit prejudices that 'contaminate' communication*.

The third level occurs when the maalim incorporates an immediate experience in his sermon. This of course goes on all the time in speech, being a feature of 'speaking in context'. For example (see page 201), during one sermon, a fight between some youths broke out. They had to be restrained. The maalim took this as an opportunity to condemn the (alleged) insolence and laziness of youth who no longer respect their parents and, instead of joining them in traditional endeavours like fishing, trade, and farming, idly spend their time smoking, drinking, dancing, fraternising, and leading an irreligious life.

The further the maalim went on in this vein, however, the more closely he in effect touched on the problem of unemployment, landlessness, and exclusion from traditional crafts and occupations which these youths suffer as a result of wider economic changes in the area, most of them due, not in fact to 'Arab' domination, but to the introduction of capital-intensive commercial fishing, tourism, and to the migration for work in the area of more skilled people from up-country.

From personal observation as a member of the congregation, one saw the maalim constantly coming close to an explanation of the youths' behaviour in these political terms but, seemingly, flinching from it. He was here controlling not an ontological but a serendipitous political U-turn in the knowledge he intended to communicate. Moreover, he made no attempt to draw out the emerging argument from the words which gave rise to it. Let us call this level *C*.

I want now to try and place these three levels in some kind of analytical framework, treating them as assumptions and beliefs about speech and knowledge. I first concentrate on levels *A* and *B*.

Level *A*, control over the means of communication, rests in assumptions made by many anthropologists. It separates propositional from non-propositional speech. It is premised on the speaker's intentionality, but also upon a belief in the self-verifying nature of propositions.

Level *B* is rather like the approach associated with Habermas's optimism that free speech is attainable through conscious disclosure of our historically constructed prejudices of intention and implication (1978: 161–86, and 371).

Thus, *B* is reflexive in a way that *A* is not and to that extent supersedes *A* in theoretical awareness. Though they are not, therefore, strictly speaking epistemically comparable (since *B* entails and encompasses A), it is instructive to treat them as if they were competing, alternative approaches, which is how they are sometimes regarded: thus, *A* positivistically sees the controllers of means of communication as determining what is communicated which is thus passively objectified; while *B* recognises the autonomy of the prejudices underlying communication which, both as means and content, shapes the outcome of utterances, almost to the extent of becoming the subject dominating the speaker as object, who must struggle to acquire subjective consciousness in order to reverse this state of affairs.

Positivistic *A* has some of the presuppositions of language as a conduit or channel inside and along which ideas are passed: bend the language and you control its content. Speech, and therefore the nature of, and accessibility to, knowledge are manipulable objects which privileged agents act upon. Dialectical *B* concerns speech which acts upon the agent or speaker in the very act of utterance. The speaker has the extraordinarily difficult task of having to distance himself from the implications of what he says, at the moment at which he says it, in order to be able to experience the falsity of his premises. *Post facto* criticism is not enough: for that entails an already-existing critical standpoint, which is therefore borrowed from the purported experiences of others.

Finally, the intentionality of *A* is uncomplicated, even naive: it presupposes a knowledge of the circumstances in which communication is controlled, of the composition of the audience, and of the effects on the audience. It uses this knowledge to reproduce or create further knowledge; i.e. it does not reflect on this original knowledge. By contrast, the intentionality of *B* is two-fold and complicated: there is the primary intention entailed in the speech act itself, i.e. the immediate and commonly held understanding it incurs; and there is the secondary intention, which we only have if we reflect on it, of uncovering the inconsistencies and distortions implied in what we say. (The primary intention of *B* is really an aspect of *A* as a whole, with its emphasis on propositional speech: that is why it was remarked above that *A* is encompassed by *B*.)

Comparing the two assumptions reveals an interesting paradox. Thus, one would think that *A*, being a naive view of speech as a safe conduit of knowledge, would easily be rebutted for its naivety. Yet, we know from observation and personal experience that we or our informants rarely attain sufficient reflexivity in the course of everyday speech to question our premises. It then follows that controlling how we speak continues very much to shape the content and outcome of what we say. Control over the means of communication retains its power. By contrast, *B* ought to enable us to be more predictable and precise in what we say and do, for it attempts to strip away underlying falsity. After all, is not an approximation to truth seen to be a route to power?

Where such approximations to truth become converted back into an empirical finding of science, and so controlled like any other objectified phenomenon, it may indeed be the case that such reflexivity gives us power. In other words, the two-fold intentionality of *B* can be a sound route to power through its alternating de-construction and verification procedures. It casts its old findings as 'beliefs' and its new ones as validated knowledge. *B* is thus based on what Ricoeur would call a hermeneutics of suspicion (Ihde *xvi* in Ricoeur 1974). Since, however, B's findings are only ever provisional, its confidence in its powers of predictability is illusory in the long term. It is like science itself.

Nevertheless, one still thinks of *B* as producing more 'amounts' of 'new' knowledge than *A*. This does not mean characterising *A* and *B* as concrete ('primitive') and abstract ('scientific') thought respectively. This and other connoted parallels are not without significance, but, as speech modalities, *A* and *B* refer to alternating aspects of discourse generally.

What is paradoxical about A is that its naïve intentionality may nevertheless 'hit upon' unintended discoveries of a sometimes radical nature. Thus, the maalim began to raise awkward ontological-cum-political questions in reaction to an unexpected event requiring comment or explanation. Just as the image of the double helix intuitively but unintendedly provided the key to understanding the structure of DNA, so it is often the 'accidental' choice of words which gives the speaker and/or hearer an unintended and novel idea. Unintended puns and double entendres and so-called Freudian slips are everyday cases of the unintended breaking into our speech. These breaks are often no more than an interlude in the discourse and do not necessarily deflect the speaker from their intended utterance. But sometimes they do and so are to that degree significant markers. They are part of polysemy: all words and expressions have multiple connotations and the slip or pun is interpreted as a frivolous aspect of this polysemy. Advertisers play on this aspect, often to remarkable effect. Nevertheless, it is the unmarked aspects of polysemy which, because they are unrecognised or hidden, are most likely to cause a change in the speaker's and/or hearer's understanding of the line of argument. For a British politician in a speech to switch between the word 'country' and 'nation' as if they were interchangeable might be an example of this potential to change a line of argument. For many hearers at least (as in 1985), to talk of the 'British nation' has connotations of 'whiteness', 'purity', 'service to the country', etc. (e.g. as veterans of World War II) that are not so strongly shared by the term 'country' alone.

Speakers may or may not realise this and so may or may not be in a position to manipulate its potential. The same stretch of speech may be regarded by one individual (either speaker/hearer(s)/writer) as of a type *A*, i.e. as dealing with unquestionable truths and therefore as best communicated in an appropriate style, while another individual may perceive hidden connotations which challenge what others regard as truths. This latter individual is taking a type *B* approach to the speech. He or she regards language as a rather unsure conduit of thought categories. The point, then, is that it is the difference of interpretation on the part of either speaker or hearer (or both) that converts the same utterance from being type A to type B. Put simply, while all speech is polysemic and encompasses, through its manifold connotations, a range of alternative worlds, this property may or may not be recognised and acted upon by language users. They can therefore see or use speech as being either (a) a safe means of controlling the communication of knowledge or (b) an entirely uncertain means of communication, full instead of polysemic traps and associations which are not intended by the speaker.

While recognising that we are here dealing with interpretive processes more than intrinsic properties of speech, we can refer to them not just as interpretations, but as 'beliefs' about language and the extent to which speaker controls knowledge or is, so to speak, controlled by it. Thus:

> *A*. Control the means of communication and you control knowledge. Knowledge is here treated as an object or commodity and can be transacted and even manipulated. Realisation of the fact that the knowledge itself can be manipulated leads to ideas of its distortion through language and to the further realisation that it is falsifiable knowledge, indeed, that it is lies. This leads through greater reflexivity, to *B*.
>
> *B*. Speakers are controlled by hidden assumptions in their speech as much if not more than they themselves control what they say. This recognition can lead away from belief A to the view that the knowledge conveyed by hidden assumptions can become the active agent and convert its speakers or enunciators into objects, who must struggle to regain their status as controlling subjects.

We move on now to the third possibility, level *C*, which I will call post-structuralism: that knowledge is not presupposed but occurs as an aspect of speaking. In other words, we make up knowledge as we carry out speech acts. Putting this another way, knowing is speaking: speaking is knowing. I have given the example of the *maalim* reproaching the youths, but, in doing so, talking *pari passu* of wider political problems. As another example, in greeting someone extensively I may come to know the state of that person, his reaction to and opinion of me, our immediate world, and even of other possible worlds, and my own reaction to him, etc. But none of this knowledge can be presupposed in advance of the speech act. The knowing and the speaking (including gestural accompaniments) are inseparably constituted in each other (see Kendall 1982).

This third possibility, which we may call belief *C*, is something of a maverick. It neither sees knowledge as an objectifiable commodity manipulable through speech, nor as an autonomous set of assumptions lurking beneath our consciousness of what we are saying. It sees knowledge as always in-the-making, neither predictable, assumed, or manipulable, nor existing as pre-ordained and active forces. It thus recognises the flaw in belief *A* and realises that though speaking may be intended as a safe conduit of thought, it nevertheless contains within itself unintended accidents of meaning; and so it is akin to belief *B*: that we do not control all the knowledge we produce through our speech.

The *C* view thus partakes of both *A* and *B*, and is not exclusively associated with either.

We can summarise A, B, and C as the following beliefs:

A = speaker controls knowledge
B = speaker is controlled by knowledge
C = knowledge is constituted in the act of speaking and neither controls the speaker nor is controlled by him: speaking *is* interacting and *is* knowing.

Both *A* and *B* rest on the idea that speaking and knowing are phenomenologically separable. *A* sees the knowing as encased in the speaking: control how it is said and you control what is said. *B* reflects on this finding and seeks the past or historically created prejudices that underlie speech. *C* rejects this phenomenological separation and, though highly aware of and attuned to the nuances of words, actions, and verbal and non-verbal ripostes, does not reflect on the extent to which the speaking and the knowing separately affect each other.

C is in fact natural language, consisting of both words and gestures, and is how we normally interact with each other. C is so unreflective that it might seem difficult to regard it as a 'belief' at all. But there are moments when people do stand back and recognise it: during the Black Power movement of the sixties in the U.S.A., a famous phrase used by the Black rhetoricians was to 'tell it like it is'. From the contexts in which it was used, this was more than an appeal for the truth. Since it was followed, in the one speech personally witnessed, by on-the-spot rhetoric of an unfolding and apparently unplanned kind, it seemed to be an appeal for knowledge and truth to come out through the very act of discourse. This distinctive Black rhetoric was the very process of elucidation. There was no subsequent epistemological framing of knowledge. 'Telling it like it is' was all that was needed for effect. In this sense it is part of that broad field which we call performative utterances and illocutionary speech acts.

Summarising still further, *A* = a belief in speaker's power; *B* = a belief in the power of prejudices in speech; while *C* = a belief in the power of truth itself as inevitably manifesting itself in natural speech.

I think that this three-fold distinction moves also through three assumptions about how knowledge is made up: *A* really refers to 'knowledge' in the sense of 'knowing how to do things without really thinking about them', i.e. unreflected-upon practical knowledge. I can walk into a room, close the door, sit down at my desk and start writing, but will not be in a state of knowing why and how I did these things until you ask me about them. Yet, clearly, it cannot be said that I did not know about these things. *B* refers more to knowledge which is, in the act of speaking, actually reflected upon. It is thought-about-knowledge, and may refer to knowledge as existential fact, as autonomous agent (i.e. knowledge doing things to us), and as a method or way of doing things. *C* is curious, for it is not as reflective as *B* is, yet has the confidence, so to speak, to by-pass active consideration of what does or should pass as knowledge, and goes immediately to a belief in it as truth. The truth will out, and in doing so, embodies knowledge which has not been passed through any filter of reflection.

The three can now be regarded as beliefs, respectively, about: speech containing unreflected-upon knowledge which is controlled by the speaker; speech containing reflected-upon knowledge which is allowed by the speaker to affect and control him/her in some way; and speech as unreflected-upon-knowledge which is immediately cast by the speaker as truth.

These three do not of course even begin to cover the many possible connotations of the word 'belief', which here, indeed, is more like that of 'assumption'. But the three do seem to offer a logically limited set of assumptions or beliefs about how the communication of words and knowing things are related. An important point to remember is that the three may co-inform the same stretch of speech, for they derive from speaker's/hearer's interpretations of the relationship between speaking and knowing, not necessarily from any intrinsic speech properties.

The three can also be seen as developing a notion of 'truth'. *A* refers more to 'believed-in' truth, i.e. speakers assume that *how* they communicate will determine *what* is communicated, and that hearers will receive this as an unquestioned truth which does not have to be demonstrated but will be clear from the rhetoric itself. The maalim, it will be recalled, intended to preach a standard religious message about the propriety of Islam. *B* questions this and related 'truths': the maalim inadvertently asks whether it is in fact God or whether it is man himself who controls his own destiny.

C neither questions nor baldly asserts truths, but has speakers drawing on visible events around them and so demonstrating the truth of their statements as they utter them: the maalim used the fight between youths to illustrate their indolence but also touched on what people believe are more fundamental politic-economic causes of their behaviour. *C* thus refers to demonstrable truth. The movement through *A*, *B*, and *C* is thus that from believed to demonstrable truth.

This progression starts out with an original intention (the maalim 's standard message, *A*), which is, however, subverted in two ways (*B* and *C*).

First, the polysemy of words used in the sermon (e.g. 'light'/ enlightenment', etc.) invites sufficient interpretive play that the maalim could quite easily contradict his original intention and be interpreted as saying something heretical. Second, the very fact of speaking to an audience which interacts with him and independently of him (i.e. is not passive), obliges him to incorporate the random events in his speech (the youths' fight) and so inadvertently draw attention to a social and political problem as well as a moral and religious one: i.e. if the young had jobs and land, then they would not go astray. This latter kind of knowledge is most easily understood as demonstrable truth because it is seen to be true at the very moment of its utterance. This inseparable seeing and uttering of 'truth ' is its most graspable testimony. Temporarily, at least, demonstrable truth subverts the believed truth conveyed by the maalim's original intention to preach the piety of Islam.

'Truth' appears to rest upon two possible understandings: that it is partial or favourable to its interpreter (as in a court's or chief's verdict), and/or that it is effective (as in the diviner's prognosis and cure).

For partiality we may substitute *believed truth*: the verdict or utterance favours me or my group and this confirms my belief in its validity. For efficacy we may substitute *demonstrable truth*: if the diviner's prescription works, then his pronouncements have been shown to be true.

The efficacy of a truth makes it more acceptable than mere belief in it. New beliefs spring up that go beyond existing efficacious knowledge. They, in turn, are subject to demonstrable tests which, if successful, strengthen their acceptability as truth, and, if unsuccessful, simply let them remain as weaker truths. This alternation of believed and demonstrable truth is, therefore, an aspect of the way speech and knowledge are related through the three levels *A*, *B*, and *C*.

We may start out by believing that power inheres in the speaker but we end up by recognising as greater that power that is shown to be effective and not simply spoken. This suggests that the power of so-called ideological argument is actually quite short-lived and must either be demonstrated or supplanted. The sway of self-verifying but undemonstrated propositions is limited, for we are ultimately all empiricists, informants and observers alike.

From Assumptions and Beliefs to Truths: Stages of Analysis

The list given below is intended to clarify what may sometimes come across in the text as conflated stages of the argument. The problem is not, however, that of analytical conflation but that the very terms 'assumption', 'belief', and 'truth', in ordinary language merge their respective referents: an assumption becomes a belief which becomes a truth, and vice versa.

Assumptions

A: Control over the means of communication
B: Control over the implicit prejudices that 'contaminate' communication
C: The intertwining of speech and experience

↓

A: Speaker controls knowledge
B: Speaker is controlled by knowledge
C: Knowledge is constituted in the act of speaking and neither controls the speaker nor is controlled by him

↓

Beliefs

A: Belief in speaker's power
B: Belief in the power of prejudice in speech
C: Belief in the power of truth as inevitably manifesting itself in natural speech

↓

A: Unreflected-upon knowledge
B: Reflected-upon knowledge
C: Unreflected-upon knowledge cast immediately as truth

↓

A: Believed-in truth
B: Deconstruction of truth
C: Demonstrable truth

Notes

(1) This distinction between two groups of Swahili is here put more clearly than is in fact the case. The complications of Swahili status are worthy of a more detailed analysis which cannot be done in the space of this short chapter.

(2) I have analysed part of one such sermon, complete with original Swahili and translation in Parkin 1985, reproduced in the preceding chapter in this volume. Some instances from that sermon are included here.

References

Bloch, M. (ed.) (1975) *Political Language and Oratory in Traditional Society*. Seminar Press, London.

Habermas, J. (1978) [1967, 1972] (tr. J.J. Shapiro) *Knowledge and Human Interests*. Heinemann, London.

Kendall, M. (1982) 'Getting to Know You' in D. Parkin (ed.) *Semantic Anthropology* A.S.A. Monograph No. 22 Academic Press. London.

Parkin, D. (1985) 'Being and selfhood among Intermediary Swahili' in J. Maw and D. Parkin (eds) 1985 Swahili Language and Society Beiträge zur Afrikanistik Band 23. University of Vienna.

Reddy, M. (1979) 'The Conduit Metaphor' in A. Ortony (ed.) *Metaphor and Thought* Cambridge U.P., Cambridge .

Ricoeur, P. (1974) [1969] (ed.) Don Ihde *The Conflict of Interpretations* Northwestern University Press. Evanston.

Salmond, A. (1982) 'Theoretical Landscapes: On a Cross-Cultural Conception of Knowledge' in D. Parkin (ed.) *Semantic Anthropology*. Academic Press. London.

11 The Politics of Naming among the Giriama

First man: Who are you?
Traveller: I am Karisa son of Muramba son of Mweni.
First man: Ah! So you are of the MwaMweni clan. Then we are brothers-in-law, for my sister was married by a MwaMweni.
Where do you come from?
Traveller: I come from Kaloleni, near Madebe's place.
Second man: My grandchild, the daughter of my son, was married to a man they call Musela.
Traveller: Yes, I know him. He is BiCharo, ...that is Kahindi Ngumbao.

This is the kind of exchange that typically occurs between strangers among a people called the Giriama, who live in the immediate hinterland off the coast of Kenya. The Giriama are an African Bantu-speaking group numbering over a hundred thousand people, among whom I have done fieldwork for various periods since 1966. Paradoxically, the longer the period of fieldwork the more intractable appear to be the problems of cultural translation.

The little encounter given above is an example. It appears to be an English translation of a meeting between strangers. Yet what is really needed for an understanding of it is a cultural translation of the society's naming system. Without that, we are reduced to guesswork. Names are no mere labels. They inform discourse and can be as much a part of its creation of surplus meaning as are metaphors.

I will not attempt immediately to make sense of this exchange of names except to say that it contains a wide variety denoting clanship, occupation, personality, and personal identity, through a mixture of what we might call orthodox and informal or nicknames. It is in fact a simple exchange. Much more complicated ones have the characteristics of a language game which builds on shifting themes. They play with the possibilities of defining and redefining people and groups as more information is brought in. As with all games there is a competitive edge in the claims made: is the newcomer's clan one that the speaker marries into, are his contacts influential, and what is his own status?

There is an enormous anthropological literature on the study of peoples' naming systems. Lévi-Strauss's early structuralist accounts, to which I turn in my conclusion, have been among the most influential (1966), and have themselves been based on still earlier ones. This is not the place to survey that and the subsequent voluminous literature, except to argue that the play of power in naming systems has been largely neglected. Naming may be a form of 'entitling' by which authority is conferred both on the receiver and donor of the name, or of objectification by which, through the choice of a particular name, the namer secures control over the named. In such situations it sometimes happens that persons anticipate such consequences by choosing or controlling the choice of their own names.

I emphasise these aspects of power and control in this essay. I try to show how among a people of coastal Kenya, called the Giriama, the naming system sets up an opposition between 'active' and 'passive' members of society, which paradigmatically also underwrites other distinctions: between active men and passive women in general but also more specifically among men between those who are deemed active and passive, and in rare instances between active and passive women. 'Active' is here taken to refer to the capacity to influence events in a publicly visible manner, while 'passive' denotes a lack of that capacity. This is the Giriama view which does not lose sight of the parallel irony: that, through witchcraft and the use of medicine, those who appear passive may well be the most powerful unacknowledged movers of events, though admittedly this is regarded as applying almost entirely to men only. Naming among the Giriama, then, articulates the micro-politics of interpersonal relations. It thus provides a yardstick by which persons are measured and so provides them with a platform for more conventional political advancement.

The distinction between active men and passive women in the realm of naming clearly has implications for other gender relations. Men's patrilineal clan names are visible markers of their entitlement to property inherited from agnates and also to men's prior right to arbitrate on such related matters as the inheritance of the widows of deceased clan-mates, while women's names make no reference to clanship nor, therefore, to transmissible property and politico-jural rights. This is not to say that women are without such rights, though they do indeed have fewer of them. However, while the jural status of a Giriama man can be gauged from his names, that of a woman is most evident through the identity of her father or husband. Nevertheless, beyond the formality of such rights and rules are hidden achievements to which both men and women aspire and which sometimes surface in the names by which they are known.

I have so far avoided referring to the category 'personal name'. This is a difficult enough notion even in Western discourse, where it may as much refer to, say, dynastic genealogy, nationhood, or religious demands (e.g. saints' names) as to the identity of a particular person. In Africa as elsewhere, as various writings have shown (Beattie 1980; Dieterlen 1973; Carrithers *et al.*, 1986), the idea of a discrete and sharply separable person entrusted autonomously with his/her own fate is rare and revealed as a Western fiction. By personal name, therefore, I refer to one that is regarded as mainly the property of a particular person (a proper name) but may also be seen among Giriama as deriving from a grandparent, some of whose qualities may go with it. Among the Giriama, also, all names, including those which we might wish to regard as personal, are seen as complementing each other and forming a system for marking life cycle phases, a system that the Giriama view as operating in large part over and above particular individual wishes.

There is, nevertheless, an area of naming, reasonably translated as nicknaming, which does catch individuals in the act, so they speak, either of carving out their own identities or, through the efforts of friends, relatives and neighbours, being sculpted by others. Among the Giriama, then, a few men, and in rare cases women, attempt to determine their own destinies or those of others, and, in doing so, seek new names that play a part in shaping these destinies and capacities.

A cross-cultural understanding of personal names must include, for example, New Guinea 'sorrow names' (Strathern 1970), Penan death names and friendship names (Needham 1954; 1971), avoidance names, descent names, teknonyms, and many others, variously subject to rules of award, transmission, and withdrawal, and involving many people in different duties and rights (e.g. Barnes 1982). While these are seen to be rule-based in the societies concerned, it is a matter for investigation as to whether and to what extent notions of self and person include at least in part the idea of autonomous agency. Among the Giriama, the area I have called nicknaming is that where individuals joust, so to speak, with the rules, by circumventing them and revealing how difficult it is to put them into practice: thus, to call someone by a nickname potentially subverts the authority of those who originally conferred, say, the clan name.

This opposition between rules and subversion has echoes of that between rule-governed society and innovative individual. Both are fictions. Thus, the concept of rule presupposes constancy, yet rules in fact change all the time. Similarly, the concept of rational individual assumes a self-determining agent, whereas in fact so-called individual accomplishments are often rationalised fantasies of plans that went wrong or were never made in the first place. But in so-called Western thinking the believed tension between society as a compulsive force and the individual as pitted against it is no less strongly felt and creates movement in each.

Giving a person a name or names is part of this tension, which can be read in various ways. From a structuralist perspective such names may be seen as mediating the contradiction between our being produced by society and therefore without individuality, and yet at the same time as able to speak about society and ourselves within it. From a post-structuralist perspective, giving someone a name draws on the tension between professed rules and facile individual fantasy and threatens to dissolve the distinction between them. That is to say, there is a point at which an increasingly unpopular naming rule may be defended by fewer and fewer people, by in fact by no more than a few individuals, while yet other individuals propagate the use of their own variously coined names. This appears to have happened with regard to the now almost obsolete clan naming rules among such other Kenyan peoples as the Digo and Kikuyu, and even, some Giriama claim, among their Mijikenda neighbours, the Jibana, Chonyi, and Kambe, and may I suppose occur eventually among the Giriama themselves.

When asked, the Giriama I spoke to first distinguished *three* kinds of names for men: clan, personal and teknonym (based on first, an eldest child's and, then, eldest grandchild's names); and *two* kinds for women, who do not have clan names. Through further conversation an additional set of names emerged which are clearly regarded as less formal and which are variously translated as those of 'boasting', 'drinking' and 'self-awarded', and are almost solely the preserve of men. To some extent they overlap with the English notion of nickname. In this way, the Giriama do make an overall distinction between orthodox and informal or nicknames.

Orthodox Names

(1) Clan name (*dzina ra mbari* or *dzina ra ndani* – literally inside name). The clan name is given to men shortly after birth at a special ceremony. It belongs to and is transmitted from the generation of grandparents, which I discuss in detail below.

(2) Personal name (*dzina ra ku-gerwa* – the given name, or the less common *dzina ra sare*). This is chosen by the mother at birth, and is normally also that of a grandparent.

Christian and Muslim names assume similar status, with the European baptismal name called *dzina ra dini* (religious name) or *dzina ra KiKristo*, and the Muslim one known as *dzina ra Kiislamu*.

(3) Teknonym (*dzina ra mwana* – child name- *dzina ra mudzukulu* -grandchild name).

Informal or Nickname

A less common term is *dzina ra kudzirava*, and more specific terms are:

dzina ra kudzigamba – boasting name
dzina ra uchi – drinking name
dzina ra kudzigera/kudzipa – self-awarded name
dzina ra mahukano – insult name, often referring to ethnic origin and used at funerals, for instance, as well as between friends, and denoting ethnic joking relations.

Though orthodox names are given or assumed according to set rules over which the person named has no choice, the informal names are in a sense competed for: sometimes they are imposed by others and the named person may be unable to resist them, but sometimes they are encouraged and even promoted in the first place by him (rarely her). They are produced by the cut and thrust of combative personalities and are not subject to set rules. There are other terms used to describe such informal names, as I have indicated above, just as there are names which are semi-formal but not identified in any consistent way. For example, after a succession of children's deaths in a family, a newborn baby may be named (usually in Swahili rather than Giriama), say, 'trouble' (*tabu*) or 'offering' (*sadaka*), with the intention, in the first case, of appearing to devalue the child in order to deter evil spirits wishing to harm and appropriate it, and, in the second, in order to appease such spirits. I witnessed such cases increasing markedly over two decades in one area of accelerated economic complexity in which I worked.

The distinction between formal and informal names is undoubtedly blurred on occasion and over time but does reflect a clash between personal styles and the explicit social rules. Older linguistic usage would refer to it as a field of rule-governed creativity, in that key elders try to enforce the rules which are therefore constraining, while the inventors of new names try to make them stick. As with so many apparently trivial areas of contestation, the field becomes politically significant as a way in which traditional authorities incorporate new sources of influence and break the rules they might at other times defend: traditional authority is seen to be fallible (or not) and innovators effective (or not).

Let me go on to show how, through the use of orthodox names, people attempt to place others within set relationships of clanship, sub-clanship, generation, age, gender and, by extension, marriage and affinity. I want then to show how this sets a scene for challenge and counter-challenge to people's thinking about power and its distribution.

Giriama Clan Names: The Fantasy of Rules

I regard the rules as fantasy since only some of them operate for some of the people some of the time. Elders sometimes speak of them as would a positivist objectifying material laws of reality, an order which clearly suits administrative and judicial thinking, but an ordering sometimes more believed in than practised. For neither they nor anyone can predict who will actually be known throughout or during part of his life by his clan name, nor to what extent and how often. Given the wide variety of name types, each person is made up of a shifting bundle of them, in the use of which we may glimpse both some operation of the rules and exceptions to them.

The Giriama are the largest of nine self-recognised sub-groups, each with similar customs whose minor differences have internal importance for the overall grouping known nowadays as the Mijikenda.

For Giriama boys there is a naming ceremony. At this ceremony, carried out before he is a year old, the boy is given his clan name (*dzina ra mbari*) by a paternal grandfather. Girls do not receive clan names.

Giriama society, like other Mijikenda sub-groups, is neatly divided into sections (*mbari*), six in the case of Giriama, each of which is further divided into exogamous clans. Each exogamous clan (also called *mbari*) is normally divided into two sub-clans, each again called *mbari* or sometimes *lukolo*. Some clans have three sub-clans. Sub-clans are the units within which a man may inherit widows. Each sub-clan is called after the name of successive sons of the senior clan founder. The clan as a whole is divided into two named generations, one called the 'fathers' (*abiatu*, literally 'fathers of the people', or simply *baba*, 'fathers'), and the other called 'sons' (*ana*, literally 'children').

Each generation has (usually) six names, none of them occurring twice. The six names in each generation are ranked by birth order of their incumbents. Taking both generations, then, there are twelve names belonging to a particular clan, one set of six being senior to the other set, and each set internally ranked. A very small number of common names are found in other clans. Provided you know which names belong to which clans, a knowledge which key elders have, you can tell a man 's clan by asking him his and his father's clan names. This is because the particular combination of, say, my name followed by my father's is not found in any other clan but my own. My father may in fact be of the generation called 'sons', but he is still my personal father and I am called X son of Y. That XY combination is unique to my clan.

The first six sons of a wife are given the six ranked names by birth order, so that you can tell which son is senior to whom. Seventh and successive sons of the same wife re-start the cycle, the seventh receiving

'Fathers' generation

1. *Mweni (the first man of the senior generation: the clan is named after him)*
2. *Masha (ku-masha = to surprise someone)*
3. *Thoya*
4. *Baya*
5. *Nyule*
6. *Ziwao*

'Sons' generation

1. *Muramba* (mulamba? = a little black bird which leads the morning singing)*
2. *Maitha ***
3. *Tsofwa (ku-tsoha = to serve out drink, therefore passive = ku-tsofwa)*
4. *Taura*
5. *Bokole (paw-paw fruit which is yellow with ripeness)*
6. *Kumbatha*

Figure 1a Names of the Mwa-Mweni clan (*mbari*)

Notes:
* The senior sub-clan is called *Mwa Mweni amwa Muramba* (the people of Mweni of Muramba)
** The junior sub-clan is called *Mwa Mweni amwa Maitha* (the people of Mweni of Maitha)
A third sub-clan would be called *Mwa Mweni amwa Tsofwa* (the people of Mweni of Tsofwa). Since new names will be added to successively differentiated sub-clans, they will in time assume the nominal appearance of distinct whole clans and may undergo their own internal differentiation.

the senior-most name, i.e. that of the first son, and so on. The sons of other co-wives are given the clan names in the same way.

At this point it may be helpful to outline the names, with some possible derivations of meaning, of two separate clans (both of the Kidzini section), in order to summarise more clearly the way the system operates, or is ideally supposed to.

Overall, the sons of one man are ranked by birth-order and not by the marriages of their mothers. Thus, the first sons of each of two co-wives will share the same clan name of, say, Baya, but the son who was born first is senior, even if his mother was the second co-wife to be married. In fact, in everyday reference and address no two living sons of a man are likely to be known by the same clan name: the junior, i.e. second-born, is the one most likely to be known by a clan name. At this level of everyday usage, then, the six clan names may be distributed by birth-order among the six

'Fathers'	*'Sons'*
1. *Baya*	1. *Yaa*
2. *Mangi*	2. *Mweri*
3. *Jefwa*	3. *Mwaro*
4. *Mure*	4. *Kitunga*
5. *Nghoka*	5. *Mwanyule*
6. *Chogga*	6. *Wara*

Figure 1b Names of the Mwa-Baya-Mwaro clan

sons of different co-wives. Let us say that one wife has the first son. He will be known as Baya. Then a second wife has three sons before the first wife has her second. The second and third sons of this second wife could then be known in everyday reference and address by the second- and third-ranked names, Mangi and Jefwa. Then, perhaps, a third wife has five sons before either of the other two wives produces a fourth or fifth son. This third wife's fourth and fifth sons will be known by the fourth- and fifth-ranked names, Mure and Nghoka. A fourth wife would need to produce six sons before the other wives produced a sixth, in order that her sixth son be known on an everyday basis as Chogga, the sixth-ranked name. In this fictitious case, each clan name of the generation would be in regular use for no more than one son in the family.

Although this spreading out of clan names in everyday usage already departs from the folk theory of naming, it is itself no more than a tendency. Quite often, at this quotidian level, only one or two sons in a family may be regularly addressed and referred to by their clan names, usually the senior-most.

Why should people seem to shy away from using clan names a great deal in daily communication? It is true that cutting down on the number of clan names for same-birth-order sons of different wives, or for first and seventh sons of a single wife, does avoid the confusion that might result from different sons of the same homestead being called or addressed by the same name. Nevertheless, everyone knows that a male must have his own particular clan name, even if it is not the name by which he is normally known. His clan name is in such cases kept in store, so to speak, for use on special occasions. In other words, Giriama males all receive or inherit clan names shortly after birth, but only a few of them are regularly known by such names.

Though hidden, however, clan names are not forgotten. Indeed, their socio-political significance is sustained by three main occasions on which men bring these names out of storage, though the extent to which they do so is largely their own responsibility.

First, a younger man may approach a 'nationally' respected elder for information about Giriama traditions, including its naming system, and perhaps membership in a secret society and its oathing procedures. A few such elders live in the Giriama traditional capital, the Kaya. The younger man, who may well be middle-aged, first offers the elder some palm wine. The elder will ask for the younger man's clan name and those of his forebears up to five generations. A possible response might be, in the case of the Mweni clan, 'My name is Mweni, son of Muramba, son of Thoya, son of Kumbatha, son of Masha ...'. The number of possible sequences is colossal. The point of the question is said to be to ensure that the younger man is truly a Giriama in the father's line. Personal names and the names of forefathers' wives may also be asked for as part of the check, if the elder happens to have some knowledge of the particular line, but it is not expected that these forefather' wives will be only Giriama: it is recognised that through inter-marriage they can be from any of the nine Mijikenda sub-groups or, rarely, from some other ethnic group.

The elders of some other Mijikenda sub-groups also insist on comparable confirmations of patrilineal ethnic 'purity' (which is more problematic among those like the Duruma and, formerly, Rabai and to some extent the once matrilineal Digo, who recognise a limited form of double descent). The knowledge of these key elders is certainly not fossilised but is used in organising modern political movements. In the past it was surrounded by tremendous secrecy and is still jealously preserved, though a combination in recent years of tourists and researchers willing to pay for information, is causing its dispersal. The younger man's recitation of clan names is said to be a means of identification, but would still seem also to be half of a symbolic symmetry: the younger supplicant brings out clan names which are often effectively hidden from everyday knowledge: while the elder, in exchange, gives out secret ritual and other knowledge, including more details of the wider clan system and its names. The clan names do not, however, as with neighbouring Muslim Swahili names, take on a special ritual, religious or mystical halo, a point to which I return at the end of this chapter.

A second occasion on which a man may have to use his clan name is while travelling in other parts of Giriamaland, as presented at the beginning of this chapter. In passing a homestead he will greet and then, since he is a stranger, be asked about his home and clan name, and that of his father and grandfather. The questioner will reciprocate by giving details of his own clanship. He may go further and rapidly trace personally known kinship links with the stranger. Even if he cannot do this, he is likely to be able to work out from the stranger's clan name and clanship some classificatory kindship and affinal links. There are only some 20-odd exogamous clans among the Giriama, and so, in the classificatory sense, almost everyone is related to each other by any number of ways. Giriama strangers can thus immediately create an impression of relatedness and even amity which either of them may try to build on if he wishes. This exchange of clan names is of course a politeness formula. But its importance is considerable among a people who travel frequently, seeking casual or permanent wage employment, herbal medicines native to a particular region or famous traditional doctors, or as petty traders. On the basis of the structural tie that the exchange of clan names creates, people can set up a personally instrumental relationship.

Third, knowing about clan names enables a person to try and structure relationships at funerals, whose social significance is considerable among the Giriama (see Parkin 1972: 77–86; 1991: 105–35). Affines of the deceased should come in large number to his or her funeral. They should also invite their affines, who should also invite theirs. This customary use of serial affinity is tied up with marriage obligations and is respected. It means that among the hundreds of people present at any funeral, there are many drawn from a distance who do not know each other personally. Stating one's clanship and having it authenticated by those who know, publicises marriageable categories and profitable possibilities. There is a boasting game played at funerals for enjoyment which reflects this emergent structuring of the event. Those neighbours and strangers whose precise clanship status is unknown to each other, may, over their palm wine, test who is the most senior. To return to the lists of clan names I have given, a man, X, may proudly announce that his clan name is Thoya (i.e. a third senior member of the 'fathers' generation of the Mweni clan), reasonably banking on the chance that his opponent is unlikely to top that grade of the senior generation. His opponent in the game, Y, may indeed not be able to do so, perhaps faring no better than the second ranked name (Mweri) of the 'sons' generation of the Baya-Mwaro clan. But, at some time, Y will come up against opponents of the 'sons' generation who have a lower name-grade than himself, and he may see the chance as worth taking. That said, one can hardly blame a man whose clan name is sixth-ranked of the 'sons' generation for avoiding such tussles if he can. But there are possible compensations. Even if a man has to concede seniority regarding his own clan name, he can seek to soften the blow and, through the names of ancestors, try to claim genealogical if not generational seniority, by demonstrating his descent from an alleged senior lineal founder, whose name is highly ranked. This challenge has more effect within a clan where relative lineal seniority is easier to gauge, but can also be made between clans as opponents vie with each other in claims to originate from a more senior point in their respective sub-clan's formation.

As with the example of the traveller politely exchanging clan names with the stranger, this game may not by itself alter events. But repeated many times between different people in the numerous small drinking groups that make up much of the male attendance at funerals, it provides a structure into which events are fitted and shaped.

To repeat, there are three occasions when a man may use his clan name, even though he may normally be known by some other name.

The system of clan names is, then, like a grid in dark but shallow waters, which, in their movements, momentarily reveal scattered glimpses of it. The structure is there but never visible in its entirety.

More recently, the clan name of a father or grandfather has, for a very few people, taken on the status of the English surname. It is a name you suffix to other names. It is a style and does not inhibit a man from revealing his own and forebear's names under the three circumstances I have described. Not surprisingly, it is also a style adopted by the very small number of educated women, who have professional status, as teachers for example, and do not have to marry. It is the inverse of the other 'Western' style of a few women who suffix their husband's clan name to their own. At least such women acquire a clan name in this way, and it is significant that these women usually stand apart from other women by virtue of their education or work. They, again, are inversely paralleled by the case of a man who suffixed the name of his mother, and who, as a prominent traditional doctor, also stood apart from other members of his own sex. The custom is uncommon though long established. A few men use both their father's clan name and mother's personal name while others switch between them, perhaps using the one to the exclusion of the other for long periods. In this way, clan names may re-appear or as easily disappear, and perhaps remain unused. Such situational usages hide the complex structure of clan names as a whole.

Let me now return to the question of why clan names should be buried, so to speak, in ordinary everyday discourse. The possibility of confusion is of course a good practical reason for not calling every man by his rightful clan name all the time. With a single clan consisting of thousands of men allocated only twelve names, there might need to be some further means of identification. But the reason for hiding the structure seems to go beyond this practical problem. For a start Giriama clan segments or sections are highly interspersed geographically. The cluster of twenty-six small homesteads in which I first lived includes people from twelve different clans, a half or so of all Giriama clans. Very few women even manage to produce six children. The people could, therefore, use many more clan names on an everyday basis before becoming confused as to who is being referred to. The people do not, so to speak, take up their full allocation of clan names. Many extended families include no more than one or two males in a generation who are commonly called by their clan names.

So, while there is indeed a practical limit as to how many males can be called by the same clan name (and who refer to each other as *somo*, namesake, and their mothers as *misomo*), the Giriama tendency to hide their clan names cannot be explained by this factor alone. I suggest that this tendency, and the corollary usage of a wide range of non-clan names, neatly denote the contrasting parameters by which Giriama men define themselves: clan names are reminders of the need to conform for the most part, while other names open up a sometimes non-conformist route to personal power and self-advancement.

An early European district officer who had worked among a number of Kenyan peoples, once referred to the Giriama in 1914 as 'democratic' and 'independent' by nature (Champion 1914), but in the disapproving sense of anarchic (Smith, 1981: 141), a view echoed by others since then and since independence. In fact 1914 was the year of the famous Giriama rebellion against the British (Brantley 1981), and so it would be surprising if Giriama did not appear to display characteristics which Champion, the district officer, evidently found unpalatable. Nevertheless, Giriama men do indeed nowadays sometimes justify non-conformity in the face of what others regard as moral rules. While rule-governed behaviour is expected, non-conformists may under some circumstances be re-described as strong and fearless. Thus, a young entrepreneur was condemned by elders for ignoring custom. But after succouring to a number of their 'needs', he was praised as a true Giriama warrior leading the people along the path to economic modernity. The Giriama view is that there are indeed times to rebel, and they are ready to cite their uprising against the British in 1914 as evidence of this. But this view in no way invalidates the strong Giriama conviction and faith in traditional legal and dispute settlement procedures, which are seen as the corner stones of Giriama identity and continuity.

Similarly, although it is always partially hidden, the structure of Giriama clan names provides a relatively unambiguous means of inclusion and exclusion. There is always the method of checking a man's clan and sub-group by asking for his clan names. The identity of infiltrators from other ethnic groups is easily located in this way, and, even if their descendants are eventually accepted as Giriama persons as a result of long residence in a Giriama area, their foreign origin is always remembered.

In fact, a number of Giriama clans are of non-Giriama origin, a fact well recognised by the Giriama themselves, and, if preservation of clan and ethnic boundaries and purity were of such great concern to Giriama, then we might expect the clan names to be used more regularly and openly. But the ecological changes and frequent and rapid population movements of the Mijikenda peoples as a whole have made it neither practicable nor always useful to adhere strictly to boundaries and group membership. Unlike the Luo of Kenya, who, to use Evans-Pritchard's phrase, expanded southwards "like a line of shunting trucks, each tribe driving out the one in front of it to seek compensation from one yet further in front" (1965: 209), the Mijikenda have for generations repeatedly moved north and south, east and west, and have alternately concentrated in and dispersed from small areas largely within the same region.

Under these conditions a flexible system of clan naming has been the most suitable: stored and therefore ready to be articulated in defence of shifting clan claims for territory or in marriage; yet not so insistently imposed that personal identities could not be given expression through other means than that of clanship. Nicknames are of course the most expressive of such alternative identities. Intermediary between them and clan names, however, are those which Giriama themselves regard as a separate type and which I call personal names, which belong to all Giriama, are not associated with particular clans, and so are less affected by customary rules of usage.

Personal Names

In view of the use of the same cluster of personal names among all or most non-Muslim Mijikenda, it is in fact these rather than the lesser used clan names that might themselves lead to confusion as to who in any grouping is being referred to, except that they are always qualified by some other name. These Mijikenda-wide names refer to roles, attributes, or events, well-known examples of which are: Karisa (the herder), Katana (child), Charo (journey, given to a child born while his father is away from home), Kazungu (European), Kahindi (Indian), Kasena (friend), Kaingu (cloud), Kalume (male), Kadzomba (Swahili person), Chembe (named after the famous district officer, Champion, whom I have already referred to, but also, as a pun, meaning the head of an arrow), and many others. They are long-established names, yet their original coining can sometimes be clearly dated, and so they make up a second layer of permanency in the structure of names, somewhat below that of the even longer established clan names.

At this second level, also, are the names normally given to women. Some have clearly traceable meanings, e.g. Kadzo (beautiful one), Kache (girl), Kadii (a long time, referring either to a long gestation period or to a lengthy birth), Kahonzi (the pounder of maize), Kahaso (blessing or medicine), Kavumbi (prolonged rain), Kademu (rag), Karembo (prettiness), Kadale (brass beads), Kan(d)ze (outside), Kahunda (bridewealth), Ndzingo (back of the house, for a girl supposedly born there and in fact derived from the verb, to commit adultery), Mwaka (south or season), Dama (termite or possibly heifer, for which the term is ndama), Jumwa (restday or week), and so on.

Other women's names are like most men's names in lacking an easily traceable meaning, e.g. Nyevu, Maku, Mbodze, Monje, Sidi, Mbua, Kizi, and Mgundo. We may note that female names which have the prefix ka, expressing diminution, are more likely to have recognisable meaning than those that do not. Among men names prefixed by ka, as given above, also carry clear meaning, as do most other men's personal names: e.g. Charo and Chembe (mentioned above), Kitsao (bullock), Kinda (young bird), Kenga (cheat), Kirao (feast), Mupati (wealthy), Ngumbao (hero, warrior), Ndago (thick, tough grass), and Chengo (new village). Indeed, there are remarkably few men's non-clan names for which there is not a recognised meaning. People do not pretend to more than guess at the previous circumstances under which these meaningful men's and women's names were first coined. But they point to the invention of such names as an ongoing process. These nicknames of the past now co-exist with clan names as the orthodox names of the present. The art of nicknaming continues, producing some names which will die with the person, if not beforehand, but others which catch on.

So, while clan names are formally and ceremoniously handed down relatively unchanged over the generations, other names are part of a public Mijikenda-wide artistic creativity which also stretches back generations. The line between established names and newly coined and therefore unique ones is marked by the use of the term *somo* to refer to or address someone with whom one shares a name, clan or non-clan, for which another term is *tsitwa*. According to Giriama, such namesakes are special friends because they share some indefinable quality that comes from names not simply labelling someone but being part of their human nature. Contrariwise, people with unique nicknames have correspondingly something unique in their personal make-up.

The easier traceability of meanings in men's non-clan names, compared with women's, suggests that there is a higher turnover of men's non-clan names. That is to say, more women's names have been used for longer periods and so have undergone phonological changes which have disguised their original meanings. Proportionally more men's non-clan names are being invented at any one time. This speculation would fit the ease with which men engage in banter about each other's names and reputations. Women, however much they also joke about other women's (and men's) personal attributes, are simply less likely to have the authority, in even an informal sense, to have these attributes inscribed as the person's name. It is an offence for men to discuss and re-name other men's women, and so, while it is true that a child's personal name is chosen by its mother, a new name for a woman is only likely to be invented when she is young on her father's authority, perhaps on the advice of a diviner treating the girl for a sickness requiring a new name.

Putting all this simply, men take a greater part than women in coining new names, and more new names are coined for men than women. Indeed, in so far as women provide their children at birth with personal names drawn from an existing pool, and given that these are often the names of a grandparent, it can be said that women reproduce the structure of names while men are more easily able to innovate within it. This is especially significant in view of the idea that by changing names persons may escape current misfortune or, to put the notion another way, can alter their character or destiny, concepts together translated by the term *mwenendo*, from the verb meaning to go or proceed. Preserving the Giriama metaphor, then, men are more easily able through name changes to alter direction in the course of life.

Informal and Nicknames

At this point we can focus on the third level of Giriama names, that of pure inventiveness and context-specific meaning. There is some overlap in time between this third level and the second as I have explained. This third is the level of nicknames invented on the spot, or of names with meanings which directly refer to a situation, attribute, or problem, sometimes seriously, sometimes humorously. In this category, for instance, would be included the sorrow names found among the Wiru of New Guinea and other societies (Strathern 1970), as well as the nicknames which are puns on or statements about situations and persons.

Since this is the level of current tides and fashions, it is where foreign names are borrowed. European Christian names were first borrowed on any scale with the advent of the missions in the late nineteenth century (earlier elsewhere) and since then at an increasing rate, especially following Kenya's independence in 1963 and the expansion of education. Swahili Muslim names have only ever been used as a result of conversion to Islam. However, an increasing number of non-Muslim Giriama children have been given as names terms drawn from the Swahili language, e.g. *tabu* (male: trouble), *juma* (male: week), *matano* (male: five things), *sadaka* (female: offering, blessing, sacrifice), *nyanya* (female: grandmother), *bibi* (female: madame), etc., without being required to become Muslim. Some of these Swahili names (e.g. Juma, Matano) are even used by Muslim Swahili themselves who, after all, are also subject to changing fashions. But every Swahili has his or her Muslim name and most are regularly known by it. This was almost entirely the case among the Swahili-Digo community of fishermen among whom I worked, whose stress on Islam corresponded with their own desperate efforts to retain land and fishing rights in the face of government and entrepreneurial pressure to relinquish them.

At this third level of borrowed, invented, and context-specific names, we can also place the change of name that a person, especially a child, may undergo if he or she has been sick. I have mentioned the example of a child's name that was altered to *tabu* (trouble, see above) in an attempt, the father said, to deceive the spirits into thinking that nothing would be gained by possessing this particular child for they would get nothing but trouble from it.

At this level, too, are the nicknames invented by a man himself, or by others for him, to denote a personal quality or the circumstances of birth. There is a continuum from those names which are imposed to those which are invented by the named person for himself. Somewhere in between are the collusive games in which persons encourage some kind of nickname and try to shape its connotations.

Imposed nicknames often have an ironic quality. A young boy-child would wander off on his own, quite unlike other children and was called *kachimbizi*, from the verb *ku-chimbira*, to run away. The intended pun is that the verb and name are normally used of women who have a habit of running away from husbands, especially older men, and have to be returned to them. They are not without sympathy, even among some men, for there are many who regard it as perfectly natural that a young woman should seek to escape a much older husband. The ambivalently regarded failings of young adult women are thus laid lightly on the shoulders of a young boy who, even when he becomes a man, will still be known by the name, a continuing oblique reminder of some of the problems of marriage. An old man was known as *Mizigo*, meaning heavy loads. When younger he had many troubles, or perhaps gave his parents anxiety, and so was always heavily burdened or a burden to others. A man born when there was plenty of cattle and grain is called *katembe*, meaning rich. Less benignly, non-Muslims refer to a woman Swahili shop-owner as *Mama sikudai*, meaning 'Don't I have a claim on you', i.e. 'Don't you owe me something?', and to another Swahili Muslim as *Kapiga Mbifu*, ('He cries tightness', with *mbifu* referring to something like an old coconut, that has dried out and become hard), because he holds back from paying those who work for him, whining that he is without money at the time. Neither of the two Muslims accept these nicknames and are each respectfully referred to by other Muslims by their formal names of Khaddiya Omar and Mzee Awadhi.

With these two exceptions, which clearly arose from tense ethnic-economic relations, nicknames are not invented and used without the knowledge of the adult to whom they apply. They are in fact spontaneously coined, or so it seems, at an informal gathering such as a dance, or when drinking or talking in small groups. The recipient is expected to take them in good humour, and usually does. But he has the right, so to speak, to denounce them. He may engage in counter-banter and thereby suggest alternatives. To the extent that a name becomes acceptable and so endures, the bearer of it has co-operated in its creation. He has publicly accepted that definition of his personality. Some men, and very occasionally women, go further than merely co-operating. They collude and encourage. They may even invent and publicise their own names. A young tourist guide who acts as one who has travelled far, seen much, and is a generous provider of palm wine, became known as *Musela*, meaning sailor, and is the person referred to at the beginning of this essay. A certain Giriama traditional doctor first introduces himself to strangers by his personal and clan name s, but then asks them to seek him out in his home area by the name of *Mwiya*, thorn. This has the connotation of power through penetration, which is a quality ascribed both to effective medicine and to vengeful witchcraft. *Mwiya*, the doctor, does indeed warn of his dangerous anger if provoked, and at the same time advertises his curative skills. In the same combative mood, a man who has for most of his life been known by the orthodox Christian and clan names of Samson Ngumbao Mugandi, and who, as a church preacher, gave Christian names to his sons, took on the name *Zhaatu*, meaning 'coming from people' and referring to his claim in a family land dispute to be the senior-most of four grandparents and, as such, the lawful head of the family. More humorously an old woman became known as *Hawe Kadzo Kinyee*. The first of these simply means grandmother and may be used of older women generally, the second is a common personal name for a woman, while the last, the nickname, has the connotation of sexual promiscuity (for both men and women). The woman has grandchildren of her own and is a strong, authoritarian figure who jokes daringly with men, and much enjoys the allusions in the nickname.

Some cases of self-naming become particularly celebrated. A famous chief of Kaloleni died in 1965 after sixteen years of considerable popularity (Parkin 1974: 160–5). He played life the people's way, not the way of colonial government. He held fine feasts, drank palm wine as well as any man, managed to collect taxes without antagonising people, was not above a little illegal ivory trading, had many wives and kept many cattle, and settled disputes using oaths in the traditional manner. Before becoming such a popular chief, he had coined for himself the name Kidugwa, which means hard fighter or competitor. He had already marked out the dominance of his character. Much later, in 1966, a young witch-finder who went on to become famous nationally, cultivated the name of Kajiwe, meaning little rock or something of enduring strength (Parkin 1968).

The judicious use of a mixture of orthodox and nicknames frequently defines an otherwise ambiguous social situation. For instance, a younger man, whom I came to know well during my first period among the Giriama in 1966, prided himself on his fearlessness. He joked with and insulted chiefs and headmen, yet stopped short of visibly incurring their wrath. Early on in fieldwork, when other people in and around my homestead were unsure as to how to address me, he called my wife *Hawe*, grandmother but also used by a man of his brother's wife. People were embarrassed: were he and I, then, no more than peers? Was I no higher in status than that? Dare he address my wife in that way? His judgment seemed sound, and anyway there was no alternative. I joked back and my status was settled. We were peers. He called himself in Swahili *Siogopi hata Ulaya*, which means 'I fear nothing, not even Europe(ans)'. The name was shortened to *Siogopi*, 'I fear nothing', and became widely used.

At one end, then, of the Giriama nicknaming continuum, people use names to shape the identities of others, including children. At the other end, men carve out their own identities. In the middle, men are offered nicknames which, through their responses, they accept or reject.

It is notable that passive nicknaming is of children and docile adults, while self-nicknaming is seen as a vigorous assertion of manhood through such motifs as fighting, drunkenness, and fearlessness. In between are men who respond to and even negotiate but do not initiate their own nicknames. Significantly, such men-in-the-middle may even, through their names, be ambivalently likened to females while clearly remaining men: it was sometimes remarked that the old man, *Mizigo*, carried burdens just as a woman does, but had the strength of a man to endure them.

It is also notable that nicknaming is neither an attempt simply to label human qualities nor only to create them. It involves aspects of both and is best seen as an on-going process of human definition. A person is both what others make him and also what he makes himself and, from the Giriama viewpoint, the shifting and sometimes negotiable line between the two is a fact of human existence. Thus, manhood in the abstract may mean assertiveness but it is up to a man himself either to insist on his own manhood by inventing an appropriate nickname for himself, risking ridicule if his bluff is called, or not to take this chance and instead wait and see how others define him, and how much he can shift this definition in his favour.

Moreover, the continuum from passive to active nicknaming represents that from non-manhood to manhood. Non-manhood rather than womanhood is here the opposite of manhood: male children can in later life reverse nicknames given them when young; and even the few women who become 'like men' may be nicknamed, as in the example given above, though this is rare. Non-manhood is thus an area of indeterminacy waiting to be defined according to a combination of factors: whether the person is male or female, of thrusting or retiring disposition, and able to earn the respect and liking of those around him or her. Gender provides the clearest tendencies. Young girls may be nicknamed but not normally women, nor do women invent their own nicknames. Men on the other hand are given the chance to name their own degree of manhood, if necessary by subverting existing definitions or supplementing clan and other names.

There is an interesting meta-level parallel. The three naming levels which I outlined earlier (clan names, established non-clan or personal names and new names, including nicknames), also represent a continuum from passive to active definitions of self. That is to say, persons do not choose their clan names which can never be changed. Neither do persons choose their established non-clan names, but at least these may fall into disuse by propagating a new name, especially a nickname, the choice of which the person may sometimes influence or control. Thus, just as within the field of nicknaming there is movement between its active and passive modes, so there is comparable movement within the wider Giriama naming system.

Naming and Gender

Since it is men much more than women who can move along from the passive to active modes, the naming system is really depicting a male struggle to escape the constraints of a definition of self imposed by others. Nicknames and personal names enable men to break away from the strictures of clan identity imposed by clan names, which nevertheless remain ineradicable and situationally retrievable although less used in everyday discourse. Men's assertiveness of the *Siogopi* type is the culmination of a journey beginning with the temporary subordination of clanship and finishing with the celebration of self-determining manhood. In other words male assertiveness is placed over and above clanship. The paradox is that clanship is only perpetuated by males among the Giriama and is in other respects regarded as being a very male phenomenon. But clanship is collective manhood, as evidenced in the male arbitration and ritual groups of which it is formed. By subordinating it partially through the use of nicknames and the public withdrawal of clan names, men create the indeterminate arena to which I referred where they can joust and assert themselves as unique individuals, only raising the obligations of clanship periodically and in a secondary manner. Individualism among Giriama males is thus a gradation. Its weakest representation is a man's clan name, for by this is connoted powerfully sanctioned collective obligations. Its strongest representation is the nickname invented by a man himself, and foisted, so to speak, on an admiring public. In between is the personal name shared with at least one other Giriama and other Mijikenda or the nickname which has been given to a man with his consent. A Giriama man's repertoire of names is therefore within his range of possible selves, though names are not the only forms of self-identification and construction. But names are important both as markers of qualities and as constitutive of them. What differentiates men from each other is not the unique nature of a particular combination of selves, but more the possibilities for self-expansion and redefinition that each creates. What is striking about Giriama views of human nature is that it is labile and not fixed, as evidenced in the dynamic concept of *mwenendo* (continuer) to denote what we would translate together as character, destiny, and even ambition. On the whole men regard this as a desirable quality in themselves but as threatening in women, a view not normally shared by women, as far as I can judge.

It is with regard to the use of teknonyms that gender distinctions are at their minimum. Only close kin and friends are entitled to address people by them. Even kinship terms can, like clan names, be used between persons of limited acquaintance who are nevertheless related classificatorily. Like clan names, however, teknonyms are rule-governed and cannot be freely chosen. Indeed, since they denote the honourable status of parent or grandparent, there would be no point in wishing to alter them. The implication in teknonymy that the birth of a child or grandchild ushers in the death of the parent or grandchild is not taken negatively, as is apparently the case in some other societies. Like clan names also, teknonyms are completely at odds with the energy and artistry that goes into creating nicknames: they are part of a person's movement through life stages and not inventively applied to him or her.

At the birth of their first child, whether a boy or a girl, the physical father and mother become known as, say, *BiKadzo* (formerly *AbiKadzo*) and *Mikadzo*, meaning father of *Kadzo* (a girl) and mother of *Kadzo*. With the birth of their first grandchild, the teknonym changes: the words for grandfather and grandmother are *tsawe* and *hawe*, and so the teknonyms referring to a (female) grandchild called *Kache* are *TsoKache* and *HaweKache*. The formula is exactly the same for boys. It is in fact an offence not to address friends or close kin by a teknonym if they have one. Teknonyms are constitutive not only of the persons named by them but also of those who use them in address, for the practice presupposes not just kinship and amity but also that all involved should be or become parents and grandparents, and that the unfortunate exceptions are victims, usually of others' witchcraft. Both teknonymy and clan names mark generational continuity. The first is used in households and close interaction. But the second, clan names, act most effectively in linking strangers wishing to locate their relatedness as well as in reproducing the alternate generations of particular clans which are geographically widely dispersed throughout Giriama country.

Terms of address among kin are too complex to be discussed here but involve the use of either teknonyms or kinship terms. The Giriama kinship terminology is of the wide-flung, open-ended Hawaiian type and so, as I have mentioned, most Giriama can find at least some classificatory affinal or kinship link with each other, which will be used in mutual address should they become well acquainted. For those who already know each other well, such kinship or teknonymic terms of address are so normal that they may rarely actually call each other by their personal or other names. There is a logic to this. Given that their names are an aspect of a person's store of possible selves, it is inappropriate or at least risky for those closest to the person to use them to their face. This would be like deciding on the person's behalf which self was appropriate, and, since this might not accord with the bearer's own choice on that occasion, might lead to resentment.

It is among associates who are known but outside this close network that personal and nicknames are used. These are people who are intermediary between strangers and family and both compete and co-operate with each other, sometimes intermarrying. They include unmarried friends and kinship peers who use these names but switch to teknonyms when they become parents. The fighting or competitiveness comes before the intermarrying, however, and so it is these who argue over definitions of selfhood. These are public and therefore political battles and act as preludes and accompaniments to seeking office in, say, the local district council, the local branch of the ruling political party, the co-operative administration, or in a traditional society.

Those men and women who have come to use teknonyms with each other, on the other hand, tend to avoid the possibility of coming into conflict. Politically they have thereby set up something of a neutral zone in the more openly visible political battle for the names that most appropriately reflect men's views of themselves and their policies. This passive, teknonymous domain, with its accompanying use of also of kinship terms of endearment and address, fits paradigmatically with the position of women who rarely experience name changes except through teknonymy: their possible selves are allocated according to predictable stages of the lifecycle. Only by subverting their primary domestic roles as wives, mothers, and marriageable daughters can women break out of the cycle: the equivalent of male escape from the generational constraints of clanship. Giriama men state that it is 'wilful' women who are most often possessed by spirits. They also recognise that it is 'wilful' women who, if they are not possessed, may run off to Mombasa or other towns and become Swahili-speaking Muslims. Men claim to regard spirit possession as the better alternative and worth tolerating.

Those few women who do run off, live independently, and assume the status of Muslim-Swahili, necessarily take on a new name as well as religion and lifestyle. They take the name conferred on them by their adopted Islamic community. The name will probably be one of a limited number of religious names, and once assumed, is non-negotiable. In this respect, though they have switched from Giriama to Swahili status, these women have entered an equally structured set of roles. The difference is that their behaviour and identity are now seen to be subject to religious authority rather than that of clanship. But at least they are no different from Swahili men in this respect and so achieve some parity of status. This is not to say that Swahili male and female roles are not sharply distinguished, nor that in all respects women have equal status. It is just that the use of relatively fixed religious names to the exclusion of others applies to both men and women and is seen by the people themselves to represent their common subjection as individuals to the will of God. Of course, individuals can still make their distinctive impression on the world through trade, business, politics, or, in the case of men, religious office. But in doing so, they do not normally use their names as a way of building up, altering, or re-shuffling a repertoire of different possible selves, as do Giriama men.

The use of names in this way among Giriama men not only distinguishes them from Swahili men and women, it also distinguishes Giriama men from Giriama women, whose name repertoire is small and relatively fixed like that of the Swahili. Pushed to the level of an hypothesis, these differences suggest that where personal names (here including nicknames) can be changed and re-combined in different ways, people are likely to see themselves as individually closer to controlling much of their own destiny (regardless of whether they in fact do so), but that where names are fixed and non-negotiable some greater agency is seen as in control: in the case of Giriama women that greater agency is their menfolk, including the witches among them who afflict their children and health; for Swahili men and women it is their God. The significant contrast here regarding names is not that between Giriama and Swahili, but that between Giriama men who are more likely to see personal name changes as a means of social and political advancement, and Giriama women and Swahili men and women together who are less able to regard name changes in this way.

Personal naming in any society makes up some kind of language game. Among Giriama men this is complex and is a form of active reflexivity through which men may change themselves through statements about themselves. Among their less advantaged womenfolk, and among Swahili Muslims, for whom Islamic names have an important religious if not sacred quality, change is less acceptable, and nicknames have little of the assertiveness of Giriama males. Here the language game is more one of passive reflexivity through which persons maintain rather than attempt to alter themselves. The distinction suggests that language games differ from each other not only in terms of their logical complexity but also as instruments of power and subordination.

Let me conclude on this point by asking how far a naming system can be explained, following Lévi-Strauss, in terms of its logical coherence, as against the strategic uses to which it is put by individuals. Let me then ask whether this distinction between logic and strategy is here tenable.

Conclusion

Lévi-Strauss does in fact touch on the question of subordination in his discussion of proper or personal names. He points out that among the Penan, studied by Needham, it is in fact only children who are known by their proper names (or autonyms), and even then only until an ascendant dies, at which point a child is known by that dead relative's name, called a necronym. When another relative dies the child is then known by that person's name, another necronym. This use of successive necronyms occurs until he or she becomes a parent and so becomes teknonymously known by his/her own child's name (Lévi-Strauss 1966: 191–5, based on Needham 1954). In other words his personal name is never used after early childhood. There are yet other aspects, but all point to the member of the community with the least power, the young child, as the only one to be known by its personal name.

At first there appear to be some elements of similarity with the Giriama naming system, in which teknonyms take over from personal names. Lacking clan names women are particularly affected, since they appear to lose their only distinctive characterisation of self, their personal name, and to remain with nothing but a teknonym. But what in fact do they lose? For a start, they are only known by their teknonyms among close associates. Other people continue to refer to them by their proper names, sometimes also as wife-of-so-and-so. Secondly, even their personal names are normally those of their father's own mother and classificatory mothers, in order of sibling birth seniority. One could say that they were not given much in the first place to express their exclusive selfhood.

Boys similarly are given clan names and sometimes even personal names after grandfathers, so much so that one must wonder how far we can even refer to the existence among the Giriama of personal names which are the sole property, so to speak, of any one individual, i.e. his/her proper name, and not already 'owned' by an ascendant. In fact, as I have explained, there are circumstances in which children may be given names which stress their personal distinctiveness (for instance, to ward off spirits). In other words, personal or proper names do exist, but only as exceptions to the rules. Otherwise the orthodox names, as I have called them, either identify people with the alternate generations of grandparents and grandchildren, or distance them from the immediately adjacent ones of parents and children, in both cases fitting them into a system of relationships. Apart from the exceptions, then, all such names play a part in subordinating expressions of exclusive selfhood.

Out of the idea of exceptions to the rules is born that of the nickname, itself governed by at least implicit conventions. Selfmade nicknames among the Giriama are the most likely creations of speech to reverse subordination. Lévi-Strauss's mention of nicknames is sparse. He equates them with descriptive names of the kind given, for instance, among the Tiwi, or to cattle among some African pastoral people. They are created anew each time for each individual, no two individuals having the same name (Lévi-Strauss 1966: 188, 206–9; see also Akinasso on the Yoruba 1981). But he only ever regards them as bestowed upon an individual by others, and not as created by that individual for himself, as is the case among certain Giriama. This is not surprising, for Lévi-Strauss's elegant account depends on the idea of an underlying classificatory logic fitting names and name-types in relation to each other, and so acting as a self-determining agent. The simple difference, however, between being named by others (whether or not we call those others a society or a logic) and naming oneself, presupposes conflicting agencies, and requires that we seek to understand the uncertain play of power in this conflict.

Early in the essay I raised the possibility that personal names mediate the contradiction between our being produced by society and yet able to speak creatively about society. I now suggest that this is based on an inappropriate dichotomy of individual and society. It is inappropriate in two ways.

First, the Giriama have ideas which indicate a gradation of individualism. At one extreme is the assertive Giriama selfnicknamer who marks himself out discretely enough to satisfy any amount of Western insistence on the autonomy of the individual. At the other is the Giriama man whose clan name is so used that he is identified with it and with his constituent sub-clan and so partially merges his selfhood with that of other clan members. There is no point along this continuum that we can say that we have arrived at the or a Giriama individual. Rather, an individual occupies at any one time a number of dispersed points along this continuum, the combination of which varies among individuals.

Second, the rule-based clan names and creative nicknames respectively echo the concepts of *langue* and *parole*, and so of society and the individual. But it is more to the *idea* of rules that the clan names appeal, for in fact only some Giriama men are regularly known by them, even though all have had them allocated. Rather like the imagined French Grammar which voluminously consists of more exceptions to the rules than of rules themselves, the system of clan naming practice allows for many 'ungrammatical' forms of usage. Inventiveness is not the sole prerogative of nicknaming. Persons use names in ingeniously novel combinations and dissolve any neat boundary between rule-based and rule-less behaviour, and so between social and individual innovation.

The names by which persons are known are not, then, allocated by rule-governed institutions but by persons in competition with each other. From our conventional perspective we might say that such politics of naming is inscribed in a people's ontology more directly than is the case, say, with the politics of land allocation. That is to say, naming someone does more than give them an identifiable label, for it is part of their personal and social construction. Giving someone land rights, or withholding them, has supposedly a less direct role in their personal and social make-up. However, I believe this to be an error. In much of Africa, as in many other agricultural societies, land is indeed coterminous with social, political and personal identity, and its bestowal or withdrawal does not simply re-define but re-constitutes persons and groups. Indeed, one could say the same about the politics of religion or of parenthood in societies where these were of fundamental concern. Systems of personal naming are certainly distinctive linguistically and encompass an immense variety. But as aspects of political process, they are like politics anywhere: the struggle for the right to determine human entitlement and even who is human.

References

Akinasso, F.N. (1980) The sociolinguistic basis of Yoruba personal names. *Anthropological Linguistics* 22, 275–304.

Barnes, R. (1982) Personal names and social classification. In D. Parkin (ed.) *Semantic Anthropology*. London. Academic Press.

Beattie, J. (1980) The self in traditional Africa. *Africa* 50, 313–20.

Brantley, C. (1981) *The Giriama and Colonial Resistance in Kenya, 1800–1920*. Berkeley: University of California Press.

Carrithers, M., Collins, S. and Lukes, S. (eds) (1986) *The category of the Person*. Cambridge: Cambridge University Press.

Champion, A.M. (1914) *Memorandum: Labour Supply and the Giriama*, Nairobi: Kenya National Archives.

Dieterlen, G. (ed.) (1973) *La Notion de la Personne en Afrique Noire*, Paris: Edition du Centre Nationale de Recherche Scientifique.

Evans-Pritchard, E.E. (1965) 'Luo tribes and clans', in The Position of Women in Primitive Society, London: Faber.

Lévi-Strauss, C. (1966) [1962] *The Savage Mind*, London: Weidenfeld & Nicolson.

Needham, R. (1954) The system of teknonyms and death-names of the Penan, *Southwestern Journal of Anthropology* 10, 416–31.

Needham, R. (1971) 'Penan friendship names', in T. Beidelman (ed.) *The Translation of Culture*, London: Tavistock.

Parkin, D.J. (1968) 'Medicines and men of influence', *Man* 3, 424–39.

Parkin, D.J. (1972) *Palms, Wine and Witnesses*, San Francisco: Chandler.

Parkin, D.J. (1974) 'National independence and local tradition in a Kenya trading centre', *Bulletin of the School of Oriental and African Studies* 37, 157–74.

Parkin, D.J. (1991) *Sacred Void*, Cambridge: Cambridge University Press.

Strathern, A. (1970) 'Wiru penthonyms', *Bijdragen tot de Taal-Land-, en Volkenkunde*, 126, 59–74.

Part 3

The Materiality of Language and Communication

The capacity of naming to 'create' a person or an object, as discussed in the last chapter, takes us directly into the materiality of language and communication. Language does not just communicate meaning. It also does things and so has physical or material effect. We are used to the idea of illocutionary speech having physical impact (e.g. 'that door is open', i.e. 'please close it') but there are other ways in which the communication of events and conditions is both itself material and has material consequences. A familiar Whorfian example is the problem of so-called 'empty' gasoline drums, which may be empty of the liquid fuel but not of the residual and highly explosive gas which workers, sitting down for a break to smoke, casually ignite by throwing discarded cigarette ends into an 'empty' drum. Ardener (1982: 3–4, 13) used this illustration of semantic materialism to show what he called the 'contamination' of our social and technical worlds by language. That is to say, the social, material and linguistic are inseparably constituted. They 'contaminate' each other and together make possible the communication as well as miscommunication of reality, a clear indictment of those who advocate language purity as an ideal to be pursued (discussed in Part 2). Here, the notion of language shadow relates to that of semantic cluster which, for social anthropology, is arguably the basis of cross-cultural comparison and a way of reconciling the analytical opposition between so-called relativity and universalism, a topic to be explored (see Parkin, 2007b, 2013).

Chapters 12 and 13 both refer to Ardener's approach: the first is a review of the posthumous collection of many of his key essays, while Chapter 13 weaves Ardener's concept of 'language shadow' into a demonstration of how the usage of cultural key terms can rise and fall according to whether wider socio-political circumstances stigmatise those identified by the terms. Thus, the term for a disease allegedly arising from 'promiscuity' and associated with a public and dangerous pandemic (e.g. HIV/AIDS) stigmatises those afflicted. Once the disease and stigmatisation have passed, the underlying behavioural and causative associations recede, fade and become a language shadow, possibly to be re-articulated later as a culturally explicit key term when the disease recurs. Or the opposite may occur; the stigmatising term is avoided altogether during the crisis to which it refers, leaving only its unspoken, culturally subliminal shadow, but, after the crisis, no longer stigmatises and so is used openly. The point here is that the key term or lexicon is not fixed but is of variable or cyclical presence and effect and that communication comprises this semantic instantiation and de-instantiation, i.e. its coming-into and out-of-being. The materiality of disease and its semantic identification thus co-vary in their expression but are inseparable.

The stigmatisation of persons triggered by the use of key terms is commonly expressed morally: e.g. an identified disease is seen as the result of 'immoral' promiscuity. In turn, such moral states may be referred to metaphorically. In standard English usage the terms, 'moral' and 'ethical', are often synonymous.

In Chapter 14, however, the moral and ethical are analytically distinguished as operating at different levels of scale and influence: the ethical is associated with society-wide authoritative institutional judgements (as by the British Medical Association) and the moral with the smaller everyday concerns of individuals. The ethical is further characterised as 'loud' because of its authoritative and sometimes punitive condemnation of delicts which flout institutional and/or professional rules (as when medical doctors fail to observe proper procedure). The moral is characterised as 'quiet' as when, say, medical delicts go unreported or patients lack the voice to protest effectively and can do little more than merely talk among themselves about problems. The dual metaphor of 'loud' and 'quiet' is used analytically to capture the way a Swahili Muslim traditional healer negotiates his status as at one level serving his everyday 'quiet' clients and at another level acceding to the 'louder' demands of more authoritative figures. These include not just the medical establishment, but other Muslims of more radical persuasion who reject his traditional healing methods. The connotation is also semantically material: 'loud' is forceful while 'quiet' is acquiescent, gentle and retiring. The two in interaction denote a familiar struggle between 'heavy' institutional and 'lighter' individual practices, in this case in the medical sphere.

Power differences thus frame communication and, through their differential impact, can set up islands of semantic density. Semantic density results when speakers (competitively) add more and more meaning to utterances in order make their propositions persuasive or to dominate conversational discourse. In their efforts to overcome or exploit power differences among them, interlocuters can try to persuade through appeal to sentiment or through so-called rational argument, which Bailey (1981, 1983) calls hortatory and cerebral rhetoric, respectively.

Chapter 15 explores a number of similar dichotomies based on this 'western' distinction between reason and emotion. Ethnography on the Giriama and other African societies shows that this distinction has a different semantic spread. It is polysemy rather than dichotomy. Thus, the Giriama names of some body parts such as heart, liver, kidney, eye refer to what may be translated into English as both reason and emotion. That is to say, the same Giriama terms denote reason and emotion as well as bodily part. This is not metaphorical but is how Giriama understand the way humans are made up. Earlier forms of English did have one or two similar examples: as in Shakespearean England, where the heart 'thinks' as well as 'feels', and the liver is the seat of the passions (*Much Ado About Nothing* III. Ii. 13).

The modern English lexical separation of terms for bodily parts, emotion and reason which are only sometimes joined as metaphor, is unlike and, in translation, distorts the more packed-in, polysemic discourse of the Giriama. The polysemic spread among Giriama is evident also in the fact that intentionality is built into emotional states, even though there is a completely separate vocabulary describing allied notions such as thinking, pondering, comparing, explaining, understanding, remembering, reminding and deciding. The chapter is then an exploration of how Giriama and other African semantic clusters index ontological and cosmological arrangements which differ significantly from those of dichotomous, Cartesian heritage.

Chapter 16 provides an example, not of such relativism as described in the preceding chapter, but of a procedure cross-culturally common in semiosis, which is the power of innuendo, allusion or insinuation as a rhetorical device. Speakers may intentionally stop short of spelling out the full meaning of a proposition but rather refer indirectly to matters. Innuendo is thus incomplete propositional argument. It is a feature of both metaphor and metonymy as in the assertion that 'George is a lion' (Sapir & Crocker, 1977). This metaphorically combines humanity and animality and metonymically identifies the human with an alleged part of animality (lion's bravery). It thus truncates but hints at the idea that George, a human, has the animal quality of bravery associated with lions. Innuendo can be powerful because it introduces uncertainty and possible ambiguity in a communicative exchange and gives the speaker leverage over the listener: does the speaker have access to information that the listener lacks and/or would rather prefer was not disclosed publicly? Or, as in commercial advertising, does the indirect message hint at promises which appeal to the consumer and persuade them to purchase the product? The ambiguity of incomplete talk is not always intended and, at root, inheres in the communicative limits of representation: propositions can always be interpreted as leaving something out depending on the interests and acuity of the listener(s). There may in fact be different interpretations varying by listener. Listener's uncertainty as to whether incomplete talk is intended or unintended adds another layer of ambiguity.

Indeed, such ambiguity puts into question whether communicative intention in the sense of controlled and planned cognition can ever be separated from unplanned social and other influences (see Duranti, 2015). That said, listeners do experience a sense of premature ending to apparently incomplete utterances whether regarded as intended or not. It is the audience response and, sometimes, counter-response that chapter sixteen analyses. This is through a detailed description of a culturally distinctive form of 'prestation' among Muslim Swahili women along the East African coast. These women wear special rectangular cotton cloths called *kanga*. The women buy the cloths but choose them not mainly for their pattern and use of colour but for the messages or sayings which are written on them. The messages are invariably oblique and need deciphering. They play on words and refer to humorous, ironic, laudatory and didactic situations involving the wearer, including those of a conjugal, sexual or erotic nature. They are a kind of prestation in being commonly directed at other women rivals for a man or husband or even at the husband himself, although most messages are for other women. To a much lesser extent, the messages refer also to economic, political and ideological issues. But mainly they are directed at a specific woman who, it is claimed, will know that she is the target of the innuendo. The messages take account of differences of age among women, with sexual innuendos much less likely to be aimed at older women, for instance. Individuals receiving a prestation of this kind are unlikely to reciprocate openly because this will be tantamount to acknowledging the message's claim or accusation. But they may of course themselves buy an appropriately messaged *kanga* as a riposte, which perhaps only the two rivals may understand. There is thus potentially in-built ambiguity which borders on communicative secrecy but which can, in principle, be deciphered by other observers of the social relations which are in effect being discussed *sotto voce*. The material of this chapter thus returns us to how semantic clusters may be unevenly experienced in even a small population. Sometimes they are expressed by and for some interlocuters as relatively unambiguous propositions, but sometimes they are implicit or hidden, so to speak, in innuendo and insinuation and understood at first by only a few.

Chapter 17. We can think of an implicit but unverbalised semantic cluster or semantic density as related to Ardener's notion of language shadow, introduced in Chapter 13, which he also referred to by such broadly comparable synonyms as 'paradigm', 'ideology', 'black box', 'programme', 'template' and as a 'simultaneity' of events, i.e. a clustering of happenings and references, which, like poiesis, produces linear 'output' in the form of 'a stream of events' (Ardener, 1989b: 86–87, 93–94). Chapter 17 explores theoretically the concept of simultaneity or synchronicity in language, communication and cognition, and its output, sequentiality.

In the 1970s the relationship of simultaneity to sequentiality was taken up by linguistic anthropologists. Paul Kay, with Brent Berlin, extended the idea that the synchronic variability of basic colour terms generated the linear evolution of more specialised colour terms, to a more general claim that 'all linguistic change has its roots in synchronic heterogeneity of the speech community' (Kay, 1975: 257). In other words, the mixed speech of a community at a particular point in time is the basis of future differences and changes in their speech, not unlike the concept of poiesis.

Using the example of divinatory or shamanic spirit speech, Chapter 17 draws on but recasts this shift. The diviner's spirit presents the client's illness or misfortune as due to simultaneous and conflicting disorders in his life but, through questioning him, reorders them as cause, effect and curative solution. It is a movement from a 'tangled state' to one that is 'straightened out'. The apparently orderless network of ideas and events criss-cross on top of each other and make up the simultaneity. This is in effect an unarticulated language shadow. It needs to be straightened out by being expressed verbally in terms of, first, diagnosis and then prognosis leading to cure. It is Ardener's programme which generates output. More than this, however, it is suggested that divination needs to set up a language shadow in the first place as a kind of puzzle, the resolution of which gives successful closure to the divinatory session and perpetuates the shared belief in the power of spirits which possess shamanic diviners.

12 Unpacking Anthropology

Review of Edwin Ardener 1989 *The Voice of Prophecy and Other Essays* (ed. Malcolm Chapman), Oxford: Basil Blackwell.

This is the posthumous volume that Edwin Ardener had once said (to this reviewer) would be the only form in which his most seminal essays would be published collectively. In fact, it did seem at one stage that the volume, or something like it, might after all appear in Ardener's lifetime. But, as if in returning to the original prophecy, Ardener died suddenly (in 1987) and the volume was indeed mainly prepared after his death. As is common with scholars who die in the prime of their intellectual life, there have been many obituary tributes. There has already been so much said, including, in this volume, Chapman 's introduction and postscripts by two other students of Ardener's, Kirsten Hastrup and Maryon McDonald, that it is difficult to avoid repetition. Let us then re-cast the exercise of the review in different terms, a task Ardener might have appreciated, and 'unpack', as he used to say, this volume in an exploratory way, discovering things about it as we define it.

Starting near the end with Hastrup's postscript, we find an exposition of Ardener's approach that is as clearly expressed as Ardener's own appeared elusive. It focuses on three of Ardener's notions: semantic density, event richness and historical density, which are neatly glossed as to do respectively with language, space and time. It is subtly expressed but also the most polished summary statement I know of the trajectory in Ardener's thought, shorn of all the inevitable untidiness that went into it, and one of which Ardener himself would have been incapable, so reluctant was he to stay for more than a moment with anything that looked like a definitive statement. As McDonald says, Ardener avoided the -isms and, as Chapman notes, he saw himself as ghosting between the interstices, difficult to pin down if you wanted a precise formulation. He regarded characterisations that began to assume theoretical status as always provisional, and no sooner had we begun to understand what a p-structure was in relation to an s-structure and how they derived from the idea of template, than we were carried on into language shadows, simultaneities and world-structures and, most intriguingly of all, as in the final chapter here ("Remote Areas" – Some Theoretical Considerations'), into such expressions of everyday English language as 'remote areas', whose excavation tells us more than any analytical term, but which may itself, as Ardener sadly warned, eventually suffer the fate of taking on analytical status.

Chapman has done a remarkable editorial job and has also provided an introduction that retains the freshness of Ardener's creative provocations. The volume comes across as autobiographical in multiple and unintended ways. The book is of and about Ardener's work and achieves that task well, but Chapman also comes through as an intelligent and sensitive interpreter who one would like to emerge from the shadows, just as Hastrup and McDonald establish their own legitimacy (the latter seeming to reflect in her comments on Ardener's empiricism something of her own remarkable experiences working in Brittany-a kind of many-mirrored imaging of Breton authenticity). This is not to say that there has been a merging of student and master, but that among the very few anthropologists who would let themselves be visibly captured by Ardener's prose and thence by his ideas, most were his students. Of course, a very much larger number have over the years moved in his direction, though rarely aware of the influence and even more rarely acknowledging the triggering insight.

All this relates directly to the book's title and, most importantly, to the heart of Ardener's mission. The title is bold and risky, as Chapman notes, but is probably right because it forces us to focus on prophecy as an epistemological problem rather than as to do with fortune-telling or the like. As Ardener says, prophets do not foretell: they tell us what is already there, but at the time we cannot understand them. They see before them what for others is neither visible nor communicable in existing language but which, through non-verbal means, eventually makes surface sense as the underlying logic of events and tendencies begins to be articulated in a style that informs common understanding. But it is not that language catches up with the underlying pattern. It is that the new language and the pattern are indissolubly formed through each other.

It has become commonplace nowadays to scoff at naïve ideas of language as referential, as principally a means by which objects are concretised and labelled. To use Ardener's early phrase, we now all accept that the linguistic and the social penetrate each other and even that the linguistic constantly 'contaminates' the social, a general view towards whose contribution Ardener acknowledges (p. 39) the work of Needham, whose *Belief, Language and Experience* (1972) also became an important landmark. But it is not always widely known how and why we arrived at this position. For this reason, it is good that Chapman included (a shortened version of) the introduction to the 1971 ASA volume, *Social Anthropology and Language*, for it has almost undergone the full cycle of datedness, and now seems ripe for re-release at a time when much of a whole new generation knows only the panic of 'relevance' and seems to be rebuilding the wall that separates the practical from the conceptual.

We have to abstract what is valuable, and it is still useful to remind ourselves of the three levels at which Ardener saw language and anthropology as being related – the technical, pragmatic and explanatory – in order both to dispose of them, as he himself did, but also to pause over historical traces that may again become interesting. For instance, Ardener was at the time writing with great adulation of Saussure and against older, reconstructionist philological work. At that time, the 'master exemplar' was *langue* and *parole* and attendant oppositions, each having relational rather than intrinsic value. 'Living philology' of the Henry Sweet kind was regarded as the non-relational interest of a Malinowski who sought meanings only or mainly 'in context'. Yet, while Ardener continued to regard meaning as resting on relational notions of opposition, his last works seem also to point in the direction of a kind of philology, as the chapter on remote areas suggests: like the apparent inarticulateness of the prophet, the everyday term or phrase (odd-job word?) hovers over an assemblage of possible actions, thoughts and language, which may or may not be realised.

It would have been instructive to have Ardener address within his scheme Lienhardt's insight (1988: 107), with which I concur, that African (and, I would say, especially Bantu) languages have extraordinarily transparent etymologies. I find that it is sometimes possible to trace complex vocabulary back to an apparently original meaning. The transparency is sometimes evident to the speakers, who therefore have their own, non-Western epistemological framing that, through its visibility, invites referential thinking; not with regard to objects, however, but to conceptual-semantic archetypes. Many Africanist ethnographers must have witnessed and marvelled at how a diviner or other sage unravels a complex semantic domain and poignantly reveals an alleged root. In such situations, less is hidden from us and we are that much closer to the apparent origins of ideas, so that the 'word' can and does take on great intrinsic significance that does not have to be explained relationally, although relational significance can be found in it too. It is at once archetype, realisation and expression.

Here we come to what I regard as an interesting tension in Ardener's work. A paper that is not in the volume, but which must stand as progenitor of the rest, is the celebrated one (1970) on zombies and witchcraft, and their co-variation with poverty and economic boom, which was first presented publicly in 1967 and published in the ASA volume on witchcraft, but which in part is found in even earlier work. Here was born the idea of the template, the underlying assemblage of ideas that can only be given partial realisation at any one time, giving the impression of surface differences, which are, nevertheless, cut from the same template. It is an idea that, unlike Geertz's (1966: xx) neat but throwaway usage in his famous paper on religion as a cultural system, was nurtured over the years and took increasingly fruitful form during the rest of Ardener's career. The tension I see in Ardener's work is between the similarity that this notion shows to a standard structuralist account and the empirical flexibility that it implies and that threatens to break the constraints of any structure.

This tension entered Ardener's own conceptualisations and language. Apart from learning in the first chapter (the ASA volume introduction 'Social Anthropology and Language') that it is not the Prague School model of phonemic opposition and distinctiveness that anthropologists should be emulating, but rather that of relational opposition and distinctiveness in general, we are introduced in the second chapter ('The New Anthropology and its Critics', the 1970 Malinowski lecture) to the idea of underlying programme, qualitative generativeness as opposed to quantitative predictability, and then in later chapters (principally Chapter 5, 'Some Outstanding Problems in the Analysis of Events', which was first presented and circulated widely in 1973) to the distinction between paradigmatic and syntagmatic structures. Ardener called the latter p- and s-structures, not just as an exercise in abbreviation, but because he wished to emphasise that they were not quite the same as the Saussurean and later Lévi-Straussian concepts, though very much related to them. But what was the difference and why the hesitancy?

The difference is three-fold: of scale, of his perception of otherness, and of his vision of loose as against tight boundedness. For Lévi-Strauss, it is the great mythological and marriage schemes of the world to which we address our analyses. For Ardener, it is the nooks and crannies of existence: alleged witches hiding under blankets in tin-roofed houses; differences between Ibo and English handshakes; women returning from the Bakweri forest to scream at their husbands under the general complaint of 'bush'; or the irony of retired Americans and other incomers maintaining and refurbishing the traditions of the Hebrides. Ardener reestablished the apparently trivial as of exemplary significance and dissolved otherness as a matter to be created (rather than discovered), as much at home as abroad.

The tension, then, is that Ardener commonly resorted, especially early on, to a vocabulary of obvious structuralist derivation (including, from among his terms not mentioned so far, 'black box', 'linear chains', 'output', 'binary distinctions' and so on), yet was practising a methodology on the small things of life that could be found anywhere and at any time, were experientially unbounded (not at all like a structure) and among which the surface/deep or signifiers/signified distinction was of the loosest kind. In this empirical respect he was closer to Barthes than to Lévi-Strauss, though he disagreed with Barthes' view that semiotics should be part of linguistics: Ardener sided with Saussure, who argued for linguistics as part of a wider semiotics.

Now it is certainly clear that Ardener subscribed to a general semiotics, in the sense that he wished to relate the different communication media through which ideas and actions inform each other. This indeed is his idea of the 'simultaneity': signification straddles different channels and alters as it is understood, explained, renounced etc. We change that which we interpret in the very act of interpretation, but it is change that is ultimately 'generated' by the phenomenon of which we have become part through our act of interpretation. This view is now familiar and has reached us in more episodic and less systematic fashion via Geertz. I say systematic because Ardener was clearly very conscious of what he had written beforehand, so that ideas are referred back and connected very precisely. Through this continuity of conceptual overlap, however, Ardener gradually substituted lateral homologues for hierarchical levels of the appearance/essence type. As the chronologically ordered chapters proceed, they rely less and less on the basic structuralist idea of surface and deep and turn instead to, at most, a distinction between the hidden and the evident (in events) that twists inside out periodically, producing what Ardener calls parameter collapse and which is probably akin to what others have called paradigmatic change. Thus, the study of marriage as an institution that legally contains among other things sexuality can so easily become the study of 'outside' marriages and thence of 'prostitution', which reverses the paradigm by showing sexuality now as 'containing' the law in the sense of commonly being outside and beyond it.

Chapman was right to arrange the chapters in the chronological order of their first appearance rather than of their actual publication. For it is in this way that we can see the shift from quasi-structuralist language to a use of vocabulary that becomes increasingly everyday and descriptive. It is indeed a shift from 'genre to life', which is how Ardener describes, in the penultimate chapter ('Social Anthropology and the Decline of Modernism'), the decline of modernism and its successor.

Yet there are distinctive sub-themes that punctuate the flow at different points, and, while it is against the spirit of his work to abstract them as separable, they are bound to be addressed as such. Thus, the issue of how to measure events and people when these same phenomena never remain sufficiently fixed to be measurable by set criteria, is especially treated in the chapters on population and ethnicity – 'Language, Ethnicity and Population' (first published in *JASO*) and 'Social Anthropology and Population' – but recurs in others. It is not just that human populations have the capacity, unlike animal species or plants, to redefine themselves (to call themselves by different 'ethnic' names) at the very point at which you put them in a category to be counted. This is one problem. Another more fundamental problem is that human 'groups' are also constantly re-evaluating the criteria by which they identify themselves. The demographer presupposes a standardisation of his/her data by resort to what appear to be such universal measures as gender and age, and so irons out the creases that would otherwise appear in the concepts that lie behind such measures. As Ardener says, the outrageous or anomalous become susceptible to a levelling-out operation. In other words, before we measure we have to define the unit of measurement, and to define it means taking into account peoples' own definitions as well as our own, which, as we know, are affected significantly by this very process. Ardener was well aware of the pitfalls of statistical 'truths', having worked in this area in early studies of fertility and divorce. He saw the above, later, chapters as keeping us on constant alert for this mutual relatedness of measurement and definition, and to the fact that to measure is always to raise problems of definition. It was, as with other sub-themes, a challenge to the tendency in social science to privilege an alleged underlying statistical objectivity and to separate it from what some might present as surface deviatory behaviour.

The same concern comes across in the chapters – '"Behaviour": A Social Anthropological Criticism' (another first published in *JASO*) and, to a lesser extent, "Social Fitness" and the Idea of "Survival" – that reject both naïve and sophisticated arguments alike that animal and human behaviour can be understood as commensurately similar. In many ways, however, Ardener presents the problem as that of the impossibility of translating across cultures according to a universally understood code: for different cultures, read animal and human, and see this allegorical. The argument for the incommensurability of cultures, echoed by Feyerabend and others, is well taken as a methodological starting point. But how would Ardener have reacted to the extraordinary bio-genetic changes that are now envisaged within science, whose implications are of patterns that go far beyond our facile distinction between human and animal? These after all are theories that in their experimental practice are wreaking havoc with even our own anthropological ideas of kinship: who is the mother of the child, or to whom does the child 'belong', and what now the significance of oppositional patterns of relatedness? Are we far from the factory-like production of babies for whom the sentiment of kinship could only arise through adoption, and could a notion of incest, and therefore of kinship *rules*, have any significance in such a system? As Strathern (1992) has been showing recently, bio-power indeed.

The mention of power raises a perennial criticism of Ardener's work, which is that, in its concern with the apparently small things of life and with semiotics as itself one of the allegedly small things, it failed to grapple with issues of tyranny, of great historical changes, and with the common questions of statehood and people. I think it is perfectly true that with Ardener's approach you can, so to speak, paint yourself into a semantic corner and, with great finesse, do no more than counter such charges with the claim that it is precisely the small things that both make up the large and act as a conceptual basis for it. Ardener would probably have accepted this point, to judge by the pleasure he took when I once remarked that his work on 'the woman question' was really a political statement, or at least a study of the mainsprings of power differences. Certainly his three papers focused on 'the woman question' ('Belief and the Problem of Women', 'The "Problem" Revisited', 'The Problem of Dominance'; Chapters 4, 8 and 12 here) reached out to a much larger audience than any of his others and played a major part in pre- and post-feminist debates. The last seemed most directly addressed to feminism and, using the origins of women's dominance by men as a 'vehicle', formulated the argument that minor, often biological differences, can become socially and then culturally elaborated to form the basis of class, ethnic and other major social divisions, but that human consciousness need not remain so 'false' and unquestioning that we are condemned to be permanently enslaved by such predispositions. The ending here, with its curious slide into an uncharacteristic universalising plea for a happy ending, is clearly weak and seems to reinforce the claim that there is a need for some kind of accommodation with history, a task that may well be that of Ardener's posthumous volume on Cameroonian coastal society over the last three centuries that we are promised.

Perhaps the best way to read the volume is to not take too seriously the earlier, though quite long-lasting structuralist-like concepts but to focus instead on the unfamiliar use of familiar terms. For example, we learn so much more about the problems both of prophecy and of how apparently different events are related to each other through the idea of 'blank banners' ('Social Anthropology and Language'; Chapter 1) and its cognate, 'hollow categories' ('Social Anthropology and Population': Chapter 7). The former describes that moment of hesitancy in the mobilisation of a 'movement' when people gather for a purpose they know to be important to them but for which they lack the language to express it. The latter idea catches admirably the conceptual awkwardness of ethnic self and other classifications, which often seem to come from nowhere: an ethnic group suddenly becomes a highly visible unit; a former group seems equally suddenly to have no substance, for its members seem mostly to belong elsewhere; in-between such apparent transformations are the areas of doubt, uncertainty and reformulation, as those who were 'dying out' seem now to have regathered while those who were many and strong are now said to be dispersed or 'lost'.

The notion of 'event richness' is especially interesting. It seems at first sight scandalous to suggest that the Bakweri are event-rich, in that everything that happens to them seems to them to be unique and so to have new and special significance, and that the Ibo, on their own admission, are event-impoverished, by virtue of the fact that they lead routine lives laced with occasional excitement whose outcome is, however, seen to be broadly predictable within a narrow range of possibilities. One is reminded of Gluckman's (1962: 34) equally scandalous remark that technologically simple societies have more ritual than complex ones. But, as an aspect of self-definition and therefore of experience, such distinctions seem inescapable, although to go beyond this broad generalisation to other more interesting statements makes increasingly imaginative demands that may well result in the analytical complexity that suffocates the inspirational value of using 'natural' language.

This takes us on to the question of whether it is at all legitimate to ask where Ardener's work leads. He himself abandoned the structuralist load that he had had to carry first (at a time when few others were believers). In turning to non-structuralist vocabulary, he makes it quite clear in the later chapters that the very process of unpacking ordinary 'natural' language subverted its openness: instead of *experiencing* the difference between a remote and non-remote area, we shall, after reading the last chapter, *classify* it on the basis of ossifying criteria. This is part of the contamination of the social, not so much by language, as Ardener put it, but by analytical terms. The salvation, however, is that new everyday terms and phrases are coined continually in every society and are consubstantive with and perhaps constitutive of events and thought-tendencies within it. There is, therefore, always more ethnography where that came from.

Ardener, it is true, used only ethnographic snippets in his papers, and it highly questionable whether he could have said more, theoretically or epistemologically, in a full-length ethnographic monograph than he did say, with such economy, in his short papers. I certainly benefit from rereading his essays, but I am also always left with a nagging worry that he offers us only succulent tastes of a meal that we shall have actually to cook ourselves. Perhaps that is a fair division of labour. Or perhaps it reflects the gap between anthropological theory and ethnographic narrative rather than any failing on Ardener's part. I would have liked to have seen Ardener write the Bakweri monograph, if only to learn what difference, if any, it might have made. I suspect none, which is no reproach, but a recognition of the need to distinguish frankly between the ethnography that painstakingly produces the insight and elegant crystallisation of the latter for more general consumption.

Others, including Chapman, Hastrup and McDonald, have written the book length ethnographies that we still demand as evidence of apprenticeship in our trade, and these books are certainly highly regarded in the subject. The question that needs to be asked is how much one can tell nowadays from reading them that these and subsequent ethnographies have been shaped by Ardener's ideas. We know their tutorial provenance and can certainly see a distinctiveness. Yet if Ardener's view of the prophet is correct, and if he was one himself, then his ideas will have passed, or will in due course pass, into common and unacknowledged usage, and as time goes on we shall not be able to recognise such distinctiveness. Prophets, after all, are unintelligible when they begin to speak, but, once their ideas are absorbed, become banal. By this definition, then, prophets only become so in retrospect, after their ideas have had their effect and become commonplace. It may be reassuring to suggest that, by this latter criterion, Ardener was not a prophet, for though he developed a language for empiricising what we may identify as a structuralist and then post-structuralist trend in social anthropology that was often difficult to understand, and although many of his ideas have indeed percolated into the body of anthropological assumptions, there remain, especially in the essays gathered in this volume, intriguing suggestions and insight that will take a good few years yet to unpack and that remain far from banal.

References

Ardener, E. (1970) 'Witchcraft, Economics, and the Continuity of Belief', in Mary Douglas (ed.), *Witchcraft Confessions and Accusations* (ASA Monographs No. 9), London: Tavistock, pp. 141–60.

Geertz, C. (1966) 'Religion as a Cultural System', in Michael Banton (ed.) *Anthropological Approaches to the Study of Religion* (ASA Monographs No. 3), London: Tavistock, pp. 1–46.

Gluckman, M. (1966) 'Les Rites de Passage', in his (ed.) *Essays on the Ritual of Social Relations*, Manchester: Manchester University Press, pp. 1–52.

Lienhardt, G. (1988) 'Social and Cultural Implications of Some African Personal Names' *Journal of the Anthropology Society of Oxford* 19 (2), 105–16.

Needham, R. (1972) *Belief, Language, and Experience*. Oxford: Basil Blackwell,

Strathern, M. (1992) *Reproducing the Future: Essays on Anthropology, Kinship and the New Reproductive Technologies*, Manchester: Manchester University Press.

13 Revisiting: Keywords, Transforming Phrases, and Cultural Concepts[1]

The verbally explicit (the said) may over time become implicit (the unsaid). Similarly, culturally prominent keywords may alternate as unarticulated cultural assumptions. The cycle is from precise lexicon to silence covering a language shadow (Ardener) and back. Mediating this shift between lexicon and language shadow are variable phrases alluding to the cultural concept. Literature on keywords explains well their significance in many languages. Unexplained is how keywords may give way to silence or allusion and, in due course, sometimes return as prominent keywords. It is suggested that the trigger for such shifts is the stigmatiaation of the condition or person-kind to which a keyword refers. The keyword goes 'underground', possibly to be re-expressed when the stigma no longer applies. African ethnographic case material spanning a gap of 50 years supports this proposition and shows the role in this process of increasing admixture of different ethnic languages in late urban modernity.

In 1969, Edwin Ardener referred to the "failure" of British 'social anthropologists to respond to the challenge of language'. He saw this as a curiosity of British social anthropology which stood in contrast to the so-called "'cultural anthropology' of the United States in which the study of language has never lost its place" (Ardener 1971: ix). Forty years later, in 2010, Ben Rampton put the same question (personal communication): why did so few British anthropologists really grasp the nettle and, through their own often fluent fieldwork-based knowledge of languages, single out language for focused study within anthropology. Why did they leave it to linguists and/or those in education studies with a linguistic background to interrogate society as made salient by language?

It is Rampton, Blommaert and others in UK and Europe who work under the label of linguistic ethnography, a term which tries to bridge the laboratory of social anthropology, which is its long-term fieldwork- and language-based holistic ethnography, with analytical concepts found in linguistics and sociolinguistics. The problems addressed are much the same.

But does it matter if linguistic anthropology, carried out by anthropologists, never got off the ground in the UK, when there is so much work being done elsewhere and under the new rubric of linguistic ethnography?[2] The reasons for its absence are anyway hard to find. It has been suggested that Radcliffe-Brown opposed development of the field in the UK, having come into conflict with its proponents in Chicago, but could his influence alone have been enough? Was the lack of development more the result of early British anthropological unease with 19th century European comparative philology? But that was over a century ago. Or was it relative British ignorance of de Saussure in the early 20th century? But American linguistic anthropology did not rely heavily on de Saussure either, being more indebted to Boas and Sapir. Why did not the post-second world war influence of Levi-Strauss inspire greater British interest in linguistic anthropology? Although, from his semiological perspective, Levi-Strauss may have seen language as no more than one of the three major universal communicative exchanges (along with marriage and economics), he did privilege myth or words over ritual and viewed linguistics as the only true science in the social sciences. Given the closeness of British and French anthropology, why didn't this inspire colleagues to develop anthropological linguistics, rather than just structuralism? Nor is it convincing to argue that the American four-fields approach offered the only framework within which anthropological specialisations could develop. This might have provided a favourable intellectual and institutional environment but its absence in the UK was hardly a cause for not creating the subfield of linguistic anthropology, for other subfields have flourished in the UK without this environment (e.g. medical anthropology; legal anthropology; material anthropology; social archaeology). As Ardener points out, valiant attempts in the 1950s and 1960s by British anthropologists to address language, such as Whiteley and Milner, simply did not catch on, nor did the much later influences coming directly from North America.

Fast forward to 2004 and we find that, even in the compendious reader of 22 specially commissioned articles edited by Duranti, there are no British entries, not through the neglect of the editor but because so few contributors at the time would have been available, though Netherlands-based Levinson would have merited inclusion, and there might have been more than four other European contributions (two from Italy and one each from Germany and the Netherlands). A comparable sociolinguistics reader would have no such difficulty in securing British and European contributors. We move now to 2011 to an even more startling case. The invaluable, inaugural virtual issue of the *American Anthropologist* appeared in that year, 2011, under the title The Anthropology of Language, edited by Tom Boellstorff. It covers readings in the field from 1888 to 2010, many of them indeed key tournants. Of the issue's 86 articles, which the editor sees as showing major themes in the development of linguistic anthropology over the 122 year period, only one or two are by British scholars (including one by Gluckman on Barotse legal terms) and only a few more by other Europeans. Clearly this is an indictment of "failure", to repeat Ardener, which indicates the minimal impact of even those few in the UK and rest of Europe who were trying to develop linguistic anthropology, an observation that does not even begin to take account of non-English-speaking linguistic anthropologists.

Of course, just as we would flinch from 'methodological nationalism' as the starting-point of any analysis of language in the face of the increasingly transnational flows and cross-overs of peoples and speech styles, so we must not presume from this sample of compendia that they exactly represent developments in the field. That said, the collections cited are evidently published for English-speaking readers and so the absence in them of, say, the few UK anthropologists interested in language from Malinowski to Ardener and Levinson, and of fellow-Europeans who have published in English, has to be an indication of how little influence they are seen to have had on the subject, and indeed how little the subject has developed in that country.

But perhaps all this will change, as we view the new, though still small, crop of linguistic anthropologists in Europe, including the UK, who are prepared to call themselves such andwho do not see their interest in language as merely fitted in, so to speak, between the layers of a multiple approach to anthropology.

However, while we may not be able to know why so few British social anthropologists over nearly a century have taught university courses in linguistic anthropology nor focused on the subject in research, there is work that is worth revisiting in what is now a relatively recent interest in the field.[3]

Ardener and the Unsaid

This paper began with Ardener and will continue with him, for his own approach to the relationship between anthropology and language may merit not just recognition but, more constructively, some development. His ideas have not become subsumed in theoretical treatments of discourse and conversational analysis, for instance. They belong to a less clearly defined area of the mutual involvement of cultural conceptualisation and speaking, and provide a distinctive slant on how humans fashion and understand cultural concepts though speech and lexicon. The examples given in this paper are monolingual to begin with but have relevance for mixed language contexts of the kind that sociolinguistic superdiversity addresses and which are presented later.

Of course people like Ardener worked in small-scale ethnographic contexts and not in those which are nowadays characterised as part of and commensurate with the global cultural ecumene brought on by extensive transnational migrations. In a face-to-face conversation of two or three people, is the effect on their talk of shared cultural assumptions similar regardless of whether they are drawn from the stereotypical category of bourgeois, middle-class members of a diaspora numbering millions, or from the co-resident members of an ethnic group of only a few thousand? The principles of conversational interaction may be the same in both cases, but the scale and nature of stereotypes and cultural presuppositions are surely different. Interlocutors are likely to have a looser understanding of the stereotype of the city financier from an elite school than they would have of that of a herbalist or diviner in the small ethnic group. The stereotype of the diviner in a small ethnic group will be part of a tightly packed set of cultural assumptions about well-being, illness, malevolence and witchcraft. That of the city financier fans out into a wider range of positive and negative assumptions, from mansions, Merecedes and monetary skills to ruthless exploitation, corruption and untrustworthiness, and many more besides.

In other words, demographic size, density and complexity do matter. We may no longer hold to the idea of the bounded speech community but we can still retain an idea of ramifying lines of interpersonally connected stereotypical assumptions. The point to remember is that the internal consistency of these assumptions may vary considerably depending on how many potential interlocutors make up one's network. The more it contains, the less the coherence of assumption. The shift from absolute to conditional presupposition is a function of the move from small to large collectivity.

Ardener and his fellow anthropologists at the time generally did work among relatively small populations, which they were happy to call speech communities, and among whom interlocutors could place each other fairly easily. Of course these small communities were more embroiled in the world through labour migration or trade than was sometimes recognised (though Ardener certainly recognised it). But, having seen changes to such communities over decades, one can argue that the relative sense of smallness had currency then in more places than is perhaps now the case. In those small communities Ardener and colleagues could observe interlocutors who did not need to invoke ill-contoured stereotypes of distant provenance in their mutual evaluations. Speakers could focus on narrowly circumscribed areas of mutual understanding which, because of the high degree of mutual understanding, were not necessarily marked by set words, terms or verbal concepts. The unsaid did not need to become the said, a process alluded to by Stephen Tyler in the title of his book (1978). By contrast, nowadays, research of the kind undertaken by Rampton, Blommaert and colleagues of the International Consortium on Language and Superdiversity (InCoLas), suggests that in many vernaculars of late modern urban superdiversity, the said occurs in proliferating modes of semiosis and makes less use of the unsaid or silence as a semantic feature.

Language Shadows

While the unsaid might not need verbal expression among people who already knew it, it could nevertheless generate different arrangements of words around the underlying sense of the occasion. It is what Ardener called a language shadow. The famous example presented by Ardener was of witchcraft among the Bakweri of Cameroons. Let me somewhat impose my own interpretation, which is influenced by my own fieldwork in eastern Africa among Giriama and Luo as well as by Ardener's account.

Although the Bakweri and other peoples have a word which we can translate as 'witchcraft', it is more through associated happenings and attitudes that they perceive and explain its presence. They do not start by saying, "there is a case of witchcraft and this explains why there is misfortune and people die". This kind of statement comes as the end of the drama, rather like the conclusion to a story. People begin rather by relating different events and behaviour in what comes across as a random pattern but which is in fact the gathering together of constituent features making up a semantic field or cultural concept (Ardener 2007: 91) There is in effect a simultaneity of talk but with different starting points of observation: one person talks of greed, another of economic slump and poverty, another of some people getting wealthy by stealing from others, another of the unusually high numbers of people dying or stricken by disease and misfortune, and yet another of the sighting of zombies who kill. These different comments eventually come together as making sense of the story, which reads thus:

> *There is poverty. People remember an earlier time of prosperity. But now only some people live comfortably. One man has the luxury of a tin roof on his house, instead of the less prestigious grass thatch. Those without are envious. They dislike the man's evident greed, for he must have taken from others to be able to afford to buy the roof. Moreover, more people are sick and dying it seems. Zombies wander around and kill and take peoples' life essence. It must be that this man was a zombie, a witch*

who has gained through others' misfortune and who must be dealt with severely, even killed in order to purge the community of the witchcraft, with allusions to its contagious nature which must therefore be stifled.

The statement, "there is witchcraft in the community" therefore is a post-hoc proposition. It says what people have been coming to know. It is an assertion of a state of being. It is also a prelude to doing something about the problem, such as employing specialist witch-hunters to attack this and other alleged witches. The word "witch" is therefore the end-effect, the summation of speculations on the inter-relatedness of inauspicious events and conditions. It is the coming together of these speculations that determine the concept of the witch.

By contrast, in times of prosperity among the Bakweri, when more people live comfortably and there seems to be less sickness and death, there is less guardedness in referring to witchcraft, for there isn't any, or what little there is applies only to minor or remediable misfortunes. Under these better conditions, 'witch' is a key verbalised concept that conversations can start with and use openly, sometimes moving on to further implicit connotations which have to be unpacked. That is to say, use of the word 'witch' is not a random feature of speech. It is structured by conditions of existence. There are times when to use it evokes fearful sensitivities but there are times when it can be used without fear. We shall see shortly how this contrary process, the use of a key term to begin a conversation, rather than coming late in the conversation, can in fact unravel implications of the unsaid.

Ardener had a number of terms to describe this unsaid or pre-articulated semantic process: "language shadow", "template" and "p-structure". This latter is, of course, short for paradigmatic structure, or the underlying idea, which generates syntagmatic or s-structures, an obvious combination of the langue/parole and essence/surface hierarchical dualisms of structural linguistics and anthropology. It is therefore more precise than the notion of 'semantic field' which has sometimes been defined as meanings clustered around a single word but sometimes as different words sharing reference to a common phenomenon (cf. Lyons's discussion of 'semantic field' and 'lexical field' (1977: 251–3)).

In Ardener's dualism of the unsaid and the said, which moves from a simultaneity of allusions to sequential proposition, it is striking that the priority for Ardener was not the word, i.e. 'witch', which for him was only a curtain between acts in the on-going drama of how to deal with disaster. The priority for Ardener was people's at first inchoate attempts at making sense of misfortunes and abnormalities. The non-word was the priority. And yet it was the non-word, presaging the presence of a 'witch', which fuelled as well as pre-signified what appears to be a cultural predilection to gather evidence cumulatively before confronting the cause of misfortune and stating that it is a witch. It is after all extremely risky to accuse someone of being a witch unless the accuser is seen to have collected persuasive evidence. Timing is all: accuse too early and it may recoil on you, but accuse by interpreting correctly others' parallel innuendoes and your timing may be effective.

In short, Ardener's language shadows generate propositional language from the base of emerging and unarticulated comprehension. This is more than the 'idea' pre-forming the 'word'. It is rather that a cultural template is invoked, whose jumbled but shared nature among observers stimulates cross-varying perspectives that come together in the word. My impression is that this process is more likely to occur in small-scale contexts of high social density where interlocutors share and are swift to grasp cultural paths to explanation. The traditional anthropological field sites of intensive study of no more than a few score people are obvious examples of such contexts as are the close-knit social segments that, despite globalisation, still act as nodes in wide-flung networks of communication.

The approach here, then, is from unspoken base to surface parole, of which we can find other instances in the literature. Sometimes the underlying cultural templates never become verbalised except minimally. Thus, ethnically self-distinguished peoples such as the Acholi, Alur and Lango in northern Uganda each reverses certain customs in relation to their neighbours. For instance, the Acholi post-partum period of a mother's seclusion is four days for the birth of a boy and three for a girl; among Alur it is three for a boy and four a girl; among Lango, who border Alur, it is four for a boy and three for a girl. This reversal of customs and sometimes, also, of word meaning, is quite common in Africa among contiguous peoples. A crude explanation is that each ethnic group thereby makes itself distinctive of its neighbour. But it is not normally talked about nor even known among peoples away from the borders between ethnic groups. Thus, while framing the identities of groups, these reversals of custom act as largely unspoken attributes of ethnic distinctiveness.

Keywords

There is, however, an approach which is other way round. This is where the starting point is not a language shadow but is explicitly a key term, whose packed-in semantic ramifications can be traced out to underlying cultural presuppositions.

I refer to anthropological work on what have been called keywords, or key cultural concepts and terms. This is the approach from established lexicon, sometimes including taxonomy, systematic classification and, as in medical anthropology, nosology, but sometimes focusing on words which at first are identified as standing alone. It goes back at least to Boas and Sapir, later taking the form of an interest in cultural themes and their verbalised expression (e.g. Benedict, Kluckhohn and Opler), and has also been a more recent European concern. While keywords may sometimes belong to culturally identified taxonomies, such systems of classification are not the focus of attention. The focus is on a salient word which is identified as standing alone, but around which recurrent or new conceptual allusions may be invoked or created during the very use of the term.

Raymond Williams's study of key words in the English language attracted considerable attention on its appearance in 1976. Following an urban ethnography of Luo explored through key words (Parkin 1978), there have since been a number of other anthropological studies, such as Moeran (1986), Goodman (1990), Hsu (1999), Krijtenburg (2007), Fu (2011) and, most notably, Wierzbicka (1997) whose meticulous account of key words in English, Russian, Polish, German and Japanese is widely cited and influential.

Wierzbicka sees key words as "focal points around which entire cultural domains have been organized" (Wierzbicka 1997: 16) and as needing special methodology such as word frequency indicators among large samples of informants and literary texts. I would add that even more important is that keywords be studied ethnographically and over time, as in the studies just cited. Let me look at some Japanese examples exhaustively and persuasively analysed by Wierzbicka (1997: 238–242) and by many other scholars whom she cites. These come across as relatively enduring Japanese emotional and moral coordinates.

Amae is a Japanese key concept that has been much written about. It is claimed that there is no single word translation in European languages, including English, but that it can be rendered through phrases, including use of its verbal root. One such phrase translation is "helplessness and the desire to be loved" (Wierzbicka 1997: 239 after Doi 1981: 22). The term has an etymological link with an adjective (*amai*) translatable as "sweet" as of taste and human relations. You can show your *amae* to someone close to you and expect to be indulged, loved and even spoiled. It can apply to any dyadic relationship. It probably has its roots in the mother-daughter relationship (Wierzbicka 1997: 240). It extends to any number of intimate relationships within and outside the family, including lovers, so much so that at one time three pop songs included the word (Wierzbicka 1997: 239).

There are numerous reports by Japanese and non-Japanese observers of the frequency and intensity of the use of the key term, and, even allowing for the fashionable repetition of such accounts, there seems little doubt that it is an example of a widespread Japanese verbal concept that enters peoples' lives and relationships in a fundamental manner, providing a model of how humans should behave towards each other. Other enduring Japanese key words discussed include *enryo* (reserve or restraint), *wa* (harmony) and, more difficult to translate, *on* (beneficence or kindness to be reciprocated, with Maussian echoes of the obligatory return of the gift) and *giri* (honourable obligation), and many more (Wierzbicka *ibid*).

Variable Salience of Keywords

Apart from the plethora of reports confirming the profoundly ramifying extent of these key terms, the Japanese case is also demographically significant by virtue of the fact that, we are told, the terms have strong currency among the total population of some 120 million.

However, in other highly industrialised countries with large populations such as Germany or Russia, there may be more variability in the durability and salience of key terms. For instance, Wierzbicka focuses on *Heimat* and *Vaterland* as fundamental to German self-definition (and their equivalents in Russia and Poland). The accounts do suggest a traditional conceptual centrality of both *Heimat* and *Vaterland*, but although the most recently cited public use of one of the terms, *Heimat*, is given by Wierzbicka (1997: 160) as 1970 in a radio discussion, much of the evidence of its centrality is much earlier. The terms evidently declined in significance following the political re-making of Germany after the second world war, especially in debates concerning the contentious status of so-called ethnic Germans. According to the Google Books Ngram Viewer[4] (https://books.google.com/ngrams), printed use of the word, Vaterland, has fallen by over a half from its peak usage during the Nazi regime and, by the year 2000, was at its greatest low and still in decline. According to a BBC report on an address by Chancellor Helmut Kohl's at the unification of Germany in 1989–1990, his use of the word Vaterland was "notable given that the word had declined in usage owing to its association with German nationalism before and during World War Two". A similar decline over the same period is recorded by the Google Viewer for the word Heimat, though with a slight increase coinciding with three series of the very popular German TV drama of the same name in 1984, 1992 and 2004, with a feature film in 2012. Even with these temporary increases, usage has still remained well below peak usage during Nazi rule. While the Google Books site is a limited measure, it matches other observations such as the BBC and popular report.

It is of course hardly surprising that *Heimat* and *Vaterland* should dip greatly in fashion as key words, having become negatively associated with earlier German territorial claims of belonging leading to conquest and expansion. By contrast, at a more subliminal level, the concept of tree (*Baum*) and its extensions (as in the regionally directed expression *woher stammen Sie*? *Where do you* stem *from*?) have recently been perceptively analysed by Becker (2002) as representing a more enduring focus on German forests as the fount of *Natur* and as intrinsic to human wellbeing and a sense of 'Germanness', and as only indirectly connected to German nationalism. Notwithstanding the brilliance of Wierzbicka's analysis, we can say that the key terms, *Heimat* and *Vaterland*, either will lose, or have lost, their overall salience in the face of the rapid increase of migrants of different origins, especially since the changes in and around 1990, which ushered in superdiversity (Vertovec 2007), or will become more prevalent if, say, appropriated by right wing nationalists opposed to such diversity. The point here is that the salience of keywords may fall and either rise again or remain a subliminal or no-longer-spoken cultural concept.

For comparison, I turn now to a smaller sociocultural canvas. Among the Luo-speaking peoples of Kenya and Tanzania, the word *chira* is probably the most written about epidemiological term among this people. It refers to a wasting disease. Although the Luo language is Nilotic, the term is of Bantu origin. We have reports on the concept from when the Luo numbered only a few hundred thousand to their present size of some six million (Mboya 1938; Whisson 1964(a), 1964(b); Parkin 1978: 149–164; Dilger 2010: 113–114; Geissler and Prince 2010: 203–209).

Chira, as a term, has etymological and conceptual similarities among a huge number of epidemiological concepts among contiguous peoples in eastern and central Africa. By tracing cognates of the term across this vast region, one sees variations of emphasis but always a concern with the sickness, death, infertility and misfortunes which result from breaking some sexual, bodily or kinship prohibition, for which ritual expurgation is the only remedy. The prohibitions are fundamentally of an incestuous or sexual nature: for instance, a man sleeping with his brother's wife or with a woman he did not know was his classificatory sister, or a mother or wife committing adultery.

But such terms vary in emphasis over time as well as geographically. Among the Luo, *chira* in the 1960s mainly came when someone broke rules of seniority within a family, for instance a younger brother marrying or building his house before his elder, or a son using his real or classificatory father's clothes or bed (Parkin *ibid*). Breaking seniority rules is of course a kind of incest for it violates family and kinship order. At the same time, actual sexual violations also brought *chira* but were cited less often as causes. The nineteen sixties was a time when many Luo extended families were being split up as a result of migration from rural to urban areas, and so the focus on family seniority more than on incest probably reflected the threats to extended family coherence which mass migration produced.

But by the 1990s and later, HIV/AIDS was recognised as having swept the country and its incidence was reportedly highest among Luo. *Chira,* whose bodily wasting symptoms are remarkably similar to those of AIDS, now was seen mainly to arise from sexual violations such as adultery, incest and promiscuity, with broken seniority rules a less frequent cause of the disease. That is to say, the causal importance had been reversed. As a key term, *chira* had retained the underlying morality of proper sexuality and respect among kin, but now denoted the more specific morality surrounding the new disease of AIDS. This moral environment included NGOs, biomedical clinicians and international campaigns and so brought these many new, external agents into peoples' conversations about sickness, death and infertility.

Nevertheless, Luo society was still sufficiently small-scale that, like other key terms in its cultural vocabulary, *chira* continued to be transacted within the tight networks of interconnected extended families and maximal lineages. It thus retained much of its saliency and yet adapted to the new changes. This is a process whose coherence as a pattern is surely more observable than in a much larger polity. Even in a large industrialised nation, it is easier to trace changes in a keyword by focusing on a small community or network within it. I could give more reported and observed examples of keywords of the *chira* kind from African ethnography.

As a keyword *chira* also went underground, so to speak, rather as I suggested might be the case for the German *Heimat* and *Vaterland*. But before it went underground with the advent of AIDS, it could be used openly and to start off conversations, for the following reason.

Traditionally, the perpetrator of the 'sin' that caused the disease of *chira* was not necessarily the victim him- or herself. The perpetrator or 'sinner' was often someone else in the lineage or village. But the effects of the 'sin' would strike an innocent relative. It would take the village or lineage time to identify the culprit. During that time the victim might recover or, even if not, cleansing rituals would remove the effects of the sin. The collective reconciliation could in due course bring about forgiveness. *Chira* could then be used to admonish and maintain morality by reminding villagers of the consequences of their 'sins'. For this reason, *chira* was, traditionally, a keyword which carried very little stigma, being seen as part of normal, fallible humanity. *Chira* could therefore be openly discussed as a cause of sickness and misfortune. Since the concept lacked significant stigma, there was no need to avoid using the term as the starting point of discussion.

With the advent of AIDS, however, two other non-Luo, Kenya-wide terms were coined to refer to the disease. One was the Swahili 'Ukimwi', and the other the English word, 'Slim'. These new terms stigmatised the sufferer as having caused their plight through their own promiscuity or carelessness. Moreover their promiscuity was heinous in threatening others with their contagion. Through their alleged behaviour, they had gone beyond the bounds of human morality. *Chira* began to share in some of this stigma, for its symptoms are similar to those of AIDS. As a result the direct use of the word *chira* in discussion and speech became less. People used innuendo to refer to AIDS, much as the Bakweri allude to witchcraft as the unsaid. *Chira* had become an avoidance term, rather in the manner of death-names or sorrow names in many parts of the world.

Nowadays, however, with the relatively high success of ARV drugs and less stigmatisation of AIDS victims, *chira* is once again being used openly as a moral concept to refer to acceptable human fallibility. It has therefore moved in a cycle: from being the moral said in its traditional context, to the stigmatised immoral unsaid during the height of the AIDS pandemic, back to being the openly said again during the period of relief provided by ARV drugs. Correspondingly, HIV/AIDS itself has also, in addition to *chira*, come to be referred to more openly by other terms in both the English and Luo languages: e.g. *amadhi yath* (I am eating/taking medicine, i.e. ARV drugs); *PLWA*, i.e. Person Living With Aids; *ingeyo status?* i.e. do you know your status (whether or not you have HIV/AIDS)? These new expressions have partially substituted for the older mixed language terms, *ukimwi* and 'slim', the latter nowadays hardly heard at all[5].

These examples of varying saliency suggest, then, that some keywords may in fact alternate between the said and the unsaid, depending on the extent to which they meet with public approval or disapproval. When likely to attach stigma to a known person, their use becomes less collectively prominent. They turn into an underlying language shadow, to become salient again when the circumstances of their conceptualisation change.

A Cycle of Denotation and Connotation

The two approaches to cultural semantics that I outlined, each summarised as that of Ardener and that of Wierzbicka, are really looking at separate stages of a cycle. The language shadow presupposes the propositional, insofar as unspoken or barely spoken suspicions and malaise may eventually cohere and result in people coming together and asserting that there is, say, a witch or AIDS among them. During boom times, however, the Bakweri can talk openly about witchcraft because few people are poor and suffering and so there must be very little witchcraft about. This is similar to how the introduction of ARVs and campaigns leading to de-stigmatisation of AIDS sufferers allows *chira* to again be referred to directly, prior to setting up ritual reconciliation. Being now more frequently used and highly salient keywords, *chira* and 'witchcraft' open up paths into a wider understanding of events and persons and of the cultural context in which they occur. The non-threatening context of their utterance frees them of the need to be avoided and hidden.

The East African coining of the early Swahili and English words for HIV/AIDS (Ukimwi and Slim) played a part in the cycle of conceptual template and keyword. They had a relational and contagious effect on the indexical use of the Luo term, *chira*. Their stigma-bearing connotation rubbed off on the Luo term, which was pushed underground, before being able to rise again during the post-ARV drugs period, accompanied by the less stigmatising, mixed language terms given above such as *amadhi yath* and PLWA. Being drawn from Swahili and English, these pre- and post-ARV terms are an example of the use of language diversity and mixing as a resource, which I now consider.

Language Diversity

In the 1960s Luo had to adjust themselves as urban migrants to the new political conditions of their residence in Nairobi city, the capital of Kenya. Across Africa, countries had been gaining their political independence from colonial powers. Having been esssentialised beforehand as discrete ethnic groups as part of imperial indirect rule, regional peoples in the new post-independence politics were pitted against each other. The conflict, commonly traduced as 'tribalism', threatened their respective political and ethno-linguistic identities. It was often especially severe in cities like Nairobi. Let me compare that situation of 50 years ago with present circumstances.

At that time Luo ethnic associations organised frequent meetings, and stimulated long discussions and passionate conversations debating how to deal with the threatened ethnic identity of Luo (Parkin 1978: 165–242).

Street conversations and the speeches at special meetings called to discuss the crisis were built around recurring keywords, not just *chira*, but others, including 'jealousy or rivalry (*nyiego*); 'the untrustworthy friend' (*jasem*) as opposed to the 'true friend' (*jagam*); 'the unrelated brotherly friend' (*omera*) as opposed to the 'real blood brother or kinsman' (*owadwa*); 'the proud or arrogant person' (*sunga*); and 'the diviner-herbalist' (*ajuoga*). These terms of amity, kinship and betrayal metaphorically indicated internal divisions among Luo as they tried to agree on a common strategy of cultural survival. Some terms denoted destructive emotions and rivalry, and undesirable person-kinds, while others denoted their more benign opposites. In making these oppositions between desirable and undesirable sentiments, aims and person-kinds, speakers had to argue with each other to make their case. For example, your true friend (*jagam*) arranges a good marriage for you, choosing a spouse and family which suits you in every respect. But you have to guard against the supposed friend who is really wanting to sabotage your marriage and happiness out of jealousy (*nyiego*) and who is no more than *jasem*, a bad friend. You should choose a friend to act as the caring *jagam* who ensures your happiness and is above petty considerations of rivalry and jealousy. For friendship, substitute political alliance, for these were dilemmas facing the Luo writ large (Parkin 1978: 289–290).

This kind of moralising peppered the speeches and conversations which juxtaposed key terms and discursive elaboration. There was therefore a dialectic of key word and propositional phraseology, which constituted the Luo internal cultural debate.

With the increasingly rapid urbanisation of Nairobi city, whose population has increased enormously in 50 years, a new urban language has emerged which combines Swahili, English and elements of the distinctive vernaculars of the main ethnic groups, including Luo. It is commonly known as Sheng, an abbreviation of Swahili-English-slang. It is mainly Swahili but with English terms inserted and with variable amounts of ethnic vernacular. Although the name, Sheng, did not become used until the 1980s, proto-forms of the language may go back nearly a century during the colonial period (Mazrui 1995: 173). In the 1960s, I wrote about a polyethnic urban youth vernacular in which "English verbs (which are) incorporated in predominantly Swahili utterances .... take Swahili pronominal and tense prefixes and English pronominal suffixes", as in the expression by a young football player, "Ni-ta-win you kabisa" (I will beat you completely) (Parkin 1977; 1978: 72). Mazrui provides similar examples, e.g. *a-li-relax*; *days i-me-elapse*, and shows other grammatical features of Sheng (Mazrui 1995: 176). Standard Swahili pronominal and noun class concordance is subsumed within novel experimentation. Blommaert also provides instances of Swahili incorporating English and developing a consistent rule pattern in what is presumably an early form of communication with features similar to Sheng (Blommaert 1999: 159–179). The digital revolution and the immigration of new groups into Kenya, including Chinese, has produced the multi-modal superdiversity of linguistic and other semiotic resources with which we are now familiar.

In Nairobi nowadays, many young Luo, and indeed members of other ethnic groups in Nairobi, were born in the city and have never fully known their ethnic vernacular. It is common to meet Luo (and members of other ethnic groups), even in their thirties and forties, who know very little of their so-called ethnic vernacular. The amount of the Luo language in their Sheng is therefore often limited and varies according to the closeness or otherwise of the speaker to the Luo homeland in western Kenya. Limited Luo is claimed to be also a feature of what is called *Ingluo*, an amalgamation of English and Luo. Such relative ignorance of their mother tongue would have been unthinkable 50 years ago.[6] Yet these Luo still regard themselves as ethnically distinctive as well as proudly Kenyan, but do so through a diverse semiotic repertoire of visual and acoustic signs.

A collective Luo concern with cultural identity has, then, not lessened nowadays. It took on prominence in the form of a national political alliance in 2013, in order to contest the country's parliamentary elections. The various Luo ethnic associations continued to hold meetings and discussions but this time in language which was made up, not just of the Luo vernacular, but also of standard Swahili, standard English, and combinations of all three, alongside the use of banners and flags. Sheng, among both young and many middle-aged speakers, did not figure greatly in the Luo public rhetoric but played a greater role in their street conversations about the problem of Luo identity.

We have then a radical transformation in the pattern of speaking about Luo cultural identity during a period of over 40 years from the 1960s to the second decade of the 21st century.

In the 1960s, Luo was the sole language of Luo public meetings and rhetoric and of street conversations on the theme of threatened identity. By contrast, English and Swahili, and the then proto-type of Sheng, occupied different domains outside the Luo cultural debate, for instance in speech with non-Luo.

As of 2013, the public debate at meetings was conducted in Swahili and English as much as Luo. In street conversation, however, Sheng was as likely to be used as much as Swahili and English and dominated speech among younger speakers, especially, according to Mazrui, those of so-called lower class.

In this transformation, the key words which people recognised and spoke about in the nineteen sixties as framing their concerns, no longer figured significantly or at all in the later period, whether in public meetings or face-to-face conversations. Instead, the only consistently recurring or salient keywords referred to the names of political parties and candidates and to topics, events and concepts such as 'democracy', 'vote-rigging', 'corruption', or 'unification' (*umwenga*), affecting the Kenya nation as a whole but not specific to Luo.

The denunciation of internal treachery among Luo in the 1960s through the use of such keywords as *jagam* and *jasem* (trustworthy and untrustworthy friend) gave way to elaborate and changing phraseology, in the various tongues available. During the 2013 campaign Luo among themselves might refer to someone allegedly betraying his regional or lineage's political affiliation by the phrase *ok en loyal* (he is not loyal) and as a 'mole' (i.e. by analogy with 'spy'). A greeting among fellow Luo, *an loyal* (I am loyal), indicated the solidarity of their support for the Luo-dominated political party (ODM). This changing phraseology attacked those inside and outside the Luo polity who were charged with threatening Luo ethnocultural integrity.

The later period has seen a proliferation of variable phrases drawing on the ample, multiple linguistic resources (Swahili, English and Sheng, as well as Luo). But now they connote rather than precisely identify these underlying concerns of cultural identity, political representation and exclusion. For these are concerns which are sensitive, contentious and potentially explosive, much like the risky stigmatising business of referring directly to AIDS and *chira* until recently. The key terms which were once the starting points of debate are now the unsaid but implicit assumptions governing the production of phrases of infinite linguistic variety but common conceptual thrust.

Conclusion

This kind of analysis explores the alternating interrelationship and dialectic of key word and unarticulated cultural template. It gets us away from seeing keywords as static. This is not to say that there are not long-standing configurations of keywords within a society which seem to endure a long time, as seems to be the case concerning the Japanese examples given by Wierzbicka. But, slowly or swiftly, keywords undergo this alternation of the said and unsaid, and as relational elements in such configurations, they have a knock-on effect on other terms, and therefore on the talk that surrounds their salience or loss of it. I would suggest that this alternation is likely to be more rapid in the current conditions of superdiversity, of which the arrival of AIDS and economic and other catastrophes is a manifestation. I contend also that this cyclical model tells us more than linear claims of the type proposed by Fairclough (2010: 189) that linguistic and intertextual movement is greatest during intense socio-cultural change

It is quite common in conversation analysis to refer to the invocation by interlocutors of 'immanent' cultural stereotypes, whether of person-kinds or of concepts. Immanence here connotes 'packed-in' bundles of related concepts or what Ardener called language shadows, templates or p-structures. Under the kinds of circumstance that I have described, it seems that the immanent language shadow can become prominent, which is another way of saying that it becomes the salient keyword. Completing the cycle, however, it follows that the prominent key word may, as a result of its stigmatising effects, become the unsaid but immanent shadow, and so on, round the cycle. While the cycle may be commonsensical, finding examples which illustrate it over the longue durée is an ethnographic challenge.

Notes

(1) A shorter version of this paper was a keynote presentation at the conference on *Language and Superdiversity: Explorations and interrogations* in Jyväskylä, Finland, June 4–7, 2013.

(2) Rampton's discussion (2014) of the linguistic anthropologist, Gumperz, indicates shared concerns.

(3) In March 2015 the author was appointed chair of a new committee of the Royal Anthropological Institute on anthropology and language formed to liaise with UK and other European anthropologists interested in furthering the field through seminars, publications and organisational links.

(4) I am grateful to Fiona Jordan for directing me to this site.

(5) I thank Gemma Jones and J. Omondi for discussing these and other terms with me.

(6) The great Tom Mboya, a Luo political leader, was condemned in the 1960s for giving political speeches in Swahili.

References

Ardener, E. (1971) (ed.) *Social anthropology and language.* London. Tavistock.

Becker, L. (2002) *Die Mythologie der Baueme.* Papyrus 1–2 (1).

Blommaert, J. (1999) *State ideology and language in Tanzania.* Koeln. Ruediger Koeppe, Verlag.

Boellstorff, T. (2011) The anthropology of language. Virtual Issue. *American anthropologist.*

Dilger, H. (2010) 'My relatives are running away from me!' Kinship and care in the wake of structural adjustment, privatisation and HIV/AIDS in Tanzania. In H. Dilger and U. Luig (eds) *Morality, hope and grief: Anthropologies of AIDS in Africa.* New York and Oxford, Berghahn.

Doi, T. (1981) *The anatomy of dependence.* Tokyo. Kodansha.

Duranti, A. (2004) (ed.) *A companion to linguistic anthropology.* Malden. MA. Blackwell.

Fairclough, N. (2010) *Critical discourse analysis: the critical study of language.* (2nd Ed.). Harlow. Pearson Education.

Fu, H. (2011) *An Emerging Non-Regular Labour Force in Japan: The Dignity of Dispatched Workers.* London and New York: Routledge (Routledge/Nissan Institute Japanese Studies).

Geissler, P.W. and Prince, R. (2010) *The land is dying: contingency, creativity and conflict in western Kenya*. New York and Oxford. Berghahn.

Goodman, R. (1990) *Japan's 'International Youth': The emergence of a new class of school children*. Oxford. Oxford University Press.

Hsu, E. (1999) *The transmission of Chinese medicine*. Cambridge. Cambridge University Press.

Krijtenburg, F. (2007) *Cultural ideologies of peace and conflict*. Doctoral dissertation. Free University of Amsterdam.

Lyons, J. (1977) *Semantics 1*. Cambridge. Cambridge University Press.

Mazrui, A.A. (1995) Slang and code-switching: The case of Sheng in Kenya. *Swahili forum* 42, 168–179.

Mboya, P. (1938) *Luo kitgi gi Timbegi*. Nairobi. East African Standard.

Morean, B. (1986) Individual, group and *seishin*: Japan's internal cultural debate. In Lebra, T.S. and Lebra, W.P. (eds) *Japanese culture and behaviour*. Rev. edn. Honolulu. University Press of Hawaii.

Palmer, G.B. (2001) Review of Anna Wierzbicka 1997 *Understanding cultures through their key words*, In *Journal of Linguistic Anthropology* 10 (2), 279–284. Copyright © 2001, American Anthropological Association.

Parkin, D.J. (1977) Stabilized and emergent multilingualism. In Howard Giles (ed.) *Language, ethnicity and inter-group relations*. Academic Press. London.

Parkin, D.J. (1978) *The cultural definition of political response: Lineal destiny among the Luo*. London. Academic Press.

Rampton, B. (2014) Gumperz and governmentality in the 21st century: interaction, power and subjectivity. Paper 136. *Working papers in urban language and literacies*. London. Kings College.

Tyler, S. (1978) *The said and the unsaid: Mind, meaning and culture*. New York. Academic Press.

Tyler, S. (1987) The Unspeakable: Discourse, Dialogue, and Rhetoric in the Postmodern World. Madison, Wisconsin: The University of Wisconsin Press.

Vertovec, S. (2007) 'Super-diversity and its implications,' *Ethnic and Racial Studies* 30 (6), 1024–1054.

Whisson, M. (1964a) Some aspects of functional disorders among the Kenya Luo. In A. Kiev (ed.) *Magic, faith and healing*. New York. The Free Press.

Whisson, M. (1964b) *Change and challenge*. Nairobi. The Christian Council of Kenya.

Wierzbicka, A. (1997) *Understanding cultures through their key words*. New York. Oxford University Press.

Williams, R. (1976) *Keywords: A vocabulary of culture and society*. London: Flamingo Fontana.

14 Loud Ethics and Quiet Morality among Muslim Healers in Eastern Africa

The professional ethics of biomedicine in Eastern Africa are usually sharply distinguished from the everyday moral concerns of patients, who may interpret healthcare treatment differently from their doctors. Biomedical doctors' pronouncements adhere to the ethical demands of formal training, while ordinary people form their own ideas about biomedicine, with the two discourses meeting only during medical-moral crises. The voice of biomedicine, therefore, is metaphorically loud compared with that of everyday talk. This hegemonic duality of biomedicine is less evident in traditional Islamic healing, where patients sometimes negotiate the moral implications of sickness with their healers, and where Islamic medical ethics may be transmitted to younger apprentices interpersonally through life histories and narrative. The differences in volume between healers' and patients' moral voices are thus less pronounced, though not absent. Nevertheless, both are subject to the higher authority of Islam, whose holy texts and clerics are the final arbiters of the symptoms, cause and consequences of sickness. It is speculated that the emerging power, influence and stronger voice of radical Wahhabism could create a hegemonic medical ethical duality based more strictly than at present on religiously prescribed practice.

Introduction

Exploring the ethical and/or moral in ordinary speech and action calls for a level of detailed ethnography that an exclusive focus on wider institutional rule conformity cannot provide. This appeal is presented by Lambek (2010a) as revealing that vital core of humanity that seeks virtue for its own sake, such that acts and statements are ends in themselves. It is indeed the case that anthropologists have tended to work from the institutional to the individual in discussing morality rather than focus on the morally implicit in human behaviour. But in this intuitive drive to fashion their moral selves, for how long can people's actions and speech remain unaffected by wider social forces? Over time, is the desire for personal virtue altered and sometimes undermined by these forces, even if unconsciously? Converting desire into personal virtue for any longer than a brief period presupposes the unfettered freedom to do so.

A 'Durkheimian' position (see Laidlaw 2002 for a critique) would claim that a focus on the ordinary, that, over time, excludes consideration of powerful institutional influences runs the risk of providing an under-interpreted and therefore incomplete picture of the presuppositions involved in everyday talk and action. This article focuses on the underlying morality or ethics of everyday speech and action; however, it suggests that the internal composition and intrinsic notions of virtue in these statements can only be fully understood by taking into account their engagement with the wider circumstances of their occurrence. The focus is not on the personal and contextual treated separately, but on their ineluctable interaction. The field explored is that of healing talk and treatment in Eastern Africa based on case material from coastal Kenya.

The Pervasiveness of Judgements about Healing

Indigenous healers in Eastern Africa share some characteristics with biomedical doctors. Doctors are professionally subject to the Hippocratic oath, but healers also observe a similar professional ethic, as in the mutually understood obligation to treat people who are not immediately able to pay the required fee, an obligation that is underwritten in the ethical code of professional associations to which many healers belong.

Everyday moral comments on the ability and virtue of a particular doctor or healer are normally shared by patients and their family and friends. Such comments are private to the extent that people close to each other talk about whether their doctor's or healer's treatment and behaviour are acceptable. The comments become public to the extent that small groups may connect and share such concerns drawn from their own particular experiences. They may become the wider-scale basis of popular but conflicting evaluations of doctors or healers and healthcare, sometimes conforming and sometimes opposed to social and cultural changes (see Robbins 2009: 70–1; 2012; forthcoming; Parkin 2013; 2014). This distinction between 'private' and 'public' talk is crucial.

Comparatively, biomedicine stands out as strictly governed by professional ethics. It is also more than this. On the one hand, a biomedical doctor who is known to violate his professional code of conduct becomes subject to state-sanctioned judgements, having broken specific, written ethical prescriptions. On the other, the quotidian expectations held by patients and intimates of their biomedical doctors and hospitals make up a more generalised morality, one that includes comments on doctors' personal qualities as well as whether they are deemed to be doing their job properly. Heuristically, these two kinds of judgement may be called, respectively, professional ethics and everyday morality, a contrast that is commensurate with other contrasts. Ethics is institutionally specific and explicit, while morality is diffuse and implicit. Similarly, Steinmuller (2013: 13) sees morality as everyday habitus and ethics as a second-level reflection on morality where there is 'moral breakdown'. Such views counter those that do not distinguish morality and ethics from each other, with, for instance, Lambek (2010b: 8–9) and Keane (2010: 65) referring to ethics and morals as 'interchangeable' terms (see also the debate in Heintz 2009: 4–5.)

I further suggest that, as well as distinguishing them heuristically in biomedicine, we can figuratively refer to them as 'loud' ethics and 'quiet' morality, taking into account the state-sanctioned and media-involved nature of the first and the interpersonal features of the second. In other words, even though the medical profession may try to keep a major medical scandal discreet, the public media may hear of it and the state – sometimes through a professional association – is then obliged to join in 'loud' condemnation. By contrast, interpersonal comments among ordinary people about their general practitioner or sources of healthcare are often contained within their own conversational networks, therefore being 'quietly' transacted. The 'quiet' may become 'loud' if and when it is taken up by the state via the media, as when a local violation of conduct is judged to be of national significance.

It has to be conceded that this picture applies most evidently to biomedicine, because it globally enforces ethics through professional bodies supported by the state. Ordinary patients' access to biomedicine and treatment is determined by this imposed structure. However, while sometimes complaining among themselves about an instance of inadequate healthcare, patients do not always do so to medical authorities. They may then be left with the option only of simply talking about what went wrong rather than acting on it.

This hegemonic status of state-sanctioned professional biomedical ethics and its discursive separation from everyday moral concerns is evident in published debates concerning healthcare access. Thus, Woods *et al.* (2005) document how a state may ultimately decide who is ethically entitled to receive biomedical health treatment, and which categories of people are debarred; for example, illegal immigrants, the uninsured, the poor and socially marginal, depending on the country concerned. But individual practitioners may decide themselves whom they treat, regardless of state law, including patients who are officially debarred from receiving treatment. In so doing, they sometimes invoke the Hippocratic oath but sometimes fashion their own personal morality of dutiful healthcare. As individuals, ordinary people may think of particular doctors acting in this way as especially moral or virtuous. However, as members of makeshift moral communities brought together over a national medical issue, ordinary people may expect all doctors to act in an exceptionally virtuous way. There is thus an inbuilt interpretive tension in the relationship between professional ethics and people's ordinary moral expectations.

Thus, in what Steinmuller (2013: 24, 227–8) calls 'communities of complicity', individuals make judgements about doctors or healers. Sometimes such judgements touch on a major ethical dilemma. Should the judgements of the community (however defined) take precedence over those of the individual, or should the reverse prevail, in which individual needs are regarded as the priority? With regard to what he calls 'biomedical ethics', Parker (2002) discusses the dilemma of a father whose daughter needs a kidney for which the father could be a compatible donor. This would replace her sole remaining but diseased kidney and could save her life. The 'community', consisting of the doctors, the father's family and society generally, would think it normal and even imperative that the father should donate one of his kidneys for the sake of his daughter. But the father at first refuses for fear that his daughter's second kidney transplant may be unsuccessful and that he would jeopardise his own future and that of his other family dependants should his own remaining kidney later fail. He first asks the doctor to lie to his family that he is not compatible and so could not donate his kidney. Though sympathetic, the doctor refuses to lie and the father, feeling the moral pressure of a family that would never understand his refusal, agrees to donate one of his two good kidneys.

Parker uses this case to ask why, in healthcare, such 'communitarian' values should prevail over the father's 'individualistic' values. Parker pits communitarian ethics against individual morality, arguing that neither should prevail. He rejects individualistic primacy for three reasons: the individual cannot make full sense of his or her moral position except through a social rather than an individual understanding of human experience; the individual is not morally and existentially free of the inter-subjective, socially embedded ethical evaluations that make up his or her identity; and, because the individual is always socially embedded, society would be harmed if individualism were prioritised. Parker argues against communitarianism also for three reasons: communitarianism cannot recognise and may suppress the distinctive moral stance of the individual; it cannot explain social change resulting from individualistic reflection, criticism and creativity; and communitarianism presupposes shared values that are neither consistently held nor easily identified in the socially diverse communities of today. Parker's 'solution' is to present 'the discursive oral subject'. He says that 'morality is elaborated' in everyday inter-subjective contexts, 'that the primary social reality is neither the individual nor the community but people in conversation and that discourse is the developmental fundamental of human experience' (Parker 2002: 33). It is in conversation that we transact and negotiate our identities and moral concerns. This prioritises neither the community nor the individual as the primary moral agent but points to the mutual creation among interlocutors of moral (and immoral and amoral) personkinds.

Parker's case touches on the difficulties faced by individuals in avoiding social pressure and becoming discursive moral subjects. The father cited above unsurprisingly could not resist such pressure, which is indirectly supported by state biomedical policy. Clearly, communitarian ethics superseded individual morality in this case. A less likely example of the reverse would have been for him to insist on his individualistic rights and incur undoubted community opprobrium. It is in the process of reaching either conclusion that we identify a discursive moral subject who straddles and/or sits between community and individual moral pressure.

How far can this pattern of conflicting communal hegemony and individual morality, and their separation as two moral discourses, be found outside biomedicine and in indigenous healing systems of the kind found in Eastern Africa?[1]

East African Healers: A Case from Mombasa

Indigenous healing in Eastern Africa exhibits much less of the ethically prescriptive duality found in biomedicine. Patients can question, challenge and negotiate with healers, who may thereby use new knowledge obtained from patients to alter diagnostic interpretations. Patients overall defer to healers' authority but are not excluded from co-constructing diagnosis in the shared border between lay and expert knowledge. Here, traditional African healing systems, including both Muslim and non-Muslim, are thus different from and independent of more authoritarian biomedicine, which they may complement as either an alternative or an addition. My account is now confined to Muslim healers.

While healthcare among Eastern African Muslim healers may sometimes invoke religious judgement (insufficient prayer or mosque attendance and neglected or wrongful practices), it has much less of the professional hegemony and judgmental dualism of biomedicine (specialist knowledge versus patient 'ignorance'). Similarly, Muslim healers do not distinguish so sharply as in biomedicine between what I call publicly ethical and everyday morality in healing. Nevertheless, a dualistic tendency does exist in Muslim healthcare even if it is less pronounced than in biomedicine. On the one hand, moral-making conversations make up the quiet talk among patients and between them and local healers. On the other, what we might call the ethical shadow of religious and political hegemony lies over the work of such healers. This is because the few but vociferously puritanical Wahhabi or Salafi Muslim preachers reject healers' methods, such as the use of spirits and witchcraft diagnosis, despite these being expected by healers' patients.

The quiet talk about and with local healers alludes to their moral virtues and dilemmas. These allusions are evident when healers speak about their own lives and how they became healers. Telling younger would-be and apprenticed healers such moral or ethical stories is part of the normal entry into training. It is often an older relative of the grandparental generation who begins, in this way, to transmit their knowledge and experience to initiates. There are many kinds of healers with distinctive specialisations, and most, as among many Mijikenda- and Swahili-speaking peoples of coastal Kenya, take seven years or so to become a healer. While such transmission of traditional knowledge and morality is set within ordinary contexts of everyday interaction, the background factors of Islamic ethical prescription and piety are always present as inextricable features of the discourse. And the ordinary and everyday are permeated by the increasing influence of radicalising Islam as purveyed by Wahhabi missionaries.

Let me give an account by a young man, Ahmed,[2] of how such reflexive, moral storytelling by healers reveals how ordinary and externally impinging ethics have both clashed and become intertwined over time. The morally implicit nature of the storytelling is evident throughout.

Ahmed is a student researching traditional healers in Mombasa, coastal Kenya, including his own family. He chose to write this account in English. Others, including those by myself, are in Swahili and/or Mijikenda dialects. The account begins with details of Ahmed's grandfather treating Ahmed's sister's son (the old man's great-grandson) but then moves on to discuss a well-known healer. Ahmed's story contains within it an account by the healer, who himself recounts comments made by his own grandfather. The healer also cites statements made by a possessory spirit, which morally justifies having taken possession of a young woman.

As I suggest below, this kind of multiply embedded narrative about healing and the teaching of healing provides insights into successive layers of moral interpretation and expectation. I refer to such insights throughout the story. A notable feature is how these expectations of healing remain largely at the level of ordinary talk, yet are nevertheless indirectly, quietly and sometimes invisibly sanctioned and controlled by 'higher' Islamic authority over healing. Healers need to balance their individual therapeutic morality with their professional ethical obedience to Islamic authority. This obligation may be less acute than that experienced by biomedical doctors in the face of their professional body, but it is recognised and expressed – just as, conversely, is their recognition of the threatening power of Wahhabism.

First, Ahmed, tells how he came to be involved with healers through his family connections. These sustain 'communities of complicity' through the way in which the healing profession is handed down to younger relatives.

> *Ahmed*: Omar Hamsi Shibe is the name of my young nephew [elder sister's son] who had been having learning problems at school. He could not understand things in class and so got the lowest marks in exams.
>
> My maternal grandmother gave him '*zinguo*' [incense fumigation]. He recovered so well that he came fifth in that term's exams. But the problem returned after a little while.
>
> My sister, Hadija, heard that I talked to traditional healers [*tabibu, sic*] and asked that I arrange for her son to have another form of incense treatment called *zinguo la jahamu* [incense of consciousness].
>
> I then took the boy to Mohammad Ussi who looked at the boy and divined that he was bewitched by old men at home. He prepared for the boy the liquid medicine called *kombe* [a Qur'anic verse is written in saffron on a small plate, and the saffron is then swallowed with rose water]. He was in a hurry to get to the mosque for evening prayer and so did not perform any *zinguo* incense treatment. He also said that the next day he needed to leave for Nairobi and so referred us to another healer in Mombasa called Bwana Bwanadi.
>
> Bwana Bwanadi first carried out a divination. He read from a small old book, while telling us about the boy's problem, which he regarded as easily curable. He said that the boy's mind was fine and that he was bright initially but, at school, deteriorated because he had been bewitched, using the circumlocution *matende* [harmful] actions, rather than the more explicit terms for witchcraft.[3] Bwanadi next gave the boy a *kombe* to drink with the further instruction that he wash his hair daily. After that he performed the *zinguo* incense fumigation for the boy. He sat him on a small stool facing west, covering him with a white cloth. He recited Qur'anic verses while spitting on the boy's head after each verse, repeating

> the action 10 times. He took a small copy of the Qur'an in Arabic, moved it about the boy's head a few times, and then told us to return for more treatment in due course.
>
> My sister told me thereafter that her son was improving in his studies, and, though still having difficulties, was trying hard every day, whereas beforehand he would just look blankly at his books and not respond to forceful pressure and never improved. She then wanted the boy to be taken back for further treatment.

The use in therapy of Qur'anic verses and the Holy Book appears to be matter of fact in this account. However, their use is indirectly implicated in an ongoing ethical dilemma and conflict. It opposes senior and high-placed Muslims influenced by Wahhabism or Salafism to ordinary Muslims. The former denounce this particular use of the Qur'an as 'superstition' and disrespectful of the Holy Book, while also accepting that God is the source of all successful healing. Ordinary Muslims, including divinatory healers, do not normally argue among themselves over the pros and cons of the Wahhabi viewpoint, preferring to go about their everyday business of using Qur'anic verses for *kombe* and the Holy Book itself as an object in healing and in talking about healing. But, as in this account, they clearly do not condemn the therapeutic use of the Qur'an; in fact, they see it as essential. They say that it is using the benefits of God's work and is therefore both moral and professionally ethical. While there is no concerted campaign against Wahhabi objections, healers, including Bwanadi, do sometimes express objection and rise up in great anger at the attacks made on their profession by Wahhabi purists.

The section also refers to witchcraft, a recurrent theme that, as shown below, draws together a range of moral and ethical issues affecting well-being and causing misfortune, sickness and death.

> *Ahmed*: Ten days later we returned to Bwanadi, catching him at the end of the day when there were no more patients. He gave my nephew *kombe* but this was free of charge, since he knew that, as a student, I couldn't give him much. On other occasions, whenever I offered him something he would always refuse to accept it.

There is a familiar reference here to the professional ethic of medical charity, which is a familiar element of healers' discourse, both Muslim and non-Muslim. Patients, or their representatives, who cannot afford to pay are nevertheless treated. Muslim healers say that their skills come from God and so cannot be withheld from fellow humans, while non-Muslim healers say that 'living' herbs and possessory spirits used in therapy similarly do not allow the withholding of treatment. For their part, patients who can pay should do so as part of the ethic.

> *Ahmed*: It was on this occasion that we got to talk about his 'license' to practice, which he said was given by the Ministry of Health. He pointed out that he also had certificates: from a research institute at the University of Nairobi and from the traditional healers' union called Jamii Tiba [Community of Healing], of which he was a branch chairman in Mombasa district.

Implicit in the turn towards a discussion of 'licenses' and 'certificates' is the increasingly popular expectation, especially in a town such as Mombasa, Kenya, that efficient and virtuous healers will have these paper qualifications and even that their work should be shown to contribute seriously to medical research at university level. It indicates a limited dualistic tendency to mark out local from wider institutional healing authorities, with the latter far short of the ethical hegemony of biomedical authority.

> *Ahmed*: I went to see the *maalim* [*sic*] the next day to continue our conversation. He first said that he had some other commitments, including work as a chairman of the KANU political party branch in his area, and that he would not be available. But I noticed a chicken in the clinic room and asked him about it. He said it was for curing the disease known as *makafara*. He was to slaughter it and use its blood in order to get spirits to leave their human victim, noting that sometimes healers use goats and even cattle.
>
> He then went on to describe more of this use of chickens in cure. The colour of each chicken is important, he said. Black ones are aimed at protecting people from unknown disasters in the future, for which people are blind and can see only darkness, such as loss of job or business or personal misfortune, resulting from witchcraft. Chickens speckled threefold with black, white and red marks are used to cure people of a plurality of threats and problems, while those bearing only two colours of any combination relieve a victim of the witchcraft of relatives rather than non-relatives. A white chicken is sacrificed on behalf of someone who wants protection in their job or health etc., again against the witchcraft of others. Covering a victim with a white cloth, as in *zinguo*, drives away harmful spirits and witchcraft and then protects that person from further attacks.

Although it is a description of a particular treatment, this section is founded on the cultural assumption that sickness and misfortune come from harmful spirits and other people's witchcraft. What is hidden is the ordinariness of these two sources of harm. They are bad but are part of everyday human normality and experience. It is said that a person can become a witch if provoked, and that spirits are everywhere in the air around one. However, they vary in the severity of their effects. Thus, while witchcraft can kill, spirits do not. As we see below, some spirits are even harnessed in the work of healers. This tells us, therefore, of a world of, on the one hand, humans of potentially limitless evil who nevertheless act out of common human emotions, and, on the other, some non-human spirits whose emotions and character do not go so far as to cause death and may even be beneficial. This moral environment is understood by both Bwanadi and Ahmed, and by any local onlookers, without having to be spelled out.

> *Ahmed*: Having given me this information on this form of curing, Bwana Bwanadi was happy to give me the story of how he learned his knowledge. He said … [See Bwana Bwanadi quoted below.]

Ahmed repeats Bwanadi's words (see below) in the form of direct speech. I interpret this as Ahmed indicating the significance of the healer's preparedness to give part of his life history in his own words. It is a key element in introducing young would-be apprentices to healing. Just as the verses of the Qur'an should not be paraphrased but should be read only in the full text, preferably in Arabic, Bwanadi alone can be trusted to convey such important details of how he came to receive the gift of healing. We could say that this aspect of the story is too highly valued to be communicated by others. It morally belongs to Bwanadi to tell.

> *Bwana Bwanadi*: When I was young, about thirteen years old, I saw my grandfather (my namesake, Bwana Bwanadi) practicing this very treatment. This grandfather had extra powers because he could even talk to spirits [he used the positive term *majini*, which is approvingly cited in the Qur'an, rather than *shetani*]. He could tell the *majini* to leave possessing a person in case they have attacked him or her, and normally they would follow as my grandfather directed.
>
> While I was still thirteen years old, my grandfather gave me the Halo [*sic* perhaps "holy"] power and the knowledge of the treatment, as follows.
>
> My grandfather said that he was growing old and that he had chosen me to be given the Halo power and its treatment and did so on that very day. I agreed to this and he immediately recited a verse from the Qur'an, after which he spat into a glass of water for me to drink. This gave me the Halo power and the knowledge to cure apart from the other processes which I would observe my grandfather doing.

> Immediately after this initiation, a small girl passed by. I looked at her and turned to my grandfather and told him that she was suffering a sickness caused by a spirit [*jini*] which had possessed her. I was able to see this because of the power which my grandfather had put into me. I instantly told the girl's mother, who was my aunt [*shangazi*, father's sister], who was very surprised. Within a day the girl in fact became so sick that people at her home lost hope that she would survive. I set out to cure the girl myself, though many people were startled by my activity.
>
> According to the people of Lamu, it is shameful [*aibu*] to be possessed by a devil [*shetani*; note the switch from *jini*], so I decided to remove the devil myself quickly and quietly so that not many people would come to know about it. I called the *shetani* and asked what it wanted from the girl. The *shetani* replied as follows:
>
> *Shetani: I decided to enter this girl today in order to protect her from other angry devils [majini]. They are angry with her because she unearthed some saucers and bowls [utensils] which belonged to them.*
>
> *Bwana Bwanadi:* But the *shetani* later agreed to move out of the girl after I met certain of its conditions. It said:
>
> *Shetani: I will agree to move away if you help me. If you help me, I will help you.*
>
> Bwana Bwanadi: I asked the *shetani* spirit how I could help it. It said it wanted rose water [*marashi*], incense [*ubani*] and a *kombe*, and for me to perform *zinguo* [fumigation] for it, to all of which I agreed.
>
> The girl's name was Momo Bakari. On leaving the girl, the *shetani* named seven other people who had been suffering problems and whom it had cured. Some had been made to run away from home and live somewhere else, but the *shetani* told their relatives what to do and they returned and stayed home.

Bwanadi's offerings to the *shetani* are made through the medium of the girl: that is, it is she who physically receives them. In his direct reporting of Bwanadi's account, Ahmed uses two Swahili words for 'spirit' in his English text. *Jini* (or *djinn* etc.) refers to spirits mentioned in the Qur'an, which many people say means that God acknowledges and approves of them, despite the admonition that there is only one God. A helpful and virtuous spirit is called *rohani*. Sometimes a *shetani* (linked to the English term Satan) acts in an apparently benign way, but they are more often seen as harmful. The *shetani* in this episode is depicted by the healer as having moral qualities: it claims that it possessed the girl because it wanted to protect rather than harm her. Healer (i.e. Bwanadi) and spirit then bargain with each other. The healer wants to return the girl to a dispossessed state, while the *shetani* seeks in return its own sustenance in the form of a mixture of pleasurable substances and digested Qur'anic verses. The *shetani* keeps to the bargain and leaves the girl, but also tells the healer of seven other virtuous acts for which it had been responsible.

> *Bwana Bwanadi*: Nowadays, Momo Bakari is an older woman but is very important in the village, because she knows in advance if there are going to be problems of disasters in the village and can tell people how to prevent or stop them.
>
> After I had cured that woman, any time I dream of her, I know that I will receive a very nice gift, such as a good watch or spectacles, etc. When my grandfather gave me the Halo power and knowledge to cure, he said I should read or recite a certain prayer, *dua*, whenever there is a problem [to solve]. This prayer, *dua*, is called *burdai*. My grandfather explained that this prayer was recited when rainfall was needed or when a disaster such as mass death [i.e. epidemic] had struck.

Bwanadi's reference to Momo Bakari as now an older woman with the power to foresee and so help prevent misfortune indicates a general process by which many healers, including diviners or shamans, go through therapy en route to acquiring knowledge: their view is that personal suffering provides understanding of the suffering of others. Echoing the case provided by Parker cited above, Bwanadi also alludes to the 'communitarian' obligation in being a healer: a *burdai* prayer is normally recited to alleviate humans suffering 'natural' disaster; this prayer or invocation should be read by a healer when providing therapy.

> *Ahmed*: At this age of thirteen years, the doctor (i.e. Bwanadi) was able to read the Qur'an very well as a result of having attended Qur'anic school [*chuo*], at which he continued even after having been given the Halo power. He learned the Qur'an and about Islam in a single class which included students of different ages, but not in the Arabic language.

In describing Bwanadi's rise to more senior Islamic recognition, Ahmed indicates the importance of Qur'anic school and alludes to another moral and ethical debate between so-called traditional Muslims and reformist Wahhabi, concerning how vital it is that the Qur'an should be in Arabic and not Swahili, which uses the Roman alphabet. This issue is not always confined to the quiet talk of a few people. It sometimes flares into competitively separate public lectures. So-called 'traditionalists' argue for greater use of the Swahili translation of the Qur'an, while sometimes accepting that children will also rote learn it in Arabic. Wahhabi argue that, since the Arabic version is the very word of God as transmitted to the Prophet, it alone should be used and it should not be supplemented or replaced by local language translations.

> *Bwana Bwanadi*: Even after my initiation to be a healer, I still had to go to Qur'anic school to read more about my religion. But now I concentrated on other subjects beside the Qur'an such as Qur'anic translation, Arabic and other subjects. But this was now in another Qur'anic school.
>
> *Ahmed*: His knowledge of curing increased through meeting other healers, as he explained:
>
> *Bwana Bwanadi*: My search for traditional cures to add to what I already had was boosted when I met my brother-in-law, Omar Abu, who was himself a respected healer and came to love me, calling me to his place to teach me for my own benefit how he treated people.
>
> *Ahmed*: When he was a young man but old enough to work, Bwanadi entered the dhow trade, acquiring his own dhows [*ma-johazi*] to carry mangrove poles to Mombasa where they were used to build houses. In 1945 he was given a contract by Alfal Khan, an Indian businessman who had been commissioned by the then government to clear trees and debris from the whole area of Shimo la Tewa.

Islamic learning and healing are intertwined, much in the way that the mosque and Qur'anic school are extensions of each other in terms of learning and dedication. Bwanadi's education as a healer continued into that of the Qur'an, Arabic and 'other subjects'. The ethics of healing and religious morality are seen to be mutually reinforcing. It is possible to meet healers who were once imams and vice versa at different points in their lives. Or they may not have worked in either of these but in trade or another form of work, as in Bwanadi's case.

> *Bwana Bwanadi*: I finished this contract in 1957. When doing the job I stayed at a place along the seashore called Kuze, later moving to Kisauni Mwandoni, where I built my permanent house.
>
> I used to treat people on a part-time basis even while I was working. I used my traditional medicine to treat people in urgent need and those who came and asked me to cure their problems. At that time I was not settled and had no permanent clinic as now, building it when I had my house at Kisauni.

Often mentioned is the fact that healers see their healing as helping humanity, justified by the acceptance that their 'gift' to heal comes from God, for which sometimes they waive or reduce a patient's payment. The commitment to heal is reinforced among Muslim healers in the Mombasa area by building a permanent clinic.

> *Ahmed*: I came to learn that Bwana Bwanadi is married with two wives, keeping one at his house in Kisauni and the other at Sparki on Mombasa island where he built his clinic. He practices here at his clinic on the island more than at Kisauni, and most of his patients know his Mombasa clinic which he does not own but rents. Another reason for preferring Sparki is that he is a village chairman of the KANU [political party] branch for Sparki, a position he has held since independence till [the] present time, being the only one to hold it. He was appointed to the position by the late Ngala, a coastal non-Muslim politician and Christian friend of Bwana Bwanadi.[4]

It is sometimes expected of prominent Muslim healers, who may also carry out specifically Islamic duties, that they also engage in party political activities. As healers working within an Islamic tradition, they are regarded as having the moral weight to take on political duties requiring the virtues of concern for people's welfare and honesty in dealing with funds, and as being more removed from the temptations of corruption than other politicians.

> *Ahmed*: Bwana Bwanadi also talked about the medicines he gave his patients.
>
> *Bwana Bwanadi*: While asleep at night, I usually dream what kind of medicine I should give to sick persons who have already come to see me. I am told what kind of medicine is appropriate for a particular sickness.
>
> *Ahmed*: But, before he can begin to cure anyone brought to him, he has to carry out a divination to find out what is wrong with the patient.
>
> *Bwana Bwanadi*: I can't cure anyone unless I know what is wrong with him or her. Is it a *shetani* which has attacked them or is it something else, which I need to know in order to select the right medicine? First, I ask the patient their name and their mother's name. I check what time it is at the moment, the day and date, following the Arabic calendar. This is vital information that I need. Then I look at the side of good things, namely the angels [*malaika*] and the side of lies, the devil, and how they are that day. From this I can know which of the two angels is at work that day and at that particular moment, either Zual or Shamsi. This will decide whether I can conduct the divination or not at this time. If Zual is at work, then I don't normally carry out the divination because I will not get correct information concerning the patient.

As his personal story unfolds, Bwandi goes into more detail about his medical treatments and the problems besetting patients. He mentions the effects on patients' health of spirits and witchcraft, his dependence on divinatory knowledge, dream revelations, and 'angels' cited in the Qur'an.

Analysis

At no point in this multiply embedded narrative are there clauses explicitly declaring or promoting a particular ethical path or moral dilemma. Yet the accounts allude to professional ethical and layman's moral considerations, as my inserted remarks suggest. The student, Ahmed, reports and comments on what he has heard, using direct speech for himself and reported speech for the healer and the *shetani*. Elsewhere, I have presented a conversation on the same theme consisting only of direct speech.[5] There, too, implicit ethical and moral commentary is not in the form of admonition ('You should do this or that'), but is part of ordinary, everyday communication about how to heal and be healed.

The various layers of ethical and moral understanding in Bwanadi's personal story and its presentation by Ahmed, and my own ethnographic interventions, suggest that, in the specific domain of medicine and healing, both professional ethical and everyday moral assumptions inform language exchanges and reports. There is a 'community of complicity' linking 'quiet' moral assumptions of what is good and appropriate therapy to occasional 'loud' expressions of professional ethics. On the one hand, the healer's narrative inculcates in Ahmed a 'quiet' understanding of the implicit morality of his 'traditional' methods. On the other, it is also clear from the narrative that the expression of professional ethics always threatens to become 'loud' when the profession needs to promote itself publicly or is explicitly challenged. For instance, we are told how healers proclaim their virtue as well as their skills by acquiring licenses and certificates from healers' associations modelled after biomedicine. Their virtuous professional reputations are recognised and reinforced when they become politically involved, for healers are trusted. More importantly, we also learn that healers constantly need to defend their 'traditional' profession against the increasing number of Wahhabi radicals who wish to eliminate spirit-based aspects of Muslim healing.

Given, then, that it is in the nature of medicine and healing systems that the ethical is already explicit and is the basis of professionalism, this may be why, in his edited volume of 2010, Lambek (2010a) asked contributors to avoid discussing studies of specialised areas of institutionalised activity, such as bioethics and, by extension, biomedicine, or other professional organisations, since they are already built on ethical considerations, often with written codes of ethics. He wished instead to capture the non-institutionalised ordinary, everyday social fact 'that ethics is intrinsic to [and implicit in] speech and action' (Lambek 2010b: 1).

The distinction between explicit and intrinsic ethics can indeed be regarded as analytically valid at any given point in time. That is to say, we can generally identify clear, institutionally bounded areas of ethical pronouncement on the one hand and examples of implicit moral presuppositions in everyday speech and action on the other. In the same footnoted comment, however, Lambek concedes that some of his contributors do allow ethically highlighted topics to 'creep back in, as it is a feature of ordinary ethics that it cannot be compartmentalized' (*ibid*).

I would suggest that it is not just that ordinary ethics cannot be compartmentalised but that here there is a dynamic process at work in which the two dimensions (everyday moral and institutionally/hegemonic ethical) are constantly invading or 'contaminating' each other. We know, for instance, that there is a field of judgmental concerns that occur in, say, medicine or anthropology that are not governed by the professional code – a field in which ordinary practitioners constantly grapple with moral concerns that, for them as individuals, crop up anew but for which existing professional guidelines are unsatisfactory. We have the familiar examples: biomedics advise against 'unhealthy' practices which are, however, key customs (for example, a communal insistence on widow inheritance even if the deceased husband died of AIDS (Whyte 2005: 163; Geissler and Prince: 2010: 33, note 11, 200, 224, note 3)); anthropologists make deep friendships in the field that some may interpret as exploitative if they result in an informant's or patient's dependency; NGOs deal with an unanticipated health crisis by providing medical and nutritional aid that cannot be sustained, and so on. In the interface between explicit institutional ethics and implicit everyday moral issues, 'quiet' interpersonal concerns can get caught up in the 'noisy' currents of institutional judgement, with even perhaps the reverse sometimes occurring, for example when 'big' issues become institutionally irrelevant and sink into everyday talk of no apparent great consequence.

No formal code of ethics covers every situation, however, and each judgement may lead into others. Thus, we are told that eating junk food is bad for children but McDonald's continues to supply it, while claiming to have improved it. This leads to the accusation that the company is lying to protect its profits. Which leads to the rage against uncontrolled multinationals, and thence to the despair with weak governments that do too little, or, indeed, need the company lobbies, and so on.

In this judgmental chain, we can make a distinction between everyday moral concerns (the ordinary folk complain to no avail) and business ethics (shareholders' profits take precedence over communal health). However, a more helpful view is to recognise that everyday morality is made explicit at key points through its sometime stark opposition to a putative but not always followed professional, business or state code of ethics. And that this is not a static distinction but a process of constant explication and redefinition.

The next task is to ask whether there is some variation in the nature of this hegemonic duality. How different in this respect are non-biomedical systems of healing from biomedicine? The brief example given of Eastern African indigenous Muslim healing suggests that there is much overlap with the everyday and wider society. Healing is part of religion. Religion pervades society. Islamic ethics are rigidly ascribed in the case of Wahhabi Muslims but more flexibly applied among so-called traditionalist Muslims - and sometimes ignored. Since, in coastal Eastern Africa, traditionalists Muslims are the majority, it is ordinary, quotidian questions, answers and judgements that prevail in therapeutic talk and action.

However, to return to the idea of process, this need not always be so. It is not beyond the realms of possibility for this majority of traditionalist Muslims in, say, Mombasa to become subject to increased Wahhabi 'radicalisation', thereby creating a much greater religious control of indigenous healing. The ordinary moralities of everyday life might then be in greater conflict with those of the new Wahhabi establishment than they are already. For instance, if a new Wahhabi regime were to rigorously enforce surveillance and a ban on the use and interpretation of spirit possession in healing, this would surely make the ordinary moralities that are intrinsic to Bwana Bwanadi's speech and actions no longer ordinary. They would no longer be seen as a 'unity of means and ends' (Lambek: 2010b: 3) but a self-consciously risky means to potentially dangerous ends (i.e. as the Wahhabi regime clamps down on healers' use of practices deemed anti-Islamic by Wahhabi).

Wahhabi influence in Eastern Africa has increased over the last thirty or so years. It is an open question as to how strong this influence may become. But the possibility of its continuing expansion highlights the variable relationship and shifting boundary between a 'loud' institutionalisation of radical religious ethics opposed to current Muslim healing practices and the 'quiet' everyday transactions of evaluative comment, conflict and agreement that make up ordinary Islamic healing morality. A Wahhabi-imposed hegemonic duality is already prefigured in the Wahhabi denunciation of *bida'a* (innovations since the Prophet), including the use of spirits, witchcraft diagnosis and other 'magical' practices in healing. This duality is still, however, less sharply differentiated than in biomedicine.

Conclusion and Wider Implications

I am aware that this analysis takes into account 'structure, power and interest' (Lambek 2010b: 1), and that the contributors to Lambek (2010a) do not wish this to be a focus in the discussion of ordinary ethics. But in the empirical material presented, it has not been possible to separate the institutional framework of power from the kind of talk that a healer and potential apprentice engage in through personal narrative. It is clear from this that, while ordinary ethics or morality may indeed be intrinsic to speech and action, there are changing institutional constraints and directives acting on and among interlocutors that make one presupposition acceptable and not another.

In his understanding of ordinary ethics or morality as tacit, Lambek sees it as 'grounded in agreement ... without calling undue attention to itself ... [and only] becomes explicit ... in respect to its breaches' or when 'the right thing to do is unknown or hotly contested'. He argues that:

> Historically, ethics has been closely related to religion, to theology and the problem of evil ... [through which] the ordinary is transcended ... However, the present book intends to go deeper; the focus is less on special cases, unusual circumstances, new horizons, professional rationalizations, or contested forms of authorization than on everyday comportment and understanding. (Lambek 2010b: 2–3)

This reverses an earlier approach (Parkin 1985): this is that ordinary morality is indeed neither marked nor celebrated, but that it is only through marked 'evil' breaches of morality and moral authority that the contrasting ordinary, tacit morality of everyday lives is highlighted. A further contrast was suggested: this is that 'unmarked', tacit, everyday morality is secured by steering between excesses on the one hand and insufficiencies on the other, both of which are the templates from which notions of 'evil' have developed in European languages and are implicit in others (Parkin 1985: 3–18; and more recently Csordas 2013). Lambek does in fact make some concession to this view in his invocation of Aristotle's *phronesis* or 'temperance' (2010b: 20–1).

I suggest that there are therefore two contrasting approaches to the study of ordinary ethics in speech and action. One is that taken by Lambek *et al.* through the analysis of everyday talk and occurrences which are viewed as heuristically insulated from contested forms of authorisation and breaches of morality, including those defined as evil. The other is to keep the focus on quotidian morality – and for a long time there have been many studies on this[6] – but to regard broader social forces as sometimes hidden but sometimes explicit influences and constraints on everyday morally inscribed talk and action, which, through disagreement and conflict, sometimes erupt as ethical crises. In such cases, ordinary morality becomes extraordinary in that it takes the form of a loudly expressed ethical dilemma. In this way, we see the transformational dynamics of ordinary morality rather than its operation in separation from more powerful ethically impinging circumstances.

Notes

(1) It may well be that the official recognition by the Chinese and Indian states of, respectively, traditional Chinese medicine (TCM) and Ayurvedic medicine, each with regulated university-level training and professional sanctions, creates similar dualities. But, if so, they do not appear to have the same hegemonic moral impact on the individual as biomedicine, whose global distribution, supported by the pharmaceutical industry and such extremely well-funded international bodies as the World Health Organization, is one of the main features of late modernity.

(2) This is a pseudonym.

(3) Educational competition at school is believed in particular to foster the jealousies behind witchcraft, especially of parents.

(4) Ngala was one of Kenya's most prominent politicians from the late 1950s until his death in 1972. He headed a pre-independence Kenya assembly, was the first leader of the KADU political party, switched to KANU, and united Muslims and non-Muslims in an attempt to secure autonomy for the coastal region.

(5) In the presentation 'Interruptions as prosody in medical practice' at the conference 'Illness Narratives Revisited: From the Semiotics of Language to the Materiality of Speech', sponsored by the University of Oxford and Max Planck Institute for the Study of Ethnic and Religious Diversity, Göttingen, held in Oxford on 6-8 December 2012.

(6) As a limited, random sample consider Augé (2002); Auclair (1982); Cavell (1988); Certeau (1984; 1998); Deshimaru (1985); Grenier (1968); Javeau (2003); Lefebvre (1991 [1947]); Masqulier and Siran (2000); Sherringham (2006).

References

Auclair, G. (1982) *Le mana quotidian: structures et fonctions de la chronique des faits divers*. 2nd edition. Paris: Éditions Anthropos.

Auge, M. (2002) *In the Metro*. Translated by Tom Conley. Minneapolis MN: University of Minnesota Press.

Cavell, S. (1988) *In Quest of the Ordinary*. Chicago IL: University of Chicago Press.

Certeau, M. de (1984) *The Practice of Everyday Life*. Translated by Steven Rendall. Berkeley CA: University of California Press.

Certeau, M. de (1988) *The Practice of Everyday Life. 2: Living and cooking*. Translated by Timothy J. Tomasik. Minneapolis MN: University of Minnesota Press.

Csordas, T.J. (2013) 'Morality as cultural system?', *Current Anthropology* 54 (5), 523–46.
Deshimaru, T. (1985) *Zen et vie quotidienne*. Paris: Albin Michel.
Geissler, P.W. and Prince, R. (2010) *The Land is Dying: contingency, creativity and conflict in Western Kenya*. Oxford and New York NY: Berghahn.
Javeau, C. (2003) *Sociologie de la vie quotidienne*. Paris: Presses Universitaires de France.
Keane, W. (2010) 'Minds, surfaces and reason in the anthropology of ethics' in M. Lambek (ed.) *Ordinary Ethics: anthropology, language and action*. New York NY: Fordham University Press.
Laidlaw, J. (2002) 'For an anthropology of ethics and freedom', *Journal of the Royal Anthropological Institute* 8 (2), 311–32.
Lambek, M (ed.) (2010a) *Ordinary Ethics: anthropology, language and action*. New York NY: Fordham University Press.
Lambek, M (ed.) (2010b) 'Introduction' in M. Lambek (ed.) *Ordinary Ethics: anthropology, language and action*. New York NY: Fordham University Press.
Lefebvre, H. (1991 [1947]) *Critique of Everyday Life*. Translated by J. Moore. London: Verso.
Masquelier, B. and Siran, J.-L. (eds) (2000) *Pour une anthropologie de l'interlocution: rhétoriques du quotidian*. Paris: L'Harmattan.
Parker, M. (2002) 'A deliberative approach to bioethics' in K.W.M. Fulford, D.L. Dickenson and T.H. Murray (eds) *Healthcare Ethics and Human Values*, Malden M.A. and Oxford: Blackwell.
Parkin, D. (1985) 'Introduction' in D. Parkin (ed.) *The Anthropology of Evil*. Oxford and New York NY: Blackwell.
Parkin, D. (2013) 'Medical crises and therapeutic talk', *Anthropology and Medicine* (special issue) 20 (2), 124–41.
Parkin, D. 'Pathways to healing: curative travel among Muslims and non-Muslims in Eastern East Africa', *Medical Anthropology* (special issue) 33, 21–36.
Robbins, J. (2009) 'Morality, value and radical cultural change' in M. Heintz (ed.) *The Anthropology of Moralities*. New York NY and Oxford: Berghahn.
Robbins, J. (2012) 'Transcendence and the anthropology of Christianity: language, change, and individualism (Edward Westermarck memorial lecture)', *Journal of the Finnish Anthropological Society* 37 (2), 5–23.
Robbins, J. (forthcoming) 'What is the matter with transcendence? On the place of religion in the new anthropology of ethics', *Journal of the Royal Anthropological Institute*.
Sherringham, M. (2006) *Everyday Life: theories and practices from surrealism to the present*. Oxford and New York NY: Oxford University Press.
Steinmuller, H. (2013) *Communities of Complicity: everyday ethics in rural China*. Oxford and New York NY: Berghahn.
Whyte, S.R. (2005) 'Going Home? Belonging and burial in the era of AIDS', *Africa* 75 (2), 154–72.
Woods, M.D. *et al.* (2005) *Vulnerable Groups and Access to Health Care: a critical interpretive review. Report for the National Co-ordinating Centre for NHS Service Delivery and Organization R and D (NCCSDO)*. Leicester: University of Leicester.

15 Reason, Emotion, and the Embodiment of Power

Dualisms as Traditions

The various dichotomies framing debates on rationality are revealing. Relativism may be opposed to rationality, but may also be opposed to universalism. The latter slides over into objectivity and so is contrasted with subjectivity. Subjectivity subsumes emotionalism, which itself is set up against reason. Thus, from rationality and relativism we move to reason and sentiment. Three issues arise from this muddle. One is the attempt to disentangle such apparent confusion. We can subdivide kinds of rationality into, for instance, cognitive and strategic (de Sousa 1980: 129), or we can distinguish arch-rationalism from anarcho-rationalism (Hacking 1982: 1–66), recognising that in all such cases a notion of objective truth is in some way implied and, with it, a potential universalism (for example, even if a society does not have a particular version of reality, it remains a possible option to be taken up from among those available to humanity (Gellner 1982: IX7–88)). We can also subdivide types of relativism, such as conceptual, perceptual, moral, cognitive, and those of truth and reason (Hollis and Lukes 1982: 6–20), and no doubt many more. Bearing in mind the many other dualistic connotations, this chapter focuses on the opposition between reason and emotion and asks how far it can be ethnographically applied.

A second issue, then, is the extraordinary resilience in ordinary English language not just of the tendency to contrast emotion with reason but also to draw further parallels. Thus, emotions are subjective states that are the responsibility of the individual and so, at the particular moment of their expression, relate to him or her alone. Reason is the property of reasonable persons who are held to be in the majority and who would, if all problems of the world could be solved, exist everywhere.

But how far are such lofty ideals put into practice? Television anthropology may temporarily convert liberal middle-class business executives to the idea that other peoples' reasonings may legitimately be different from theirs. But when dealing in their offices next day with Third World import and export deliveries, they may easily revert to less charitable explanations in terms of 'different mentalities'. Nor are the beleaguered businessmen alone.

That the one-and many-mind distinction in ordinary English language is unlikely ever to be altered by academic debate need not surprise us. It is a variation of the distinction between human and less-than -human which seems to be employed in different ways by peoples the world over and is a frequent topic of anthropological concern (Southall 1976; Arens 1979). What is interesting is the way in which this contrast becomes re-cast as that of reasoning selves and emotionally irrational others (e.g. Chapman's popular and scholarly portrayals of Celts as "irrational" over the centuries (1982)).

Third, then, it is not the seemingly unsuspecting ordinary English speaker alone who uses the opposition of reason to emotion as the basis of further argument. When they are not reflecting on its epistemological inappropriateness, academics use it too, the most recent example being a model of political language proposed by F.G. Bailey, who distinguishes between hortatory and cerebral rhetoric, the former depending on the evocation of sentiment and the latter on rational argument. A third mode is called pseudo-cerebral. It is speech which poses as rational but uses specious argumentation. For an English-speaking readership Bailey's account is convincing (1981). As he also shows (1983) the strategic use of emotional display may be the most appropriate and so, in the circumstances, the most rational means of persuasion. But could such alternating rhetorical devices work in a culture that did not distinguish clearly or at all between reason and emotion? Indeed, are there such cultures?

I mention Bailey's work because, in 'Western' speech, people figuratively distinguish the 'heart' and 'head' as the separate loci respectively of sentiment and intellect, irrationality and logic, or emotion and reason. This folk distinction is a part of the Cartesian heritage that has surely shaped the questions raised by the debate on rationality. If there was no such folk distinction of heart versus mind, would 'Western' speakers have moved on to ask whether other peoples are equally rational, and, if not, in what ways they differ? In other words, perhaps out of the heart-versus-mind dichotomy has grown that of relativism and rationality. It may be therefore that the grand academic debate is itself epistemologically couched in folk usage.

Speaking thus of a Cartesian heritage is admittedly glib, for it is a modern popularisation of Descartes' views on mind and body. Nevertheless, why has theoretical popularisation apparently reduced Descartes' complex argument to a simple duality?

It is perfectly acceptable to say that Descartes' distinction between mental phenomena (mind) and physical phenomena (body) is dualistic. Within each of these the dualisms continue: mind is composed of intellect (which refers to ideas outside the mind. e.g. God) and of will (consisting of attitudes to these intellectual ideas, e.g. God exists or does not exist). Physical body consists of matter and of motion. Confining ourselves to mind, we find a further intriguing duality in the distinction within the will between two types of attitude towards ideas of the intellect. One is desire-aversion and the other assertion-denial. The former leads into a concern with volition, including the emotions of love and hatred. The latter, assertion-denial, is the basis of judgement. As long as these dualities and sub-dualities are regarded as parts of an overall scheme, then one can continue to think in terms of an encompassing dichotomy of mind and body.

But two factors dislodge the simplicity of this dichotomy. The first is the difficulty of controlling, so to speak, a concept like volition or emotion. In the English language we often speak of desires and hatreds overwhelming judgements calculated on the basis of factual assertions and denials. Emotion, that is to say, frequently subordinates reason. It assumes inordinate significance. In doing so, volition or emotion may seem to stifle not only judgement but intellect itself, in so far as it shapes our ideas of the things supposedly existing outside our minds. The second discomforting factor is the tendency among some philosophers, including Descartes, to add to the dualism a third, independent agency (not always regarded as such, however). Thus, Socrates sees *thumos* as mediating and monitoring thought and 'appetite'[1]. Plato does propose a dualism of the soul and the body-senses, from which a soul must escape in order to achieve clarity of thought as well as immortality. But his soul is tied in one direction to mental functions and in the other to the eternal Ideas through eros or transcendental love: soul thus looks to emotion, a third agency, as a route to intellect. Aristotle specifically suggests a trinary characterisation: there is nutritive soul designed for ingestion and procreation; animal soul for perceiving, remembering, and imagining; and rational soul by which humans alone are endowed with the capacity for thought. For Descartes himself, his early idea of mind as an independent homunculus inside the body seems to become incompatible with his later dualism of mind-soul and body. Thus, on the one hand he sees mind as receiving sense impressions from the brain, a part of the body, and of acting upon matter, including the body. On the other hand, in identifying mind with soul, he describes the latter as able to exist independently of the body, capable indeed of leading a disembodied life (Rée 1974: 91–117). Putting his point very simply, mind can only operate on and through matter, including the body, while soul can exist independently of matter. Yet mind is supposed to be identical to soul. The dualism of mind and body comes across rather as an unacknowledged triad of mind, soul, and body.[2]

Such triads arise because a place has to be found in the scheme for a transcendental link with God; soul provides this link. Soul as part of mind can judge (or err), while soul as part of God can love (or hate). But even when, in the post-enlightenment period, a link with God is no longer thought necessary, a triadic scheme persists. Thus, while Tönnies distinguishes natural will (our emotions and general volition) from rational will, he adds a third, social will which is concerned with what he calls three great systems, order, law and morality (1955 (1857))[3]. In other words, instead of God providing the necessity for a third independent agent or will, we have society itself. Tönnies did not consciously seek to substitute society for God in his triad of wills, but this is in effect what happened, as with other post-Enlightenment scholars. Indeed, the substitution anticipates Durkheim 's observation that, as a definition of a social fact, God is society.

When did these triads or triadisms give way to the dualisms commonly spoken of in modern times. It may have stemmed from Durkheim's own opposition of society and individual. The primacy of society over individual was his attempt to crush the explanation of social institutions through psychology. Psychological explanations of the individual, including his volition and emotions, were rendered irrelevant. Saussure, basing his opposition of *langue* to *parole* on that of society and individual, also privileged *langue* and regarded *parole* as the analytically irrelevant utterances of individuals. What mattered was *langue*, the generative powerhouse of utterances, a dualism which was later given a firm Cartesian pedigree by Chomsky. So, Cartesian dualism became Chomskian dualism. Somehow, the triadisms, not always clear or acknowledged, got lost.

Feelings and Power as Rationality

The shift from ambiguous triadism to firm dualism has brought two other developments. First, the dualism is not simply that of opposed but equal concepts. Rather, as with *langue* over *parole*, the concepts are ranked. Second, though it is individuals who create the unique utterances we call *paroles* or performance, they are depicted as doing so without emotion. Competence or langue is the knowledge of rules or grammar, while *paroles* are the rule-governed creations which individuals, however innovative they may be, refer rationally to the collective reason enshrined in *langue*.

In recent years some anthropologists have reacted against this reliance on intellect in structuralist explanations of culture, arguing that ratiocination is sustained more by intuition, aesthetics and emotional factors than by a neutral calculation of logically possible alternatives (Milner 1969 after Bergson 1975 and Lewis 1980; Tonkin 1982; Parkin 1982; Rosaldo 1980). People may aim for a rationality unaffected by emotion, but whether or not they are aware of it, their thinking remains framed by personal values and inner states. They may evaluate a decision differently in the light of apparent or possible consequences and of their changing moods and dispositions.

Although it is a modern reaction against structuralism in anthropology, this second view shares affinities with Hume's dictum that passions do and should rule reason, and that reason should be the slave of passion (Baier 1980 *passim*). Thus, whereas dualists, including structuralists, privilege rationality (via rules) over sentiment, Hume reverses this priority.

Baier notes that Hume classifies passions in a number of ways: direct and indirect, violent and calm, agreeable and uneasy, regular and irregular (reciprocated and unreciprocated), instinctive and acquired, activating and passive, and so on (Baier 1980: 404). The focus is on the force of passions in their struggle to master reason. Baier notes parallels with the distinctions of Spinoza between free active passions and unfree sovereign ones, of Nietzsche between sovereign-free sentiments and those that are slavish and reactive, and of Hume himself between self-sustaining pure and other-directed impure passions. Implicit is a vocabulary of hierarchy and conflict. 'Pride' is taken as an emotion that embodies this battle. For Hume, if pride is properly socialised by the collective moral sentiment then it will not become self-conceit but will applaud virtue: 'I am proud of my nation's achievements but not chauvinistic'. It will insist on 'morally proper' reasons for decisions: 'My society's values should be respected but not arbitrarily imposed on others'. These metaphors of force, control and struggle in depicting the interplay of emotions with each other and in the domination of reason, are significant. For they are part of the language used by proponents who compete to have their versions of 'reason' or of 'emotion' accepted, thus revealing the inevitable power and political dimension of such imposed definitions.

There is, however, a third view which, as far as ordinary language will allow, merges reason and emotion. Taking an example of this 'coherence' from Wilson (1972: 182–89), we can say that what makes a human different from a highly intelligent robot is that a person makes sense of a decision they have made not only in terms of whether it will secure the goal they have set themself, but in terms also of whether it fits one's feelings and attitudes towards the object of decision. Certain kinds of 'transactional' anthropologists might counter with the view that, in taking decisions, people do balance the emotional and pragmatic costs of a goal. But this comes close to tautology if the argument is that all acts are utilitarian because, whatever we do, it is part of a means to an end. Wilson's point is that, unlike robots, people seek a coherence of feeling and attitude in the things they (decide to) do, and that this makes nonsense of the dichotomy between reason and emotion. In other words, no reason can be given for an act or decision that does not also involve the actor's emotions, however weak or strong. There is here no conflict between reason and emotion.

The three views (reason over emotion, emotion over reason, and their 'equal' coherence) map out some of the ways in which actions are justified. English idioms reveal this. 'He is hot-headed', meaning that he should train his reason to curb his passions. 'He is a cold fish', meaning that more sentiment and less calculation are needed. But, 'He dedicated himself to the task with a passion', meaning that he balanced reason with emotion quite well. Many other phrases indicate one or other priority or preference. They reflect the persistent difficulties underlying the dualistic attempt to think only in terms of reasoning mind and body and excluding sentiment. A dualistic hierarchy may appear more 'scientific' (though modern scientists rarely associate themselves with it anymore), but departs seriously from folk views. The ambiguous triadism in such concepts as mind, soul, and body, or reason, passion, and body, more accurately reflects the way ordinary people approach, explain, and justify situations and their involvement in them.

Again, as a paradigm of three views of society, they denote fixed hierarchy (as in reason, langue, competence, and society, being over and against emotion, *parole*, performance, and the individual); permanent struggle to gain or retain mastery (as in Hume's assertion that passions must rule reason); and harmony and equality (as in the mutual embeddedness of reason and feeling). A history of ideas thus turns out to be an analogue of social possibilities as well as the way people may map their individual actions.[1]

Moreover, the views define the conditions of rationality. First, rationality intimates a capacity to repair disturbed hierarchies of values, to reconcile conflicts of opinions and interests, and to bring them into supposed order and harmony with each other. Second, rationality entails decision-making and choices and therefore conflicts, contradiction, struggle, force, power, and control. Third, however, rationality as coherence presupposes that reason and emotion are not in conflict but are shaped by each other and convince more through an apparent rightness of 'feel' and 'fit' than by any demonstrable proof. For example, the awe of a man gazing at an indescribably beautiful scene may, for those moments, make the idea of the non-existence of God irrational and unacceptable to him. These views may now be illustrated ethnographically.

Rationality is commonly described as action based on the most efficient means to a particular end. But this raises the Weberian question of whose interpretation of means and ends is accepted as the most efficient: peoples themselves may disagree and so the outside analyst steps in authoritatively with their interpretation. We can reverse this and instead start with interpretive disagreements recognised by actors themselves: some may see a conflict, while others do not, a difference which itself constitutes a conflict in their interpretations (i.e. some seeing interpretive conflict and some not). The concept of rationality, then, simultaneously presupposes disagreement and the possibility of consensus. It therefore concerns the politics of personal rivalries, loyalties, interests, and identities. At stake is not only who gets the most land or property, but also how much of one's selfhood is left of whoever loses the fight to have one's interpretation accepted. Among the Giriama of Kenya, this primacy of selfhood for some, though not all, makes sense of their habit of bankrupting themselves by selling land and trees to pay for lavishly prestigious mortuary rituals for a family member.

Two reasons may be given, or be apparent, for this habit. First, the shame in losing personal esteem through being judged ungenerous is greater than the shame of bankruptcy. Another reason for expensive ceremonies is that they have been called at the request of an ancestor or must be held in honour of one, including a recently deceased member of the homestead. Certain Giriama may publicly acknowledge these as just reasons. Through careful planning a few of them stage lavish rites but keep enough of their property 'hidden' to re-establish themselves. Such successful farmers do systematically relate means to ends in what they see as the most efficient way to conserve and expand wealth. But this interpretation of ceremonial obligation conflicts with that of other farmers. Those other farmers claim that a sponsor should be unstinting even to the point of bankruptcy either because to do so otherwise is shameful to self, family, and clan, or because one or more ancestors will be offended and will punish the family. However, entrepreneurial farmers reason privately among those they can trust that, provided a sponsor is *seen* to be generous, then both ancestors and communal honour will be satisfied (Parkin 1982).

If this was all there is to the situation, we would say that these simply represent alternative rationalities, each of which characterises a particular category of person. But the situation is inconstant. The role of emotions enters into it through the opinions and expressed feelings of other people and of the ancestors which shape the interpretation of what has been or might be done. To offend those who hold other opinions is to incur their displeasure, anger, and even vengeance. Taking the 'right' decision is not only a question of reaching a particular end, but may be an attempt to avoid personal fear and guilt, as well as the wrath or mere ridicule of others. Moreover, avoiding the effects of others' as well as one's own sentiments, or seeking approval through them, may become more important than preserving one's own property. We often redefine our aims which have already been reshaped through our changing emotions. Thus it is that the once successful entrepreneurial farmer visibly loses his grip and joins the ranks of the poor. He (or a member of his family) has become sick and, fearing ancestral vengeance or the witchcraft of jealous neighbours, no longer makes a secret of his property holdings and so soon loses them through the obligation to fund ceremonies and proffer gifts and help. In Giriama society, as elsewhere in Africa, there are many examples of rapid fluctuations in family fortunes within a single generation as well as between them, for which the standard of economic explanation of insufficient liquidity is not the only one and itself only scratches the surface.

A reason can, then, always be found for acting in a particular way, and more than one reason may be held. Ceremonial generosity may be the means to avoid shame, the effects of others' envy, or ancestral displeasure, or to satisfy communal expectations and so seek support in a subsequent endeavour. If it is convincing, any reason will stick. Even madness may be interpreted as a rational attempt to escape the impossibility of meeting the otherwise rational demands of everyday life. A personal or cultural flow chart of alternative reasons for decisions would not indicate a fixed number of logical possibilities but, given people's imaginative creativity, an expanding list in which preferences and priorities would constantly be changing, and in which deletions and substitutions would also occur.

Here, it is important to stress that this imagination is not simply the play of an innovative intellect which refuses to recognise logical bounds. Such a view would reduce interpretative creativity to the infinite articulation of different possible judgements. The argument here instead is that emotions can be nonjudgemental shapers of decisions. That is to say, emotions act autonomously, or at least appear to do so, in giving sense to an interpretation, not through comparison with other possible decisions but by making that particular interpretation seem fitting. Emotions thus make for aesthetic as well as functional appropriateness.

For example, homoeopathic magic makes sense not necessarily because it is seen to work but because it presents a pleasing and persuasive picture, image, or metaphor of feasibility. Many such pleasing images involve the use of people's bodies. Thus, magicians often heighten the drama of their performance through stylistic movements and gestures. Bodily drama and emotion here draw on each other and at the same time result in acts, decisions, and suggestions that are regarded as reasonable as well as pleasing. Among the Giriama, the stalk of a certain herb oozes a white sap when broken. The stalk is stroked gently by the herbalist and is offered into a prepared liquid which is then drunk by a mother having difficulties breastfeeding her child, each phase being given stylistic emphasis and accompanied by ancestral and other incantations. The breaking, oozing, stroking, offering up, and recitation evidently arouse a range of feelings, a number of which are obvious and appear to be commonly held.

A Moving Together

We would be missing much of the sense of the occasion simply to call this therapy. I suggest that it is an instance of aesthetic appropriateness and has to be thought of as a moving-together of reason, emotion, and body. The ideas of both Sartre (1958) and Merleau-Ponty (1962) are relevant here, as well as those of a number of anthropologists who have looked ethnographically at the bodily loci of reasoning emotions (e.g. Blacking 1977; Lienhardt 1980; Rosaldo 1980; Heelas 1981; Harris 1978; Lewis 1980).

There are some standard observations on the various ways in which the body and its parts are associated with social power and authority. Familiar examples are the grid:group dichotomy proposed by Mary Douglas (1970), by which different bodily postures correspond socially with either individualism or conformity; the hierarchy of head and loins among the Fipa described by Willis (1967, 1980) which underwrites centralised political legitimacy; and the association of right- and left-handedness with authority and submission respectively (Needham 1973).

Other ethnographers will generally accept these kinds of correspondences between the human and social body. But, taking account of how they were elicited, they are intellectual classifications. That is to say, people in the society concerned will explain to the ethnographer or to uninformed fellow-members what is socially represented by the dichotomy of head and loins, or of right and left, or of loose as against stiff bodily posture. Sometimes, further associations are accounted for by the ethnographer themself, but the initial dualism can generally be explained by some members of the society.

This being so, those same members of the society will comment on the correctness or appropriateness of bodily usage. Thus, on the rare occasions when a Giriama woman is allowed to drink alcoholic liquor, she must do so holding the gourd from which she drinks in her left hand. Since the occasions are so rare, she may have to be reminded of this obligation. Similarly, there are appropriate burial positions for ordinary men and women and for special men who are members of a secret society. Sometimes there is dispute as to the direction in which the deceased's head must face. But that there are rules concerning this is not disputed.

In all such cases, and there are many, people have to be told what to do. Usually they accept this without question as an authoritative statement from someone in a legitimate position to make it: elder to young man, man to woman, adult to child. Sometimes people are also told what dire effects will ensue if the custom is not carried out. This is the realm of command and explanation. It is an area of discourse which places reason in control of body. But there is another area of discourse which reverses this. Spirit possession, madness, hysteria (the three are distinguished lexically as well as conceptually), witchcraft, and persistent violence, drunkenness, and thieving, must be explained by a diviner. Such behaviour is explained as the result of what we might loosely call imbalances in human nature. I call them imbalances because the Giriama do not believe that a person can be intrinsically or irredeemably evil: at some stage, usually remarkably quickly, they will be brought back into the fold, even if they subsequently leave it again. A large number of terms, roughly translatable as greed, lust, envy, jealousy, malice, resentment, anger, are used to refer to these imbalances of character and the accompanying behaviour. In English we would say that emotions are seen as controlling the body and its actions.

However, to describe such behaviour as due to imbalances of character presupposes that the Giriama regard the morally proper person as balanced and others as deviating from this. But this is a Western imposition. The Giriama view such alternations of virtue and vice as that which makes up a human being: a purely virtuous or a purely wicked person does not exist, so why bother to set these up as polar models? Thus, while there are rules governing the use of the body (e.g. left or right hand) which privilege reason and indicate reasonable behaviour, there are other kinds of bodily behaviour (spirit possession, causing illness through witchcraft, theft, violence) which are regarded as caused by such emotions as desire, resentment, greed, envy, and malice, which all people experience at some time or other.

We can go beyond the view that, for the Giriama, reason controls body in the field of ritual prohibitions, but that emotions govern body where there is destructive behaviour. This is because key terms for the sources of these emotions themselves refer to parts of the body. Moreover, the same key terms refer, ambivalently, to reason. In other words, the same terms may refer to what we call body, reason, and emotion. Using such English language terms analytically denoting the separateness of emotions thus distorts the more packed-in, polysemic discourse of the Giriama themselves.

The key terms in Giriama that show this polysemy, as probably in most Bantu languages, refer directly to heart, liver, kidney, eye, and possibly head, each with derived terms and meanings:

> *moyo* = physical heart, life, selfhood, reason, mind, determination, but also feelings, innermost sentiment, hope, willingness, will, and desire and thence to
>
> *choyo* = (literally little heart) = greed, selfishness, envy, but also palpitating spot in veins, blood, and also *m'fundo moyo* or *fundo ra moyo* (lit. knotted heart) = malice, envy. The idea of innermost feelings is also found as one of the meanings of the word for liver, thus
>
> *ini* = physical liver, core emotion (usually negative, like *ifu* kidney), and thence to
>
> *kiini* = (lit. little liver) = innermost part, kernel of nut, stone of fruit, yolk of egg, heart of tree, and core of meaning or argument
>
> *dzitso* = physical eye and spring of water, but also greed, envy, more usually in the form of
>
> *kidzitso* = (lit, little eye) = envy, covetousness, and directly associated with witchcraft. The plural form is
>
> *matso* = physical eyes, but, unless qualified (e.g. *matso mai* bad eyes = a kind of witchcraft), lacks the sinister, emotional connotations of the singular. Instead, as in expressions such as *matso mafu* (open eyes) or *kukala matso* (to be awake) there is the sense of being alert and in a stable, reasoning frame of mind.
>
> *Kitswa* = physical head, top or higher part, that which leads, authority, but also pride, arrogance, including
>
> *dzitswa-ro* = (lit. that large head) = stupid person

The inclusion of the word for head reveals the author's Western bias. As will be seen it only marginally touches on all three aspects of reason, emotion, and body. It is certainly part of the body, but, except that to be an authority requires wisdom, and that leaders tend to be proud, the co-associations are weak. The greatest sources of feelings and thought are the heart, liver, and kidney, and, to a lesser extent, the eye and eyes. All three, including eye with its secondary meaning of spring of water, refer to internal origins, the innermost being those of heart and liver. This accords with Lienhardt's findings among some non-Bantu African peoples, the Nilotic Dinka and Luo of Eastern Africa (1980). Outside Africa, as in Shakespearean England, the heart 'thinks' as well as 'feels', and the liver is the seat of the passions (*Much Ado About Nothing* III. Ii. 13, cited by Gregory 1984).

Other bodily terms are important among Giriama. *Milatso* is blood and can, when used in aphorisms, stress the reasonableness of marriage and affinity ('blood follows cattle', i.e. that cattle exchanges make marriages which make children). It can also refer to 'natural skills', e.g. *ana mulatso wa kufuga ng'ombe*, he knows how to keep cattle (Lit. he has the blood to keep cattle). In its adverbial form, *kilatso*, the term refers to blood guiltiness (i.e. spilling blood in battle or in sacrifice) and to bad fate. Blood is contrasted with flesh, for which the word is *nyama*, which also means meat, live animal, and spirits which possess people and so denotes a general principle of animation.

Other bodily terms are also used metaphorically and show their potential for indicating existential dilemmas, e.g. *ku-nyerezeza mukono* is to offer one's hand gently in respect, while *ku-kala na mukono* is to 'stay with the hand', i.e. have a tendency to pilfer. The hand is for giving as well as for taking. However, none of these other terms goes as far in this respect as heart, liver, kidney, eye, head, blood, and flesh.

On the one hand, then, the heart, liver, kidney, and eye are the seat of conjoined reason and emotions in general. On the other hand, particular kinds of reasoning and emotional behaviour are identified by terms that have nothing directly to do with the body, though etymologically they may originate in practical, bodily actions. With regard to the latter, what is impressive is, (a) the large number of terms for what we might translate as emotions and reasoning faculties; and (b) how possible it is to distinguish these as such. In other words, while the Giriama see the origins of reason and emotion in particular parts of the body, they nevertheless distinguish reasoning from emotion in specific references to actual cases of behaviour.

There are terms denoting grief, loneliness, longing, love, lust, greed, envy, jealousy, malice, anger, fear, doubt, despair, disgust, shame, pride, trust, hope, determination, and others. Many such translations into English miss the different ways in which emotions may be linked among the Giriama. Thus, to take just one example, *utsungu* means poison, bitterness, resentment, and anger, on the one hand, but also grief on the other. It is the feeling experienced at a funeral of a loved or respected relative or friend. A man or woman is grieved at the loss but also bitter that it has happened at all, and angry with the witch who caused the death. Since the witch will be made to pay, the sentiment carries within it both the consequences of the loss of a dear one and the intention to avenge his or her death.

Intentionality is thus built into descriptions of emotional states, and yet a completely separate vocabulary exists to describe acts of thinking, pondering, intending, comparing, explaining, understanding, remembering, reminding, and deciding. Two underlying notions figure prominently: making clean, clear, or bright, and aiming or pointing in a particular direction. Cleaning, clearing, lighting (the way), and directing are practical, purposive activities. They are premised on intentionality, as we would call it, just as are the descriptions of emotions.

Thus, to take some examples, *ku-ng'alira* means to shine upon (moon, sun, or fire), while the passive form, *ku-ng'alirwa*, is to understand, i.e. to have made clear to one. Similarly, *ku-aza* can be translated as to reflect or consider possibilities, and is etymologically related to *ku-aka*, to bum brightly. Derived forms are *ku-azuka*, to reach a decision after thinking about it, and *ku-azya*, to cause someone to think about something. 'To make the way clear' becomes linked to ideas of direction. Thus *ku-era* means to be or become clean or clear, and the derived form *ku-erekeza* has the sense of to aim at and thence to intend. The act of pointing a way opposes destination to departure and so the word has an additional sense of to be opposed and therefore to compare. The causative *ku-erekezanya* means to explain to one another or come to an agreement, while the static form, *ku-erekezeka*, is to be capable of settlement and of explanation, and therefore to be thinkable. The many forms of inflection in Bantu verb stems allow for a wide range of increasingly abstract ideas to be developed out of a basic term for a practical act.

The Case of Divination

While the specific terms for emotions presuppose intentional acts, the terms for thinking are etymologically rooted in intentional or purposive acts. But both can be seen as making up a complementarity. The intentionality behind terms for emotions is always to return a fragmented part of the self back to its core, or to avenge its fragmentation by another. A diviner's diagnosis travels, so to speak, over different parts of the patient's body, indicating different emotions as symptoms and causes of the patient's affliction of misfortune. The diviner finishes his/her diagnosis by fixing on a particular part of the body as the one which is out of order.

S/he then suggests therapy, to be carried out by another doctor, which will re-establish bodily-emotional harmony. In acting autonomously, bodily emotions wander off or split off from the core of the innermost self. The diviner indicates both the source of the trouble and a means of bringing back together the wayward parts (Chapter 18 and Parkin, 1979). The diviners' intentionality, embodied in the idioms of pointing and explaining, complements the intending grief, love, hatred, anger, or malice of the patient or his attacker. The result will be to return them to heart and liver, the innermost loci of what we call reason and emotion.

Divination has a powerful performative aspect. Its apparent empirical success depends on the persuasive artistry of diviners. Their knowledge of local social ties and enmities may sometimes be a necessary condition of accurate predictions, but their dramatic skills make them convincing and credible. It is impressive to see how Giriama diviners, and sometimes other ritual experts, bring their own bodies into the performance. They may sing, move in a rhythmic manner, alter their voices when possessed, go into trances, jump out of them, and assume dramatic airs. They bring together not only their own bodily parts, but also their judgements and feelings into an aesthetic whole. This aesthetic moving-together is what gives sense to the divination. It reduces conflict between judgement, emotion and the body and so presents them as an appropriate response to disorder.

Thus far, we can see how this Giriama coordination of body, reason, and emotion might seem to conform to Merleau-Ponty's phenomenology of perception (1962, 1945). That is to say, the diviner achieves their own unity of body, mind, and feelings through interaction with that of their patient. Indeed, they create their own unity at the same time as creating that of the patient. They dissolve the distinction between themselves as subject and the patient as object, making them both an inter-subjectivity, to use Merleau-Ponty 's concept. Neither reason, nor emotion, nor body, prevails one over the other. Nor does the diviner's unity prevail over that of the patient, nor that of the patient over the diviner's. The simultaneity or, as I would prefer, the moving-together, extends over the complete range of perception and interaction. It materially expresses the polysemy of heart, liver, kidney and eye.

Where in this, however, are the powers and forces mentioned above as allegedly characterising Western ideas of emotions as being potentially out of control and in conflict with each other, with the body, and with reason? The view from Merleau-Ponty establishes their harmony. Sartre, with whose work Merleau-Ponty is associated, suggests a radical extension to this view (1958, 1943).

For Merleau-Ponty, the uniqueness of the individual, i.e. of myself, which you can see but I cannot, and of yourself, which I can see but which you cannot, creates an ambiguity which leads us into further understanding of the world. The possibility of reflecting upon this unseeable aspect of ourselves expands our horizons. But for Sartre this capacity of the other to see myself as I cannot (e.g. by catching me looking through a keyhole and causing me to feel shame), alienates myself from that other (1958: 259–63). Alienation may be unfortunate but it is what is basic to human relationships and makes up our being in the world. Thus, through my body I act upon the world, as a subject acting upon an object. But I am also ultimately an object for another observer other who can always catch me in *flagrante delicto*. S/he has the upper hand over me and so alienates my body from me. I do the same for her, but unfortunately that helps neither of us. For Merleau-Ponty our body optimistically reveals possibilities, while for Sartre it entails alienation before revelation (Rabil 1970: 30–31).

Where does this leave the Giriama? The Giriama diviner's ideas concerning illness and misfortune are understood by him/her to be held by no higher authority than oneself or some other diviner. S/he may privately concede that other (though rarely if ever), or that all diviners rely on spirits. But all are part of the same Giriama authority. However, with the advent first of Arabic and later of Western medicine, this has for a long time and perhaps always been a fiction. New ideas compete with old and clients seek them. This obliges a diviner to incorporate them. But s/he can only do so by making concessions to the world-order or episteme of which the new ideas are part.

Thus, at an earlier time in Giriama society diviners had to compete with the growing power of Arabic Islam which diagnosed and prescribed through the use of numbers, astrology, and the Qur'an, as well as through herbal remedies. Two kinds of diviners emerged, non-Muslim Giriama and Muslim so-called Swahili. The latter were, and still are, regarded as more efficacious. They are also more expensive. With the advent of European missions and British colonialism in the nineteenth century, Western medicine offered new competition. Its metaphysics of diagnosis and prognosis insist on still further specialisation: a doctor must have education, training, and facilities, which are way beyond that available to Giriama diviners, who can only imitate them at best.

In the first case, the Islamic concept of *dini* (religion) confronted the pre-Islamic one of *uganga* (traditional medicine). In the second case, Western medicine acted through Christian schools and hospitals and opposed both traditional and Muslim divination, strongly resisting synthesisation. The political power underlying its introduction was that much greater. In the case of both Muslim and Western medicine, the Giriama diviner was, so to speak, caught at the keyhole by the other. He could, however, move into Islam without too much difficulty, and gain mastery of Muslim divination. A common feature of both Muslim and non-Muslim divination facilitating this is the reciprocal roles of diviner and client in helping each other reach a mutually satisfactory diagnosis and cure through the use of vocal, facial, and other bodily cues. With Merleau-Ponty we can say here that the reciprocal revelation widens horizons of understanding.

However, while a Giriama diviner might become Christian (though I know of none), he could not move into Western medicine. The epistemological boundary between himself and Islam was that of religion, which technically he could cross. But the barrier placed against him by Western medicine was a specialised concept of reason, to which access could only be had through training which, given its scarcity, was inevitably privileged: a chief's son, residents of localities with mission schools, those living near roads, shops, and 'European' towns, and, more recently, the children of successful farmers and professional workers, were the ones most likely to have this privilege. It is a barrier which divides those shamed by their inadequacies from those proud of their achievements. It matches the alienation of allegedly ignorant patient from their allegedly omniscient, Western-trained doctor, and accords more with Sartre's observation. The patient can never 'know' that part of him which the doctor diagnoses as symptom and disease for s/he is regarded as lacking precise scientific medical understanding of cause and effect. But nor does the doctor 'know' that his supposed omniscience is false and that s/he, too, depends on his/her patients' cues and cooperation in reaching diagnoses.

Doctor and diviner/herbalist are further alienated from each other in that, while a herbalist's or diviner's apprentice is first their client and friend or relative, a patient can hardly ever assume the status of his 'Western' doctor, who in turn may lose the capacity to empathise with those s/he treats.

Whereas the traditional diviner might be little more than an ordinary elder of a small neighbourhood, perhaps one day becoming more famous, the modern, the bio-medically trained doctor is from the beginning marked out in a number of distinct ways. Not only does s/he have access to knowledge and equipment that no local elder could attain, s/he is also distinguished physically. S/he dresses differently, has fixed premises which are set apart from the village, and is subject to recall and redeployment to other areas, rarely one's natal one. Doctors' physical isolation and separateness contrast with the manner in which diviners and their practice merge with and operate through their surroundings. Moreover, the 'Western ' doctor stands over, so to speak, the patient who is rendered passive and not held to play a rhythmic, reciprocal role in the interaction. The doctor diagnoses and prescribes authoritatively as one body acting not through but upon another. S/he literally here embodies the power of an imposed Western rationality. Patients, for their part, are required to remain mute, any expression of pain, distress, or concern becoming easily labelled as emotionalism, neurosis, or some such.

Some Giriama are beginning to adopt this popular Western distinction, with its echoes of so-called Cartesian dualism, between reason as most fully expressed through education, and emotion as ideally under reason's control. This view co-exists with beliefs in the efficacy of traditional diviners and herbalists, who often do not so much reach curative decisions as exchange roles with their patients in a drama out of which come mutually acceptable suggestions. We may say that this latter is a rationality whose sense derives from a coherence of mind, body, and emotion. The 'new' alternative is a rationality evincing the non-reciprocal power of modern, 'Western-style' specialists most of whom normally live and were trained outside the society of their Giriama patients.

Notes

(1) We are reminded that Socrates' three parts making up the human soul (thought-reason, *thumos* or 'regulatory spirit', and the appetitive and impulsive) paralleled the three classes of educated governors or kings, soldiers-police, and lower classes, making up his Ideal State.

(2) Curiously, in the same passage that he claims not to distinguish between mind and soul, as distinct from body, Descartes nevertheless refers to mind and soul by the different French terms (*ésprit* and *âme*) (cited in Rée 1974: 117).

(3) "I distinguish between the will which includes the thinking (the natural will) and the thinking which encompasses the will (the rational will) ..." (1955: 119, my bracketed inclusions).

References

Arens, W. (1979) *The Man-Eating Myth*. New York: Oxford University Press.

Baier, A. (1980) Master Passions. In A. Rorty (ed.) *Explaining Emotions*. Berkeley: University of California Press.

Bailey, F.G. (1981) Dimensions of Rhetoric in Conditions of Uncertainty. In R. Paine (ed.) Politically Speaking. Newfoundland Institute for Social and Economic Research. Philadelphia: ISHI.

Bailey, F.G. (1983) *The Tactical Uses of Passion*. Ithaca and London: Cornell University Press.

Bergson, H. (1975) *The Creative Mind*. Totowa, NJ: Littlefield, Adam.

Blacking, J. (ed.) (1977) *The Anthropology of the Body* (ASA Monographs 15). London: Academic Press.
Chapman, M. (1982) 'Semantics' and the 'Celt'. In D. Parkin (ed.) *Semantic Anthropology* (ASA Monographs 22). London: Academic Press.
Deed, F. (n.d.) *Giryama-English Dictionary*. Nairobi: Church Missionary Society.
Gellner, E. (1982) Relativism and Universals. In M. Hollis and S. Lukes (eds) *Rationality and Relativism*. Oxford: Basil Blackwell.
Gregory, A. (1984) Slander Accusations and Social Control in Late 16th- and Early 7th-Century England. D. Phil. Thesis, University of Sussex.
Hacking, I. (1982) Language, Truth and Reason. In M. Hollis and S. Lukes (eds) *Rationality and Relativism*. Oxford: Basil Blackwell.
Harris, G. (1978) *Casting out Anger*. Cambridge: Cambridge University Press.
Heelas, P. and Lock, A. (eds) (1981) *Indigenous Psychologies*. London: Academic Press.
Hollis, M. and Lukes, S. (eds) (1982) *Rationality and Relativism*. Oxford: Basil Blackwell.
Lewis, G. (1980) *Day of Shining Red*. Cambridge: Cambridge University Press.
Lienhardt, G. (1980) Self: Public and Private. Some African Representations. *Journal of the Anthropological Society of Oxford* 11, 69–82.
Merleau-Ponty, M. (1962) [1945] *The Phenomenology of Perception*. London: Routledge & Kegan Paul.
Milner, G. Siamese twins, Birds and the Double Helix. *Man* n.s. 4, 5–23.
Needham, R. (ed.) (1973) *Right and Left*. Chicago: Chicago University Press.
Parkin, D. (1972) *Palms, Wine and Witnesses*. San Francisco: Chandler.
Parkin, D. (1979) Straightening the Paths from Wilderness. *JASO* 10, 147–60.
Parkin, D. (1982) Introduction to his (ed.) *Semantic Anthropology*. London: Academic Press.
Rabil, A.J.R. (1967) *Merleau-Ponty*. New York: Columbia University Press.
Rée, J. (1974) *Descartes*. London: Allen Lane.
Rorty, A. (ed.) (1980) *Explaining Emotions*. Berkeley: University of California Press.
Rosaldo, M. (1980) *Knowledge and Passion*. London: Cambridge University Press.
Sartre. J.-P. (1958) [1943] *Being and Nothingness*. London: Methuen.
De Sousa, R. (1980) *The Rationality of Emotions*. In A. Rorty (ed.) *Explaining Emotions*. Berkeley: University of California Press.
Southall, A.W. (1976) Nuer and Dinka Are People: Ecology, Ethnicity and Logical Possibility. *Man* n.s. 11, 463–91.
Tonkin, E. (1982) Language vs. the World: Notes on meaning for Anthropologists. In D. Parkin (ed.) *Semantic Anthropology*. London: Academic Press.
De Tönnies, F. (1955) [1857] *Community and Association*. London: Routledge & Kegan Paul.
Willis, R. (1967) The Head and the Loins. *Man* n.s. 2, 519–34.
Willis, R. (1980) *State in the Making*. Bloomington: Indiana University Press.
Wilson, J.R.S. (1972) *Emotion and Object*. Cambridge: Cambridge University Press.

16 The Power of Incompleteness: Innuendo in Swahili Women's Dress

From Dichotomy to Infinite Suggestiveness

A number of dichotomies have been used to illustrate rhetoric, political language and oratory: e.g. "straight" and "veiled" talk (A. Strathern, 1975), *kabary* and *resaka* (Keenan, 1975), "ideology" and "programme" (Parkin, 1975), and so on. They commonly echo the European distinction between metaphorical and literal language. Such a distinction has come under attack. Ricoeur (1975), Parkin (1982) and Hesse (1986) argue that all language is metaphorical, though with different degrees of live and dead metaphor. Even with regard to the theoretical language of anthropology, spatial metaphors are basic and premised on a root metaphor of knowledge as a landscape that has to be held in sight, captured and conquered (e.g. Salmond, 1982).

It was part of the post-modernist trend to dissolve such dichotomies. But we can never completely eradicate dichotomous ways of speaking. All we can do is to try constantly to expose their false assumptions of substance and fixity. Thus, so-called literal language no more conveys referential information about objective reality than so-called metaphors; for neither literal nor metaphorical language can ever do more than approximate and partially represent objects, states, conditions and events. Representational completeness is a chimera, for each representational attempt both raises new images and so, in that very act, leaves out some other associated imagery.

I have argued elsewhere, however, that we may refer to a process of "rotating deconstructionism" (1984 and see Chapter 15), by which I mean that we can indeed deconstruct dichotomies of description and judgement but that, because popular, everyday language and thinking are commonly preserved in such dichotomies. We need to recognise also, and to be alert to, the creation of new dichotomies. We have already come to acknowledge that polythetic thinking in terms of overlapping signifiers, and not just in terms of dichotomies and dualities, informs popular imagination, as well as, for instance, recent television advertising whose fantasised merging of realities possibly derives from post-modernism's love of ironic juxtapositions and differs radically from an earlier contrastive either/or kind of advertising (i.e. 'good' versus 'bad' product).

What most characterises this trend is perhaps a recognition of the powers of incompleteness in talk: that is to say, the matters hinted at but not spelled out. Thus, so-called indirect advertising, in which the product's name is hardly mentioned, has been shown to sell more goods than advertising which directly communicates and focuses on the name of the product (O'Barr, 1982).

The power of incomplete talk seems to be the most salient feature of metaphor used in rhetoric. Metaphors draw on the attention-focusing qualities of paradox, by referring to two distinct domains of meaning but actually making them similar. Sapir's well-known example, "George is a lion", first separates humanity and animality and then collapses them, with George and the lion thereby sharing in each other's qualities (Sapir, 1977). In other words, metaphor makes incomplete use of a semantic dichotomy. A complete usage would take the form of a syllogism:

George is human.
A lion is an animal. Humans are not animals
Therefore, George is not a lion.

While metaphor is a supreme example of the power of incomplete propositional argument, I here concentrate on a different though related genre of examples.

In English, for instance, we recognise the term *innuendo* as hinting, not just at meaning, but at shades and differences of meaning around a theme. Synonyms are *allusion*, *insinuation* and *nuance*, which are also the French terms which translate the term *innuendo*. Innuendo is therefore a kind of polyvalent metaphor, linking not just two semantic domains but an array of them as infinite as the imagination will allow.

Innuendo thus partakes of a paradox in the concept of the incomplete. At one level an innuendo stops short of a full statement or proposition. It hints at a condition but leaves the hearer to complete the phrase and image. On the other hand, the number of possible propositions that can be developed out of the innuendo, hint, or allusion, are as many as there are different hearers, each individually creating their own interpretations and statements, some of which may coincide, others of which may differ and conflict. In this second sense the innuendo is not only incomplete but incompletable.

The very word "innuendo", in connoting such apparent synonyms as "hint", "allusion" or "insinuation" implies also "half-truths" or "half-falsehoods" and so arouses the suspicion in the hearer that some information is being withheld and kept secret.

Secrets, as secrets, need never be hinted at. The surest way of keeping them is never to admit that there are any. For the rhetorical power of secrecy to be utilised, however, the existence of secrets must be acknowledged. Since the secrets cannot be presented as propositions (for they would then cease to be secrets), they can only be hinted at, revealing what an audience has to be persuaded is at least a partial truth.

Secret societies provide an obvious case in point, for their power, authority and capacity to tyrannise partly derives from their having persuaded outsiders or novices that they have access to guarded truths and knowledge which cannot, however, ever be used openly, whether for good or evil. The societies reveal enough of the secret to persuade an audience to continue listening and believing, but not enough for them consistently to draw complete conclusions.

However, innuendo is also a powerful feature of other kinds of rhetoric and political language, and indeed of the combative language of the inter-personal relations that make up the small politics of everyday life. For a spouse or a lover, or an employer to an employee, to hint darkly at an unpleasant possibility in the relationship is a colossal act of power if the listener is persuaded to believe in the possibility. Even lighter hints at more welcome possibilities may, for the same reason, provide the speaker with a decisive instrument of control: parents often temporarily exert control over children in this way, and whole series of children's festivals in Western culture, including the hinted promise of gifts at Christmas, the New Year, Easter or birthdays, may provide some parental control.

A question now is to ask whether the power of innuendo is most effective politically in small groups and inter-personal relationships, or in larger-scale political discourse. I suggest that the politician addressing his or her audience, or the religious cleric his congregation, do significantly increase their rhetorical effect through the use of innuendo.

I have examples of speeches by Muslim religious leaders which skilfully stop short of expanding on "sinful" events occurring in the community, and which, from the tone, manner and context in which they are presented, suggest dire consequences for the perpetrators of the events. A *maalim* may thus refer to "happenings in the area involving some of you in this audience which the holy occasion today inhibits me from discussing".

Is the *maalim* here hinting at the possibility that some people in the congregation have been seeking the help of Muslim diviners and medicine to reverse the effects of witchcraft, or to take "pagan" oaths? Or is it that they have been tapping their coconut palms for the (forbidden) sale of alcoholic liquor or have been eating unblessed meat or prohibited food? And so on (see Chapter 9 and Parkin 1985).

The skill with which innuendo is used is obviously crucial, but should at least be recognised as a rhetorical device which draws its efficacy *not* from its direct propositional force, but rather from its propositional incompleteness.

In referring at this point to the skill of an orator or speaker, I touch on a further distinctive element which qualifies innuendo. For, while innuendo can be intended for persuasive effect, it can easily misfire, should the audience not believe in the possible consequence being hinted at. I may allude to a problem threatening you as a result of your behaviour, but you may laugh in my face if you are not convinced that the harmful possibility exists.

Structurally, there is something in common between innuendo and jokes that fall flat, and also with ritual performances which are deemed to have gone wrong or to be nonsense.

This fallibility in speaker's control over what s/he says and intends has to be seen against the formal but abstract qualities of such rhetorical devices as metaphor, other tropes, innuendo and jokes. It is certainly the ambiguity of these devices and their capacity to touch simultaneously on surprise, credibility and secrecy that comprises their effect. It is also part of their ambiguity that neither the audience nor, especially, the speaker can know for sure what this effect will be.

Innuendo, then, presupposes endless 'différance' (Derrida 1982: 17)[1]. Analytically it may at first appear peripheral to the main features of political language and everyday rhetoric, such as style, formal or informal delivery, and direct or indirect propositional modes. But, in fact, by fitting into none of these dichotomous categories, and indeed by slipping between them, we see that innuendo occupies an area of paradigmatic importance. By being off-centre structurally, it is often of central significance conceptually.

The ambiguity is at the very heart of the persuasiveness of rhetoric. Ricoeur asks in what respects such persuasion can be distinguished from what he calls the most subtle forms of violence, that is to say, flattery, seduction, and threats (Ricoeur 1975: 16). I would suggest that innuendo most closely approaches seduction, for it offers and withholds at the same time. But it is not necessarily an agreeable form of seduction, for the allusion may contain threats as well as promises. It is thus a perfect tool of political and therefore rhetorical challenge and control.

Aristotle's portrayal of the imitative nature of poetics and its concern with depicting tragedy suggests a full and perhaps complete form of representation. By contrast, rhetoric is deliberate under-representation and partial concealment, concerned with not telling the full story. Insofar as this distinction between poetics and rhetoric may be sustained, innuendo is a more likely property of rhetoric. Yet, it is difficult to deny the role of the incomplete in poetics, and to this extent innuendo and allusion are also part of it.

Perhaps it can be suggested that the "violent" uses of innuendo most likely typify rhetorical persuasion and the more pacific and evocative uses inform poetics. But even this comes close to yet another tautology and one suspects that the problem here is that rhetoric and poetics have been defined as separate discourses rather than as overlapping styles within a single field of discourse.

The Stuff of Debate

Let me turn now to ethnography. Rectangular cotton cloths, measuring about 150 cm by 110 cm and bearing patterns made up of two to three dominant colours, are worn by Swahili-speaking women along the East African coast, especially, and inland in some areas. The cloth is known as *kanga* or *leso*, the latter term largely confined to Kenya. The term *kanga* means guinea-fowl and refers to some early patterns of white spots on a dark background, while *leso* is derived from the Portugese word for handkerchief. A useful brief history of the *kanga* or *leso* and its development is found in Linnebuhr (1992; see also Beck, 1995), who includes references to earlier German and Dutch texts and in Hilal (1989), while Handby and Bygott (1985) discuss numerous ways in which *kanga* may be worn. In addition, there is a vast literature on proverbs and riddles and their use generally and not just those worn on *kanga* (see Barwani-Sheikh and Samsom (1995) and Mtoro (1981: 194–198, 326) and bibliographies).

This paper concentrates on the contemporary and recent use of the proverbs, riddles, sharp comments and slogans, (sayings in short), which adorn the *kanga*. Other women's cloths do not bear these messages and I will not be concerned with them. The messages carried on the *kanga* are commonly plays on words and situations of a humorous, ironic, laudatory and didactic nature, often with conjugal, sexual or erotic innuendos. The poetics of these sayings are, however, certainly part of the everyday rhetorical struggle inherent in both public and face-to-face social relations, particularly those between women who see each other as rivals, and, also, privately in the bedroom between wife and husband.

Since it is women themselves who submit their suggestions for sayings to the manufacturers of the *kanga*, in return for a small cash payment or a new *kanga*, the garments become for the women a major medium for communicating their own distinctive views on the nature and conduct of social relations and status, particularly as regards their relations with men, but including also those with rival women and with neighbours, friends and family, including mothers. The central concern, however, in the recent and contemporary period is certainly that of rivalry between women, which they acknowledge and will refer to as "women (competitively) riddling with each other" (*wanawake wanafumbiana*).

Before moving to discuss this, however, it is important to mention the private bedroom context in which *kanga* are also used, for this provides an intimate backdrop against which more public innuendos are communicated.

In many, if not most, Swahili households in Zanzibar at least, following the evening maghrib prayer, wives may aromatise selected *kanga* with incense (*kufukiza kanga zao*). *Kanga* are sold in pairs (*doti*), so that, in the bedroom context, one part of a selected aromatised one may be used by the wife and the other by the husband. Through her choice of *kanga* and therefore message, she communicates her feelings to her husband and her love. For his part, the husband never wears his *kanga* outside the bedroom nor in front of anyone else: for this moment, it is his wife's intimate prestation to him alone (though, at a later time, the *kanga* and its message become visible to family, friends and neighbours when the wife wears it while, say, washing, cooking or cleaning the courtyard). This is unlike the situation on the mainland where, in "hotelis" for instance, a man may be seen leaving his bedroom at night to go to the bathroom wearing a *kanga*, allegedly an unthinkable act for a "true" Swahili, who would rather change and don some other cloth such as a *saruni*, *kikoi* or *shuka*.

Within the Swahili household, also, close female family members, such as a mother, mother-in-law, aunt or grandmother, may sometimes prepare the bedroom for the couple, perhaps sprinkling jasmin blossom on the bed sheets and laying out on the bed a pair of *kanga* chosen for its message, which may be directed at one or both of them, "for they will know for whom it is intended". The bedroom thus provides a context for *kanga* usage which may extend from the confines of husbandwife intimacy to a concern by other members of the household. It then extends further into the more public domain of neighbours, friends and other relatives outside the immediate household.

Linnebuhr (1992: 85) correctly notes that there may be some variation in the themes addressed by the sayings, such that in the late seventies and eighties, apparently, polygamy became a thematic focus, while in the late eighties there was more emphasis on economic issues. She notes also that in Tanzania politically motivated self-improvement slogans appeared on *kanga* during the high period of socialism and self-reliance (*ujamaa* and *ku-jitegemea*), while these were absent in Kenya. There is also some variation by age, in that, for instance, an older woman would not wear, nor be given, a *kanga* which referred to sexual relations. In other respects, however, I can confirm from observation that the themes of the proverbs have remained broadly the same over at least a thirty-year period (c. 1970–2000), principally focusing on men-women relations and sexuality, though sometimes behind an apparently innocent and even pious declaration.

Two published collections (Farsi, 1958; Abudu and Baruwa, 1981) include a large number of sayings, many of them going back at least 30 or 40 years before such publication, and in some cases to the 19th century. Few are presented as having sexual and gender-based innuendos and most are of an explicitly nonsexual moralistic or didactic nature. Some, however, once transposed to the even more interpretively liberal context of the *kanga* are given further "double meaning" (a feature noted by Mtoro for 1903 (Mtoro, 1981: 194)), which may extend to the sexual or erotic.

That said, out of a sample of sixty-six proverbs, riddles and sayings on *kanga* being sold in shops in Zanzibar town, and which I systematically collected during a two-week period in January 1993 by sitting in the shops in Zanzibar town in which they were being sold, only a few were found among the 787 recorded by Farsi in 1958 (557 "proverbs", 93 "riddles" and 137 "superstition" as he distinguishes them). I also have a much smaller number collected unsystematically in Kenya at various times during the period 1966 to 1991, none of which featured in Farsi's list. This suggests that women are producing *kanga* sayings that constitute a separate thematic domain and activity from those in which other proverbs and riddles are produced. Or, it may be that nowadays the women's is the main and perhaps only domain.

It has to be remembered that Abudu, Baruwa and Farsi, and before them Taylor (1891) and Shabaan Robert (1954: 36–38), aimed to display the immense range and variety of Swahili sayings, but were not specifically concerned with those used on *kanga*. The themes reported by these authors tend to be of a didactic and moral nature, and not sexually and erotically suggestive. The erotic sayings are then a part of the visual communication of sexual and gender issues among women especially, and also between women and men, made possible by the bodily site of the *kanga* as a kind of publicised private space. Linnebuhr's informants even claimed that the first printed texts on *kanga* towards the end of the nineteenth century emerged when women persuaded cloth merchants to print erotic and other sayings which the women themselves had composed. She remarks that, by 1912, the colonial authorities had noted the popularity of these erotic allusions on *kanga* and had tried, unsuccessfully it seems, to ban them (Linnebuhr, 1992: 90).

Particular sayings are not repeated in successive years. Nor would a woman normally wear a *kanga* whose maxim is regarded as in some way outdated, that is to say, belonging to the previous year (though very old ones are sometimes re-cycled and, under some circumstances, a saying from a recent year may be especially apt and so worn pointedly on a specific occasion). The same sense of datedness extends to the *kanga* designs themselves, which are too numerous to be described here. As a result there is a colossal proliferation of *kanga* and therefore of sayings. My impression from observation is that *kanga* designs of the early sixties were less complex than those of the seventies and eighties and were generally of a higher quality cotton than modern ones. In the mid-nineties those made in China had a reputation for thicker cotton, but tended to have a limited number of proverbs and patterns repeated in different colour schemes, while those from India were thinner but more diverse in proverb and design (even if sometimes badly printed), with Kenyan and Tanzanian *kanga* similarly diverse but of variable cotton quality, those from Mombasa in Kenya in particular being regarded as of high quality.

The status of the *kanga* as a garment appears also to have undergone change. As mentioned above, it consists of two parts or "sheets". One is worn from the top of the body to the ankles and the other over the shoulders or head. In the 1960s the dress was worn by Swahili-speaking women in their homes and, out in public, as an informal alternative to the formal black head-to-foot attire locally called *buibui*. Increasingly over this period, the *kanga* has also been bought and worn by non-Muslim women of the Kenya coast and immediate hinterland, principally the Mijikenda. In Tanzania its inland use by both Muslim and non-Muslim women goes back much further. To illustrate such change in Kenya, there has been a marked shift among Giriama non-Muslim women who, during the middle nineteen sixties still wore the traditional cotton *hando* or skirt and remained bare-breasted but who nowadays are hardly ever seen in this way and who wear either *kanga* or "European" dresses.

Although there is local variation, Swahili-speaking women generally still buy *kanga* for indoor use (including domestic activity and extending to weddings and mourning ceremonies) but less often outdoors, sometimes wearing instead the black *buibui* or, recently, the more expensive "Arab" *hijabu*. The *hijabu* is an ornate hood, worked into spider-like patterns in gold and silver thread, and, in its most elaborate form, is imported from the Gulf states of the Middle East. Some women also wear the white scarves associated with Iran. Alongside Iranian influence, there is thus a pronounced "arabisation" of outdoor dress among those Swahili-speaking women who can afford it. There is no evidence nowadays for Linnebuhr's suggestion, made with reference to the mid- and late-eighties, that the importation of second-hand European clothes was likely to oust the use of *kanga*, although this is interesting as an indication of how rapidly women's dress opportunities and preferences may change. There was for instance, little opportunity for women to "riddle with each other" during the immediate postrevolutionary period in Zanzibar, and to some extent on the mainland, when *kanga* with sayings on them were banned, while in Kenya they continued to be produced.

As another example of rapid change, I noticed a difference in Zanzibar between the situation in December 1992-January 1993 and August-September 1993. The first period was one of radical Muslim demonstrations and marches, and the use by women of the black *buibui* and of the *hijab* was much in evidence. Men instanced this as evidence of female support for their religious radicalism. I was struck during the second period, only seven months later, that far fewer women were wearing these religious garments, with the colourful *kanga* being worn more publicly. Some men said that the change corresponded with the virtual disappearance of public radical Muslim protest, but some women claimed that they had, in each case, treated the changes as those of fashion determined by women themselves, and certainly, even behind the veil, took pleasure in using it to make statements about themselves (one women admitting to her women friends that, underneath her black head-to-toe *buibui,* she was wearing a bikini). The changes are therefore part of an ongoing female aesthetics and not just determined by the presence or absence of religious affirmation. Despite, therefore, some re-definition from time to time of what constitutes a *kanga*-wearing domain (in effect a redrawing of the relationship of domestic to public), the *kanga* appears to adapt to and so survive such changes. The history of the *kanga* is therefore that of a garment which speaks at two levels: through the different statuses of those who wear it; and through the sayings written on it.

In this paper I deal with the latter, the written "announcements", which range from clear-cut assertions hinting at broader issues to complex riddles which are sometimes difficult to decipher. *Fumbo*, a Bantu term, can roughly be translated as riddle, *methali*, of Arabic derivation, means proverb, *vijembe* denotes cutting remarks, while *jina* or *msemo* mean name or statement/saying. Sauda Sheikh ranks some of these according to their verbal acuity (*ukali*), with *vijembe* the most and the *misemo* and *methali* the least cutting, and *mafumbo* in between (Sheikh, 1994: 7), so indicating Swahili-speakers' recognition of how complex and rich this verbal domain is, with the proverbs (*methali*), most likely to encapsulate folk wisdom (BarwaniSheikh and Samsom, 1995).

Since all types are found on *kanga*, I shall in English refer to them in general as sayings. In all cases, even where folk wisdom is communicated, there is a sense of incompleteness, for the situations and tensions to which the proverbs, riddles or assertions refer provoke further exegeses. They are, for instance, more "secretive" in their insinuations than the slogans nowadays found on Western-style T-shirts.

Swahili women themselves constantly say that the number of interpretations to be made of any riddle/proverb/saying depends on the person's own viewpoint and interpretive ingenuity and so is potentially limitless. I spent many hours over some weeks in Zanzibar discussing with three wives of friends such interpretations and was judged, after some time, to have myself become quite expert in my own skills. The point here is that, as the women say, no meaning is necessarily fixed, and that, although it is in some cases difficult to go beyond a single bland assertion, in many others a wider latitude is possible and that this is often an ideal to be aimed at in composing a riddle. In addition, there is the situational context of meaning generated, for instance, by the nature and circumstances under which the woman buys the *kanga*, by who accompanies her at the purchase (and who can therefore spread word of the choice of saying), and, especially, by the occasion and manner in which the *kanga* is worn and its message displayed.

As well as buying for themselves, women may also buy *kanga* for their mothers, sisters and other female relatives and friends, but it is principally for themselves that purchases are made. Moreover, I observed that, if the message on the *kanga* is inappropriate (whether for herself or someone else), she will not buy it, regardless of how much she might like its design and colour. The wording counts for more than the pattern's aesthetic appeal (see also Linnebuhr, 1992: 82).

There must of course be a certain income level enabling frequent purchases of *kanga* to be made. The inhabitants of Pemba, like Mafia island as studied by Pat Caplan, are generally much poorer than those of Unguja island or Mombasa (though pockets of poverty exist in all areas). Women's capacity to enter into competitive *kanga* games is, therefore, much reduced by being poor, and indeed the very ability to play is an index of at least minimally high socioeconomic status. It may well be that, in areas of considerable poverty, men will buy *kanga* for their womenfolk, as appears to be the case in Mafia island, so further limiting the possibility of competitive *kanga* games among women. Lacking these material means, the women of Mafia use instead their *kalewa* dance and deploy the same verbal techniques in competitive singing both against each other and sometimes against men (Pat Caplan, personal communication). The inscription of aphorisms on dress rather than in song privileges the visual over the acoustic but clearly does not prevent the geographical spread of aphorisms.

Emphasising, perhaps, his view of *kanga* sayings as essentially didactic, Farsi (1958: Volume One iii-iv) speaks of "old women (*wanawake wazee*)" having the duty of educating children with "an inexhaustible fund of riddles and stories" conceding that no one person could collect them all, while Maryam Abudu (1978: iv) acknowledges many more remain to be collected than are in her published sample. Together, the claims indicate an enormous productive capacity of women to compose these *kanga* messages. The sayings indicate different regional Swahili spellings and pronunciations, as Maryam Abudu (herself a woman) notes (1978: iii), declaring herself sensitive to such regional variation but unable nevertheless to encompass all areas.

Given the existence and availability of these and other published sources, it is interesting that the designers and manufacturers of *kanga* do not consult them but prefer to make use of sayings, and in some cases designs, sent in by the Swahili women consumers themselves. Although it would be inaccurate to refer to this as a case of consumers controlling the producers in their choice of commodity, for in fact the manufacturers benefit from this form of very cheap expertise, the end result is a product, the *kanga*, which carries in its messages references to personal and sometimes public interests which are always likely to be topical. Yet, topical though they may, the frequent ambiguity of the sayings makes them opaque and may create uncertainty as well as provoke debate.

Let me now give some examples of this ambiguity giving rise to propositional incompleteness coupled with multiple interpretability. I first provide a mixed bag of *kanga* sayings collected over a prolonged period in or near Mombasa, Kenya.

Mombasa (mid-sixties – c. 1990)

1. *Tutakula nao wenye waume zao*
"We shall eat with those having husbands." (c. 1990).

This is said to be the kind of oblique reference that a man's mistress might make to his wife. But there are varying interpretations as to its meaning.

(a) It is said to be a way of belittling the wife, of indicating to her that she is obliged to share her husband with another woman: it is an assertion of competition between women for men.
(b) It is said to be a commentary on modern marriage, for infidelity is alleged to be common and women find themselves sharing the same men.

It is clear from even this contrast that each assertion, and there are certainly other possible interpretations, sets up a whole chain of assumptions that constitute separate discourses.

Thus, the first view privileges the idea of men as a scarce and valuable resource sought after by women. I have, however, heard women as well as men offer this interpretation, despite its undermining of women's autonomy.

The second view is less common and is more often expressed by women. It expresses not so much competition between women as a sense of sisterly irony that, in a system of unstable marriages, women find themselves obliged to "taste" the same "food" (there are of course numerous analogies between sexuality and food consumption). Men are not here privileged but are, rather, reduced to the value of consumer objects, to be taken up, put down and handed on to other women at will. The sentiment relates strongly to a view I commonly heard expressed by women that it was they, rather than men, who initiated marital separation: *Si ni desturi ya wanawake kuachana na wanaume*? Translation: "But it's the custom of women (nowadays) to leave men, isn't it?". It points to a whole set of strategies that women are alleged to be able to adopt in and outside of marriage in their relations with men, within an overall situation in which both men and women are often too poor to "satisfy" consumer demands.

There are three points I wish to make here. First, this discussion concerning relations between men and women and among men and women themselves can, of course, continue indefinitely. The proverb inscribed on the *kanga* not only triggers the discourse but prescribes its infinitude and incompleteness. Second, like different myths that may be said to be incomplete in themselves but, together, constitute fragments over time (and space) of a larger myth-design, so the proverb relates to other sayings worn on women's *kanga* and, indeed, to yet others which are spoken as well as written. Third, there are many such proverbs that may be linked to each other in this way. Just as wits may joust with each other by reciprocally quoting relevant proverbs and thereby creating a web of verbal significance, so the *kanga* maxims can be regarded as similarly linked as "interlocutors". Thus, to take another example from many such possibilities, there is the following:

> 2. *Mwenye pupa hadiriki kula tamu*
> "A hasty (and therefore) over-passionate and lustful person cannot taste the sweetness." (1966).

Whereas, proverb No. I pointed to a circulation and possible abundance of sexuality and, by analogy, of food and consumer items, No. 2 is a sobering reminder of the loss people incur through haste and lust or greed. It fits with the Swahili admonition to be moderate in all things. Alongside this advice is expressed the innuendo that rapid coitus results in unsatisfactory sex, or that a fine meal is spoiled by gobbling it. Once again, this can lead into other discourses: from the unsatisfactory nature of greed and lust to its immorality, as when avarice leads to hoarding or the exclusion of others from one's own good fortune and enjoyment, and thence to the vengeful effects of malice and witchcraft. Despite the time difference of about 24 years between their respective first appearances, each saying is of on-going existential relevance and can be interpreted to make sense in terms of the other. That is to say, the discourses run into each other regardless of the time and occasion of their enunciation. In any event, sayings recur over the years in different forms.

Part of the recurring context is certainly the inter-meshing of ideas about sex and food as subject to the pleasures and problems of consumption. The entailed morality in such ideas, including notions of excess or wise management, are evident in the following:

> 3. *Wape wape vidonge vyao wakavila wakavitupa ni shauri yao*
> "Give them their pills (tablets) – whether they eat them or throw them away, that's their business." (c. 1990).

This line is adapted from a famous *taarab* song performed in Zanzibar in 1992 (*Wape wape vidonge vyao, wakimeza wakitema, ni shauri yao* – Give them their tablets, whether they swallow or spit them out is their business). It is a chorus line probably derived from and incorporated in other songs and has found its place also on *kanga*. The reference in the song is in fact to men being offered peace of mind by their women: it is up to the men as to whether they accept that their women love them and to act on this accordingly.

Two women offered a further interpretation which was not accepted by another. This is that the saying may refer to persons who will be punished for their delicts if they do not improve themselves, having been given the chance to do so. Such homilies are an invariable feature of a *maalim*'s sermons, as I indicated above, and will be justified in terms of Islamic dictates, although they are also seen in everyday non-religious contexts as underlining "good manners" (*adabu*), an expression and sentiment that underlies much Swahili discourse, but whose definition in particular cases causes disputes which are resolved by religious clerics and sages.

The moral element in such *kanga* proverbs ranges from oblique exhortations to "proper" behaviour: (as in the examples so far) to more straightforward admonitions, which involve much less word-play. Thus, we have:

4. *Jirani mwema ni asi(ye)sengenya*
"A good neighbour is one who doesn't backbite." (1991).

The tensions of co-residence in a homestead, village or urban quarter are, as everywhere, most obviously expressed in fears of being maligned in neighbourhood gossip and clearly shade into fears of being bewitched and perhaps of being accused of witchcraft. Since it is women who are most likely to have to live with these neighbourhood tensions on a daily basis, the *kanga* proverb is said to apply mostly to them.

Another, at first even more simplistic and straightforward admonition on the same theme, though this time in the spirit of conciliation rather than condemnation, is the following:

5. *Tusigombane*
"Don't let's quarrel." (1966).

The appeal not to quarrel can refer to couples as well as neighbours. What is particularly interesting here, however, is that there is reportedly a double-entendre: namely, that not only should we not quarrel, but, on the contrary, we should get together in a sexual liaison. This is an example which indeed appears to justify the oft-repeated claim that the most innocentseeming *kanga* maxims have a second and often sexual meaning. For instance, note the following:

6. *Mama nipe radhi yako*
"Mother, give me your blessing." (c. 1990).

At one level of signification, this can be regarded as an expression of filial respect: the son or daughter seeks the blessing of the mother. The man-friend of one woman suggested that it could refer to a man asking a woman for sexual favours or to set up a relationship with her, though other women hotly denied that *radhi* ("a religious term") could be used in this way. It might also be an appeal for maternal blessing for something illicit carried out by a perpetrator.

An element of innuendo through mysterious allusion is more certain, if complex, in the following:

> 7. *Utabaki na labuda langu hutalijua*
> "You will be left behind and perhaps never know what my (e.g. sexual) business is. i.e. You think you know, but you'll never know what I'm up to." (1990).

The double-meaning is contained within the very expression: there is the sense of physically being left behind and at the same time of being outside crucial knowledge. It might be said by a lover or by rivals, but is especially an allusion to relations between women and men and plays on the uncertain knowledge each has of the other's feelings and activities.

The sense of uncertainty and hesitation surrounding manwoman relationships extends to ideas of male impotence or male inability to follow through a relationship, as in the next proverb:

> 8. *Chura watajia maji lakini kuyaogelea hawezi.*
> "The frog(s) will come to the water but cannot swim in it." (c. 1990).

Frogs should by nature be endowed with the ability to swim and yet, according to this saying, we find them unable to do so.

The most obvious allusion is to male impotence. Such anomalies also refer, it is said, to certain kinds of people who yearn for something yet cannot cope with it when they get it, or, more specifically, to men who make a woman they love pregnant and then run away from the relationship, or to the dilemma of some men who want to marry a woman but feel unable to retain her character as it was before.

This last example, with its range of related but broad interpretations, which could surely be expanded through more extensive questioning, emphasises again the incomplete nature of the proverbs.

Zanzibar (c. 1992–1995)

Some of the above sayings appear on *kanga* worn in Zanzibar, either through use of the same riddle on a Tanzanian made cloth or through importation of a Kenyan *kanga*. A more systematic sample of those found in Zanzibar indicates much the same range of sexual and gender-related themes, often around the concept of either romantic or sexual love, expressed by women, the sense of which I leave largely unpacked. Indeed, although I group them under putative relationship headings, their ambiguity sometimes allows them to be placed in the context of other relationships.

From woman to man:

9. *Chelewa chelewa, utamkuta mtoto si wako*
"Delay, delay, and you'll find the child is not yours."
(If a lover/husband neglects his wife, she'll find another man).

10. *Bwana Bakari, karibu ugali*
"Mister Bakari (personal name), come close to the food." (Come and make love).

11. *Utatembea bucha zote, nyama ni ile ile*
"You can visit all the butchers, but the meat is the same." (You can visit many women but the love/body is the same).

12. *Isikuhadae rangi, tamu ya chai sukari.*
"Don't be cheated by the colour, the taste of tea is sugar." (The sweet person/body beneath the pleasantly brown skin or finery is what counts).

13. *Alaye kazini hashibi maishani.*
"He who eats on the job isn't satisfied in life."
(Warning not to cheat at work and to remain honest: a general homily or possibly oblique challenge to a lover or husband).

14. *Mahaba machoni, uhuru moyoni*
"Love in the eyes, (but) freedom in the heart."
(You show love to someone, but your heart remains free to love someone else. You are not a slave to love).

15. *Penzi ni jeraha, nipende nione raha*
"Love is an ulcer/sore; love me so that I feel happiness." (A clear, direct and personal call for love).

16. *Chunga chungio, usinichunge mimi, si mke mwenzio*
"Look after your own affairs, not mine, for I am not your co-wife." (Woman asserting her independence).

17. *Kula zabibu, urudishe majibu*
"Eat grapes, so that you may return your answers."
(You have to know what the taste is like in order to respond).

18. *Mchunguliya bahari si msafiri*
"Someone who (just) looks out at the sea is not a (real) traveller."
(Looking is not the same as acting. A person of action does not hesitate).

19. *Kwa mwari hoi hoi, kwa kungwi je?*
"With a sensual girl like that, what can her instructress be like?"
(This explicitly erotic message shocked and delighted women when it appeared. It can refer to the wearer proudly announcing herself to desired men or rival women, or even refer obliquely but disapprovingly to a particular woman for having raised a girl in her own lewd image. Kungwi is a Swahili sexual instructress. Some women did wear it).

20. *Nakuomba leo siyo kila siku*
"I ask you today, but not every day; or, I ask for you today but not every day."

Woman to other interfering, rival woman/women:

21. *Pilipili usizozila, zitakuwashaje*
"How could hot pepper/chillis that you didn't eat burn (hurt) you?"
(Don't take on what or who is not your business or is far from you). The reference to hot peppers as burning/itching/irritating can have an underlying sexual connotation.

22. *Unapita mpakani kwangu, hala hala kuna mtende wangu.*
"You are crossing my boundary, be immediately careful of my date tree."
[You're getting too close, lay off my man (to rival woman), or, keep away from my sweetness (woman to man)].

23. *Fitina lako ni baraka kwangu*
"Your backbiting is my blessing."
(Two friends may quarrel or backbite but the third knows that the friendship will endure, *or* the third benefits since each will seek her friendship).

24. *Nahodha hana neno, hofu ni abiria*
"The ship's captain (i.e. the one who has power, perhaps a husband) is not the one you have to worry about; your concerns should be about the passenger."
(i.e. the common man or, in a sexual relationship, a lover).

25. *Hiyo kwangu mnahangaika*
"You (gossipers) are just troubling yourself for nothing as far as I am concerned."

26. *Kusemwa kusemwa sitaki leo niwaeleze ukweli*
"I don't want to be talked about, (so) today I'll tell them (or you) the truth."
(e.g. people may be gossiping about a relationship, but the woman has had enough and wants to make it clear to the slanderers that all is well between her and her man).

27. *Vikao kaeni, umbea acheni*
"Let the households meet together, (but) leave off the indecent gossip."
(i.e. people pry into our domestic relationship, but they should stop).

28. *Msinionee wivu wenzangu, nilivumilia*
"Don't feel jealousy friends (note that my husband and I are always quarrelling), for I have endured a lot."

29. *Mpenzi wangu ni zahabu (dhahabu), kumpenda si ajabu*
"Since my love is pure gold, it's no wonder he's so lovable."
(i.e. woman recognising the value of her man and triumphantly acknowledging other women's jealousy and designs on him).

30. *Maneno si mkuki, msemayo si shituki*
"Words are no spear, and I don't fear who says them."
(Backbite as much as you like, I'm not worried).

31. *Mengi nimeyasikia, lakini navumilia*
"I hear a lot (of backbiting), but I carry on regardless."

32. *Heri paka kukamata panya kuliko binadamu*
"Better a cat to catch rats than a human."
(Warning off rivals by reference to their inadequacies).

33. *Kila unalo wasema, na hili pia kaseme*
"You backbite them on everything, so talk about this too."
(i.e. showing the saying on the *kanga*).
(I know that you backbite, but you should know that I know you do).

A few sayings are in praise of a mother or refer unambiguously to topical problems and concerns, e.g. AIDS and politics. Bland messages, "I chose you" (*Nimekuchagua wewe*); "Calm your heart, I am yours" (*Poa moyo wako, mimi ni wako*), were, at the time of fieldwork (1992–95), sometimes found on "marriage cloths" (*kisutu* or *kanga za harusi*), but with exhortations aimed at the groom wearing a red, yellow and black cloth around his waist, and his bride and women guests wearing those of other colours. Although I have not seen it, a few people said that the *kisutu* is also worn at a funeral (*msiba*), but over the shoulder in such a way that any words printed on it cannot be seen. Overall however, in Zanzibar as in Mombasa, most messages occur on *kanga* for ordinary internal and external dress and most are nowadays aimed at rival women, and also husband and male lovers, with other referents much less common.

They are part of a wider mode of unvoiced competitive communication, in which, while others may comment or speak, a woman becomes her own silent agent. Thus, women's rivalry in Zanzibar extends also to the part they play in an audience listening to certain kinds of *taarab* musical concerts, which are distinctive of Zanzibar island and only ever imitated elsewhere, though originating in India and the Middle East. At these *taarab* performances, women wear lavishly colourful dress ("western",

Indian and Arab), gowns and jewellery and predominate in the audience. When the singer, a man or a woman, expresses a sentiment that touches on a particular woman's perception of her relationship with a man or her personal situation, the woman walks up boldly and places a sum of money at the singer's feet, to indicate that she knows which woman rival is backbiting her or seeking the attentions of her lover. A number of women do the same, each triggered by a phrase uttered by the singer appropriate to their circumstance, so forming a procession which grows and even accelerates as the song continues, with each woman throughout the evening laying out often large amounts. These will include unmarried as well as married women, though all relatively young (Parkin, 1995).

Like the messages on the *kanga*, those of the *taarab* performances are communicated to a rival by a woman not through use of her own voice but visually, silently and through bodily movement and adornment. Thus, while women in the *kanga* and *taarab* contexts are orally passive, they are nevertheless active in promoting their interests within a general field of performative communication. Whatever may be the social and interactional constraints to which they feel subject, such as the alleged opinion and actions of neighbours, friends, lovers and family, they exercise choice both in the purchase of *kanga* and in making symbolic payments to the *taarab* singers. There is no equivalent male field of communication, and men's dress, though governed by rules, does not become such a dense means of message-making. To be sure, at certain festive rites held in the mosque, such as the *maulidi* celebrations, men dressed in *kanzu* and *kofia* may link arms while seated and rock from side to side, perhaps reaching a trance-like or even ecstatic crescendo in their chanting. But this expresses solidarity not rivalry and it is more in the institution of the secular, quotidien *baraza*, a seating area around a house or mosque, that men will engage in talk about each other as well as on other topics. For women, the *kanga*, whose sayings some of them compose, and the *taarab*, whose songs may also be written by women, provide means of communicating at a second, silent remove which, in ordinary everyday spoken discourse, cannot he directly voiced by the "victims".

Conclusion

I have five observations. First, the number of examples could be much greater than is provided. My own Zanzibar sample collected during January 1993 is, for instance, 65 but the number produced over the years is immense. At one level, they could be reduced to a limited number of broad themes: love, sex, tensions between man and woman, neighbourhood harmony and disharmony, family duties, loyalty and disloyalty among friends, and personal autonomy. On the other hand, the very fact that something can be said in a similar but not identical manner immediately makes possible a divergence of view: slight variation can lead to sharp difference; or, differences can be made to arise out of broad similarities. Methodologically, also, it is probably as fruitless to catalogue examples in terms of types as it is to classify cases of witchcraft and their explanations. For it is not as a system of classification that speakers use the sayings. The messages evoke overlapping questions and issues for those who read them.

Second, therefore, the proverbs cannot be reduced to the logic of binary reasoning. They cannot be answered or interpreted in terms of standard two-valued logic of the yes/no type. Third, they comprise both poetics and rhetoric. They draw on some features of wordplay and, although I have not been able to demonstrate this, of Swahili verse-form, while at the same time seek to persuade and seduce.

Fourth, their often elliptical character is also said to be typical of a society whose stress on concealment (*setiri*) and secrecy (*siri*) is paradoxically part of proper manners (*adabu*) as well as the cause of tension (*fitina*). That is to say, it is proper to act discreetly and to withhold personal details and sentiments from all but the closest confidants. Yet this very lack of openness and its connotation of secrecy may sometimes produce the ambiguity and conditions of uncertainty under which suspicions of backbiting and covert enmity, including witchcraft, arise. Fifth, this uncertainty is reflected in the content and medium of the *kanga* maxims themselves. They are written but not spoken. They are carried on women's garments and are chosen for their content: sometimes the choice is for a saying that is complexly ambiguous and suggests a number of possible innuendos, while at other times the choice is of a more assertive exhortation, which, although more complete in itself as a proposition, nevertheless raises issues and questions in the discourse to which it may be interpreted as belonging.

A final, more general point is that these *kanga* sayings, while achieving their effect by remaining unspoken, are more like ordinary, everyday language than might at first appear to be the case. Ordinary conversation is rarely reducible to propositions which have mutually consistent truth-value. People shift their positions in the course of discussion and move towards either harmony or a polarisation of sentiment and views, or towards an unsettled indeterminacy. I would suggest that this is not just because speakers seek to maximise the number of possible interpretations open to them in any discourse. It is also a common feature of talk that it often remains propositionally inconclusive or incomplete. The speaker who controls this incompleteness is also better able to initiate new directions and, possibly, to reach a conclusion to his or her advantage. The use of innuendo and insinuation fall short of full assertions and are part of this incompleteness. Their inscription on women's *kanga* makes them in this respect much more than the spoken aphorisms that we normally regard as the source of folk wisdom. They do encode wisdom. But they do so as moving, transactable and *visible* markers, which are usually set in the context of women's rivalries over men, including relationships with men themselves. As such they can, if interpretations continue to be made, become the cut and thrust of unresolved and sometimes unresolvable existential debates[2].

Notes

(1) The concept was designed to combine the idea of deferral with that of difference and so captures well this aspect of innuendo.

(2) I thank Sauda Barwani-Sheikh, Pat Caplan, Ridder Samson and Farouk Topan for invaluable comments made on this paper, and to numerous, mainly women, Zanzibaris who let me discuss and interpret with them *kanga* usage and "names" during fieldwork on this subject in Zanzibar and Mombasa at various times in the late eighties and early nineties. The paper was widely circulated after its first presentation in May 1992 and I am grateful for the interest shown in it by other researchers in the field.

References

Abudu, M. (1978) *Methali za Kiswahili*. Volume One. Nairobi. Shungwaya Publishers.

Abudu, M. and Abdalla, B. (1981) *Methal za Kiswahili*. Volume Two. Nairobi. Shungwaya Publishers.

Abudu, M. and Abdalla, B. (1981) *Methali za Kiswahili*, Volume Three. Nairobi. Shungwaya Publishers.

Barwani-Sheikh, S. and Ridder, S. (1995) Sprichwörter und ihr Gebrauch. In G. Miehe und M. Wilhelm (eds) *Swahili-Handbuch*. Köln. Rüdiger Köppe Verlag. pp. 347–355.

Beck, R.-M. (1995) Text als Textilie: die *Kanga*. Wortwechsel. *Sprache und Kommunikationsnetze*. (*Beitraege zur feministischen theorie und praxis* 40). Köln.

Damman, E. (1955) *Sprichwörter aus Lamu*. Berlin. Westermann Festschrift.

Derrida, J. (1982) Différance. In *Margins of Philosophy*. Chicago and London. University of Chicago Press. p. 17.

Farsi, S.S. (1958) *Swahili Sayings*. Volume One. Nairobi. Kenya Literature Bureau.

Farsi, S.S. (1958) *Swahili Sayings*. Volume Two. Nairobi. Kenya Literature Bureau.

Hanby, J. and David, B. (1984) Kanga: 101 Uses. Nairobi. Ines May Publicity.

Hesse, M. (1984) The Cognitive Realms of Metaphor. In J.P. van Noppen (ed.) *Metaphor and Religion. Theolinguistics* 2. Brussels.

Hilal, N.M. (1989) (June), Khanga – A Medium of Communication among Women. *Sauti Yo Siti? a Tanzania Women's Magazine* No 6. Dar es Salaam.

Keenan, E. (1973) [1975] A Sliding Sense of Obligatoriness: The Polystructure of Malagasy Oratory. In M. Bloch (ed.) *Political Language and Oratory in Traditional Society*. London and New York. Academic Press.

Linnebuhr, E. (1992) Kanga: Popular Cloths with Messages. In G. Werner (ed.) *Sokomoko: Popular Culture in East Africa*. Rodopi. Amsterdam. Atlanta. Georgia.

Mtoro bin Mwinyi Bakari (ed. and trans. by J.W.T. Allen) (1981) *The Customs of the Swahili People*. Berkeley and London. California University Press.

O'Barr, W.M. (1982) *Linguistic Evidence: Language. Power and Strategy in the Courtroom*. New York. Academic Press.

Parkin, D. (1975) The Rhetoric of Responsibility. In M. Bloch (ed.) *Political Language and Oratory in Traditional Society*. London and New York. Acadamic Press.

Parkin, D. (1982) Introduction. *Semantic Anthropology*. ASA Monograph No 22. London and New York. Academic Press.

Parkin, D. (1984) Political language. *Annual Review of Anthropology* 13, 345–365.

Parkin, D. (1985) Being and Selfhood among Intermediary Swahili. In J. Maw and D. Parkin (eds) *Swahili Language and Society*, Beiträge zur Afrikanistik. Band 23. Vienna. Institut für Afrikanistik der Universität.

Parkin, D. (1995) "Blank banners": Islamic Consciousness in Zanzibar. In C. Anthony and R. Nigel (eds) *Questions of Consciousness*. London and New York. Routledge.

Ricoeur, P. (1975) *La metaphore vive*. Paris. Editions du Seuil.

Robert, S. (1954) *Kielezo cha Insha*. Johannesburg. Witwaterswand University Press.

Salmond, A. (1982) Knowledge as a Landscape. In D. Parkin (ed.) *Semantic Anthropology*. ASA Monograph No 22. London and New York. Academic Press.

Sapir, D. (1977) The Anatomy of Metaphor. In J.D. Sapir and J.C. Crocker (eds) *The Social Use of Metaphor: Essays on the Anthropology of Rhetoric*. Philadelphia. University of Pennsylvania Press.

Sheikh, S. (1994) Yanayoudhi kuyaona mafumbo na vijembe vya Kiswahili. In *Swahili Forum* 1, 7–11, Edited by Rose-Marie Beck. Thomas Geider and Werner Graebner. (Also see Barwani-Sheikh, Sauda above).

Strathern, A. (1975) Veiled speech in Mount Hagen. In M. Bloch (ed.) *Political Language and Oratory in Traditional Society*. London. Academic Press.

Taylor, W.E. (1891) *African Aphorisms, or, Saws from Swahili-land*. London. Society for the Promotion of Christian Knowledge.

Velten, C. (1907) *Prosa und Poesie der Wasuaheli*. Berlin.

17 Simultaneity and Sequencing in the Oracular Speech of Kenyan Diviners

A convergence of ideas that has occurred in linguistics and semantics has relevance also for social anthropology. In 1975 Marshall Durbin proposed formal models for distinguishing simultaneity and sequencing in human cognition. He noted the recent popular usage of this explanatory contrast in linguistics especially. Also in 1975, Paul Kay saw synchronic variability in basic colour terms as generating a roughly linear evolution of more specialised terms. Kay's study demonstrated the more general hypothesis in lexical semantics that "all linguistic change has its roots in synchronic heterogeneity of the speech community" (1975: 257). Finally, in a paper published in 1978 but delivered in 1973 at a conference I attended, Edwin Ardener distinguished between a simultaneity of events and their output as linear chains. A simultaneity is verbally unspecified, marked only by a "language shadow," while a causal sequence of events is distinguished more precisely in speech. Though they differ in other respects, these three views treat synchronicity or simultaneity as in some way generating sequential behaviour, vocabulary, or events.

Sequentiality is, of course, the only logically possible alternative to simultaneity. One "becomes" the other, though we tend to place the emphasis on sequenced events as emerging from a previously synchronic state and so as "produced" by that state. But the reverse direction is certainly possible, as when myths lump together events in overlapping and spatiotemporally contradictory ways. On the whole, though, the cases we present are of how sequential "order" comes out of synchronic "disorder." We see this sequence as people at their most creative. A point I want to make is that this creativity consists not simply in answering the puzzles posed by cognitive simultaneity but also in setting up the simultaneity in the first place.

Jung clearly understood our fascination. His view of the synchronicity of events was that their coincidence in space and time meant much more to us than mere chance. Events occurring simultaneously showed a special interdependence with each other, and, through our psyches, with us as observers (Jung: 1968; xxiv; cited in Jackson 1978: 117). Indeed we do often ascribe a hidden causality to what we interpret as coincidence, which in that sense is taken as something prior in us. But when we look at certain social events, we see people actually creating a pool of meanings, first by speaking and thinking of different events as if they occur simultaneously, even in contradiction, and then by relating events to each other in causal sequence. That is to say, through an event initially evoking the idea of simultaneity, people reorder events and make the new combinations intelligible to a wider public.

The event I shall look at is that of divinatory speech among the people with whom I have worked. But first I shall suggest some more universal aspects of the contrast and relationship between simultaneity and sequencing.

An Archetypal Contrast

Let me begin with a biblical text, Mark 1:3 on John the Baptist: "The voice of one crying in the wilderness, Prepare ye the way of the Lord, and make his paths straight." The idea of confusion suggested by the crying in the wilderness and the implication that the confused paths of the Lord need to be straightened represent two common archetypal ideas which we conventionally associate with religion and ritual.

The first archetype can be seen in the many expressions of tangled, crossed, or confused states: the sins of incest and some forms of adultery; the ritualisation of breech and other abnormal births; the dangers of improperly conducted rites of passage or of neglected relations between juniors and seniors; the use of key terms for witchcraft which relate to the idea of trapping and ensnaring and even the celebration of the Christian *Cross* (Easter) and the Jewish Passover as central events at about the same time of year.

The second archetype may be thought of as an attribute of the broad contrast between nature and culture. It is the contrast between wilderness and wandering on one hand, and fixed, secure clearly narrowly defined (often home) bases on the other. We have the biblical examples of Jesus and John the Baptist going off into the wilderness but returning new "straightened-out" men; the parable of the prodigal son forgiven and welcomed back from his aimless debauchery in the wastelands of the outside world; prophets coming into the small-scale society from a wider, alien, outside world; and, in at least some societies (including the Giriama and Swahili of Kenya who are the subject of this essay), sick patients going off, sometimes in trances, to the forest or the bush, impelled by an inner understanding, to gather the correct medicines required for their return to the now legitimate, i.e., "straight", role of the diviner.

First then, tangled states become "objects of the ritual attitude." Like cases of boundary confusion, they may be thought of as sources of power, sometimes beneficial but sometimes so dangerous for the society and the transgressing individual that he has to withdraw from it. Second, victims are straightened out as a result of having wandered into the wilderness.

Linking the two archetypes, we can say that the geographical transition from wilderness to straight paths parallels the individual's movement from social or mental confusion to clarity. As a metaphor of change between personal states, this characterises divination among the Giriama and Swahili of Kenya. This movement is evident more from their speech than from their actions. By concentrating on the speech of diviners among the people I have studied, I am able to understand a little more about the thought processes associated with the two archetypes I have described.

Diagnosis of problems is arrived at through divination; treatment (i.e. attempted cure) takes place after the divination and at a set place and time. Diviners may be of either sex and are paid between two and five Kenya shillings for their diagnosis. They usually recommend that the patient be treated by a specialist doctor. This treatment is much more expensive and is much more profitable than divination.

There is a hierarchy within these occupations, which include exorcism of spirits and reversal of witchcraft. It is based on the (sometimes cross-cutting) criteria of sex, age, and ethnic religious group. Doctors who provide only therapy but not divination are always men. Diviners may be men or women among non-Muslims but only men among Muslims. "Arab" diviners and doctors (who are always men) are generally held to be the best, and are the most expensive; they are regarded as having mixed Arab-Swahili-Mijikenda ancestry. "Swahili" (i.e. Muslim Africans) are usually regarded as the next most efficacious, and "Giriama" (i.e. non-Muslim Mijikenda) as the least (see figure). Oracular techniques vary between these categories, and patients try a range of practitioners. Thus an individual Giriama may in fact achieve exceptional renown. Complicating the matter still further is the fact that non-Muslims say that all diviners must be Muslims, for the spirits that possess them will include "Arabic" (i.e. Muslim) ones. However, claims to Muslim status are graded in East Africa, and those who are most widely acknowledged as "full" Muslims do distinguish between Muslim and non-Muslim diviners. This practice of grading Muslim status and the inconsistency of the contrast between

Muslim and non-Muslim is a result of the shifts from partial to "full" Muslim status, which often take more than one generation; it is reflected in the loose hierarchy of divinatory and medical prowess. That is to say, the social is reflected in the ritual hierarchy.

Following this Durkheimian line, it might be possible to show how changes in judgments made about the diviners in terms of their ethnic group, religion, sex, and age amount to statements about the wider, changing social relations. But diviners of all kinds use the idea of moving from a boundless to a bounded realm of existence in their diagnoses. Such archetypal usage seems unaffected by difference of rank and status among diviners. By investigating the diagnoses of a social range of such diviners I think we are able to understand their thematic logic and its relative imperviousness to variations in the social circumstances of diviners.

Three Cases

I reproduce in condensed form and comment on the diagnoses of three diviners: an "Arab", a "Swahili," and a "Giriama," as they are locally identified. First a few introductory remarks about them.

A client approaches a diviner without notice. The client is not necessarily the patient. Indeed it is often argued that he or she should not be. But some are. The late middle-aged "Arab" diviner runs his profession like a true business; he uses a pocket watch as an oracle. Clients sit around in his ample, well-stocked homestead waiting to be seen, the humbler receiving shorter divinations than the more influential, though the fees are the same (five shillings). He presses clients to agree to his carrying out the therapy on an appointed day after the divination. The "Giriama" diviner, in this case a woman past childbearing age, differs in a number of respects. She divines through spirit possession. She may be found sitting in her mud and wattle hut, unseen from the outside, and apparently withdrawn from the world. The client enters the hut, makes his greeting, and responds to her polite, euphemistic requests for tobacco by placing the two-shilling fee in front of her. The divination begins slowly. Punctuated by sweet refrains, gasps, and whistling as the spirits pause in their reflections, it consists of dramatic use of voice tone and vocabulary. The third diviner, the Muslim Digo (referred to by his fellow African Muslims as "Swahili") is a little less dramatic. His divination is punctuated by the spirits speaking in other ethnic tongues rather than in refrains of song. He accepts the same fee as the Giriama woman, and like her, he puts time and effort into the divination. The range in style from the least to the most dramatic among these three diviners does not alter certain common themes covered in their divinations. The diviner is not expected to know anything of the victim's affliction nor indeed whether the person in front of him – the client – is him/herself the victim or a caring relative come to ask for diagnosis on the victim's behalf.

The "Arab" Diviner

The "Arab" diviner speaks in Swahili. His client has come on behalf of his 10-year-old son, who talks to himself, whoops and yells as if possessed, plays alone, and not with other children, and is easily angered.

The diviner's spirits first make these points:

> He [i.e., the victim] is troubled because of his trade – the trade carried out from his home – I mean the trade that results from a man marrying a wife and having a child by her. I mean that trade – for the wife is the investment and the child the profit. Women are the loads which we men trade with, feeding them, and hoping to trade further with.
>
> But the wife can't or won't get out of your body – she is the owner of it – it's your trade but she is the owner ... and she can say I don't love you and she can leave you ... but your child can't say that.
>
> That is why I say it is your business which is disturbing you [i.e., he refers to the victim by addressing the client].

By converting one metaphor into another (trade into domestic relations) and by using the metaphors inconsistently, the diviner simultaneously links a number of possible sources of distress: the victim's occupation or trade, the costs of running a family, a dominant and unloving wife, and the loss of a child through her desertion. Of particular note is the fact that the wife is locked in the victim's body, possessing it – perhaps even consuming it – and yet also leaving it. Bodily possession is also of course normally attributed to spirits, though as yet spirits have not been mentioned. The implicit proposition, therefore, is that the victim's wife is a controlling spirit. This is combined with another proposition, which states that the victim is troubled by his trade or occupation. Home and the outside are thus simultaneously linked as sources of distress. As yet, such propositions are only hinted at; they are not clear enough to be judged true or false by the client.

We see in the next section of paraphrase, however, that the diviner successfully locates a child as the victim. As usual, a positive response from the client has helped him. Clients do this by words of encouragement and agreement throughout the divination. The diviner says:

> I am looking at the [victim's] head, circling around, going now to the stomach, to the joints, circling all the time ... and the child is suffering in all parts of the body-head, heart, stomach-but the stomach pain is ceasing, now it is the back which is troubling.
>
> And yet this child has been sent to hospital, but vomits. This is caused by the heart, for the disease is in the heart. And the head aches.
>
> He was given tablets but was sick on taking them. ... He is constipated for two or three days. Isn't this so? [The client is asked, but courteously denies that the child is constipated.] He is constipated one day but not the next. He goes and then the stomach can be heard rumbling at his umbilicus. Where do you live? [The question is addressed to the client, who tells the diviner.]
>
> You saw something astonishing in his house, didn't you – like a wild animal from the forest going in? Now that animal came up to the child, who fell asleep and went "Haw haw" [the noise of an animal]. And even the next day, when he's about to recover, the sickness goes away a little but then comes right back. The disease then comes and goes every two days, with the child going "Haw haw" at its onset. For now there are spirits active there, which must be seen to quickly.

There is an interesting kind of two-part syllogism here, the first of which uses metonymy. First: the child is approached by the animal (which is understood to rasp); the child is approached by the sickness (initiated by a rasp); therefore the animal is the sickness. Second: the animal is from outside (i.e., the forest); spirits are from the outside; therefore the animal is the spirits (therefore to treat the spirits is to treat the sickness).

The diviner then follows up his admonition to treat the spirits with explicit instructions about the medicines needed for the treatment: "Get a cock, a hen of different colours, a white loin cloth, and materials for making an Arabic charm which can be drunk. The child has spirits, including the ape-spirit to which he is attracted. Get these spices: Ambari, Miski, Kafuri, Zafarani, Marashi, and also a sheep – a surrogate will do – even a sheep's hoof (literally, shoe)." After further instructions and then some open discussion, a date, time, and place are set for the treatment for which these items will be needed.

The first part of the divination links home and the outside world as simultaneously producing a number of sometimes conflicting sources of distress. The second repeatedly probes different areas of the body, then focuses on the home, which is entered by a wild animal from the forest (perhaps echoing the equation of home with wife in the first part). Merged ideas are broken down into separate ones through the idiom of following separate parts of the body. This is followed by a specific statement of the cause of sickness: outside spirits intruding and requiring appeasement. The final part of the divination carries still further the ordered sequencing of ideas and actually spells out the list of medical requirements and the time and place of their application. The shift is from conceptual simultaneity to sequencing.

The "Swahili" Diviner

The "Swahili" (Muslim Digo) diviner's client is a young unmarried man who has come on his own behalf. He seems to be suffering from venereal disease. This diviner also begins with a complex linking of concepts: man, woman, sadness, sympathy, lust and longing, including the supreme symbol of suffering, the shoe (*kirahu*). The word derives from the verb "to go here and there" (*ku-kira-kira*). The reflexive *ku-dzi-kirira* means "to walk about aimlessly" (see Deed 1964: 9).

> Why is there this need for sympathy my friend [addressing the client]? There is a woman loving a man ... The love is puzzled. The man loves the woman. The man loves with longing/lust [using the word *thamaa*, which can also stand for penis]. There is longing and there is the shoe. You [i.e., the client] have even followed the shoe [i.e., you have really "suffered"; suffering is implied by the notion of wandering endlessly on foot.] Why is there sickness as well as longing here?

Here the interlinked notions of longing, lust, and metonymic penis are denoted by the one word and merge into that of sickness. The use of the word *shoe* and the verb *followed* anticipates the more extensive treatment of the theme of wandering, as in the previous divination.

> He [i.e., the victim] is a man and is sick and wandering ... this way and that ... He comes out quickly ... He can't cope [for which the verb *kukola* is used, which also means to penetrate] ... He runs about here and there ... struggling, but to no avail. He goes to doctors but to no avail.
>
> Why has he this disease of the shoe? He can't stay in bed with the sickness. He wanders with it. Why is it a disease of the top [i.e., the head]? It has gripped his head, but why the head, my friend? The head goes round and round and becomes dizzy. And because of the dizziness it becomes senseless and loses its memory. His [senseless] mind tells him to cry and produce tears.

> The disease is in the chest … and in the stomach … in the solar plexus [*chembe cha moyo*] … and even his heart is bursting … It is worn out from beating at great speed. The heart goes fast yet it wanders. It [the disease] is in the arteries and veins [*mishipa*] and his legs are lazy.
>
> Now the sickness is descending. It's in the middle. It is a male's sickness … to do with [sexual] satisfaction … It's between the kidneys. Now we find it in the veins of the penis [for which an orthodox word, *kilume*, is used] … and right beneath the umbilicus. Why is there fire burning there … like peppers … ? The disease makes one mindless. When you urinate it's a war, and even injections have not helped.

Now the diviner, having located the distressing parts of the body, proceeds to itemise the causative agents:

> You [i.e. the client, now identified as the victim] are caught by the [witchcraft] trap [*tego*] which prevents you defecating [*ya zindika*], by the trap which prevents you urinating [*tego ya mkufu*], by the trap which causes irritation [*ya lwambe*] and by the traps called peppers [*pilipili*], laziness [*munyegero*], the needle [*sindano*], black ants [*minyo*], and safari ants [*tsalafu*]. [Most of these traps indicate the sensations of itching, pricking, and stinging].
>
> Have you entered someone's house? [The victim answers no.] I don't really mean a house, I mean a human house [i.e. a woman, and this the victim does not deny … You have had this sickness a long time, not a long time, yet a long time, but you have been wandering around with this sickness, and you are surprised that it has stayed with you. But you must cure the first causes [i.e. the witchcraft causes which have physical effects].
>
> Also, my friend, you have the following [other kinds of] witchcraft. [Here the diviner also uses the term *muhaso* but later *utsai*; both have mental rather than physical effects.] These are: the witchcraft of self-hatred [*utsai wa dzimene*], of senseless babbling [*mbayumbayu*], of indecisiveness and lack of concentration [*shulamoyo*], and of restlessness [*mtango*]. These witchcrafts want to turn you into a perpetual nomad, wandering unthinkingly around the world, never settling at home, with your heart burning … and feeling numb in your head. You also have the witchcraft [*nzaiko*] which makes you cry when combined with those that make you indecisive and gibbering.
>
> The disease comes from the west … You had a job there. Maybe you were learning there, but people are bad there and gave you these things.

The diviner next shifts from a focus on the causes of the affliction to a precise statement of the items needed for the cure: "Find me seven loaves made out of ashes, seven loaves of bread, seven sides of sand from a termite mound, a chain, seven wild tomatoes [?] and with these we shall make you free." The diviner shifts for a moment back to the focus on cause, then reverts to the medical prescription:

> Your school absences and lack of concentration were due to bad people. You humans really were bad to each other ... Do you hear, my friend?
>
> Anyway, now also find a chicken [later called a cock] of mixed colours, and a red hen; these are for the witchcraft traps. For reversing the mental effects of the second kind of witchcraft and getting your memory back from God, you need a chicken with frayed and tufted feathers [*kuku wa kidemu*], a newly hatched chick, and an egg which never hatched.
>
> I could mention the names of those who wanted you to become a vagrant and who caused your apathy, while your friends forged ahead, but I [i.e. the spirit] am asked only to "name" the sickness [i.e. to find its cause and remedy].
>
> Don't think that by going off to another country you will resist them – you *must* be cured – your body must be treated ... and then you will be somebody, settled with a job and money and able to face people ... The day for the treatment is next Tuesday, 10AM to 3PM.

With this divination, we also have an initial amassing and overlapping of ideas: man and woman, loving and longing, following the shoe, getting sick. My translated abstract misses the polysemy of certain words used: *kimako* means sympathy, sorrow, astonishment; *thamaa* means hope, longing, lust, penis; *ku-kola* means to overcome or penetrate. The word used in divination for woman is *figa*, which normally refers to one of three stones making up a stand for cooking pots; the word used for man is the normal word for five (*tsano*), which admirably projects the five-limbed image of masculinity. The word for shoe (*kirahu*) carries the meaning also of wandering and therefore of random sickness. Conflicting innuendos are created through such polysemy, which heightens the ambivalence of concept. The listening client can try and judge for himself but may not be certain of what precisely is being proposed, while the diviner himself can always retreat from an unpromising lead and take up another through the use of the same words.

The theme of uncontrolled wandering follows on easily from such ambivalence. It occurs first in undefined outside space, then in pursuit through different parts of the body, eventually settling, in this case, on the genitals. But the young man is clearly mentally as well as physically distressed, and so his mind's wanderings are described. The physical and mental troubles are each explained by a different kind of witchcraft.

Finally, there is a well-ordered list of requisites for cure, interspersed with more direct admonitions not to wander. The subject of wandering may at any one time have been the sickness, the pain, the victim, the aggrieved relative of the victim, or even the agent causing the distress. The admonition by the spirits not to wander places these phenomena (the subjects of wandering) in fixed rather than indeterminate relations to each other.

The "Giriama" Diviner

In the final case of divination, which I will summarise even more briefly, a Giriama woman about 10 years past childbearing age treats a young man who has also come on his own behalf and who suffers from continual stomach pains, which, the diviner comes to assume, necessarily affect his sexuality.

The diviner opens with a short song in Giriama, which is mutually intelligible with Digo: "The spirits are coming with sympathy, and we are traveling along with that sympathy, and with our human hope." The spirit switches from song to speech.

> We [i.e., the spirits – though perhaps the plural pronoun is used to denote respect for the client, who is a member of an adjacent generation and therefore a "father"] have stood with a female, but the sick person is a male .... Isn't that so? [The client agrees and the diviner responds with song.]
>
> We are swaying like an eagle; Kayumba [name given to client] has come, yes, and the sick person is asking ... I want to sleep, brothers. [The song ends.]
>
> We have gone with our male ... he is small ... and yet big ... he can speak [i.e. is not a baby; the client assents to this]. He has a problem sent by God [i.e. not caused by witchcraft, *utsai*]. He has the shoe.

The diviner (i.e. spirits) repeats the previous refrain and then speaks of the journey through the body.

> We have tried the head and left it. Now we are down in the chest, and not the heart. My mind [i.e. that of the spirit, standing as the patient] is confused, isn't that true? [The client agrees and the diviner repeats the refrain.] Now we are down to the stomach. [To which the client assents readily: "The stomach, yes, the stomach, that's it!" And the diviner continues.] It is constipated and burning, and something in it gets up and stands erect and clings to the heart .... My heart is being pulled. And now we travel down to my back. [The client assents.] My back, my back. It is my loins/genitals [*thamaa*] isn't it father? It affects my legs, my hips, my *thamaa*.

The client asks what has caused the affliction and the diviner recounts a phase in the victim's childbirth when he was put in a lake and could not breathe, but he lived and has suffered ever since.

The diviner then suggests in detail three separate sets of causative agents: spirits, harmful exposure to a family tradition of the occult (the man's mother is also a diviner), and, as in the previous divination, witchcraft traps – which contradicts her earlier assertion that witchcraft was not involved. The diviner then spells out the curative plants, animals, and cloth that will be required, giving precise instructions as to the identification and whereabouts of the plants, indicating by which lake, in which area of bush, etc. A time for the exorcism of the spirits and reversal of the witchcraft is set for the same afternoon at the victim's home.

This Giriama diviner creates the same overlapping metaphors through use of the same polysemic vocabulary as does the Digo ('Swahili') diviner. However, one expression used by the Giriama and not by the Digo is worth noting. It is a phrase for human being (*magulu mairi mudamu ludzere*), which literally means "a two-legged human with hair." The expression perhaps illustrates the underlying idea that though spirits are like humans in some aspects of their nature and in the forms some of them may assume, only "real" humans are of "real" flesh, blood, and hair.

The Giriama diviner also at first refers to the spirits she talks to by the term used for "ancestral spirit" (*koma*), but later uses the normal word for "possession spirit" (*pepo*). The Giriama people stress patri-lineage relationships and ancestry more than the Digo, and this initial reference to dead ancestors is therefore consistent. Otherwise, in both divinations there is the same idea of a wandering soul in distress who joins up with equally nomadic but undistressed spirits to search through the different parts of the body and locate the source of pain. Bodily and mental problems are eventually distinguished, as in the Digo's divination, but the bodily ones are emphasised. The final stage of the Giriama's diagnosis distinguishes three causative agents: spirits, having a diviner in the family, and witchcraft, which are further subdivided in some descriptive detail, whereas the Digo diviner confines himself to two kinds of witchcraft, one producing physical and the other producing mental distress.

A Common Logic

Such differences of detail in the diagnoses of the three diviners represent their individual creativity. It is, however, a creativity which operates within the successive frameworks I have suggested: jumbled ideas and metaphors that suggest various possible interpretations give way to their ordered sequencing and to more limited interpretations; they are finally superseded by an unambiguous classification of the causes of the sickness and the material needed to cure it.

This process of semantic disentanglement and clarification runs parallel with the idiom of movement from a wilderness to a set place and time. Taking the cases as a whole, this "spatial" idiom can be expressed as follows:

The victim, or perhaps we would say his soul, wanders aimlessly outside his body and home. The spirits wander too. They are always "unsettled," as diviners say. But it is part of their nature to be so. The human patient, whose nature it is not to be disembodied but rather to be settled in time and place, joins up with the spirits and with them frantically travels from one part of the body to another. Though the journey is frantic, it does at least exhibit a rough sequence. It always starts from the head and moves downward to the area of the genitals and, in the intermediary area of the trunk, alternates probingly between heart, stomach, chest, solar plexus, back, joints, hips and legs, usually linking up again with the mind.

Once the victim's source of pain has been located, the spirits, through the mouth of the diviner, can advise on its cure. In concentrating their advice on a fixed bodily area the spirits are themselves settled, at least while the remedy is effective.

In advising on the curative materials and methods to be used, the spirits order and classify, and so are turned from wanderers into busy *bricoleurs*. Indeed, the suggestion may now have become clear from my summaries of the divinations that the unravelling of ideas and their ordered reassembly as diagnosis and potential cure well fits the description of *bricolage* given by Levi-Strauss (1966: 16–22).

It is true that it is the diviner (or his/her spirits) rather than the patient who converts "debris" and "chaos" into "order," or we might properly say, jumbled thought into sequential thought. But the patient is not only figuratively carried along the paths from wilderness to settlement; he is also a point of reference and guidance along the way. That is to say, by his nods, cues, and statements of agreement, the patient helps the diviner, encouraging him/her to proceed from one possibility to another. So, while we may think of the patient as being led to a cure by the diviner, the patient also guides the diviner in this attempt to reach a satisfactory diagnosis, converting an unmanageably large number of interpretations into a more limited number.

This view, that the patient guides the diviner as well as being guided by him/her, suggests more than a mutual dependency of the two roles. It suggests that they may be seen as mirror images of each other. The further implicit idea that each person is both doctor and patient is reinforced by the process through which diviners achieve their position in the first place. They first suffer severely as a patient and then, as part of the cure, are instructed by a diviner's spirits to seek certain plants and medicines in the bush, thereby also coming to possess divinatory powers. Only a few patients become diviners, but all diviners were once patients. It is as if in order to become a psychotherapist, one would first need to be a "schizophrenic" patient and become a psychotherapist as part of one's "cure." Indeed, the parallel may not be without significance.

Just as divinatory diagnoses suggest bricolage, so also the idioms and language used to describe the patient's distressed state suggest at least some features of what we call schizophrenia: disembodiment, personal withdrawal into a "private" world of spirits, the creation of a "false self" which denies the diviner's "real" identity, and what I continue for the moment to call jumbled speech. Yet, once again, these are features which are as much, if not more, the creation of the diviner as they are attributable to the patient. Both the patient and the diviner participate willingly in this diagnosis, with the patient allowing himself into the "private" spirit world of the diviner. Also, both appear to be in control of the way in which the diagnosis proceeds. It may well be that cultures like those of the Swahili and the Giriama provide structured events and roles by which what we call schizophrenia is legitimised and thereby brought under the control of those who suffer from it. Be that as it may, it is not here my intent to claim that the diviner and patient are in some degree schizophrenic. What is interesting is that the diagnostic themes in the divinations appeal to thought and speech processes which, when very marked, we would label schizophrenic.

Does this mean, then, that divinatory diagnosis is both *bricolage* and schizophrenia? Or, to put the equation another way, that *bricolage* (or myth-making thought, as Lévi-Strauss alternatively calls it) and schizophrenic thought are basically the same thing? Schizophrenic thought has moreover been viewed by some scholars as resting on a basis similar to that of artistic thought (Wilson 1978: 97); does this further mean that *bricolage* and schizophrenic and artistic thought are equivalent? This seems absurd and perhaps, in reaching this equation, I have merely allowed myself to be captured by the terms and have merged their respective referents.

On the other hand, absurd though the equation might seem, the fact that it can be reached at all suggests some further consideration of Lévi-Strauss's threefold distinction between *bricolage*, art, and modern science as modes of thought. Art, it will be remembered, is placed halfway between *bricolage* and modern science. The artist is said to partake of both. He is a *bricoleur* in creating a model or structure, a recognisable painting for example, out of pre-existing images. So does the myth maker. But he also works by design, like the modern scientist or engineer in producing, as well as reproducing, structures. That is to say, the picture only exists as a painting on canvas and remains under his technological control as creator. He can, if he wants to, alter it so as to signify new directions, as would an impressionist (Lévi-Strauss 1966: 22, 25).

Likewise, we are told that intellectual *bricolage* in the form of myth-making has a poetic quality and can achieve brilliant intellectual results (Lévi-Strauss 1966: 17, 21). Much the same could be said of divination, which, as well as offering opportunities for dramatic and semantic creativity, solves the practical problem of mental as well as physical distress. The Digo and Giriama diviners, it will be remembered, elaborated to a greater extent than the "Arab" and in ways much more aesthetically pleasing. As well as being *bricolage*, and even touching on modern medical science in its diagnostic parallels with psychotherapy, the divination is also an art form.

Lévi-Strauss himself notes that the difference between the myth maker and the modern scientist, or the *bricoleur* and the engineer, with the artist in between, is not absolute, and the distinction remains an important general approach complementary to the recent discussion whether "primitive" thought is based on two- or three-valued logic, and whether it may be said to exist at all (Cooper 1975; Salmon 1978; Hallpike 1976, 1977; Williams 1977; Warren 1978).

But there is another approach which, on the basis of my data, I would state as follows: analysis of the diviner's speech reveals two parallel patterns. One concerns the language used, the other the narrative theme. To take the linguistic dimension first, the diviner starts with what I called jumbled speech, or what we may now refer to as inconsistent and mixed use of metaphor, false syllogism, some reversals, and an apparent lack of path control, i.e., straying from one concept to another and back again inconsequentially. Though intended (we assume) rather than involuntary, these are features common to some degree to the speech of all of us but in excess may characterise so-called schizophrenic speech (Werner and Levis-Matichek 1975). These features are rectified as the divination proceeds. The speech and argument become clearer and culminate in perfectly precise instructions based on a crisp classification of causative agents and remedial plants, animals, and other substances.

The narrative theme starts with the idea of aimless wandering in an unspecified and we may assume empty area, which is alien and remote. Within it, paths crisscross confusedly, but eventually, through the idiom of bodily exploration, lead to a settled point and prospective cure. We can see that the shifts from jumbled to sequential speech and from aimless wandering to purposeful direction "say" the same thing. But it would be difficult to conclude that one is an epiphenomenon of the other.

One view might be that the logic governing both may be said to lie in the contrast between deep-structure and surface semantics. Gerald Leech offers us a linguistic example with the sentence *I saw the girls crossing the street* (1974: 288). At a deep semantic level the crossing and the seeing occur at the same time; they are a "junction of two interacting events" (288). But the sentence orders them sequentially; the seeing comes before the crossing. It also subordinates the second clause (*crossing the street*) by embedding it in the main clause (*seeing the girls*). As Leech remarks, the truest "copy of the structure of events and circumstances we recognize in the reality around us" (288) is in fact the synchronous picture, or what he calls the orderless network of deep semantics. Sentence order "distorts" the "true" picture by separating events in time and ranking them. Events do of course occur which "in reality" are indeed sequentially ordered and may be ranked in utterances by entailment and presupposition. But even here, sentences used to describe them can never fully overcome syntactic and phonological restraints and approach the semantic accuracy of personally rather than grammatically ordered words. Like the painter and the poet, the schizophrenic speaker can say things with a shocking but brilliant poignancy that conventional sentences rarely attain. As with the initial jumbled speech of diviners, they operate more freely at a level closer to the orderless networks of deep-structure semantics.

The shift from deep-structure to surface (sentence) semantics analytically parallels the shift in the diviner 's speech style and narrative theme. We can recast what others call deep-structure semantics as the area of the most creative, artistic, poetic and schizophrenic thought, and surface semantics as that of classification and taxonomy, i.e. of *bricolage*. To complete the model, modern science may be regarded as reflexive surface semantics, i.e. language used to refer to itself, including its deep-structure (which is what I have attempted in this essay).

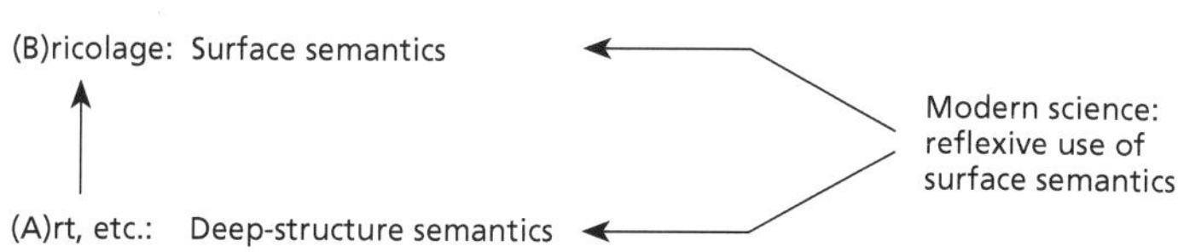

The place of the two archetypes with which I began this essay can now be seen. Categorical overlap, crossing, or confusion (orderless networks) make up the area of deep-structure semantics and art. We are accustomed to the idea of this archetype being an object of the ritual attitude. More properly, we should say that it poses the intellectual puzzles which people seek to solve through aesthetically pleasing methods. The second archetype takes off from here and, in depicting the return from random wandering in the wilderness to straight and narrow paths, represents the movement from deep-structure to surface semantics, A > B, or, in the particular case of divination, from jumbled to clear speech.

We see, then, why the basic styles and themes of divination, at least in the society I have studied, are the same, regardless of the social circumstances of the diviners. For they are part of a wider logic by which we must solve problems as puzzles: by untangling them, and so clarifying and recognising them. For that logic to operate we have to posit a simultaneity of confusion in the first place. This is the point at which I can bring the analysis to bear on the question in social anthropology of the innovative individual.

Innovating Individuals

To argue for a common logic in puzzle solving is not to deny the diviners choice in their proposed solutions. We have long known that many possibilities can emanate from a single logic (e.g., Leach 1961). It follows that diviners are perfectly able to comment socially. When they specify different kinds of witchcraft, or witchcraft rather than spirit possession, or whatever, as causes of misfortune, and when they hint at social relationships in which these differently valued acts may have arisen, they variously support, tear, or repair the social fabric. The many studies by Turner (1961) and others show this role of the diviner, and I could show the different ways in which Kenya coastal diviners do this. In this essay, however, I have tried to make the point that, however much such commentary may be viewed as sometimes reflecting social changes and continuities, the diviner and client together make up a cooperative enclave. Together they create a range of possible interpretations of cause and effect and then choose from within that range. They are in a good position, therefore, to articulate new ideas in the society which have not yet come into general currency.

This innovative power of the diviner-client relationship derives from the initial simultaneity of packed-in propositions which become progressively unpacked. That is to say, it is the initial tangled state or puzzle that inspires the discourse. This inspiration is commonly what we understand by events having become objects of the ritual attitude, and which I have glossed as incest, some kinds of adultery, breech births, badly performed rites of passage, crossing the generation gap, and the use of physical and verbal symbols which include the idea of crossing over. Such tangled states pose questions which demand answers.

This is a quite different view of the innovative individual from that held by Barth in his early work (1966). Even allowing for the fact that Barth was not specifically concerned with speech, he saw redefining roles by imparting to them new value or varying amounts of old value. The diviner and client clearly cooperate more than they compete, both inspired to disentangle a puzzle. Barth's view represents one dimension of individual innovation. Mine represents another. A tempting conclusion might be to locate Barth's innovative individual in the micropolitics of everyday life and mine in rituals dealing with tangled states. That is fine as far as it goes. But the phrasing is simplistic because it assumes a single definition of ritual and ignores the fact that what we call rituals may be conservative rather than innovative. Skorupski (1973) usefully redefined the contrast between the secular and the mystical as that between observable and hidden causality. This contrast may better illustrate the difference. Barth's individual innovates in the context of visible connections. For him/her the causality is already laid out before him: it is up to him to provide a new causal sequence of events or roles. My innovative individual is faced with a simultaneity of hidden causalities. He must straighten them out before he can see them and explain events through them. And to do this, he must cooperate with at least one other person.

For this reason tangled states generate social man, while straightened-out ones generate competitive man. Small wonder that so many leave for the wilderness.

Notes

Versions of this essay were presented in seminars at the Universities of California (Berkeley and San Diego), Sussex, Belfast (Queen's), and Oxford and appeared in the Journal of the Anthropological Society of Oxford 1979: 10 (3), 147–60 and Paideuma 1982: 28, 71–83. Research was made possible by a grant from the SSRC. I thank this and the aforementioned institutions for their help and comments.

(1) Two kinds of simultaneity and sequencing seem possible, a problem I shall deal with elsewhere. The present essay introduces the contrast and illuminates it.

(2) The Giriama are a subgroup of the Mijikenda, who speak mutually intelligible dialects.

(3) Technically, we should refer to the Giriama and Digo practitioners as shamans rather than simply diviners, for they speak through spirits which they also control. This is not, however, a distinction I wish to belabour here, though it is important for other analyses.

(4) The root verb is in fact *ku-kira*, meaning "to cross" or "to go too far." From this is derived the noun *kirwa*, which refers to a disease arising from a breach of certain sexual prohibitions. Morphological variations of *kirwa* abound as key concepts in Bantu and, through lexical borrowing, Nilotic cultures (Parkin 1978: 150–51, 327–30).

References

Ardener, E. (1978) "Some Outstanding Problems in the Analysis of Events." In *The Yearbook of Symbolic Anthropology*, vol. I, (ed.) Schwimmer, E. 103–21. London: Hurst.

Barth, F. (1966) Models of Social Organization. London: Royal Anthropological Institute.

Cooper, D.E. (1975) "Alternative Logic in 'Primitive Thought.'" *Man* n.s. 10, 238–56.

Deed, F. (1964) Giryama-English Dictionary. Nairobi: East African Literature Bureau.

Durbin, M. (1975) "Models of Simultaneity and Sequentiality in Human Cognition." In *Linguistics and Anthropology*, (ed.) M. Kinkade, *et al*. Lisse: Reter de Ridder Press.

Hallpike, C.R. (1976) "Is There a Primitive Mentality?" *Man* n.s. 11, 253–70.

——(1977) "Is There A Primitive Mentality?" Correspondence in *Man* n.s. 12, 530.

Jackson, M. (1978) "An Approach to Kuranko Divination." *Human Relations* 31 (2), 117–38.

Jung, C.S. (1968) Foreword to *The I Ching or Book of Changes*, trans. R. Wilhelm. London: Routledge.

Kay, P. (1975) "Synchronic Variability and Diachronic Change in Basic Color Terms." *Language and Society* 4, 257–70.

Leach, E. (1961) "Rethinking Anthropology." *Rethinking Anthropology*, 1–27 London: Athlone.

Leech, G. (1974) *Semantics*. Harmondsworth: Penguin Books.

Levi-Strauss, C. (1966) *The Savage Mind*, London: Weidenfeld and Nicolson.

Lewis, I.M. (1971) *Ecstatic Religion*. Harmondsworth: Penguin Books.

Parkin, D. (1978) *The Cultural Definition of Political Response*. London: Academic Press.

Salmon, M.H. (1978) "Do Azande and Nuer use a Non-standard logic?" *Man* n.s. 13, 444–54.

Skorupski, J. (1978) *Symbol and Theory*. Oxford: Oxford University Press.

Turner, V.W. (1961) *Ndembu Divination*. Manchester: Manchester University Press.

Warren, N. (1978) "*Is there a primitive mentality*?" Correspondence in *Man* n.s. 13, 477–78.

Werner, O., and Levis-Matichek, G. with Evans, M. and Litowtiz, B. (1975) "An ethnoscience view of schizophrenic speech." In *Sociocultural Dimensions of Language Use* (ed.) M. Sanches and B. Blount 349–78. New York: Academic Press.

Williams, R. (1977) "Is there a primitive mentality?" Correspondence in *Man* n.s. 12, 530.

Wilson, P. (1978) "The Outcast and the Prisoner: Models for Witchcraft and Schizophrenia." *Man* n.s. 13, 88–99.

References: Introduction and Parts 1–3 Commentaries

Ardener, E. (1982) Social anthropology, language and reality. In D. Parkin (ed.) *Semantic Anthropology*. London and Orlando: Academic Press.

Ardener, E. (1989a) (ed. M. Chapman). *The Voice of Prophecy*. Oxford and New York: Blackwell.

Ardener, E. (1989b) [1978] Some outstanding problems in the analysis of events. In E. Ardener. *The Voice of Prophecy*. Oxford and New York: Blackwell.

Arnaut, K. and Harris, R. (2013) David Parkin in interview: Anthropology, language and diversity. *Working Papers in Urban Language and Literacies*. Paper No.110. Kings College London.

Arnaut, K., Blommaert, J., Rampton, B. and Spotti, M. (2016a) Introduction in Arnaut *et al.* (eds) *Language and Superdiversity*. New York and Abingdon: Routledge.

Arnaut, K., Blommaert, J., Rampton, B. and Spotti, M. (eds) (2016b) *Language and Superdiversity*. New York and Abingdon: Routledge.

Arnaut, K., Karrebaek, M.S., Spotti, M. and Blommaert, J. (eds) (2017) *Engaging Superdiversity: Recombining Spaces, Times and Language Practices*. Bristol: Multilingual Matters.

Arnaut, K., Karrebaek, M.S. and Spotti., M. (2017) Engaging superdiversity. The poiesis-infrastructures nexus and language practices in combinatorial spaces. In Arnaut *et al.* (eds) *Engaging Superdiversity: Recombining Spaces, Times and Language Practices*. Bristol: Multilingual Matters.

Bailey, F.G. (1969) *Stratagems and Spoils*. Brighton: Pavilion Press. Blackwell.

Bailey, F.G. (1981) Dimensions of rhetoric in conditions of uncertainty. In R. Paine (ed.) *Politically Speaking*. Newfoundland Institute for Social and Economic Research. Philadelphia: ISHI.

Bailey, F.G. (1983) *The Tactical Uses of Passion*. Ithaca and London: Cornell University Press.

Barth, F. (1966) *Models of Social Organization*. Glasgow. Royal Anthropological Institute.

Bauman, R. (1975) Verbal art as performance. *American Anthropologist* 77 (2), 290–311.

Bauman, R. and Briggs, C.L. (1990) Poetics and performance as critical perspectives on language and social life. *Annual Review of Anthropology* 19, 59–88.

Besnier, N. (1991) Literacy and the notion of person on Nakulaelae Atoll. *American Anthropologist* 93 (3), 570–587.

Black, S. (2019) *Speech and Song at the Margins of Global Health*. New Brunswick and London: Rutgers University Press.

Bloch, M. (ed.) (1975) *Political Language and Oratory in Traditional Society*. London, New York: Academic Press.

Blommaert, J. (2009) Language, asylum and the national order. *Current Anthropology* 50 (4), 415–441.

Blommaert, J. (2018) *Dialogues with Ethnography: Notes on Classics, and How I Read Them*. Bristol: Multilingual Matters.

Boerllstorff, T. (2011) *American Anthropologist*. Virtual Issue: The Anthropology of Language.

Bosire, M. (2009) What makes a Sheng word unique? Lexical manipulation in mixed languages. In A. Ojo and L. Moshi (eds) *Selected Proceedings of the 39th Annual Conference on African Linguistics* (pp. 77–85). Somerville, MA: Cascadilla Proceedings Project. See www.lingref.com, document #2188.

Bowen J.R. (1993) *Muslims Through Discourse: Religion and Ritual in Gayo Society*. Princeton, NJ: Princeton Univ. Press

Brenneis D.L. (1986a) Shared territory: audience, indirection and meaning. *Text and Talk* 6 (3), 339–47.

Brenneis, D. (ed.) (1986b) The audience as co-author. *Text* 6 (3).

Brenneis D.L. and Myers, F.R. (1984) Introduction. In D.L. Brenneis and F.R. Myers (eds) *Dangerous Words* (pp. 1–29). New York: New York Univ. Press.

Briggs, C.L. (1985) The pragmatics of proverb performances in New Mexican Spanish. *American Anthropologist* 87 (4), 793–810.

Chernela, J.M. (2003) Language ideology and women's speech: Talking community in the northwest Amazon. *American Anthropologist* 105 (4), 794–806.

Duranti, A. (1993) Truth and intentionality: Towards an ethnographic critique. *Cultural Anthropology* 8 (2), 214–245.

Duranti, A. (2015) *The Anthropology of Intentions*. Cambridge. Cambridge University Press.

Ervin-Tripp, S. (1964) An analysis of the interaction of language, topic and listener. *American Anthropologist* 66, special issue 6, Part 2, 86–102.

Favret-Saada, J. (1980) [1977] *Deadly Words: Witchcraft in the Bocage*. Cambridge: Cambridge University Press.

Finnegan, R. (2002) *Communicating: The Multiple Modes of Human Interconnection*. London and New York: Routledge.

Frake, C. (1964) How to ask for a drink in Subanun. *American Anthropologist* 66, special issue 6, Part 2, 127–132.

Friedman, J. (2003) Globalization languages: Ideologies and realities of the contemporary global system. *American Anthropologist* 105 (4), 744–752.

Friedrich, P. (1989) Language, ideology and political economy. *American Anthropologist* 91 (2), 295–312.

Githiora C. (2018) *Sheng: Rise of a Kenyan Swahili Vernacular*. Woodbridge, UK and Rochester, NY: James Currey.

Goebel, Z. (2015) *Language and Superdiversity: Indonesian Knowledging at Home and Abroad*. New York: Oxford University Press.

Greenberg, J. (1955) *Studies in African Linguistic Classification*. New Haven: Compass.

Grillo, R. (ed.) (1989) *Social Anthropology and the Politics of Language*. London and New York: Routledge.

Gumperz, J. (1958) Dialect differences and social stratification in a North Indian village. *American Anthropologist* 60, 668–681.

Gumperz, J. (1961) Speech varieties and the study of Indian civilization. *American Anthropologist* 65, 976–988.

Gumperz, J. and Hymes, D. (eds) (1964) The ethnography of communication. *American Anthropologist* 66, special issue 6.

Guthrie, M. (1948) *The Classification of the Bantu Languages*. London: International African Institute.

Haviland, J.B. (2003) Ideologies of language: Some reflections on language and US law. *American Anthropologist* 105 (4), 764–774.

Hymes, D. (1964) Introduction: Towards ethnographies of communication. In J.J. Gumperz and D. Hymes (eds) The Ethnography of Communication. Special issue of *American Anthropologist* 66 (6), Part II: 137–54.

Gumperz, J.J. and Hymes, D. (1972) *Directions in Sociolinguistics: The Ethnography of Communication*. New York: Holt, Rinehart, & Winston.

Hymes, D. (1983) [1974] Traditions and paradigms. In D. Hymes (ed.) *Essays in the History of Linguistic Anthropology* (pp. 345–387). Amsterdam, The Netherlands: John Benjamins.

Keane, W. (1997a) Religious language. *Annual Reviews in Anthropology* 26, 47–71.

Keane, W. (1997b) From fetishism to sincerity: On agency, the speaking subject, and their historicity in the context of religious conversion. *Comp. Stud. Soc. Hist.* 45, 185–191.

Keane, W. (2018) On semiotic ideology. *Signs and Society* 6 (1), 1–24.

Kay, P. (1975) Synchronic variability and diachronic change in basic color terms. *Language and Society* 4, 257–270.

Labov, W. (1964) Phonological correlates of social stratification. *American Anthropologist* 66, special issue 6, Part 2, 164–176.

Labov, W. (1972) [1977] Rules for ritual insults. In *Language in the Inner City*. Oxford: Blackwell.

Laitin, D.D. and Gomez, G.R. (1992) Language, ideology and the press in Catalonia. *American Anthropologist* 94 (1), 9–30.

Leppänen, S. and Elo, A. (2016) Buffalaxing the other: superdiversity in action on You Tube. In K. Arnaut, J. Blommaert, B. Rampton and M. Spotti (eds) *Language and Superdiversity* (pp. 71–88). New York and Abingdon, UK: Routledge.

Levinson, S.C. (1983) *Pragmatics*. Cambridge: Cambridge University Press.

Makihara, M. (2004) Linguistic syncretism and language ideologies: Transforming sociolinguistic hierarchy on Rapa Nui (Easter Island). *American Anthropologist* 106 (3), 529–540.

Mazrui, A. (1995) Slang and code switching: The case of Sheng in Kenya. *Afrikanistiche Arbeitspapiere* 42, 168–179.

McIntosh, J. (2010) Mobile phones and Mipoho's prophecy. The powers and dangers of flying language. *American Ethnologist* 37 (2), 337–353.

Meyerhoff, M. (2018) *Introducing Sociolinguisics*. London and New York: Routledge.

Paine, R. (ed.) (1981) *Politically Speaking: Cross-Cultural Studies of Rhetoric*. Philadelphia: Institute for the Study of Human Issues.

Parkin, D. (1971) Language choice in two Kampala housing estates. In W.H. Whiteley (ed.) *Language Use and Social Change: Problems of Multilingualism with Special Reference to Eastern Africa* (pp. 347–363). London: International African Institute. Oxford University Press. London.

Parkin, D. (1974a) Language shift and ethnicity in Nairobi: The speech community of Kaloleni. In W.H. Whiteley (ed.) *Language in Kenya* (pp. 167–188). Nairobi: Oxford University Press.

Parkin, D. (1974b) Language switching in Nairobi. In W.H. Whiteley (ed.) *Language in Kenya* (pp. 189–216). Nairobi: Oxford University Press.

Parkin, D. (1975) The rhetoric of responsibility. In M. Bloch (ed.) *Political Language and Oratory in Traditional Society*. London, New York: Academic Press.

Parkin, D. (1976) Exchanging words. In B. Kapferer (ed.) *Transaction and Meaning* (pp. 163–190). Philadelphia: Institute for the Study of Human Issues.

Parkin, D. (1977) Stabilized and emergent multilingualism. In H. Giles (ed.) *Language, Ethnicity and Inter-group Relations* (pp. 186–210). London and New York: Academic Press.

Parkin, D. (1980) The creativity of abuse (Curl lecture 1979). *Man* 15, 45–64.

Parkin, D. (1982) (ed.) *Semantic Anthropology*. London and Orlando: Academic Press.

Parkin, D. (1984) Political language. *Annual Review of Anthropology* 13, 345–365.

Parkin, D. (1985a) Being and selfhood among intermediary Swahili. In J. Maw and D. Parkin (eds) *Swahili Language and Society*, Beiträge zur Afrikanistik. Band 23 (pp. 247–260). Vienna: Institut für Afrikanistik der Universität.

Parkin, D. (1985b) Controlling the U-turn of knowledge. In R. Fardon (ed.) *Power and Knowledge* (pp. 49–60). Edinburgh: Scottish Academic Press.

Parkin, D. (1985c) Reason, emotion and the embodiment of power. In J. Overing (ed.) *Reason and Morality* (pp. 135–151). ASA Monograph No. 24. London: Tavistock.

Parkin, D. (1989) The politics of naming among the Giriama. In R.D. Grillo (ed.) *Social Anthropology and the Politics of Language* (pp. 61–89). Sociological Review Monograph No. 36. London and New York: Routledge.

Parkin, D. (1991) Simultaneity and sequencing in the oracular speech of Kenyan diviners. In P. Peek (ed.) *African Divination Systems* (pp. 173–189). Bloomington: Indiana University Press.

Parkin, D. (1992) Unpacking anthropology. *Journal of the Anthropological Society of Oxford* 23 (1), 57–65.

Parkin, D. (1994) Language, government and the play on purity and impurity: Arabic, Swahili and the vernaculars in Kenya. In R. Fardon and G. Furniss (eds) *African Languages, Development and the State* (pp. 227–245). London: Routledge.

Parkin, D. (2000) The power of incompleteness: innuendo in Swahili women's dress. In B. Masquelier and J-L Siran (eds) *Pour une Anthropologie de l'Interlocution: Rhétoriques du Quotidien*. Paris: L'Harmattan.

Parkin, D. (2007a) The visceral in the social: the crowd as paradigmatic type. In D. Parkin and S. Ulijaszek (eds) *Holistic Anthropology: Emergence and Convergence*. New York and Oxford: Berghahn.

Parkin, D. (2007b) Wafting on the wind: Smell and the cycle of spirit and matter. In a special issue of the *Journal of the Royal Anthropological Institute*. Edited by Elisabeth Hsu and Chris Low.

Parkin, D. (2013) Balancing diversity and well-being: words, concepts and practice in eastern Africa. In P. Horden and E. Hsu (eds) *The Body in Balance: Humoral Medicines in Practice*. Oxford and New York: Berghahn.

Parkin, D. (2015) Revisiting: Key words, transforming phrases and cultural concepts. In *Working Papers in Urban Languages and Literacies*. Paper 164. Kings College, London.

Parkin, D. (2016) Multilingual classification to translingual ontology: A turning point. In K. Arnaut, J. Blommaert, B. Rampton and M. Spotti (eds) *Language and Superdiversity* (pp. 71–88). New York and Abingdon, UK: Routledge.

Parkin, D. (2017) Loud ethics and quiet morality among Muslim healers in Eastern Africa. *Africa* 87 (3), 537–53.

Rampton, B. (2007a) Neo-Hymesian linguistic ethnography in the United Kingdom. *Journal of Sociolinguistics* 11 (5), 584–607.

Rampton, B. (2007b) Linguistic ethnography and the study of identities. *Working Papers in Urban Languages and Literacies*. Paper 43. London. Kings College.

Rampton, B. (2008) Disciplinary mixing: Types and cases. *Journal of Sociolinguistics* 12 (4), 525–531.

Rampton, B. (2009) Dell Hymes's visions of enquiry. Special issue of *Text and Talk* – 'On Hymes' 29 (3), 359–70.

Sapir, J.D. and Crocker, J.C. (eds) (1977) *The Social Use of Metaphor: Essays on the Anthropology of Rhetoric*. Philadelphia: Pennsylvania University Press.

Scherzer, J. (1987) A discourse-centred approach to language and culture. *American Anthropologist* 89 (2), 295–305.

Schieffelin, B.B., Woolard, K.A. and Kroskrity, P.V. (eds) (1998) *Language Ideologies.* New York and Oxford: Oxford University Press.

Silva-Fuenza Lida, I. (1949) Ethnolinguistics and the study of culture. *American Anthropologist* 51 (3), 446–456.

Silverstein, M. (1976) Shifters, linguistic categories, cultural description. In K. Basso and H. Selby (eds) *Meaning in Anthropology.* Albuquerque: University of New Mexico Press.

Silverstein, M. (1992) The indeterminacy of contextualization: when is enough enough? In P. Auer and A. Di Luzio (eds) *The Contextualization of Language* (pp. 55–76). Amsterdam and Philadelphia: John Benjamins.

Silverstein, M. (2014) The voice of Jacob: Entextualization, contextualization, and identity. *English Literary History* Special issue. R. Copeland and F. Ferguson (eds).

Silverstein, M. and Urban, G. (eds) (1996) *Natural Histories of Discourse.* Chicago: University of Chicago Press.

Stasch, R. (2011) Ritual and oratory revisited: the semiotics of effective action. *Annual Review of Anthropology* 40, 159–174.

Street, B. (1985) *Literacy in Theory and Practice.* Cambridge: Cambridge University Press.

Stromberg, P.G. (1990) Ideological language in the transformation of identity. *American Anthropologist* 92 (1), 42–56.

Swartz, M.J. (ed) (1968) *Local-Level Politics.* Chicago: Aldine.

Tambiah, S. (1968) The magical power of words. *Man (N.S)* 3 (2), 175–208.

Vertovec, S. (2007) Superdiversity and its implications. *Ethnic and Racial Studies* 30 (6), 1024–1054.

Vigouroux, C. and Mufwene, S.S. (eds) (2008) *Globalization and Language Vitality: Perspectives from Black Africa*. London: Continuum Press:

Whiteley, W. (ed.) (1971) *Language Use and Social Change: Problems of Multilingualism in Eastern Africa.* London: International African Institute. Oxford University Press.

Whiteley, W. (ed.) (1974) *Language in Kenya*. Nairobi: Oxford University Press.

Wolfgram, M. (2012) The entextualization of Ayurveda as intellectual property. *International Journal of Cultural Property* 19 (3), 313–343.

Index